PATTON
AND
ROMMEL

MEN OF WAR
IN THE
TWENTIETH CENTURY

DENNIS SHOWALTER

With an Exclusive History Book Club Introduction by the Author

BERKLEY CALIBER, NEW YORK

THE BERKLEY PUBLISHING GROUP
Published by the Penguin Group
Penguin Group (USA) Inc.
375 Hudson Street, New York, New York 10014, USA
Penguin Group (Canada), 10 Alcorn Avenue, Toronto, Ontario M4V 3B2, Canada
(a division of Pearson Penguin Canada Inc.)
Penguin Books Ltd., 80 Strand, London WC2R 0RL, England
Penguin Group Ireland, 25 St. Stephen's Green, Dublin 2, Ireland (a division of Penguin Books Ltd.)
Penguin Group (Australia), 250 Camberwell Road, Camberwell, Victoria 3124, Australia
(a division of Pearson Australia Group Pty. Ltd.)
Penguin Books India Pvt. Ltd., 11 Community Centre, Panchsheel Park, New Delhi—110 017, India
Penguin Group (NZ), Cnr. Airborne and Rosedale Roads, Albany, Auckland 1310, New Zealand
(a division of Pearson New Zealand Ltd.)
Penguin Books (South Africa) (Pty.) Ltd., 24 Sturdee Avenue, Rosebank, Johannesburg 2196, South Africa

Penguin Books Ltd., Registered Offices: 80 Strand, London WC2R 0RL, England

This book is an original publication of The Berkley Publishing Group.

Copyright © 2005 by Dennis Showalter
Cover design by Richard Hasselberger
Photos of George S. Patton and Erwin Rommel courtesy of DPA/Landov
Text design by Tiffany Estreicher

ISBN 0-425-19346-2

PRINTED IN THE UNITED STATES OF AMERICA

ACKNOWLEDGMENTS

This book had its origins in a conversation with my agent, Frank Weimann. I thank him for the inspiration and for his constant support and assistance. The editorial staff at Berkley supplied patience, sound advice, and technical skill in equal proportions. My colleagues at Colorado College, the U.S. Air Force Academy, and the Society for Military History bore my enthusiasms and frustrations with more goodwill than they merited. Special thanks in that regard to Sandy Papuga, Office Coordinator of the CC History Department, and to Diane Brodersen, our interlibrary loans coordinator.

I owe a particular debt to a longtime friend who, when I was floundering in the early stages of writing, offered the advice that straightened me out and kept me on track until the finish. The book is dedicated to John Wheatley, with thanks for a lot of good years.

INTRODUCTION TO
THE HISTORY BOOK CLUB EDITION

IT is a particular pleasure to write a special introduction to the
History Book Club edition of *Patton and Rommel: Men of War in
the Twentieth Century.* My association with HBC as a reviewer has
been one of the most gratifying aspects of my career as a historian,
because it has offered an opportunity to link authors and readers from
a broad intellectual community. From its nineteenth-century inception
as an academic discipline, history has been at its best as a public discipline. Its great days have been when it addresses broad themes for
wide communities, eschewing the temptation of pursuing arcane subjects through opaque methodologies.

That is especially true when the subject is war. Our world and its
civilizations has been shaped for good and ill by organized, armed
conflict. Periodic efforts to demonstrate prehistoric or prelapsarian
societies innocent of that condition have foundered on an increasing
body of archaeological and anthropological evidence. In other words,
humanity has been making war for a long time. Yet, in the metaphor
of Carl von Clausewitz, war remains a chameleon. Its nature, its conduct, and its consequences continue to be as baffling in the twenty-
first century as four millennia earlier, when Egyptians and Hyksos
clashed at Megiddo in history's first recorded battle. Perhaps most baffling are the men who wage war. Are they part of a community of
"universal soldiers," responding to stimuli and circumstances essen-

tially constant over time? Or are they products of the particular: institutions and ideas specific to times, places, and cultures?

Within military systems, leaders compose a special category. Here the questions are more pointed: Born or made? Rational or reflexive? Representative or set apart? The emphasis on leadership reflects war's nature as an organized activity. Instinctual behavior plays a relatively small role. Someone, many someones, have to make war happen. And those who do it well are few and far between in history's pages. A lawyer can console his mistakes on visiting day. A doctor usually buries his one at a time. Generals are routinely responsible for hecatombs. More than that, they are responsible to the societies that entrust them with the lives of sons, husbands, fathers. There is a profound reason why wars are associated with their commanders. Even the "new military history," with its emphasis on the intellectual, cultural, and structural factors of warmaking, tends to present outcomes in personal terms: victory for General X; defeat for General Y. In the final analysis it is Lee who surrenders to Grant at Appomattox.

It is in those contexts that I offer *Patton and Rommel* to History Book Club's members and readers. Each man is a defining figure in the history and the mythology not merely of World War II but the twentieth century. Each man's legend transcends his actual achievements—which in both cases are substantial. Each man is a product of synergies between their self-definitions and the *mentalities* of the armies in which they served and the societies to which they belonged. Taken together, their stories offer readers with a broad spectrum of interests and specializations a springboard for inquiry and discussion on the fundamental theme of war.

PROLOGUE

GEORGE Patton. Erwin Rommel. Each is a name to conjure with—especially on the cover of a book. Their names and faces are regularly used to advertise large-format, general-reader volumes on armored warfare, on World War II, and on great battles and great captains. They are available in varying scales to model-builders and collectors. While "Patton's Sherman" has not yet made an appearance, in the 1960s Monogram offered "Rommel's Rod"—a "Krazy Kommand Kar" complete with decals.

Patton and Rommel play central roles in the writing of military history. Their names. deeds, and ideas run like threads through academic monographs and professional military writing. Ronald Lewin, Sir Hubert Essame, Martin Blumenson, Davvid Fraser, Carlo D'Este, Stephen Ambrose, Russell Weigley—these are only a few of the soldiers and scholars who address the operational performance of these generals, as supporters or debunkers.

In the 1960s, Patton and Rommel were featured in Ballantine's classic series on commanders of World War II. They are highlights of Brassey's contemporary *Military Profiles* series. Each is the subject of a classic film. They appear regularly in science fiction and alternate history. Patton has the title role in John Barnes's *Patton's Spaceship*. Rommel is the central character in Matthew Costello's *Time of the Fox*. In *Fox at the Front,* Douglas Niles and Michael Dobson even have Patton and Rommel fight side by side to prevent the Soviet overrunning of Germany after Hitler's assassination! Each man has not one, but two massive biographies by major authors, each a commercial and literary success: David Irving's *Trail of the Fox* and Sir David Fraser's *Iron Cross* for Rommel; Carlo D'Este's *Patton: A Genius for War* and Stanley Hirshson's *General Patton: A Soldier's Life*. A Google search, that twenty-first-century standard for measuring significance, turns up about 156,000 references to "Rommel" and about 174,000 for "George Patton."

Men of War is nevertheless the first book-length joint study of these familiar figures. This is a dual military biography. It seeks to integrate three focal points: the men, their wars, and the systems they served. It also seeks to be reader-friendly, by eschewing the academic apparatus that so often gets in the way of the story. And this is quite a story—of heroism and posturing, of honor and self-serving, of courage and betrayal. It depicts two complex personalities in the contexts of their military cultures and the countries that sustained them. Focusing on the generals, it compares the U.S. Army and the Wehrmacht as military instruments, and American and German ways of war.

Patton and Rommel were in part their own creations. Each man was his personal construction of what a soldier should be. They are also constructions of their enemies. In the middle of the North African campaign, Winston Churchill, the last great romantic, paid tribute to Rommel in the House of Commons. The Desert Fox was so admired by British soldiers and officers that "doing a Rommel" came to be a synonym for anything executed competently and with flair. Long before the end of the war, Rommel became for British and Americans alike an embodiment of the general who led from the front, saw for himself, and shared the hardships of his men. In America's service academies, he remains for cadets an archetype of what a leader should be: what contemporary military analyst David Hackworth calls a "warrior stud," a general with muddy boots and operational genius.

Rommel is also an enduring symbol of the "good" German: the man who fought a clean, honorable war, untainted by the ideology or the institutions of National Socialsim. His forced suicide in 1944 did not make him a martyr, but it did link him to the German resistance and give him status as one of Hitler's victims. That made him an iconographic figure in an emerging Federal Republic, which adopted the Rommel mythos with enough enthusiasm to name one of their navy's major ships after the army general! The other side of the story is that German soldiers and military analysts have no particular regard for Rommel as a general—"a good division commander" is the phrase I have most often heard in forty years of discussing the subject. To men trained in the schools of Clausewitz and Moltke, the qualitites Americans admire in Rommel are exactly those that merit criticsm: acting on impulse, favoring spontaneity over planning, trusting to luck for logistics.

For the German professionals, on the other hand, Patton remains a general who understood how to wage modern war and whose system gave him the tools he needed. Patton was imaginative, aggressive. Patton understood operational art. Patton saw that the tank made it possible to paralyze an enemy, then destroy him at low cost. "Patton!" the old Wehrmacht hands and their successors of the Bundeswehr reflect. "There was a true master of mobility. Had he been given a free hand by your Eisenhowers and your Bradleys, the war would have been over by November. Shermans would have been rolling down Unter den Linden before the Russians ever saw the Oder."

Americans are less comfortable with Patton. Sixty years after his triumphs he remains the bad boy become general—the profane, posturing, soldier-slapper whose extroverted lack of self-discipline made him a loose cannon to his superiors and constantly landed him in hot water with the media. To an American people still reluctant to acknowledge the role of war in American society, Patton's ebullient enthusiasm for conflict makes him disconcerting—a figure to respect but not to identify with. He is like an athlete admired for performance but not judgment—a uniformed cross between Barry Bonds and Dennis Rodman.

The horse cavalry had a song about a resting place called Fiddler's Green, where the grass is always lush and the beer is always cold. It stands along the trail to hell, but no trooper ever reaches that grim destination. Instead, he stops off at Fiddler's Green and stays to drink with his friends. Patton and Rommel never faced each other in battle. But surely Fiddler's Green must have made room for tanks and those who ride them. And just as surely, two old tankers hold court eternally under the trees.

1

FRAMEWORKS

G EORGE Patton grew up in a United States experiencing a social paradox. Founded as a republic, it moved during its early national period toward a democratic configuration: Jacksonian egalitarianism compounded by social mobility epitomized in the phrase "shirtsleeves to shirtsleeves in three generations." Alexis de Tocqueville, perhaps the most perceptive of any outside commentator on the American experience, remarked on the potential difficulty of maintaining the identity of a country with such a protean matrix. Between the Civil War and the twentieth century, however, the United States seemed well on its way to developing an aristocracy. "Establishments" combining wealth, talent, heritage, and service moved to center stage in the Northeast and the post-Reconstruction South, merging through intermarriage and common educational experiences. Across a midwest and west, they found imitators anxious to move away from the dirt-farm model familiarized by Hamlin Garland and Ole Rolvaag.

I

The Pattons of California traced their ancestry to a Scot who reached the New World around 1769 as an indentured servant, then made his way as a successful merchant in Fredericksburg, Virginia. He married above his birth, and one of his sons became a prominent lawyer and politician.

John Mercer Patton in turn sent four of his nine sons to Virginia Military Institute, and in 1861, when Virginia seceded, the Pattons, by then relocated to the Shennandoah Valley, took up arms in its service.

Sixteen Pattons fought for the Confederacy. Three died under its flag, including the first George Smith Patton, mortally wounded at Winchester in 1864. With the war's end, the family was reduced to subsistence farming in the literal sense: following a plow mule and dropping seed into the furrows. In the fall of 1866, the Pattons' fortunes changed—and did so in a fashion inviting description as "typically American." George Patton's brother-in-law had settled in California before the war and sat out the conflict in comfort. Now he contacted his widowed sister Susan and asked her to bring her family west. He underwrote the request with six hundred dollars. It was more hard cash than many Virginians had seen in years.

The Pattons' links with the South were renewed when, in 1869, George Hugh Smith settled in Los Angeles. A cousin and close friend of Susan's late husband, Patton family history also has it that Smith had long been in love with Susan and now felt free to court her openly. Apart from any romantic feelings, Susan Patton had poor health, little money, and four young children. She hesitated no longer than propriety demanded before accepting Smith's proposal. They were married in 1870.

Smith, by all accounts, was a model second father and never tired of telling his oldest stepson George stories of his birth parents' heroism and nobility. It was scarcely surprising when the young Patton determined to follow his father and his family heritage and attend the Virginia Military Institute (VMI). He proved outstanding both in the classroom and the corps of cadets and might have remained in the east—there was a girl—but his mother's illness impelled his return to Los Angeles.

Ambition may have played a role as well. California was wide open, boom country compared to a Virginia increasingly preoccupied with its past. Admitted to the California bar, young George Patton developed a reputation as an eloquent speaker in an era when high-flown rhetoric was an art form. In 1884, he followed a Patton tradition of marrying upward when he wed Ruth Wilson, daughter of one of California's most prominent families. Their first child was born on November 11, 1885. The parents named him George Smith Patton, Junior—a tribute to his father and his grandfather, an affirmation of a lineage continued.

Patton grew up in an extended family with dynamics and subtexts that would have intrigued Sigmund Freud, just beginning to establish his reputation as an alienist in a culture seemingly a polar opposite from rural California. But the doctor who treated Anna O might have found fruitful ground in what came close to a *ménage à trois,* at least emotionally, of Patton's father, his mother, and her sister Annie, who had been no less smitten with the elder Patton and compensated for finishing second in the marital race by moving in with the family and developing an extremely close relationship with their first-born son.

"Aunt Nannie" built her life around young George, indulging his behavior and making many of the decisions about how he was raised. Patton's daughter later wondered how "Georgie" grew up to be the man he was with two strong-minded women "baby-sitting him until he married . . ." One answer is implied by the survival of the childish nickname: to the end of Patton's life, his intimates called him Georgie. That both Nannie and Patton *père* were heavy drinkers even by the standards of a drinking age might also have given Ruth enough everyday leverage in the relationship to keep the triad stable. More positively, the Patton household normally included a large number of people—close and distant relatives, hangers-on, and acquaintances. Emotional connections that in a more limited environment might have proved spectacularly dysfunctional were instead diffused in a wider dynamic.

Economics influenced Patton's growing up as well. His father had given up his legal and political careers to handle the affairs of the Wilson estates and became embroiled in a family feud that lasted for fifteen years and resulted in foreclosure. The senior Patton landed on his feet as a manager for Henry Huntington, but there was no doubt that he had come down in the world. Enough money remained in the family to sustain an affluent lifestyle, with a cottage on Catalina Island. There was nevertheless irony in another Patton pursuing another way of life that eroded under his feet. It was something for a man to think about over a drink—and something, perhaps, to forget by telling stories and reading aloud to his son from such works as the *Iliad* and the *Odyssey.* Aunt Nannie kept pace with similar heroic classics, ranging from Xenophon's *Anabasis* and Plutarch's *Lives* to *Pilgrim's Progress* and the Bible—above all the Bible, three or four hours' worth of it a day.

From the classics and from Scripture, young George Patton absorbed a sense of the importance of struggle against evil, against fate, and against a cosmos ranging from indifferent to actively hostile. His fundamental inspiration, however, came from human sources rather than literary ones. The elder Patton's stories of the Old South and the Civil War lost nothing in the telling. If reinforcement were necessary, there was the presence of grandfather George Smith—an authentic hero whose more matter-of-fact depictions of his experiences tempered, if they did not quite balance, his stepson's "gunpowder and magnolias" perspective. And as a final mentor, Patton enjoyed the periodic company of John Singleton Mosby. Famous—or notorious—for his Civil War career as a partisan leader, Mosby had adapted well to the reuniting of America. Pardoned for his wartime activities, he became a political supporter and confidant of President Ulysses Grant, served as Minister to Hong Kong, then moved to California as an attorney for the Southern Pacific Railroad—all without losing his Confederate cachet. A frequent guest of the Pattons toward the end of the century, he repaid their hospitality with tales of the war that left young George in particular dazzled.

Patton's father did more than talk to his son. He taught him to ride—using the very saddle on which his grandfather had been mortally wounded. He taught him basic swordsmanship. He bought him a .22 rifle and a succession of shotguns, and George responded by developing an affinity for firearms that stayed with him throughout his life.

Almost every account of George Patton's childhood and youth describes him as having been pampered or spoiled, depending on the author's choice of words and degree of sympathy for the man Patton later became. A reasonable conclusion at this distance is that "Georgie" benefited from relatives and friends seeking to repay his parents' kindnesses, but he was also a likeable child. Young Patton seems to have been appreciative of things done for him —a point usually significant for an adult favor-giver. Whatever he was, he was not a brat. He could safely be indulged because he never pushed his boundaries to excess. The trouble he got into was usually the kind of trouble parents even today are prone to interpret as a sign of spirit and energy, especially in a boy.

Until Patton was eleven, he received no formal schooling, instead being tutored at home. This was not unusual in the Pattons' social sphere. The Pattons extended the experience because of Patton Senior's belief that childrens' education must progress in stages, based on developing levels of readiness—John Dewey's ideas applied by someone who was unaware of them. Georgie's home schooling was also extended for practical reasons: he was unable to read and write until he was eleven or twelve.

Carlo d'Este, arguably Patton's most perceptive biographer, has made a strong case for Patton as dyslexic: suffering from a problem of word reversal in reading, writing, and spelling. D'Este notes that dyslexic children tend to grow up feeling stupid, no matter how intelligent they may actually be. Anything but a crude reductionist, d'Este argues that both the adult Patton's driving ambition and the macho warrior personality he created to express it manifested, at least in part, in his childhood learning disorder.

Stanley Hirshorn, author of a much less sympathetic biography, argues that the weight of evidence is against Patton as dyslexic. Patton had no trouble with mathematics, read voraciously once he learned how, and in later life was a masterful public speaker and a successful writer. He was able to plan campaigns and visualize complex, changing battlefields with a facility few have matched. The only symptom of dyslexia that Patton manifested was an enduring inability to spell. Patton's spelling was so bad he joked about it in a way he never did about his other shortcomings. It also can be cited as the first set of rules Georgie could not be bothered to learn and keep.

For all the impossibility of determining precisely whether Patton had a learning disability, Patton's parents, and his aunt, must have varied over time, and from time to time, in their reactions to his situation. Was Georgie a bit slow? Was he poorly motivated? Bone lazy? Just not interested? No one was willing to confront the issue seriously. The family's choice for Patton's first formal school was a private, small-enrollment "classical academy"—not the sort of place to put heavy pressure on the son of one of the region's prominent families. Georgie's grammar, punctuation, and spelling remained atrocious. But his ability to express himself verbally and in writing flourished—particularly when he was dealing with a military topic. He also cultivated the ability to memorize large amounts of print.

It was during his final year at the school, in 1902, that Patton finalized his decision to make a career in the military. He was under no direct
pressure to follow the drum. The Patton family still commanded sufficient resources to sustain the ambience of landed leisure—and there was
always the other Patton way of acquiring wealth by marrying it. "Marrying up" through a family's daughters was so common as to be almost
de rigeuer. And in the summer of 1902, Patton had met Beatrice Ayer,
daughter of a "new money" Boston family long acquainted with the Pattons. The teenagers were mutually attracted—enough to call it a first love
that generated the usual fumbling correspondence.

Patton, however, faced a matter of deeper and more immediate concern: how best to take the first steps in his chosen field. After the Civil
War, the officer corps of the U.S. Army was dominated by men commissioned before 1865 who liked the Army well enough, or lacked equivalent prospects in civilian life, to stay on. Chances for senior rank might be
limited, but they were willing to accept the slow pace of promotion and
the often mind-numbing conditions of service for the sake of retiring as a
colonel. By 1898, no fewer than seven of the eight commanders of the geographic departments that provided what structure there was above regimental level were Civil War veterans who had risen by seniority. They
had their counterparts in the staff bureaus of the War Department in
Washington—filled by seniority, permeated from top to bottom by men
committed to keeping the system's wheels moving and its parts meshing
in perpetual motion.

These officers prided themselves as practical men for a practical
country, who concentrated on the actual requirements of service. When it
came to wider questions of military policy and its integration with national affairs, they tended toward principled indifference. Such things,
they argued, were matters best left to civilians, mandated by the Constitution as beyond the province of soldiers whose proper function was as
work tools of the state.

On the other side of the issue stood the visionaries. These officers'
immediate goal was an Army comparable, unit for unit, with its European
contemporaries—something difficult to conceive of in the existing system
of small garrisons and ad hoc flying columns, where a regiment's compa-

nies might never serve together in a quarter-century, and where the concept of service amounted to an agreement between the soldier and the
government to exchange labor for wages. That ambition sought support
from a developing expansionist/internationalist movement, claiming a reformed army could serve both as a power projection force and an emergency instrument of "homeland security."

The Spanish-American War lasted just long enough to confirm most
preconceptions on all sides of the major debates. The administrative system worked well enough once it found its feet. The same might be said for
the field army and its officers. The institutional result in the first years of
the twentieth century correspondingly amounted to a compromise. Under
Secretary of War Elihu Root, the regular Army's strength grew to a hundred thousand men—a fourfold increase from 1898. The concept of a
power projection force was realized when soldiers were assigned responsibility for the security of America's new Pacific holdings. The National
Guard was elevated from its previous status as a force of strikebreakers to
the nation's second line of defense. The General Staff Act provided for a
permanent military planning body. And the Army's educational institutions were overhauled to provide an officer corps capable of managing the
enlarged system and responding to the increased responsibilities.

Since its founding in 1802, the Military Academy at West Point had
been something of a paradox. Frequently criticized for being an un-
American nursery of elitism, before the Civil War it had functioned primarily as an engineering school on one hand and a socializing institution
on the other. Military thought played a subordinate role in the curriculum. Tactical training, as opposed to close-order drill, was neglected.
Cadets were allowed to request the branch of service they preferred, and
by tradition, the best and the brightest opted for the engineers, with the
infantry and cavalry bringing up the rear.

Things changed little after 1865—not least because many of the permanent professors made permanence an art form, retaining their positions long after their counterparts at civilian institutions would have
retired. The Academy's aim in practice was not to produce Army officers,
but to graduate second lieutenants with the potential to become Army officers. The curriculum, centered on mathematics and engineering in their

most abstract forms, was intended to provide mental discipline. The Academy's routines were designed to socialize youths into the "Army system." The rest would be done in the field.

West Point graduates did not automatically side with the visionaries in the "great debate" of the post–Civil War years. Active service often had an opposite effect. The image made most familiar to most Americans by generations of movies is the lieutenant fresh from West Point who sheds his irrelevant book learning under the eyes of grizzled experience. This construction was encouraged by the Army's failure to develop a body of writing and doctrine on frontier operations to which junior officers could turn for guidance. The voice of experience was the only voice available—however wrongheaded its principles frequently proved.

The frontier pattern prevailed elsewhere as well. Whether the junior officer was assigned to an infantry company at Fort Snelling, Minnesota, or an artillery company in a New York fortification, he learned the details of his job by observation, osmosis, and mentoring. And the details tended to be all there was to bother about in America's last decades of absolute free security.

In one sense, George Patton was born about five years too late. He might have fitted well—almost perfectly—into the system of officer development as it existed before the turn of the century. West Point's classes were conducted sufficiently by rote to fit his learning style. His personality would have probably gained him the same kind of approval at the Academy, and in his first assignments, that he had won in Patton family circles. But after the Spanish-American War, matters became different.

First of all, appointments to West Point were becoming more difficult to secure. Since the Academy's founding, its composition had been a matter of political patronage, depending on a presidential or congressional appointment. But appointment did not mean admission. West Point's entry examinations were noted for their rigor. Many congressmen had taken to using some version of an exam to determine their own selections. Those who did not were usually at pains to choose candidates whose school records suggested they would be at least competitive after they became cadets. In the aftermath of 1898, it was risky to open oneself to the charge of playing politics with the nation's military effectiveness.

The California Pattons had ample leverage in theory. Patton's father was, however, disappointed when he contacted regional congressmen about securing his son a place at West Point. Their replies, which usually mentioned the demanding examinations and the increasing competition, led the senior Patton to reevaluate his son's educational experience with a more sober eye. The scion of the Patton line might be of "good old American stock," with a pedigree to rival a blooded racehorse. He had "passed through" algebra and geometry; he was "well up in English composition—and very well up indeed in history." But "he has never studied any Greek or German at all—and only very little Latin and French. He is also a bad speller in English . . ."

It was, all things considered, a remarkably objective analysis by a doting father. In its context, the best next step seemed one that had always been in the family's mind as a sure-thing backup: VMI. Although the phrase "legacy admission" was a century away, the Institute took care of its own. Nor was its academic program so formidable that a young man with the right connections, the right attitude, and basic physical endurance was likely to be "found" by the classwork. In September 1903, George S. Patton enrolled at the Institute. He was an instant success. He may have entered as a first-year "rat," the lowest form of Institute life. He was also a Patton, which even three decades after the Civil War still meant something. The fear that he might not live up to the demands of his heritage put an edge on an already strong motivation. George Patton was an archetype of the spit-and-polish cadet, on every occasion buffed to a high gloss, with a military bearing that drew general admiration. And for one of the few extended periods of his life, he held his tongue through anything the upperclassmen could throw at him.

It was scarcely remarkable, then, that Patton thrived in the VMI atmosphere. His grades improved significantly relative to his classmates— which might say more about the intellectual climate at VMI than any breakthrough in Patton's study skills or intellectual development. Here again the institution's goals must be kept in mind. VMI's connection to the world of higher education at this period was peripheral. Its relationship to the U.S. Army was only slightly less marginal; especially in the post–Civil War years, relatively few graduates sought regular commissions. VMI existed to provide an elite white male leadership cadre for Virginia, and by courtesy, those other states that provided students. George Patton fit its templates perfectly.

Throughout his year at VMI, Patton nevertheless remained focused on entering West Point. His eventual patron was California Senator Thomas Bard. Patton's father had been cultivating him for several years previously, and Bard was one of the congressmen who conducted an examination for the appointment. Patton finished first out of sixteen applicants. In June 1904, he reportd to West Point for his plebe year.

The Spanish-American War and its imperial aftermaths had given the armed forces fresh publicity. No longer were they seen in Civil War terms, as aging men festooned with the ribbons of veterans' organizations marching in parades and angling for pensions. America's military establishments were increasingly presented in contexts of modernization: as cutting-edge symbols of the new century. The Navy, with its growing fleet of battleships brave in white and buff, had a visual edge. But West Point benefited from a major construction program, had its Corps of Cadets expanded from 400 to 500, and experienced a heated discussion of academic reform. Superintendent Albert Mills owed his selection to the favor of President William McKinley, rather than the traditional Army patronage networks. His tenure at West Point was stormy and short. By 1906, he had made enough enemies among enough old guards that he was replaced. But Mills also created a climate of institutional uncertainty that favored cadets who did not quite fit the traditional West Point mold—cadets, it turned out, like George Patton.

II

Patton went through the initial socialization of "Plebe summer" and the initial assignment to a cadet company with no problems he was unable to handle. His size—as one of the tallest plebes, he was assigned to A Company, the right flank of the Corps—and his VMI-cultivated fitness gave him an edge over most of his classmates. So did his familiarity with button polish and boot cream, the preservation of creases in a parade uniform, and the exact angle to wear a shako.

Perhaps Patton confused these skills with what the Academy called "military aptitude." West Point and VMI were not quite the institutional rivals they later became. But for a plebe to say as Patton did that the VMI "brace," the position of exaggerated attention, was more rigid than the West Point version was to invite attention of the wrong kind. Patton's skill at polishing brass and keeping his uniform spotless also made him a target: the purpose of the plebe system was to socialize new cadets, and someone who already commanded its key details was an uncomfortable anomaly.

As Patton settled in, however, the thing that most distinguished him from his fellow cadets was a burning, unconcealed ambition to succeed as a soldier and an officer—to be, indeed, the first of his class to achieve the rank of general. Here again Patton ran afoul of a paradox. No army can sustain effectiveness with an officer corps dominated by *routiniers:* ambition is as necessary to armed forces as oxygen is to breathing. West Point's own academic system, then and for many years, was structured around the principle of every cadet being graded every day in every subject. Class standings were calculated to tenths of a percentage and constantly updated. A similar pattern persisted on the military side, epitomized by a demerit system that precisely punished every observed lapse, from leaving a button undone to dropping a rifle on parade. Where a cadet stood had significant consequences for his present well-being and his future career.

At the same time, ambition unchecked can be devastating. The Army's experience of officers commissioned during emergencies was that they were obsessed with gaining the highest rank possible regardless of their ability to fulfill its responsibilities. The Civil War in particular had spawned a mythology of "political generals" who had led brigades, divisions, and corps to disaster while deserving and unassuming West Point–trained professionals were overlooked. The result in Academy culture was a certain cognitive dissonance in which cadets were expected to seek brass rings and yet be unobtrusive about it. A cadet such as Patton threatened an entire behavioral system perceived as centrally important to the Army's well-being.

For Patton, the West Point system was a good corrective to any initial delusions of grandeur. Academics gave him trouble from the first, especially English. His instructor immediately discovered his "utter lack of knowledge" in grammar, and in standard West Point fashion sought to bring him up to standard by drill and recital in class. Under that kind of public pressure, Patton's already limited composition skills deteriorated perceptibly, as indicated by his letters home. His morale slumped accordingly: "I am a characterless, lazy, stupid yet ambitious dreamer who will degenerate into a third rate second lieutenant and never command more than a platoon," he informed his father in the early winter of 1904.

Things are seldom as bad as they can seem to a teenager, and Patton was no exception. Though he failed to make the cut for the varsity football team, he made the track team, excelling as a hurdler. He developed an interest in fencing that quickly became a passion, and he became one of the best cadet swordsmen in the Academy. His grades improved—especially his English marks, with some thanks to a section transfer. He passed his December examinations creditably. His relationship with Beatrice Ayer progressed to the point where he described himself as "probably suffering from a bad attack of puppy love." While George Patton would never be a typical anything, he was well along the path of integration into the West Point matrix. Then, in the spring of 1905, he was for the first time caught in the Army's machinery.

It began with Superintendent Mills's efforts to overhaul the West Point curriculum—specifically, its historic emphasis on science and mathematics. Mills declared that their current place in the curriculum fostered an excessively theoretical emphasis. The professor of mathematics responded by declaring that the Academy's standards in his subject, far from being excessive, were not high enough. In the spring of 1905 semester, he declared 40 percent of the third class deficient. Unpleasant consequences have a way of running downhill. Fourth classman Patton fell foul of a general tightening of standards, failed plebe math, and was "turned back" to the next class.

Patton had many of the same ideas about officer formation that Mills entertained. He, too, was critical in his undergraduate fashion of what he considered an excessive emphasis on abstract book learning in the academic curriculum, at the expense of military history and what today are called "war studies." He was no less shaken by the turnback. In his do-over year, he built on his plebe experience to lift his academic standing to the top third of his class. Though his academic standing dropped as his classes moved into material he had not previously covered, Patton passed his examinations. He made the football team, albeit as a third-stringer, until sidelined by an injury. He ran track. His emphasis on appearance, discipline, and performance made an increasingly favorable impression—particularly on those who did not experience it directly.

Patton first made rank as a third classman: corporal, with an accompanying assignment to the cadre of plebe summer camp. He was promptly reduced for driving the new intake harder than even the unwritten laws of the Point approved—but his second-class year saw him restored to corporal once more. The end of the year saw him promoted to Cadet Sergeant Major, the highest position then available for a second-year man. In February 1908, his first-class year, Patton made cadet officer and was appointed regimental adjutant.

The appointment was an acknowledgment of Patton's military attitude and military bearing—that last enhanced by his pattern of changing his uniform, as he described it, "fifteen times a day." But Patton told his father of a dream: "I was the adjutant and I was having a fine time, then next night I dreamed I was found and I was having a hell of a time. Everybody was pointing their fingers at me and calling me stupid." Performance-anxiety dreams are common among young adults. This one suggests the unusual effort Cadet Patton devoted to developing his ideas of what made a successful soldier and a great captain.

Even before his collision with the mathematics department, Patton had been working seriously and systematically on the construction of a persona. By the end of his first year at West Point, he had developed a justifiable sense of inferiority—he *was* inferior, as a student, in mainstream athletics, and as a cadet personality. Not least of his trials was a high-pitched, almost squeaky voice whose timbre climbed under stress and kept alive the nickname "Georgie"—not intended as a compliment in the hypermasculine Academy society.

For the sake of an ideal, Patton submerged his more sensitive, warm-hearted side beneath a stern, autocratic, hard-bitten veneer. Patton's oldest daughter describes her memories of him standing in front of a mirror, practicing his warrior face and his martial diction. This was not—and is not—unusual behavior at West Point. Young men coming from the surface egalitarianism of small-town and neighborhood America often found it difficult to exercise authority in the approved Army fashion, with a "command presence" based heavily on a loud voice and a mean look. "Command" within the Corps of Cadets was always a somewhat artificial construction, exercised among age-mates in the same situation. As a result, a good many cadets developed on- and off-duty faces: a pattern remaining familiar in the Army officer corps. Patton was unwilling or unable to maintain that kind of balance between personalities. Instead, he lived the role until eventually George Patton was more or less as he seemed to be.

It is easy enough to satirize the contents of any diary or commonplace book, particularly one composed by a young man. In the entries to the one he kept, Patton fused and focused the stories he heard and the books he read as a child, the aphorisms repeated in the classrooms and on the drill grounds and athletic fields of West Point, and his own determination to transform dreams of glory as a warrior and success as a soldier into reality. On one hand, Patton emerges from these pages as seeking the praise of men; on the other, he demonstrates a determination to deserve it. Success for Patton was not a function of inspiration, but of perseverance, desire—and not least, study. Never a long-term star in formal classroom situations, Patton turned the cadet library inside out, reading not only the classics of war but the technical literature as well.

If it is possible to reduce a complex schema to a single idea, Patton's defining concept was that war allowed no second chances. Do it right the first time. Make an attack and carry it through to the last man. Above all else, allow no second thoughts. Doubt was the enemy of command in battle. It represents no disrespect to an earnest and determined student to observe that these ideas were the common stuff of military thought on both sides of the Atlantic in the first years of the twentieth century. Western armies at any rate, and those modeled on them, were infused with a cult of determination—an emphasis on seeing through a decision whatever the cost—that in 1914, drove them into each other's fire as one might push candles into a blowtorch.

To a degree, that approach reflected a changing intellectual climate, one that emphasized volitional as opposed to material elements. Friedrich Nietzsche, Henri Bergson, even the often-condemned Sigmund Freud: each in his own way asserted the importance of will in shaping an indifferent universe. Rudyard Kipling's poetry, the strenuous-life gospel preached by

Theodore Roosevelt, and a hundred counterparts took that concept into daily life—particularly for a middle class whose male members were at less and less direct risk in their everyday lives. Few in the factories, in the coal mines, and on the muscle-powered farms needed reminding that life was a high-risk enterprise that no one left alive. For the others, new forms of high-risk sports like skiing, mountain climbing, and the early versions of rugby and American football tested abilities to make decisions and stick with them. Fiction aimed at boys and young men increasingly depicted the triumph of pluck, whether on the football field, in the boxing ring, or in more serious tests. It was scarcely surprising that the emphasis on will spread into the armies, drawing more and more officers from the schooled, if not always educated, classes.

The new concepts fit specifically military developments as well. The exponentially increasing size of armies had, for practical purposes, outrun both traditional, muscle-powered means of communication and the newer electronic media, the telegraph and telephone. The drastic imbalance between mass and nervous systems made managed battles in the eighteenth-century sense impossible. Even the flexible campaigns and battles of the Napoleonic era were widely accepted as impossible without a Napoleon orchestrating them. Instead, the successful modern general was expected to make his plans, make his decisions, and stick to them in the face of all temptation to try to respond to particular situations. A flourishing literature on future and imaginary wars preached the gospel of willpower on every page.

III

It was intellectually unremarkable, then, that a well-read, autodidactic young soldier ambitious to succeed should distill a similar set of mantras for himself. Less usual is the determination with which young Patton sought to internalize these intellectual principles. And genuinely unusual was the milieu Patton chose to begin applying them. For someone who sought in the depths of his soul to become a great captain, seeking a commission in the cavalry seemed, in the year of grace 1909, to be a contradiction in terms. For a century and more, the cavalry had been a declining institution in Western armies retained, only as an apocryphal horse soldier suggested, "to give tone to what would otherwise be just a vulgar brawl." The mass charges of a Seydlitz and a Murat were a thing of the past. Even the small-scale attacks delivered in the Franco-German War had produced much mutual admiration, but also resulted in casualty rates of more than 60 percent. The cavalry's other historic task of reconnaissance was being challenged by the rapidly proliferating airships and aircraft. When the high costs of horses and equipment and the longer time required to train an effective horse soldier were factored in, the cavalry seemed doomed to the fate of a niche arm, fighting a rear-guard action for its place in orders of battle.

In the United States, however, things were different. The cavalry played a major role in the Spanish-American War, contributing one of the Cuban Expedition's three divisions, conducting the entire campaign dismounted as a matter of course, and leaving nothing to choose between its "fighting power" and that of the infantry, even when Theodore Roosevelt's grandiloquent paean to his Rough Riders was discounted.

The troopers came correspondingly well out of the increase in force structures in the new century. Indeed, their importance increased: the infantry expanded from twenty-five regiments to thirty; the cavalry's strength grew from ten regiments to fifteen. Because the official strengths of the regiments were almost identical, the cavalry made up almost a third of the Army's fighting strength and proved its worth in the tropical environments of the new American empire. The apparent degeneration of Mexico into a "failed state" in the decade before the 1910 Revolution offered an even more obvious field of opportunity.

Cavalry training stressed versatility. "Cavalry country" to a twentieth-century officer was anywhere a horse could walk or be led and the pack mules could follow. American troopers were armed with the same rifle the infantry carried. They specialized in mounted pistol charges—though the prospects of hitting anything with a Colt .45 automatic from the back of a moving horse had to be largely theoretical. Soon they would have the world's best thrusting sword as well—courtesy of Lieutenant George Patton.

The new cavalry was horse-conscious in a way its predecessor was not. Horse shows and polo, the latter borrowed from an East Coast gentry that in turn lend-leased it from England, were becoming part of regimental routine even in the larger garrisons of the West. And the cavalry still possessed ample panache. Some of it reflected the frontier experience, embodied in old-timers like "Tommy" Tompkins of the 7th. Some was manifested in the tailored uniforms and elegant lifestyles of officers like the 8th's "Lord George" Langhorne. Second Lieutenant George Patton was not simply giving in to the romantic side of his character when he put his name in for cavalry service and was assigned to the detachment of the 15th Cavalry stationed at Fort Sheridan, Illinois.

Patton had another asset as well. Like a fair number of his classmates, he married immediately after graduation. Beatrice Ayer's father was a self-made millionaire who got his start manufacturing patent medicines and first met the Pattons while vacationing in California. The Ayers were rock-ribbed Republicans, the Pattons (though none of them would have used such a vulgar expression) yellow-dog Democrats, and the two paterfamilias enjoyed arguing politics in loud voices. Beatrice had the polish money could buy at the turn of the century, and a character money did not damage. She was also beautiful. Their correspondence ripened into a courtship—with a few ups and downs—while Patton was at West Point. If he made most of the early running, he does not seem to have had to run too fast. Bea enjoyed herself thoroughly as a single girl, but women of her class were expected to marry early and well. What the Pattons lacked in money they made up in ancestry, and there was much to love about young George—not least the emotional vulnerability he poured into his frequent letters. Bea's parents liked him because he had a promising career; officers were a good catch in a way they had never been in the previous history of the Republic. The wedding, on May 26, 1910, was one of the social events of the year.

As a general rule, the Army was unenthusiastic about married second lieutenants. Apart form the issue of supporting a family on a subaltern's pay, a new officer was expected to spend his early years of service learning all the things West Point did not teach. But when the father-in-law is a millionaire, much can be overlooked. Bea's father, as was the custom, made her a generous personal allowance, which, as was also the custom, became joint income. George could afford to purchase his own horses instead of depending on government mounts. He performed his regimental duties well enough to be named an acting troop commander in his first year. He also translated French articles on the cavalry; sought assignment to the Cavalry School at Fort Riley, Kansas; and considered pushing to be sent back to West Point as a tactical officer. The ambition that marked him negatively at West Point had an opposite effect on his superiors and contemporaries in the 15th Cavalry. The Army produced a transfer to the squadron of the 15th Cavalry stationed at Fort Myer, Virginia, residence of the Chief of Staff and just across the Potomac River from Washington D.C., the beating heart of Army national politics.

Washington was essentially a small Southern town. It was not quite true that everyone who was anyone knew everyone else—it was rather that the opportunities to cultivate acquaintance were comprehensive. The squadron's duties were essentially ceremonial, and Patton's dress, demeanor, and horsemanship caught the eye of civilians as well as soldiers, notably then Secretary of War Henry Stimson. Then an unexpected opportunity emerged. The recently revived Olympic Games expanded their proposed list of events for 1912 to include a modern pentathlon. Sometimes called the military pentathlon, it was expressly aimed at soldiers, who would compete in five events ostensibly based on the ancient Greek competition. It was important for the U.S. Army to be represented, and to make a strong showing. Among potential candidates, one stood out. Patton was already known for his horsemanship and swordsmanship. He had run track at West Point. He had learned to swim in California currents. He was a good hand with a pistol. And he possessed that indefinable quality called style.

The Olympic Games were still a venue for true amateurs, and Patton gave the training and the events his all. He finished fifth—no shame when the three medal winners had been preparing for months. In the fencing competition, arguably the most physically demanding and certainly the one with the greatest crowd appeal, he defeated twenty of the twenty-nine opponents he faced and won plaudits for his slashing, all-out attacking style, a sharp contrast to the more defensive tactics favored by the best European military swordsmen. When he returned to Fort Myer, he was soon able to count Chief of Staff Leonard Wood as a dinner and riding companion beguiled by stories of an ideal test of manhood and character, where participation counted for more than victory.

George Patton was on his way. His Olympic experience led the Ordnance Department, normally among the Army's most solipsistic institutions, to consult him on the design of a new cavalry sword. The weapon adopted as the U.S. Saber Mark 1913 was designed to his specifications and rapidly acquired the cognomen of the "Patton sword"—a personalization like that of the Garand and Kalashnikov rifles of a later era, and no mean tribute to a mere lieutenant. The weapon also suggested something about its creator. Unlike its predecessors, whose curved blades made them suitable for defense as well as offense, the "Patton sword" was straight-bladed, designed for thrusting—a kill-or-be-killed instrument of war.

In June 1913, Patton was authorized to continue his sword training at Saumur, site of the French Cavalry School. It would be at his own expense, but his father-in-law knew a good investment when he saw one. Enough money was forthcoming to ship not only George and Bea, but the family auto to France while their year-old child stayed with her grandparents.

Patton's time in France was a personal and a professional success. He attended lectures at the Cavalry School, developed his French, impressed his instructors, and toured the Loire Valley's historic sites. Patton's conviction that he had fought there in a previous life is the first recorded instance of a belief in reincarnation that did much to shape his later mentality. Patton's experiences were also part of the U.S. Army's growing French connection. At first glance it seemed anomalous. The Imperial German army was by contemporary standards the finest in Europe and had a record of hospitality to those seeking to learn from it. Japanese, Turks, even Chileans and Bolivians sent missions to Germany and incorporated German methods. The Americans, however, from the beginning of their systematic encounter with Europe, focused on France as a school of instruction in modern war.

This Francophilia owed something to a generalized respect for French ways of war going back to the American Revolution, and to the influence of Napoleon and Jomini. West Point had for a period a cadet "Napoleon Club," while both Union and Confederate generals sought to internalize the emperor's military axioms. The decisive element, however, was the West Point library. Sylvanus Thayer, who gave the Academy its definitive form, built the collection around more than a thousand military works he purchased on a trip shortly after Napoleon's fall. French, moreover, was the principal foreign language taught—for much of the Academy's history the only one. Although after 1871 the library collection was supplemented with books in German, the number of cadets who could comfortably read the Gothic print was vanishingly small. Not until after World War II did American soldiers cultivate the systematic admiration for the German way of war that one contemporary observer calls "Wehrmacht penis envy."

The overwhelming majority of officers who spent time improving their military knowledge in France enjoyed the experience mightily. Few had ever been to Europe; many had grown up on isolated farms or in drab small towns. If they were not in the financial position to take the kind of advantages open to Patton, they nevertheless returned with an effervescent admiration for the historic sights, the natural beauty, the cuisine, the wine, and—discreetly, for the bachelors and adventurers—the women. Both by their contributions to professional journals and their reminiscences at regimental social functions, they laid the groundwork for the institutional cooperation of 1917–1918 that shaped the modern U.S. Army.

Patton's Olympic achievements had established him as the Army's paramount swordsman; his time at Saumur showed he was more than a public performer. The Army awarded him the title "Master of the Sword" and transferred him to the Cavalry School at Fort Riley, Kansas. The first of these accolades might seem the counterpart of being dubbed "buggy-whip champion" by America's harness makers. Within months of Patton's arrival in Kansas, a war began that marked the end of the fifteen-hundred-year reign of the *arme blanche* in battle, and some of Patton's contemporary rhetoric on the "spirit of the sword" is all too evocative of similar European fustian. But the Mounted Service School at Fort Riley was by no means an institutionalized atavism where worshippers of the horse led "the life of Riley." Since 1892, it had been the center of instruction for junior cavalry officers in a branch of service that expected to be employed on missions from small-scale patrolling, through screening and raiding, to commitment in divisional strength in the American southwest or across the border in Mexico. The sword was a corresponding weapon of opportunity, no longer primary but still useful in more than the "nice to have" category.

Yet for all its perceived usefulness, swordsmanship had become something of a lost art in a U.S. cavalry that had spent the past half-century performing essentially constabulary roles on the Great Plains, and whose greatest combat achievements during that period had been achieved dismounted, in the Cuban campaign of 1898. Patton, though a student in the school, was promptly pressed into service as an instructor, which he called "the hardest job I ever tried." He wrote the drill regulations for the new sword he had designed. In May 1914, he graduated from the Mounted School. In June, he was selected a member of the next U.S. Olympic team. With the help of some judicious string-pulling, he was also chosen for a special course, an extra year at Riley given to promising junior officers. At twenty-seven, George Patton might still be only a second lieutenant. He might periodically indulge in bouts of dissatisfaction at what he considered his limited achievements. His early story is of a prince asserting his heritage.

IV

Erwin Rommel's story, by contrast, is one of making a new place in a new society—a society that had as many frontiers as its American counterpart, only less visible ones. Rommel was born a citizen of a country only twenty years older than he was. The German Empire had been cobbled together from two dozen independent states ranging from the great-power Kingdom of Prussia to vest-pocket sovereignties from the world of operetta. Its unity had been imposed from the top down. Its founding treaty was signed on foreign soil in 1871. National identity was slow in coming to a culture of regions, where horizons seldom extended beyond the sound of village church bells and neighborhood factory whistles.

Erwin Rommel was also part of one of Germany's most distinctive regional heritages. He was a Swabian. The medieval duchy of Swabia had long since been incorporated into the Kingdom of Wuerttemberg, but the characteristics attributed to its inhabitants had survived and flourished.

Swabians were—and still are—expected to be careful and rational in their approach to life—close with money, reserved to the point of dourness, level-headed rather than imaginative. Swabians are not to be brought to battle by the flash of a lady's eyes or the rhetoric of preachers and politicians. But once engaged, they never let go, and once they have your back, they will die covering it.

The soldiers of Wuerttemberg had proven their loyalty and their effectiveness as allies and clients of Napoleon in the first years of the nineteenth century. Wuerttemberg's diplomats proved no less effective defending the small state's independence and sustaining its rights under the German Confederation from 1815 to 1871. The treaties establishing the Second Empire reaffirmed Wuerttemberg's autonomy in a federal constitution. The state controlled its own railroad and postal systems. Its king retained his throne. Wuerttemberg's army was incorporated into Prussia's but remained a separate army corps, administered by a Wuerttemberg government that also retained the right to appoint most of its officers.

That last concession was of central importance both to the Second Reich and to Erwin Rommel. The mass conscript army that won the mid-century Wars of German Unification and sustained Germany's great power status was chronically short of officers. Its Prussian predecessor had strongly favored restricting commissions to a limited basis: nobles by birth or service, supplemented by the sons of interest groups closely affiliated to the aristocracy, particularly clergymen and civil servants. Even before 1871 that pool was too shallow. Increasing numbers of officers were drawn from a middle class characterized by property and education: a middle class willing to integrate itself into the Imperial establishment and become aristocrats by ascription.

Rommel was born into that zone of upward mobility. His father, also Erwin, was a secondary-schoolmaster in the provincial town of Heidenheim an der Brenz, deep in the heart of Swabia proper. A man with a local reputation as a scholar, especially in mathematics, he had married a bit above himself socially. His wife, Helene von Lutz, was a child of Wuerttemberg's service nobility: a category of senior officials and army officers who, though commoners born, could reasonably expect to receive an eventual title as part of their "benefit package," with corresponding prospects for their descendants. Helene's father was a *Regierungspraesident*. In many parts of Prussia, that was sufficiently above a secondary-school teacher to make the marriage a bit of a *mésalliance*. Wuerttembergers, even Swabians, were both more practical and—dare it be said—perhaps a bit more romantic underneath the dourness.

In any case, the Rommels had four children, a daughter and three sons. Erwin was the second child, born in 1891, and in his youthful years thoroughly unremarkable. His friends and siblings recalled an easygoing boy who at times cultivated the aesthetic sensitivity expected of a German middle-class youth, but as he moved into adolescence, he developed his physical side, including a taste for the relatively new sports of skiing and bicycling.

By comparison to George Patton, Erwin also seems to have been self-contained. His relations with his family show nothing of the intimacy—or the enmeshment—characterizing the Patton household. Although no one really knows what goes on behind closed doors, that pattern was hardly unusual among Swabians, who frequently regard a firm handshake at Christmas and on birthdays as a year's worth of demonstrativeness. Rommel's mother provided the family warmth—a common division of labor in Imperial Germany's middle class. Erwin Senior is usually described by some variation on "strict" and "authoritarian"—again, no particular anomaly in turn-of-the-century Germany. He was ambitious, earning promotion to head of the secondary school in the small town of Aalen; and caring, providing private elementary tuition for his oldest son instead of sending him to a primary school he apparently considered inadequate.

While Swabian culture values self-reliance, young Rommel came nowhere near deciding on a career by the time he graduated from secondary school. He was sufficiently, if vaguely, interested in aircraft to consider seeking a post at the Zeppelin factory at Friedrichshafen. His father had another idea. The elder Rommel had done his own compulsory service in the artillery, but the family had no other connections with the army. Nor were the Rommels inflamed by the romantic patriotism that was so much a part of the Patton heritage. In his father's mind, what the army offered Erwin was the prospect of a solid career, with enough outdoor physical activity to satisfy him and a mentality that suited his increasingly practical orientation. Like Patton Senior, Rommel's father appears to have suffered no inflated ideas of his son's capacities. In recommending him as a potential officer, he described Erwin as thrifty, reliable, and good in gymnastics—not exactly a glowing endorsement, but sufficient for the purpose.

Rommel's route to a commission was one by the turn of the century, followed by more than half the army's career officers. In contrast to the American system, built around passage through a single military academy, Germany employed essentially a "direct-entry" process. Its details were periodically revised, but the essentials remained constant. The candidate must complete some advanced secondary schooling; he must pass an "ensign's examination" qualifying him as a cadet officer; and he must secure the approval of the officers of the regiment in which he proposed to serve.

Rommel possessed the necessary academic paperwork. Even so, the ensign's examination was no bagatelle. It involved three days of written exercises lasting from 8 A.M. to 3 P.M., followed by another day of oral examinations—all taken in full evening dress, complete with formal coat and white gloves. Failure rates might have been low, but the test was nevertheless taken very seriously by the vast majority of youngsters subjected to it. And it was only the first step.

The process of securing the approval of a candidate's prospective fellow officers is frequently misinterpreted. It was certainly designed to maintain certain standards and attitudes by screening out social and religious elements considered as "outsiders": Jews, Social Democrats, laborers, and small shopkeepers, to name a few. Participants, however, generally understood the system as fair. Though hardly democratic, it neither excluded merit nor demanded extraordinary achievement. Efforts by the War Ministry to raise the barriers by requiring all officer candidates to pass the *Abitur* examination that qualified them for university admission foundered on a broad spectrum of public protest, much the same way as standards-based testing in the United States founders when the children of the affluent middle class fall below the success line in significant numbers. Even regarding the particularly sensitive "Jewish issue," contemporary critics of the German officer corps tended to consider regard the exclusivity that cut off opportunities for reserve commissions more important than the opportunities to pursue a career as an active officer that exclusivity also denied.

Given the German army's size and complexity, the right of each regiment's officer corps to approve candidates for a commission also created a kind of free market. A candidate *prima facie* unsuitable in one regiment might be acceptable, even welcome, in another. The respective criteria of particular units were sufficiently well known to limit overt humiliation, even in the early stages of the recommendation process. The candidate's formal qualifications were also known beforehand. A direct applicant, like Rommel, he frequently had been introduced socially to his prospective comrades, sometimes even before taking the ensign's examination. That allowed ample opportunity for raising and addressing objections of any nature before the final, public step of the colonel calling for a vote that was usually unanimous. Significant dissent at that stage was considered to reflect badly on all parties involved and was correspondingly rare.

For most serious applicants, the principal problem involved finding a vacancy that matched their interests and desires. Rommel's first inquiries were to the local field artillery regiment. The colonel replied that he expected no vacancies in the foreseeable future. That was less surprising than it might seem. Once the army's red-haired stepchild, the artillery had become a high-status branch in the years after 1871, next only to the cavalry in prestige—not because of its scientific and technical aspects, but because its rapid and continuing expansion offered good promotion prospects, and because it was closely associated with horses. Young men whose incomes or social standing might not reach to the levels expected of a cavalry officer could at least share in a major element of the cavalryman's life style. By the early twentieth century, it was common for families with sons interested in joining the artillery to begin cultivating good relations with the local gunners while the boy was still in school—a kind of informal preregistration that made it difficult for a late decider like Erwin to find a place in the queue.

Rommel's technical interests next led him to the pioneers. That branch of the army was historically the most "scientific," and in the years

leading up to the Great War had focused particularly on the craft of be-
sieging and assaulting fortresses. Unfortunately, the army of Wuerttemberg maintained only a single pioneer battalion with a total officer
establishment of around three dozen, and an even longer waiting list than
the artillery.

There remained one alternative—the same one prospective officers
have been following as a last resort since the days of Julius Caesar. The
124th Infantry Regiment, the 6th Wuerttemberg, bore the title "King
William I," after a former Wuerttemberg monarch now remembered only
by doctoral candidates. The army's lineage experts traced its heritage as
far back as 1673, but its history recorded no spectacular achievements.
Its garrison of Weingarten had received the status of "city" only in 1865.
Although preferable to the small towns of Alsace and the villages of East
Prussia, Weingarten was still a *Kleinstadt,* a "home town" remarkable
primarily for its baroque architecture. But the regiment needed officers
and welcomed a young man with Rommel's stated qualities of character,
physique, and intellect. With a brief sidetrack for a hernia repair, he
joined the 124th as a cadet in July 1910.

When the old Prussian army was destroyed by Napoleon in 1806, the
reformers who evaluated its weaknesses concluded that one major defect
had been the remoteness of too many junior officers from the men they
were supposed to lead and command. The solution, which endured in
one or another form until the end of World War II, was to require every
candidate for a regular commission to serve approximately six months as
an enlisted man. During that time he would be instructed in the duties of
a junior noncommissioned officer (NCO), then put the knowledge into
practice by serving brief terms as a corporal and a sergeant. His company
officers, his battalion and regimental commander, kept him under observation for that period. In practice the process involved a significant degree of window dressing. A candidate already screened and accepted by
the officer corps was likely to receive the help he needed when he needed
it. The rest was a final hazing process, a rite of passage designed to keep
the youngster off-balance, keep him from thinking too well of himself as
he moved toward the final step on the way to a commission.

Rommel's regimental service lasted from July 1910 to March 1911.
Pushing all the right buttons as junior NCO, he found himself assigned to

the War School in Danzig. Since 1810, a network of "War Schools" had prepared students for the officer's examination. Sometimes confused with the War Academy, the army's principal institution of higher military learning, the War Schools are better compared to the contemporary U.S. Army's Officer Basic Schools. Their curricula included only military subjects: tactics, fortification, administration, gymnastics. Their purpose was not to act as "keepers of the gate," but to bring as many ensigns as possible to levels of proficiency, enabling them to pass the examinations qualifying them for a commission. That pattern is common to entry-level education/training systems everywhere in the Western and Westernized military world. Standards are set to be met; hurdles are designed to be jumpable. High failure rates indicate not rigor but incompetence on the part of the institution's administrators. Common sense and reasonable application were enough to carry most ensigns through; behavior and attitude were at least as important for students as formal class work. Certainly the examination was not as widely feared as its predecessor, the ensigns' test.

Sending a Swabian to a land of pickled herring and constant fog may have seemed an example of what author Robert Graves call the "Practical Joke Department" that exists in all armed forces. In fact, it reflected the army's concern for breaking down local and regional identities in favor of a German mind-set. That was seen as particularly important for cadets from small-state contingents, where particularism might become an obstacle to effectiveness instead of a spur to competition.

On graduating, Rommel was described as "quite good" in rifle and drill practice, "good" in leadership, and "competent" in everything else of significance. Physically still developing, Rommel possessed firm character, strong willpower, high enthusiasm, and a sense of duty. He was punctual, conscientious, and a good comrade. Although not exactly boilerplate, these comments are best understood as the German army's counterpart of the "health and morals" recommendations written every semester for B+ students whom one really does not remember all that well. Rommel, in other words, made the impression of a young man as yet mostly potential, but likely to become a useful soldier.

Rommel also seized the opportunity to fall in love. Lucie Mollin, like Rommel, was the child of a school director. Her father dead, she had her own way to make and had come to Danzig to study languages—a respectable career for a "higher daughter" at a time when university attendance stamped one a bluestocking. Dark haired and slender, the direct antithesis of the Brunhilde archetype, an accomplished dancer and more than something of a flirt, her relationship with Rommel invites the cliché of opposites attracting. But Lucie was attracted by his steadiness, and Rommel also showed a lighter side as a suitor, wearing a monocle in defiance of regulations, then concealing it whenever an officer appeared on the horizon (rebellion is relative!) and conducting a daily correspondence once he returned to his regiment.

Rommel considered them engaged, or the next thing to it. Lucie, or Lu as she was universally known, was not quite so sure, and her mother seems to have been even less impressed by the relationship. At least Erwin felt constrained to address his correspondence to the post office rather than Lu's home address. This maternal reluctance may seem surprising to readers brought up on images of the officer as Imperial Germany's most desirable catch. But Lu was young, and Wuertemberg was far away. Lu was Catholic and Rommel Protestant at a time when such mixed marriages were not common. And above all there was the *Kaution,* the marriage bond.

An officer's bride was required by regulations to provide a dowry. Usually deposited in the German equivalent of a blind trust, this was intended to prove the woman's financial independence, and by extension the couple's ability to live according to the standards appropriate to the husband's rank and status. The practice, often described as designed to keep "unsuitable" women from contaminating the Kaiser's elite, had other roots as well. A junior officer's pay, although increasingly low by comparison with civilian society, could support a single man if he was reasonably prudent. It was not a family salary. The marriage bond safeguarded army wives from becoming camp followers. The sum, although not insurmountable, probably acted as a practical deterrent to romance in the case of Erwin and Lu. And even when the bond was easily forthcoming, young love—or its equivalents—encountered the convention, amounting almost to a regulation, that junior officers were to remain unmarried, instead devoting their full attention to mastering their profession.

Small wonder then that Rommel conducted a long-distance, low-key romance when he returned to his regiment in the spring of 1912. The

124th had no reputation as a high-living outfit, so his abstence from to-
bacco and alcohol stood out less than it might in a more flamboyant regiment. He spent more time studying than was usual for a newly minted
lieutenant—a probable reaction to his experience at Danzig, where the
academic side of the curriculum had given him the most trouble. And like
every other junior officer in the Imperial German army, Erwin Rommel
trained recruits.

Germany's conscription system made every male of twenty eligible
for military service—two years in the infantry, three in the cavalry and artillery. (The difference was justified by the extra time considered necessary to teach recruits horsemastership.) That meant half the men in an
infantry company at any time would be mastering the basics. It meant
constant personnel turnover, at levels that would shock an officer in any
contemporary Western army. Officers were also scarce. Various forms of
detached service kept the usual number at two or three per company, and
on any given day, one of them was likely to be performing some regimental assignment. The German army had no room for career privates,
the professional rear rankers who did so much informally to shape British
and American recruits. For practical purposes, a company's only old soldiers were its noncommissioned officers. These served for a minimum of
twelve years, in return for a pension and generous preferences in civil-ser-
vice appointments. A fortunate company might have eight or ten of them,
ranging from polished instructors and professional role models to brutal
dipsomaniacs.

German training correspondingly tended toward the slipshod—a fact
demonstrated in the first weeks of the Great War, when recalled reservists
who barely remembered how to load their rifles made attack after attack
in mass formations best described as columns of flocks, less because of
regulations emphasizing shock tactics than because their two reflex actions were to follow their officers and huddle together for protection that
turned out to be ephemeral against modern firepower.

Full days on the drill ground accompanied by long nights of administration drove any dreams of martial glory out of most junior officers'
heads soon enough. Although the Kaiser's lieutenants, unlike their British
counterparts, were not expected to participate in sports with their men,
the German army did embody a strong paternalistic element. Twenty-

year-olds away from home for the first time could find a plethora of ways to get themselves into trouble, both in barracks and on pass. Military service had become a generally recognized rite of passage to adulthood for Germany's young men. In practice, that usually meant losing one's virginity, drinking far more than one could hold, and engaging in brawls over turf and women with civilians or men from other regiments.

Like most of the Imperial army's regiments, the 124th managed to keep the balance. Its court-martial records and its company punishment books were gratifyingly slim. If occasionally a recruit was taught the facts of his new life by a couple NCOs, or received "a visit from the Holy Ghost" at night in the barracks for drawing the sergeant's attention and wrath onto the whole section, those were not matters that a lieutenant was expected to address. A joke known to every German private involved a senior officer catechizing a new recruit. "Who is the father of your company?" "The captain, Herr General." "And who is the mother of the company?" "The *Feldwebel* (First Sergeant), Herr General!" "And what do you want to become in the army?" "An orphan, Herr General!" But then, an easy rite of passage is a contradiction in terms, and as long as there were no wars on the horizon, the officers of the Kaiser's army could count on a regular intake of tractable recruits—every autumn, one following another, until the proverbial lieutenant's destiny of "dying in a ditch outside Paris" might seem a welcome alternative.

A correspondingly crucial element of junior officer development was to keep them interested in their craft, as opposed to the "lieutenant's banes" of strong drink, poor cards, slow horses, and fast women. Even Rommel, normally a model of repressed rectitude, suffered his lapses—one in particular. In the summer of 1912, he met Walburga Stemmer. Their daughter was born the next year. Rommel was a single man, with no more than an informal understanding with Lucie. But the army's regulations and its unwritten laws alike forbade an officer marrying the teenage daughter of a seamstress, even if somehow the *Kaution* might be forthcoming.

On the other hand, a father who avoided public scandal while acknowledging and supporting his child was not considered to forfeit his honor. He could count on the support of his superiors and an army reluctant to lose a good officer for a "gentleman's failing" (*Kavaliersdelikt—*

the corresponding euphemism for gonorrhea was *Kavalierschnupfen,* or "gentleman's cold"). Nor did the mother entirely lose social standing and marriage prospects in her community, especially if she had been a "good girl" before her "misstep." *Fehltritt,* the common euphemism for such a situation, acknowledged the simultaneous powers of passion and custom in a caste society.

Although Rommel occasionally mused about making a new life with his new and unofficial family, he confined the feeling to late-night correspondence. In the harsh light of day, he does not seem to have extended the liaison unduly, nor did he hold out serious hopes of marriage to a girl who in any case presumably knew the rules or had them explained by her own mother. Rommel did all the right things for an officer and a gentleman who had made a mistake. He supported the mother and child financially. He kept in regular contact with his daughter—signing his letters "Uncle Erwin." He bit the bullet of telling Lu the story, though the circumstances of the conversation remain unknown. In his later, successful years, with women of every kind available and in a wartime sexual environment increasingly permissive, when not promiscuous, Rommel joked about his opportunities and slept alone. His daughter married in 1942 and had a son of her own. Not a fairy-tale outcome, perhaps, but better than it might have been. Walburga's apparent suicide shortly after Rommel's son was born might even have been coincidence.

Omelets and eggs—Lieutenant Rommel had a career to make, and in the decade prior to World War I, the army had grown increasingly concerned with improving the coordination between infantry and artillery. As the gunners increasingly adopted techniques of indirect fire from concealed positions, senior infantry officers grumbled at the risks of diminished morale among riflemen who would no longer be able to see their supporting guns and know their crews faced the same risks as the infantry. To bridge the gap, junior officers were frequently exchanged for brief tours of duty. It was an assignment usually considered a plus point in career advancement; no colonel wanted to risk embarrassing himself, his regiment, and his arm of service by sending any but his best. On March 1, 1914, Lieutenant Erwin Rommel was attached to the 49th Field Artillery, one of the divisional regiments supporting the 124th. He was commanding a platoon in its 4th Battery on August 1, 1914.

2

TESTS

I N the decade before 1914, not merely Europe's great powers, but such middle-size states as Belgium, Serbia, Greece, and Rumania energetically overhauled their military systems. The near-exponential expansion of armed forces after 1905 was accompanied by a near-obsessive symmetry in their structuring. Conciliation was at a corresponding discount not only in Berlin, but in Vienna, Paris, London, St. Petersburg, Belgrade—even Brussels, as a rearming Belgium prepared to defend its neutrality by force against all comers. Colonel Edward House, dispatched on a fact-finding mission by U.S. President Woodrow Wilson in May 1914, described the atmosphere as "surcharged with war and warlike preparations . . . militarism run stark mad."

Yet for all the sound and fury, Europe continued to dodge the bullet. Crises came and went; crisis management techniques repeatedly proved their equal. Armies drilled and paraded; war plans remained in general staff pigeonholes. The summer of 1914 was one of the calmest periods in a decade. When Archduke Franz Ferdinand, heir to the Dual Monarchy's throne, was assassinated in an obscure provincial city on June 28, initial reactions in foreign offices, war ministries, and newsrooms alike reflected nothing so much as a sense of *déjà vu*. It was just one more damn fool thing happening in the Balkans: the stuff of speeches and headlines for a week or two, music-hall jokes for a little longer. When the mobilization notices began going up on official bulletin boards, no one was quite sure what had happened.

I

In the German army, summer was a time to pause for breath. Officers contemplated furloughs and cures. NCOs finishing their careers began evaluating job openings in the civil service. Privates in their final weeks in uniform invested in beer mugs, pipes, and photos celebrating their approaching transition to reserve status. Regimental and brigade exercises were over. It was time to prepare for the autumn grand maneuvers. Rumor said that this year they were supposed to be more realistic than ever.

International crisis or no, there were still schedules to meet. Early in the morning of July 31, the 4th Battery of the 49th Field Artillery took its turn on the exercise ground. Lieutenant Rommel's mind was on returning to his own regiment: it was, after all, supposed to be a short war. The next day he rejoined the 124th. The barracks was a scene of purposeful chaos. Reservists reported to pick up uniforms presized and equipment presorted. New faces appeared in the officers' mess and in the ranks of the NCOs, as reservists took the places of men transferred as cadres to the reserve regiment forming as the 124th's clone.

Like its continental counterparts, the German army of 1914 was essentially a force of mobilized civilians. Even an "active" regiment like Rommel's 124th included more than 50 percent reservists, who had had no more than brief refresher courses—and many not even that—since completing their tours of duty. Before the war, an increasing gap had developed between the number of twenty-year-olds eligible for service and the number the army was actually authorized to conscript. The remainder were assigned to an *Ersatz* reserve that received no training at all and was expected to serve as a replacement pool, should the war last that long.

What all this added up to was that an army of virgin soldiers was expected to implement one of the most demanding plans of campaign in modern military history. In twenty previous years of preparing for a great continental war, the German General Staff had come to the conclusion that Germany's only chance for victory lay in an all-out offensive. The conclusion in 1894 of an alliance between France and Russia did not by itself create an irresistible impulse for that strategy, despite the inescapable image it generated of Germany as a watermelon caught in a vise. Arguably more important was the growing conviction of its military experts that German society could not sustain a long war under any circumstances. It was possible to develop a defensive strategy in which Germany could keep the field against enemies on both its eastern and western frontiers. The domestic stress resulting from the protracted conflict that strategy entailed would, however, bring disaster as surely as would a military defeat.

By the first years of the twentieth century, the General Staff had developed an operational plan that integrated mobilization, deployment, and maneuver in a single, seamless web. The Schlieffen Plan, named for its principal architect Alfred von Schlieffen, chief of staff from 1891 to 1905, proposed to solve Germany's two-front dilemma by leaving only a minimum force in the east and throwing every available man and gun against France. Its distinguishing feature was a massive sweep through northern France and Belgium that was intended, according to long-standing conventional wisdom, to outflank the French army, drive it away from Paris, and inflict a decisive defeat, enabling Germany to redeploy against a Russia that would probably be willing to negotiate peace with its principal ally driven from the field.

The invasion of Belgium, whose neutrality was guaranteed by the European powers, was considered certain to bring Britain into the war. But an Anglo-German antagonism that had been steadily growing since the 1860s, most recently fuelled by Germany's challenge to British maritime superiority by constructing its own battle fleet, meant Britain was unlikely to remain neutral in any case. Given the numerical weakness of Britain's professional army, there were arguably even strategic advantages to dealing with it at the same time as the forces of France.

The Great Plan's success depended on the army. The Second Reich possessed neither significant numerical nor material superiority in the decisive Western theater. But from Chief of Staff Helmuth von Moltke down, the army believed war's decisive elements lay in the realm of morale. The nation's will to fight must be channeled through it's armed forces. Bravery, discipline, leadership—these were the qualities that would see Germany to victory.

Popular enthusiasm for the war in Germany was less widespread and much shallower than the grainy newsreels of cheering crowds in public places suggest a century later. An initial carnival spirit rapidly gave way to what the editor of a major Berlin newspaper described as not "what one calls mass enthusiasm, but the release of an enormous inner tension." Germany's people understood the war as a defensive conflict against a coalition of implacable enemies, evoking a sense of duty that would survive four years unlike anything all but a few apocalyptic visionaries had been able to imagine. That did not exclude a certain sense of excitement as the reservists reported; donned their uniforms; and renewed friendships, acquaintances, and enmities cultivated while on active duty. Neither did it quench a certain anticipation as the troop trains rolled into the stations, the boxcars absorbed their quotas of men and horses—40 of one or 8 of the other; the size of freight cars were standard in western Europe—and everyone set out for the great adventure.

Rommel was in one of the rear echelons, not leaving for the front until August 5. The 124th, part of the XIII Corps, was assigned to the 5th Army, nominally commanded by the Crown Prince of Prussia. The heavy intellectual lifting was the responsibility of the army's chief of staff, Major General Konstantin Schmidt von Knobelsdorff. But among the seven German field armies initially deployed on the Western Front, the 4th's mission was the easiest and most obvious. It was the pivot force on which the three armies of the right wing swung through northern France and Belgium, while the two armies to its south fought a delaying action, pinning the French firmly in Alsace-Lorraine. The 4th Army's schedule called neither for the man-killing marches demanded of its northern neighbors, nor for the sophisticated tactics of a fighting retreat. All its three active and two reserve corps had to do was keep pace with the great wheel.

The major problem confronting the 4th was terrain. Its sector was the Ardennes Forest, whose impassability would twice be a mistaken article of faith in a later war. Rommel was twenty-three years old and fighting fit. But after only three days of marching, he collapsed on the field of honor after his first experience of combat, ". . . not least the terrible condition of my stomach had sapped the last ounce of my strength." Defecating for one's country was almost as bad as dying for it—almost. A quarter of the 124th's officers and almost a fifth of its men were down: in earlier wars a casualty list to inspire ballads, but just a normal day on the emerging Western Front.

Rommel's reconstruction of his Great War experiences, first published in 1937 and correspondingly polished by memory, was intended as a guide to junior infantry officers, not a memoir. Rommel's self-portrait was correspondingly a construction of the ideal infantry officer. The combat narratives he presents, while by no means fictionalized, are structured, for instructional purposes, around what Lieutenant Rommel should optimally have thought, ordered, and done. The image that emerges nevertheless reflects Rommel's actual behavior: someone increasingly committed to taking charge of a situation immediately, without waiting for orders all too likely to be irrelevant if they arrived at all.

The heavily forested terrain through which the Germans were advancing put a premium on that kind of leadership by encouraging the breakdown of larger units. Forty years later, the same thing would happen to American infantry only a few miles north, in the Huertgen Forest. The French army had eschewed field howitzers and heavy guns for their artillery in favor of concentrating on the flat-trajectory, rapid-firing, 75-millimeter field gun. Equipped only with shrapnel rounds that were not much use against dug-in targets, Mademoisellle Soixante-Quinze was nevertheless deadly against anything in the open. Field entrenchment was not a craft initially valued by the offensive-minded German army of 1914. The French guns made believers in a hurry; after a few weeks, even the battalion staff worked alongside enlisted grooms and orderlies to dig themselves in when the first rounds exploded overhead.

Rommel himself spent a lot of time on his stomach, hugging the ground. But unlike the open country of Picardy and Flanders, where conspicuous movement made one a clear target and tended to make aggressive leadership a one-time event, the Ardennes enabled a man with Rommel's rapidly developing situational awareness to take advantage of cover and concealment to implement fire and movement at small-unit levels. And as is the usual case with survivors at the beginning of a war, he built a reputation in spite of himself. In early September, he was appointed adjutant of the 124th's 2nd Battalion. The adjutant was the commander's factotum, his man of all work, and Rommel found himself alternately acting as a liaison officer to other units, commanding leading reconnaissance patrols, and accompanying the battalion's leading companies on the march or in an attack.

By mid-September, the 4th Army's advance was beginning to stall. Continuous rainy weather turned unpaved secondary roads into mud. Bogged-down supply wagons meant delayed rations. In an army unused to living off the land, that, in turn, meant hunger—or massive digestive problems, as men ate whatever they could scrounge, and ate it raw or half-cooked because no one had the energy to supervise proper preparation. Tension also contributed to digestive issues. Rommel, who as a headquarters soldier had the best of what was available, suffered from constant stomach trouble during this period—agonizing cramps that wore him out so thoroughly that on one occasion he fell into a comalike sleep from which it took a day to recover. His "normal" sleep was plagued with nightmares. And Rommel was among the toughest officers in the regiment.

Against this backdrop, senior officers sought to sustain the advance by taking chances. On one occasion, the colonel of the 124th ordered a night attack in an effort to gain surprise and escape the deadly French artillery fire. The idea had worked for other German units earlier in the campaign. This time there was no reconnaissance. Orders failed to arrive. The men stood in ranks under a cold rain. The advance did not begin until 3 A.M.—about ninety minutes from sunrise. Despite all this, the initial attack succeeded, only to bog down in the face of unexpected French counterattacks. The 124th spent the rest of the day more or less vainly seeking shelter from French guns. Casualties were more than 200, and the Germans would never get any closer to the fortress of Verdun than they did on that day.

On September 12, the 124th received orders to fall back. The French pursued cautiously. Not until September 22 was Rommel's battalion sent back into action: ordered to make a frontal attack. The commanding officer (CO) was new, and listened when Rommel suggested instead a withdrawal from the position the battalion occupied, an approach march through concealing woods, and a charge against the French from an unexpected direction. Abandoning ground without orders was enough to cost an officer his command, but Major Salzmann was willing to trust his adjutant's advice. The 2nd Battalion took the French by surprise just as Rommel predicted, capturing fifty prisoners, a couple machine guns, and best of all, field kitchens with the French dinner almost ready to eat. An entire French brigade withdrew precipitately for a cost of four German dead and eleven wounded—pocket change in the new conditions of war.

There was nothing unusual about the maneuver itself. Both the Infantry Drill Regulations and the army's collective wisdom enjoined that kind of flanking operations. What was significant was Rommel's ability to impose his solution—and his will—on his superior officer, take the lead in executing the movement and the assault—and walk away with a whole skin.

Rommel's numbers nearly ran out two days later. When the lead company stalled under fire, Rommel went forward to get the advance men moving. He took a rifle from a wounded man—officers carried only a pistol, useless at anything but point-blank range—and immediately got into a close-range fire fight with five Frenchmen. The German *Gewehr 98* held a five-round clip, and it was by good luck as well as good shooting that Rommel dropped two of his opponents before his weapon clicked empty. German infantrymen went into action with their bayonets fixed; bayonet training was an important part of the peacetime training program, and Rommel considered himself a skilled bayonet fighter. As he tells the story, he was getting ready to rush the three Frenchmen still standing when a bullet from another direction put a fist-size hole in his leg. Two of his men carried him out of the fight. Then it was three miles back to an aid station, a joltingly painful ride by horse-drawn ambulance to the field hospital, and another transfer to a base hospital in the town of Stenay, later famous as the headquarters of the Crown Prince during the battle of Verdun.

Again Rommel was lucky. His was the kind of wound that easily led to amputation in World War I, either because of initial trauma or secondary infection that generated gas gangrene. As it was, he required further surgery, but in October, he was on his way to Germany and a convalescent hospital with what his army called a *Heimatschuss*, the British a "Blighty," and the Americans a "million-dollar wound." He also had a medal: the Iron Cross, Second Class.

The leg kept Rommel away from the front until January 1915. He missed the three months in which open war gave way to the stasis of the trenches and maneuver became a thing of the past. He missed the initial weeks of adaptation, when casualties were especially high among officers constrained to take ever greater risks as the original complements of their platoons and companies gave way to replacements who too often had either forgotten their training or received only superficial instruction in loading their rifles and brushing their teeth.

Rommel also returned as a certified hero whose achievements had lost nothing in the retelling by the old hands who survived. His new assignment was as commanding officer of the 2nd Battalion's 9th Company—a little more than 200 men on paper, including men detached to do everything from carry rations to dig latrines. A "trench strength" of 120 was about standard for the period. On January 29, the 124th and the rest of its division were ordered to undertake a series of diversionary attacks to pin down the French to their front. The 9th Company was initially detailed as flank guard, but when the 3rd Battalion's adjutant dashed over, declared his battalion's attack was going well, and asked if the 9th wanted to join the party, Rommel answered "Naturally." It spoke for his leadership that most of the men followed him. It spoke for his sense of ground that he led them, first running and then crawling, unobserved to within a hundred yards of the main French positions before again coming under rifle and machine-gun fire. To stay put or to attack—either option would be costly, and Rommel was juggling alternatives when he heard the 3rd Battalion's bugles sounding "charge." He ordered his own bugler to repeat the call, and the 9th Company followed its commander through three lines of French defenses, driving their occupants before them and suffering no casualties at all.

That kind of local success was by no means unusual at this stage of the war. The French army was no better trained than the German and had suffered even heavier casualties in the war's first months. The trench systems were by no means continuous, and the unexpected appearance of Germans on a flank or in the rear was likely to induce precipitate withdrawal. The charging 9th Company's real problem began when it came under a heavy cross fire and simultaneously ran into a wire entanglement, heavier than anything Rommel had ever seen. He went ahead, found what looked like a passage through, and shouted for the company to follow. This time no one moved. Perhaps some of the veterans remembered other occasions when what looked like a gap in the wire turned out to be a dead end with a machine gun covering it. Rommel crawled back and told the commander of his leading platoon to follow orders or Rommel would shoot him on the spot.

An empty threat? Perhaps. The German army had its rules and regulations—none of which covered summary execution of a subordinate in combat. But Rommel's words were enough. George Bernard Shaw once observed that one may call a man pirate, bully, or brute, and he will feel a secret pride. Call him coward, and he will give up his life to disprove the charge. First the platoon, then the company, moved through the wire and into the abandoned positions beyond—and found themselves surrounded as French infiltrators cut off their line of retreat.

This again was a common course of events in the Great War: a local success that, when left unsupported, threatened to become a disaster. When a runner shouted an order to withdraw to the 2nd Battalion's main position, Rommel saw that going back through the wire was impossible. He dismissed surrender as "unthinkable." Instead, he led an attack forward, broke through the surprised French, and swung back to the German lines by an unobstructed route. Incredibly, the operation cost only five men too badly wounded to be moved and so left behind for the French, plus the usual number of scrapes and nicks dealt with by company aid men and not reported on the official casualty lists.

Rommel's initiative in supporting the 3rd Battalion's initial advance was thus part of a respected tradition. His success in getting farther than anyone else in the regiment, and the achievement of bringing back his company intact—those were triumphs beyond the normal standards of duty. A week later he was awarded the Iron Cross, First Class.

This was not usually a junior officer's medal, and Rommel was the first lieutenant in the regiment to sport its black-and-white ribbon. He had also by this time become a near-legendary figure to the men of the 124th. Not only did he look the part, with his piercing eyes and erect carriage, but he lived up to his reputation by sharing the dangers and privations of the front line to a greater degree than many officers, especially the youngsters. Lieutenant Rommel did not have a sore throat—the polite euphemism for a glory hunter anxious for the feel of medal ribbons around his neck. Nor was he the kind of officer who took chances from a sublime and heedless belief in his own immortality. Instead, his watchword was *"erst waegen dann wagen"*: "first consider, then risk." He wanted an opportunity to be something more than a cog in the machine, a target for enemy shell fire. New weapons, hand grenades and flamethrowers, trench mortars and small cannon were making their appearance. New tactics, emphasizing small groups attacking separately and coming together only upon reaching the objective, were being discussed and tested. On March 2, 1915, the War Ministry ordered the formation of an Assault Detachment (*Sturmabteilung*) as a test bed for these innovations.

Rommel remained with the 124th through the spring, fighting in the same sector as the trench lines stabilized and the trench systems became more elaborate. At the start of the war, some officers had been left in the regimental depot to supervise training recruits and replacements. Now they were being rotated to the front, and one of them, senior to Rommel, took over the 9th Company. The regimental commander proposed a transfer. Rommel refused, preferring to stay with men he knew and trusted. He reverted to platoon command—most probably with a certain degree of *Schadenfreude* as his green replacement coped with having a highly decorated regimental hero looking over his shoulder!

The German army was chronically short of officers, due in good part to a reluctance to expand the social and educational limits of the pool of eligible candidates. Officially a rifle company should have had five; two was a more usual figure. Rommel's record made him a logical choice as a regimental troubleshooter, transferring from company to company as commander or executive officer, then reverting to platoon command in the 9th as men senior returned from hospital, furlough, or detached duty. He had his own spell of home leave in July, was slightly wounded in the shin, and in September was promoted to First Lieutenant (*Oberleutnant*). Then his destiny changed utterly.

II

Beginning in the mid-nineteenth century, Italy, France, and Austria had begun organizing units specializing in mountain warfare. They soon discovered that the challenges of the terrain called for high standards of leadership from the officers, initiative from the enlisted men, and fitness from everyone. Mountain troops developed into *corps d'elite* wherever they existed—which was why the German army eschewed their use before the Great War. The General Staff believed modern war made impossible the deployment of specialist elites to the particular place they might be needed. Only two battalions, the 8th and 14th *Jaeger,* whose peacetime garrisons were in Alsace-Lorraine, had some mountain training. The German troops originally assigned to hold the line of the Vosges mountains were overwhelmingly reservists in their thirties, who could barely climb the steps of a *Gasthaus* without pausing for breath.

In December 1914, the French began moving their mountain troops into the sector. The *Hartmansweilerkopf,* the *Vieil Armand* in particular, became the site of a series of bitter battles in early 1915. German troops from the flatlands held their ground but were consistently and embarrassingly outperformed by the *chasseurs alpins.* Bavaria was the center of prewar mountaineering in Germany, and as early as October 1914, the Bavarian army began improvising a "snowshoe" battalion. Wuerttemberg, which had mountains of its own, established tables of organization for a snowshoe company in November. The Wuerttemberg company first saw action in the Vosges in January 1915. It spent the next eight months proving that a company-strength unit was too small for the Great War, even at high altitudes.

Meanwhile, the entry of Italy into the war on the side of the Entente in May 1915 found Austria-Hungary's southern frontier denuded of troops. As local home guards composed of adolescents and grandfathers held the passes of the Tyrol against the best of Austria's *alpini,* the Habsburg high command appealed to Germany. The Germans responded by organizing the "German Alpine Corps." This formation, an unusual combination of Prussian and Bavarian units, was doubly mistitled. It was not a "corps," but a division, with extra allowances of mountain artillery and pack trains. And it was not "alpine" in the sense of being trained for combat at high altitudes. Instead, its normal employment was in the foothills and valleys of mountainous regions. That reflected the German opinion that true mountain fighting usually resulted in standoffs because of the impossibility of bringing heavy supporting weapons into play and keeping them supplied. Rifles, bayonets, and a few machine guns cancelled out each other. On the other hand, a "German Foothills Division" was unlikely either to inspire or intimidate anyone.

During 1915 as well, Wuerttemberg's War Ministry authorized reorganizing and expanding its snowshoe company into the Wuerttemberg Mountain Battalion (*Wuerttemberg Gebirgs-Battaillon*). The WGB, as it was universally known in an army fond of acronyms, broke ground in several ways. It was the first large German unit to be trained intensively in skiing and rock-climbing. Although never a truly "alpine" unit like some of its French and Italian counterparts, the WGB could operate comfortably on higher ground than the Alpine Corps, and for much of the war the two units would work together.

The WGB's structure and the tactical doctrines developed to accompany it were pathbreaking. At this stage, all armies were rigidly configured. Chains of command were formal. The WGB was organized along task force lines. In its developed form, it consisted of six rifle companies and three machine-gun companies, a mortar company, and not least an entire signal company. The rifle companies, although seldom reaching their table of organization strength of almost three hundred men, nevertheless were usually strong enough to operate independently. The men traded their long Mauser rifles, the "cowfeet" of army slang, for the shorter cavalry carbines that, slightly modified, would become standard issue in the World War II Wehrmacht. As they became available, the rifle companies also received an increasing number of so-called "light" machine guns—water-cooled, bipod–mounted beasts with the tactical mobility of an engine block, but an indispensable source of close fire support in broken country. Each machine gun company eventually had around 200 men and twelve of the heavy water-cooled Maxims that were the backbone of the German infantry throughout the war. The mortar company had a half-dozen "grenade throwers," the rough equivalent of the U.S. 60-millimeter light mortar of World War II and Korea fame, and four "light mine throwers." These last, often described as mortars, had nothing in common with the tube-and-base-plate configuration that word usually evokes. The German "mine thrower" instead resembled a light cannon. It had a wheeled carriage, a rifled barrel, and a range of 1,300 yards with a ten-pound shell. It could be used either for high-angle fire or as a direct-fire weapon, and was particularly effective against the early tanks—a formidable weapon for a formidably armed organization.

From the beginning, it was obvious that this complex combination of units and weapons, more than 2,000 strong on paper and usually between 1,500 and 1,700 in the field, could not be commanded in the orthodox way, by a single officer and a single headquarters. Instead the WGB fought in *Abteilungen,* or detachments—first three and later two. These had no permanent organization. Instead, they were built around various combinations of rifles, machine guns, and mortars—combinations that changed even during an operation, depending on the development of the action. This flexibility facilitated reinforcing success and exploiting opportunities—the two greatest tactical challenges of the Great War. It also enabled taking advantage of the qualities of the battalion's officers, tailoring men, missions, and force structures to individual capacities.

Finally authorized in September 1915 and initially built around the Ski Company and its depot, the WGB was brought up to strength by volunteers from every branch of the army. Twelve hundred of the seventeen hundred "originals" were Wuerttembergers. The rest came from everywhere in Germany. Their average age was twenty-four. Three hundred were "war volunteers" from the glory days of 1914. Others were "encouraged" to volunteer by first sergeants seeking to be rid of troublemakers and misfits. There were draftees thinking anything was preferable to the trenches. There were a few cavalrymen, bored with rear-echelon service in a war that had no place for horsemen. Some were winter-sports enthusiasts. Some had never seen a real pair of skis. A hundred fifty of them wore decorations for bravery.

The officers were an equally mixed bag. Originally there were thirty-nine of them, including thirty with reserve or wartime commissions. One of the nine regulars was the newly promoted First Lieutenant Erwin Rommel, assigned to command the 2nd Rifle Company. Rommel expressed retrospective regret at leaving the 124th, but this new unit offered possibilities far greater than a line regiment in the trenches. Its commander was Major Theodor Sproesser, late of the 125th Infantry—a fellow Wuerttemberger. Forty-five years old, tough and ambitious, he was in many ways an archetype of the middle-ranking officers the war was bringing forward in the German army. The WGB was Sproesser's big chance, and he closely supervised the battalion's training.

The general expectation was that the WGB would be sent south to the Italian front. Instead, it went back to the Vosges, taking over its first sector on New Year's Eve 1915. For the next ten months, the WGB carried out raids and patrols in a region that had become almost inactive since the fighting of early 1915. The main positions were as far as 10,000 yards apart. The French were willing enough to accept a policy of "live and let live." It was a perfect opportunity for the battalion to shake down and find itself—an opportunity unusual on the Western Front, where losses were consistent enough and high enough that unit cohesion and skill transmission were major problems.

The WGB's first serious engagement was an exercise in coping with fog and friction matching anything experienced in 1914. The Balkan kingdom of Rumania entered the war on the Allied side in October 1916, partly from opportunism and partly under pressure from Tsarist Russia. A German high command seeking victories for a war-weary populace welcomed an adversary not mired down in trench warfare, and within three weeks dispatched more than a hundred thousand men to the new theater to reinforce the Austrians already on the ground. Among them was the WGB.

Rumanian plans included a two-pronged offensive supported by a Russian contingent and coordinated with a breakout of the Anglo-French-Greek-Serb forces blockaded for more than a year in "the world's largest internment camp" of Salonika in Greece. The Germans and Austrians turned the grand design to waste paper in a series of coordinated strikes that by early December destroyed Rumania's army and overran those parts of the country worth occupying—in particular the oil fields, increasingly valuable in a war where horsepower was everywhere giving way to the internal combustion engine.

The Rumanian army had shown well enough fighting its neighbors in the Balkan Wars of 1912–1913. But its enlisted men were largely illiterate peasants; its regimental officers inexperienced; its generals incompetent.

The WGB profited from Rumanian shortcomings even before coming under Rumanian fire. Despatched in October by rail, then by truck, and finally on foot to a front line running along the prewar frontier between Habsburg Transylvania and Rumania proper, the battalion was immediately sent forward into the mountains, without pack animals and without the equipment appropriate for heights of more than 4,000 feet.

Lieutenant Rommel was part of a two-company advance guard. Their clothes and packs were frozen onto them by the time they reached forward positions he describes as consisting of a single hole in the ground and fifty half-frozen horses. A rainstorm turned into a mountain blizzard. When the captain commanding the detachment requested permission to pull back, he was threatened with a court-martial if he gave up a single meter of ground. The prewar motto *"halten, was zu halten ist"* ("hold everything you've got") persisted even in the face of the medical officer's dire warning of mass frostbite and worse. After losing forty men in what Rommel calls "a horrible night," a relief force with mules and firewood allowed the detachment to seek lower and more hospitable ground. Throughout all this there was no sign of the Rumanians, who could have wreaked havoc in the German ranks by offering hot coffee. The WGB learned to keep its supply echelons close at hand. A few days later, on another mountain, Rommel cheerfully reports, "We were heating our tents with small charcoal fires built on suspended tin cans."

The WGB pushed forward, and on November 11 put in a model attack against Mount Lesului, two and a half companies flanking a Rumanian garrison that had been fixed in place by the rest of the battalion, then driving it off in a coordinated rush. Three points stand out in the reconstructions of the fight by Rommel and by the WGB's historian. One is the emphasis on using terrain to screen movement. The second is the use of machine guns in direct support of an attack—even the sled-mounted heavy Maxims, that weighed more than a hundred pounds in firing position, were expected to keep pace. The third crucial factor was keeping casualties limited. Rommel's company lost only one man wounded—unheard of for a frontal attack in 1916, even against a less-than-first-class enemy.

By mid-November, the WGB was moving out of the high country, toward the Rumanian heartland. This was open warfare, not in the style of 1914 with inexperienced, partially trained men fumbling for contact, but shock attacks mounted one after the other by an experienced, worked-in unit at the top of its form. Rommel stood out again for his energy, his situational awareness, and his capacity for taking pains. In his later notes, he stressed the importance of scouting, of keeping contact with neighboring formations, and above all of exercising command from the front. All would characterize his approach to command in a later war.

In the WGB, officers were able to lead from the front because they were able to keep conditions unpredictable. "Deceive, divert, and pin the enemy down," Rommel noted, as the WGB once again moved back into the mountains. Do not disregard cold, wet, and hunger, which sap energy and judgment. Instead, take advantage of them. Hunger makes men enterprising. On a night too cold to bivouac in the open, shelter can be seized from the enemy. Fog is the attacking infantryman's best friend.

Rommel put his aphorisms to use in January 1917 in an advance on the fortified village of Gagesti with his own 2nd Company and a machine-gun platoon. There was a foot of snow on the ground, a dense fog, and temperatures so low the machine-gun crews were thawing their weapons with alcohol. Reaching Gagesti around 10 P.M., Rommel planned to seize a few outlying houses, rest and feed his men, and continue the advance at daybreak. But his advance elements got to within point-blank range before being spotted, and Rommel saw his chance. The machine guns and part of his riflemen opened rapid fire, another platoon charged, and everybody made as much noise as they could—"as loud as a battalion." Rumanian resistance collapsed; Rommel's detachment tallied 360 prisoners—three times its own strength—without losing a single man wounded.

At midnight the next day, the WGB was relieved by units of the Alpine Corps. After a seven-mile night march, the 2nd Company and its commander were settling into the first comfortable quarters they had seen in days when a dispatch arrived announcing an enemy breakthrough and ordering an immediate return to the threatened sector. The demand, which included a hill climb in the middle of the night, was "almost beyond human strength," but the Wuerttembergers completed the march— only to find that its presence was unnecessary. Rommel says the Germans returned "in gay spirits" to their previous billets, where mail from home helped compensate for the army's latest practical joke. It is likely that

Rommel described this incident to make one of his favorite points: further effort is always possible.

Rommel had good reason to await the mail. In November, he had taken advantage of a brief leave to get married: a quick wartime ceremony, a foreshortened honeymoon, and a return to the front. Unlike many other war brides, Lu was not left pregnant. Times were hard enough in blockaded Germany during the "turnip winter" of 1916–1917 without carrying a first baby to term. Shops, theaters, even schools were closing for lack of coal for heating. A potato blight cut the harvest of that German staple by half. The prewar Reich had its glaring inequalities, but on the whole it was a country where one could eat well. Now meat was unobtainable and butter rationed by pats. Coffee was made from tree bark. Bread was adulterated with sawdust and chalk.

The traditional image of a "front experience" that isolated the Great War's soldiers from even their closest family members at home has given way in recent years to an understanding of the comprehensive synergies that in fact existed between home front and fighting front. Furloughs, while never as generous as the soldiers wished, were nevertheless common enough that even just before a major offensive, a typical battalion might have more than 10 percent of its men on leave, or more or less permanently detached somewhere in the army's rear echelons.[1] Mail was monitored, but not censored until 1917, and soldiers who were the products of the best elementary education system in the world took full advantage of the opportunity to let off steam at what they regarded as "injustice" and "*misstaende.*" Serious physical and psychiatric casualties were returned to Germany—to a point where by 1917 the country seemed at times one vast hospital, and grievously mutilated convalescents were restricted from appearing in public for the sake of civilian morale.

Whether Rommel allowed himself to consider the consequences of defeat remains unknown. His image in the battalion left in any case little

---

1 In contrast to contemporary practice, the armies of the Great War assigned a high proportion of their men to front-line units, then detached them as necessary for service and administrative duties while still carrying them on the regimental and company rolls.

room to exchange those kinds of confidences with his fellow officers, to say nothing of enlisted men. In January, with the Rumanian front stabilizing, the WGB returned to its old sector in the Vosges and spent most of the next six months training and patrolling, developing in particular the use of the hand grenade as an assault weapon. The German *Stielhandgranate,* the familiar "potato-masher," had a relatively long range because of the leverage its wooden handle provided. Its fragmentation effect, however, was relatively limited. A single grenadier was more likely to alert than destroy an enemy position. A half-dozen, however, had a good chance of keeping heads down long enough for the riflemen to close in and finish the job—especially if they were covered by machine-gun fire and willing to charge into the explosions of their own grenades.

Then in August, the Wuerttembergers were reassigned to Rumania, which the German high command had decided to take out of the war altogether. The WGB was ordered to secure Mount Cosna in the Carpathians, one of the major strong points securing what was left of the country. By that time, the Rumanian army had learned a good bit about modern war, and the middle weeks of August saw Rommel's nerve and skill tested to the utmost. He became Sproesser's right-hand man, the one the major turned to routinely for the battalion's critical missions. On August 9, he began by infiltrating two companies through the Rumanian front, clearing five successive positions, and securing the high ground eleven hundred yards behind the original main line of resistance.

The next day, when neither the battalion's own mortars nor the supporting mountain guns were able to get far enough forward to provide fire support, Rommel, now reinforced to five companies, turned to his heavy machine guns. The cumbersome weapons' presence in his forward positions reflected full credit on the pack animals that carried them through the early stages, the crews that carried them the rest of the way, and Rommel's ability to be patient when necessary. In defiance of conventional Great War wisdom that attacks should begin at first light, it was exactly noon when ten Maxims opened fire and the rifle companies went forward. Rommel ordered his men to shout and keep shouting as they charged. It helped German morale; it might demoralize the enemy; and in theaters where front-line noise was not so overpowering, it was as good a way as any for a commander to keep some sense of where platoons and companies expected to act on their own initiative had actually gotten to.

This time, instead of breaking as expected, the Rumanian first line fought it out. A runner shot one man aiming at Rommel at a range of fifty feet—point-blank with a modern rifle. Shortly afterward Rommel took a bullet in the forearm. The German attack stalled; the Rumanians were on the verge of mounting a counterattack when part of the detachment caught them in a flank and broke the effort. Even though reinforced by most of the rest of the battalion, when Detachment Rommel dug in for the night, it was still short of Cosna's summit and under increasingly heavy fire.

Major Sproesser came forward and around 10 P.M. informed his subordinate that the WGB had been ordered to storm Mount Cosna the next day. He then asked for suggestions from his senior officers—a recurring pattern in the WGB, and one contributing significantly to its success. The result was a collectively developed plan for a two-pronged advance. Five WGB companies would go forward and attract the Rumanians' attention; four more, with two battalions of a flatland regiment attached, would flank the Rumanian positions from the right. Sproesser requested Rommel, despite his wound, to take command of the frontal attack.

According to Rommel, "the new and difficult task was most attractive." He remained with the battalion—though to do otherwise in the face of Sproesser's request would have cost most of his reputation. And against all odds, he managed to surprise the Rumanians on the morning of July 11, taking advantage of undefended high ground to envelop the Rumanians' flank, storm their positions, capture several hundred prisoners, and begin digging in his forward elements on a knoll a half-mile from Cosna's summit under increasingly heavy machine-gun fire.

Company after company straggled into the new position, exhausted by a day of marching and climbing, depleted by straggling and the minor injuries that inevitably accompanied moving quickly in the high country. The WGB was a shock unit, most effective when its numbers—never all that large—were multiplied by careful reconnaissance, hot food, full cartridge pouches, ammunition belts, and canteens. No less important was reorganizing platoons and squads disrupted by casualties and straggling. The battalion depended heavily on its corps of enlisted leaders—the veteran NCOs who commanded the squads and most of the platoons. For them to function at their best, in turn, it was important that everyone knew exactly who was in charge of what.

Rommel correspondingly decided to rest, reorganize, and reconnoiter. Around 1 P.M., Major Sproesser arrived at the head of two "straight-leg" battalions, less than pleased to find his subordinate apparently taking its ease short of the objective. Rommel informed his CO that he proposed to resume the attack in an hour. Two WGB rifle platoons and a half-dozen machine guns formed the front line, with two rifle companies echeloned behind each flank in a loose wedge formation. The orders and tactics were by-now vintage Rommel: advance using local cover, under overhead frontal fire from the Maxims; throw showers of grenades right and left of the breakthrough sector as a diversion; then the assault. Break in; roll up the enemy flanks; push through to the second line and beyond if possible; dig in as reinforcements came up to consolidate. Rommel's Detachment cracked open the Rumanian lines in minutes, and in a few minutes captured Cosna's summit.

Most of the garrison escaped. When the Germans started down the far slope after them, they encountered such heavy machine-gun fire that Rommel considered it impossible to continue. Later that night, his patrols made contact with the battalion's other detachment. It had taken heavy losses, was pinned down only six hundred yards from strong enemy positions, and urgently requested support.

Sproesser's solution was to use the two fresh infantry battalions to finish the job in a dawn attack, while the hard-hammered WGB followed to exploit the expected breakthrough. Instead, the leading elements were stopped almost in their tracks. Rommel contacted Sproesser by phone, suggested further movement was impossible without strong artillery support, and offered to act as forward observer for the guns. His time with the 49th Field Artillery had not been wasted. After a few false starts, he managed to get the Rumanian position ranged in—only to be told that the artillery was ceasing fire the rest of the day because of ammunition shortages.

Being out of contact with its main lines was not exactly new for the WGB. But this time it was pinned down in front of positions apparently too strong to rush, at distances too short to retreat without suffering heavy losses. Rommel made a quick decision: storm the Rumanian trenches with the force on hand. "I knew my men could do it," he later declared—and better to be a hammer than an anvil! For a man who had been on his feet for almost two days, nursing an arm wound that by now almost immobilized him, it was a demonstration of what later generations would call "the right stuff."

That last merits developing. The front-line medics of World War I had nothing like today's spectrum of sophisticated analgesics and stimulants. Painkillers meant something so strong as to knock out the recipient. Alcohol, armies' traditional sovereign remedy for light wounds, could only be used sparingly by an officer in Rommel's position. Nor could the arm be fully immobilized without making it impossible to keep one's balance on Cosna's steep, broken, slopes. Every time the arm moved, the bleeding began again and the pain grew worse. A serious part of Rommel's responsibility, in short, was to decide when his judgment was affected to a point where he must relinquish command.

Rommel was just ready to order the machine guns into position when his phone rang. It was Major Sproesser, announcing an enemy breakthrough farther north and ordering Rommel to notify the infantrymen, cover their retreat, and then get his own force out. It went like a maneuver, the companies falling back through and around each other while the Rumanians on their front remained passive. Rommel reported to Sproesser, and this time he asked for permission to report to the hospital. Instead, around midnight Sproesser called him to a council of war. The enemy counterattack was continuing, and the entire force—WGB, infantry, and several Hungarian battalions by now also under Sproesser's command—was on the point of being cut off. Sproesser asked Rommel for his opinion.

Sproesser, who himself had small hope of retreating successfully through broken country in the dark, was probably sure of what his subordinate would and did recommend: organize for all-round defense, and fight it out. That was the kind of optimism needed to put steel into the spines of the German and Hungarian strangers and the WGB's own worn-out captains and lieutenants. To close the deal, Sproesser "urged" Rommel to take command of the WGB's sector—naturally the most demanding on the front. Rommel later said the seriousness of the situation and his concern for his men impelled his agreement. But he also credited "the stimulation of the difficult task" with keeping him on his feet and on the line for the next five days as Sproesser's battle group fought it out with a desperate and superior Rumanian force.

For the first time in his career, Rommel was responsible for a major defensive operation. His guiding ideas reflected both his own experience and the hard tactical lessons that were beginning to permeate the German army in 1917. Prewar doctrine of holding every terrain feature in a sector whatever the cost was giving way to a concept of defense in depth. Germany's front-line infantry was now expected to "resist, bend, and snap back," giving ground when necessary, mounting local counterattacks to keep a temporarily victorious enemy off-balance until a final, large-scale strike swept him back to his original positions. Rommel needed no advice from the General Staff to decide he had no reason to hold the summit of Mount Cosna, no matter how heroic such a stand might look in the communiqués. Instead, he proposed to cover the high ground with his ubiquitous machine guns, establish two company-strength forward positions on Cosna's reverse slope, and keep the WGB's remaining four companies in reserve to plug gaps and mount counterattacks.

The Rumanians gave the WGB everything it could handle in a series of desperate attacks that saw Rommel once again showing a gift for being where he was needed: bringing up reserves, rallying stragglers, leading counterattacks to support positions on the edge of being overrun. The Rumanians climbed slopes so steep that to aim a rifle at them required leaning far forward, suicidally exposing head and shoulders. When the defenders resorted to grenades, the fuses proved too long and the usually reliable potato-mashers just kept bouncing down the ridges.

With casualties mounting, ammunition running out, and phone lines cut, Rommel turned over command and went looking for reinforcements and supplies. Leaving a fight in the middle was not usual practice for a German regular officer. Rommel's behavior reflected confidence in his position within the battalion. No one was likely to suggest he was shirking or seeking to save his skin. He discovered, however, a situation in his rear almost as serious as the one facing the forward units. The Rumanians had infiltrated through gaps in the German lines and were pressing so closely that companies Rommel considered his reserve were in fact committed on a perimeter that was on the edge of caving in.

Grenade supplies were almost exhausted; ammunition was so low that some of the machine-gunners were defending their positions with pistols; and the Rumanians kept coming. By a stroke of good luck, the telephone lines to Sproesser's main headquarters were still intact, and Rommel called to request immediate help. This time it was two "leg" companies that bailed out the mountain troopers, reinforcing the perimeter and bringing a welcome supply of ammunition with them. Rommel was finally able to reduce the numbers in his forward positions to form counterattack detachments. German and Austrian artillery, often firing by map instead of direct observation, responded to an injunction the same in all armies: "Lay it close and keep it coming." Time and again the gunners broke up Rumanian charges before they could get started, or inflicted such losses that the survivors were vulnerable to counterattack. When one of his rifle companies reported casualties so heavy that it no longer could hold its sector, Rommel ordered two machine-gun platoons to range the position, then told the infantry survivors to run for it. The German machine guns shot the closely pursuing Rumanians to pieces; the company reoccupied its trenches.

In a war in which communication was a major tactical problem, the signalers of the WGB played a major role by their success in laying and maintaining phone lines. By late afternoon, Rommel could count on double connections to Sproesser's headquarters, and to at least some of the more threatened forward positions. Nevertheless, the German situation was verging on desperate. The Rumanian attacks persisted well into the night. Rommel ordered his men to dig—after overcoming the resistance of some WGB officers who had no experience in this kind of sustained close-quarter fighting and preferred to remain above ground. In between inspecting positions, Rommel oversaw the distribution of rations and ammunition to the forward companies and their stockpiling in a battalion reserve. He made sure the signalmen laid a fresh double line to the artillery fire direction center. He checked with his medical officer on the number and condition of the wounded, and on what supplies the aid station and the company medics needed for the next day. And in his spare time, Rommel prepared a report for Major Sproesser.

It was 4 A.M. when Rommel finished. Unable to fall asleep, he embarked on one more circuit of the WGB's positions. He had not had his shoes off for five days straight; his bandage had not been changed; his coat and trousers were stiff with dried blood. "I felt very debilitated," he recorded, in what to the comfortable reader of these lines must seem a remarkable understatement.

Fortunately for Rommel, and perhaps for the men under his command, the next days were relatively quiet. The Rumanaian offensive, like so many of its Great War counterparts, was able to break in, but failed to break through or break out. Successful counterattacks in other sectors opened an opportunity for the WGB to retake Mount Cosna. The Wuerttembergers spent two days preparing. Rommel devoted much of that time to working with artillery forward observers in locating targets. Once again he was acting as what the Germans were now calling the "Battle Force Commander," or *Kampftruppenkommandeur.* One way of overcoming the communications problem, developed on the Western Front during the 1916 battles of the Somme and Verdun, was to make the commander of the troops in the front lines responsible for directing the actual fighting. His superiors behind the lines were responsible for feeding in reinforcements and supplies. Command was by mission and not seniority. Thus a major bringing up a support battalion acted under the orders of the commander he reinforced, even if the officer was only a captain. A regimental commander, a lieutenant colonel or a colonel, could always make his way forward and take charge. He did so, however, at the risk of being relieved if he did not achieve an outstanding success—he was not supposed to be doing his subordinates' work.

The revised German approach to battle command persisted, albeit in modified form, throughout World War II. It has been widely praised by those in the best position to know: the armies that fought against it. It nevertheless posed its own unique set of problems. In particular, it depended on a steady supply of high-quality captains and majors—which in turn meant the presence of even more good lieutenants to step up and replace the losses. Casualty rates were high among officers expected to lead from the front and keep on the move among high-risk situations. One battalion of a war-created reserve infantry regiment serving on the Western Front had twenty-four company commanders during a single month in 1918.

Higher orders provided for a one-hour artillery bombardment of Cosina before the attack went in. Rommel proposed instead to rush the first Rumanian line during the barrage, then shift the guns onto the second line and attack that. It was a bold plan for a trench operation, and Rommel stacked his deck by sending forward a ten-man patrol and a telephone squad, with orders to reconnoiter his proposed line of advance and clear away obstacles wherever possible. When the squad was spotted, Rommel pulled it back and turned the WGB's organic mortars on his intended breakthrough site. A series of feints threw the defenders off-balance; the main force closed in with grenades, pistols, and sharpened entrenching tools. Once again the German machine-gunners kept pace and better, despite carrying loads averaging more than a hundred pounds. Their fire did as much as the redirected artillery to clear the way for a second successful rush. When the smoke cleared, the WGB had taken and consolidated seven hundred yards of the Rumanian second line. The way seemed open for a major breakthrough—especially when Rommel was able to contact Sproesser by phone and describe the opportunity.

Instead he learned that the regiment on the WGB's flank was hung up. Sproesser promised to send Rommel everything he had: the WGB's remaining three companies, followed by the infantry battalion still attached to the battle group. Rommel dug in, sent out patrols, and salivated as his field glasses showed him a major Rumanian base less than two miles away. The streets of the town of Tirgul Ocna were crowded with wagons; the railroad station clogged with trains. Thirty minutes, Rommel fumed retrospectively—that was all it would have taken to cut off resupply to the entire sector. But there was no sign of the reinforcements. The Rumanians were beginning to recover from the shock of the WGB's initial attack; their artillery and machine guns were beginning to range Rommel's improvised entrenchments.

Rommel stood down for the night, only to face a full-scale counterattack next morning. The WGB beat off somewhere around twenty attacks during the day, borrowing squads and platoons from temporarily quiet sectors to meet threats as they developed. A single blow, properly supported and properly coordinated, might have overrun the position.

Such an operation, however, was well beyond the capacity of a Rumanian command that throughout the day dissipated its efforts everywhere
along its front of attack in a small-scale imitation of the tactics employed
earlier by Russian General Alexi Brussilov.

Rommel by afternoon was unable to move, commanding from flat on
his back. The fever accompanying his partly treated wound took hold to a
point where he became periodically delirious. In the evening, he walked
down the ridge to Sproesser's headquarters and the battalion doctor. The
WGB held on for five more days until relieved. It suffered more than five
hundred casualties—a third of its field strength. Rommel was sent on convalescent furlough, joining his wife on the Baltic coast, as far away from
mountains as was possible to get. "A few weeks' leave," he recorded, "restored me to tip-top form." In October, he rejoined the battalion.

The fight for Monte Cosna merits description in greater detail than
some of Rommel's better-known Great War achievements because it illustrated and confirmed the approaches he would use in Italy and develop
in a mechanized context during World War II. Personal influence at the
decisive point, throwing the enemy off-balance by getting inside his so-
called "Boyd loop," the cycle of "observation, orientation, decision, action," and exploiting victories to the final limit of available resources:
that was Rommel's style of command as it had developed by 1917. It
owed a good deal to the German army's doctrine and experience—but it
owed much to the man as well. To the naked eye at least none the worse
for wear, Erwin Rommel seemed at the top of his form as the WGB
boarded trains for its new theater of operations.

III

Italy had been an ostensible ally of Germany and Austria-Hungary before
1914. When it declared neutrality in 1914, its government called the policy "sacred egotism." Everybody else in Europe knew what Italy really
was—all that remained was to establish a price. The Allies were able to offer the kinds of concessions, territory to be taken from the Habsburgs, and
imperial prospects in the Middle East—impossible for the Central Powers

to match. In May 1915, Italy launched a massive offensive against the mountain chains separating it from Austria-Hungary. Two years later, its armies were in essentially the same positions, having fought no fewer than eleven battles, each carefully numbered, along the Isonzo River.

Throughout 1917, Austro-Hungarian intelligence had compiled an impressive amount of data on Italy's war weariness. It required no mastery of the more arcane aspects of secret warfare—just an ability to monitor headlines. Strikes and demonstrations were increasing to the point where a cavalry division had to be deployed in north Italy, usually considered the bastion of the kingdom, to back up the *carabinieri* and the local police. The Vatican intensified its half-century cold war with the Italian kingdom by mounting a peace offensive from Italian pulpits and in European chanceries, calling for an end to "useless slaughter" essentially on the basis of status quo ante bellum. Its success would negate the Italian state's sacrifices. Left-wing speakers and politicians grew ever bolder, with one deputy demanding in Parliament itself, "No one be in the trenches this winter." Commander in Chief Count Luigi Cadorna complained that domestic unrest was affecting the morale of soldiers returning from furlough. The government replied that soldiers on leave fueled dissent by describing the army's mistakes and shortcomings.

Put together, the situation seemed promising for a major Central Powers offensive. For three years, military victories had not translated into political consequences. Italy, however, seemed ready to collapse if its armies were hit hard enough. The Austrian General Staff made its pitch to Berlin. The Italians were particularly vulnerable in the high ground around Caporetto in the northern Isonzo sector. A few hundred guns and a few divisions—no more, and it would be enough.

The German High Command was dubious. Erich Ludendorff, whose innocuous title of "First Quartermaster General" belied his true status as the army's chief decision-maker, believed the proposed operation was too limited to have any long-term results. But professional courtesy required him to send an observer to report on the project firsthand. Lieutenant General Konrad Krafft von Dellmensingen was a Bavarian General Staff officer—one of the best. Before the war he had made a systematic study of breakthrough operations. In 1915, he was given command of the

Alpine Corps and led it through Rumania before being transferred back to staff work. There was no better man to evaluate the feasibility of the Austrian proposal.

Krafft returned a definite maybe. The operation verged, he said, on the limits of the possible. But it could be done—with the right generals and the right units. As was often the case in the German army, the views of the man on the spot carried weight. General Otto von Below, who had been building a record as one of Germany's best senior officers since the Battle of Tannenberg, was given command of a new army; seven crack divisions. There was the German Jaeger Division, with its nine battalions of rifles, and the 200th Division, whose high number belied its experience at high altitudes. The Wuerttemberg 26th Division had seen some of the hardest fighting on the Western Front. The Alpine Corps was a natural choice. As an insurance policy, Krafft was appointed Below's chief of staff, responsible for executing the campaign he had supported. And the WGB was ordered south as a last touch.

With the Rumanian campaign closing down, the WGB took time to lick its wounds and integrate its replacements. The battalion also benefited from a new piece of equipment. The introduction of the light machine gun in 1917 multiplied small-unit fighting power and made small-unit tactics increasingly depend on fire and movement by mutually supporting small groups. Initially, the guns were centralized at company level, but they were rapidly absorbed into platoons. A strong platoon of the new model might have two or three squads of riflemen/grenadiers and two light-machine-gun crews. A weaker one would organize around its guns, with the riflemen in effect becoming spare gunners and ammunition carriers. In each case, the platoon, rather than the company, became the basic unit of both offense and defense. Rommel had utilized light machine guns in Rumania, "borrowing" them wholesale from line infantry units, and he welcomed the firepower and the flexibility they brought to the rifle companies. No longer would close support depend on the ability of machine-gun crews to hand-carry their bulky weapons in broken terrain.

On reaching its new theater of operations, the WGB was informed of such vital issues to the alliance as the fact that saluting distance in the German army was six paces while the Austro-Hungarians were satisfied with three. The battalion was also attached to the Alpine Corps. It was a fortunate pairing, though neither party to the relationship always thought so. The Alpine Corps possessed organic pack trains and mountain artillery that could be attached to the WGB as necessary. Its infantry had enough mountain training and experience to keep pace with—and sometimes surpass—the Wuerttembergers.

On October 18, the WGB, with for the first time a battalion of mountain artillery under its command, began moving toward the front. It marched by night to avoid Italian aerial reconnaissance. Air power had not been a serious consideration in the battalion's earlier experience. Now it was becoming uncomfortably acquainted with war's new third dimension. Rations too were slim—a reflection of Austria-Hungary's declining logistic capability. The Germans were enjoined to requisition from Austrian civilians only in an emergency.

Sproesser had used the time since the end of the Rumanian campaign to work with his officers in evaluating the battalion's tactical experience. He collated the conclusions in a seven-point order issued on November 5:

1. Keep applying pressure at the head of the attack; do not be distracted by flanks and secondary objectives.

2. Establish and maintain communications day and night, using human and electronic means.

3. Send written messages promptly and use reliable runners. If sketches of terrain or positions are included, keep them simple.

4. Headquarters to be alert at night, monitoring communications closely.

5. Advancing units are to mark the route clearly for their supports.

6. Avoid carrying unnecessary captured material. (This was an injunction not against looting in the conventional sense, but against picking up discarded weapons and supplies rather than take the risk of a logistics failure.)

7. Keep pressing on. Pursuit without pause saves casualties.

There was nothing especially profound there, but every word had been paid for in blood—and not all of it Erwin Rommel's.

By October 23, the XIV Army was in position. It consisted of four corps, with a total of seven German and five Austrian divisions plus an army reserve of five more Austrian divisions. The Habsburg high command had done its best to match the German quality, contributing its *Tiroler Kaiserjaeger* division and the experienced mountaineers of the 22nd *Kaiserschuetzen* Division, as well as a number of elite mountain guide and assault companies. Two thousand guns, from light mountain howitzers to the heaviest railroad pieces, were in support. For the first time in this theater as well, the Central Powers made sophisticated use of gas, which proved unusually effective in the steep Alpine valleys, where it sank close to the ground without dissipating. The barrage opened at 2 A.M. on October 24. Six hours later, the first assault waves went forward. This was another innovation of German artillery specialists, who saw the advantage of taking enemy positions under overwhelming fire by surprise, as opposed to the longer, more systematic bombardments of the war's early years. It would be developed with devastating effect in the German offensives of 1918.

The attack caught an Italian 2nd Army disorganized and demoralized from the summer's casualties, in poorly prepared, poorly coordinated defensive positions. Some German and Austrian units advanced ten miles the first day as Italian resistance disintegrated. The WGB was posted on the right flank of the Alpine Corps, in a sector including some of the most difficult terrain on the entire front of the attack. Its eventual objective was a piece of high ground undramatically dubbed Hill 1114 from its height in meters, a key position in the Italian defenses along the Kolovrat mountain range. The ground in front of it was so broken that the pack mules had to be left behind; once again the machine-gunners took their pieces into action on their own backs.

Rommel led the way with two rifle companies and a machine-gun company. Served as well as ever by his scouts, he bypassed the forward positions and found a supply trail leading deeper into the Italian defenses. It was a cold, rainy day, and detachment after detachment of the defenders were taken by surprise in their dugouts. The Rommel detachment

captured seventeen guns, including a battery of eight-inch howitzers complete with an ammunition dump.

By noon the rain had stopped, and the WGB waited briefly for reinforcements, meanwhile eating the Italians' lunch: a hot meal eked out by
captured rations. Around 7 P.M., Rommel's detachment reached the Italian
third line, still without encountering significant resistance, and found elements of the Alpine Corps's Bavarian Guard Regiment (*Leib-Regiment*)
pinned down by fire from Hill 1114 by Italians apparently uninclined to
yield any more ground without making a fight for it. The officers on the
spot agreed the attack was best resumed the next morning, after a systematic artillery preparation. The senior Bavarian officer, a major, told Rommel
he was assuming command of the combined force. Rommel replied that he
took his orders from Major Sproesser. The major tapped his insignia—
metaphorically at least—and declared that the Guards would lead the attack; *Leutnant* Rommel and his WGB could follow along and mop up
anything the Bavarians left.

Unit rivalry is as old as armed forces. This one was slightly more
complex than the pairing of two good dogs in a tandem harness. The
Bavarians were their king's personal household troops, the counterpart of
the Prussian Guard, the regiment that led the peacetime parades through
Munich's main streets. But the *Leib-Regiment,* to give its official title, was
more than just a social elite. Selected for conversion to mountain troops
in 1915, it was a fighting elite as well, with a record second to none on
flat land or in high country. Its hard chargers now intended to be first on
the Kolovrat. The WGB was not so old in the German army list but not
so young at its trade of mountain warfare, and its hard-bitten young officers were unwilling to give way to the fine gentlemen of the *Leiber.*

The opinions of the enlisted men of the respective outfits were neither
requested nor recorded. But if Bavarian morale in World War I had a subtext, it was dislike for the *Saupreussen* who were increasingly blamed for
getting Germany into the mess in the first place. The WGB for its part still
sustained a volunteer image, though its replacements included an increasing number of draftees; and its composition was strongly Swabian
and north German. Rommel himself, unused by now to being stood to attention in such obvious fashion, sent an officer to find Sproesser. By the

time the WGB's commander arrived, Rommel also had an alternate plan: to swing west, outside the Bavarians' sector, and mount a surprise attack without artillery support, while the Guards were still on their start lines.

Sproesser liked the idea well enough to send Rommel forward immediately with three companies. When the Bavarian major showed up to demand the WGB support the Guards' attack, Sproesser thanked his colleague but answered that the WGB's advance guard was presently engaged with the enemy in response to Sproesser's orders, and its progress could be observed through field glasses.

It is an exaggeration to say that Sproesser and Rommel put their respective careers on the line that day. The German army was not inclined to relieve officers for that kind of squabbling over command—some of it, indeed, was expected among young officers with the right stuff. On the other hand, more than mere bragging rights were involved, and by day's end, Rommel and the WGB made Sproesser look very good.

Rommel's detachment advanced as patrols cleared its front of Italian outposts and skirmishers. By this time the WGB was as skilled in that craft as any special operations force in either World War. A good reason why Rommel so often achieved initial surprise in his attacks involved the difficulty of sounding the alarm with a bayonet at one's throat. Another good reason for Rommel's success was his pattern of seeking dead ground a few hundred yards away from the main enemy position, where his men could catch their breath and stragglers could come up unobserved. There is almost always dead ground in mountains; this time it was a small hollow. When a patrol reported the ridge line unoccupied, Rommel ordered a rush that caught most of the ostensible defenders in their bunkers, secure from an expected barrage that never materialized. Bringing them out was a simple enough process: a shout of *"Raus! Haende hoch!"* (translation: "Outside! Hands up!") sufficed—with a grenade bounced down the stairs for effect if the occupants proved recalcitrant.

It was a good morning's work, especially because, by the sounds from the Bavarian sector, the Guards were having difficult going. It also left, Rommel quickly noted, his detachment in a salient, confronting trench system too strong for his small force to clear, and a counterattack too strong to face head-on. One of his rifle companies, by now reduced to only eighty men, was pinned down almost immediately. Sproesser had promised reinforcements, but they were still climbing. Rommel moved his other rifle company, unobserved, to the Italians' flank and rear. Two machine-gun crews managed to bring their weapons forward to support an attack that brought 2nd Company's survivors out of their positions and into the Italians from the opposite direction.

By 9:15, Rommel's detachment had taken fifteen hundred prisoners—three times and more its own strength. The Germans had also torn a half-mile hole in the Italian defenses of Kolovrat Ridge. They were taking heavy fire from Italian machine guns on even higher ground, and reserves were assembling for a counterattack, some of them arriving by truck from the rear area.

Rommel's initial adrenaline-inspired reaction was "Bring 'em on!" It did not take long, however, for him to change his mind and decide instead to continue the attack, pushing forward toward Mount Kuk. At 10:30, Sproesser arrived with four more companies At 11:15, German artillery opened fire, and Rommel's own machine guns began blasting the forward Italian positions. He had sent two strong patrols forward to probe the defenses. One encountered resistance; the other met Italians who surrendered when the Wuerttembergers waved handkerchiefs at them. The way seemed open for a rush to the summit. Then Rommel saw another opportunity. The Italians had constructed a camouflaged supply trail to their summit positions—a trail leading down the Italian side of the ridge and into their rear.

The half-dozen WGB companies by themselves could not simultaneously deal with Mount Kuk and charge off into the blue. But elements of the Bavarian Guards, their initial attack stopped, had followed the route taken by the WGB and were close at hand. As battle zone commander, they came under Rommel's authority—a mere lieutenant commanding a force of near-regiment strength. Leaving the Guards to deal with Kuk, Rommel led four WGB companies literally on a dead run down the track. His men had marched most of the night and fought all morning. But they were as physically fit as any soldiers in the German army, and no one was shooting at them. Perhaps the most impressive feat of the charge was the machine-gunners' continuing to carry the heavy guns on their backs and shoulders as they overran supply dumps, battery positions, and command posts one after another with no more than a few random shots fired. They raced through the village of Ravna, scattering soldiers and pack mules indiscriminately, and Rommel led them deeper into the Italian lines, toward the Luico-Savogna valley. Block that, and the Italians in the entire sector were trapped.

Again the Germans moved at the double, snatching eggs and grapes from the baskets of abandoned pack mules, stumbling through bushes and small woods downhill toward the valley floor. At 12:30, the detachment's leading elements—including Rommel and his staff officers—appeared like wraiths from the underbrush alongside the main road. As surprised Italians scattered in all directions, Rommel's troopers, the relatively few who had not fallen out along the way, cut the phone wires and began digging in. Italian trucks and wagons continued using the road, and hungry Germans enjoyed the chocolate, jam, and white bread included in their cargoes—delicacies that had disappeared from German rations long ago.

Business was booming, Rommel observed, and morale was wonderful. But there was still no sign of reinforcements, and one of Rommel's scouts reported a long column of Italian infantry marching toward the roadblock. Rommel by now still had only about one hundred fifty men, but they possessed every advantage of surprise and position. He let the Italians move into the killing zone of his machine guns, then sent out a parliamentarian under a flag of truce to demand surrender. It was scarcely surprising that the Italians, part of the elite 20th Bersaglieri Regiment, did not comply—especially because Rommel's negotiator had forgotten to remove his pistol. The eight rounds in a Luger's magazine were not exactly intimidating under the circumstances, but the technical violation of the laws of war prescribing negotiators must be unarmed led the Italians to take the man prisoner, and in the process rough him up slightly.

When Rommel and a few of his staff tried to attract the Italians' attention by waving handkerchiefs, the response was a scattering of shots from the head of the column. Rommel blew his whistle; German machine guns swept the road; and the Italians fell back. A ten-minute firefight ensued, punctuated by desperate Italian efforts to break through the roadblock. Then resistance collapsed. Fifty officers and two thousand men surrendered to less than a tenth of their number, because less than a tenth of them had a chance to get into the fight.

As his men were disarming and sorting out this new bag of POWs, Rommel mounted a heavy machine gun on a captured auto and drove into Lucio. There he found Sproesser, the rest of the WGB, and the Guards battalion, which had taken Kuk and moved on the town from a different direction. Again Rommel urged action. His detachment, he argued, should move cross-country immediately to the next high ground, Hill 1096. That would put the Germans even deeper in the enemy rear, in a position to cut the main Italian supply routes north.

Sproesser gave Rommel his blessing and six companies, including all the WGB's heavy machine guns. Even by Rommel's standards, the advance rapidly turned into a demanding climb, with more and more men falling out or dropping out with minor injuries such as twisted ankles. When his patrols reported strong Italian positions ahead, Rommel camped for the night while his scouts searched for an alternate route forward. Not until 4:30 did one of the officers report that there was a way. An hour later, the Germans moved out—and hit the Italians on Hill 1096, where the defenders were on the alert and ready to make a fight of it.

There was no time and no room for Rommel to follow his usual practice of pulling back and seeking a way round. Instead, the Wuerttembergers went up and went in. By 7:15, they were in control—at a price. Every man had been committed to the attack; no reserves were left. Casualties among the leaders had been heavy. Every officer in 2nd Company was down. So were too many of the senior NCOs on whom Rommel so depended to lead patrols and assaults. Rommel himself became a target for an Italian machine gun. But in addition to several hundred prisoners taken during the fighting, a further sixteen hundred Bersaglieri, cut off on the lower slopes, surrendered, marching into captivity fully armed and equipped.

The next objective was Mrzli Peak, and Rommel pushed toward it so quickly that he lost contact with his own rear echelon. His vanguard, 2nd Company, now commanded by a platoon sergeant, was down to a third of its men, plus a couple of light machine guns. It took until 10 A.M. to assemble the equivalent of three companies from the men who had followed him that morning. As his improvised and attenuated force moved forward, Rommel, leading the way, saw—and heard—what seemed like around three battalions' worth of Italians. Everyone was armed, but there seemed to be too much noise being made to indicate troops reliably under discipline. Rommel considered it worth the risk to walk forward waving a handkerchief and calling on the men to surrender. Suddenly the mass broke and scattered in all directions. Hundreds of Italians started running toward him, throwing down their rifles and shouting "Long live Germany!" The first to reach him hoisted Rommel on their shoulders. An officer who seemed reluctant was shot by his own men. About that time, the vanguard of Rommel's detachment appeared on the scene and began the process of disarming more than fifteen hundred men of the Salerno Brigade.

The rest of the brigade, prisoners informed him, was occupying Matajur and would fight. Rommel was preparing to oblige them when he received an order from Sproesser to withdraw. The major had arrived at Hill 1096 and, on seeing the mass of prisoners, assumed the fighting was over and Matajur to be in German hands. Even in a context of "mission tactics," a direct order could not simply be disregarded even though it showed ignorance of the true situation. But in as neat a piece of superior-finessing as war's history shows, Rommel sent most of his detachment— and its officers—back to Hill 1096 as instructed. He kept a hundred riflemen and six heavy machine-gun crews with him: enlisted men, who would not be court-martialed for following the orders of their immediate superior.

A hundred-odd men against a regiment might not seem too promising. But Rommel, apart from his belief that one of his mountaineers was worth twenty of any other soldiers, saw that the ground in front of him was too broken to support an interlocking defense system. He was confident that his small force could infiltrate the Italian position and break it from the inside out. A small force, indeed, might well be more useful than a large one in that kind of operation. But as his men came in sight of Mount Matajur, the firing died down. Rounding a bend in the road, the Germans saw another twelve hundred Italians, the other regiment of the Salerno Brigade, downing arms and surrendering.

Matajur's summit was still a mile away and a two-hundred-meter climb, but what remained of the garrison rapidly unraveled under no more than slight pressure. At 11:40, Rommel sent up the flares announcing

Matajur was in German hands. He gave his men an hour's rest while he dictated his report to Sproesser. Then, relieved by other German troops, the Rommel Detachment moved slowly back down the Kolovrat Ridge.

In a war where gains were measured in hundreds of yards and losses in tens of thousands, the saga of the WGB reads like military melodrama. In fifty-two hours of marching and fighting, a force never much stronger than five hundred men at the contact point accounted for nine thousand prisoners; eighty guns; and more horses, mules, and assorted supplies than anyone had time to count. When the last German stragglers were accounted for and the final combat losses tallied, the price was six dead and twenty wounded. Small wonder that Sproesser turned Nelson's blind eye and basked in the Alpine Corps's order of the day, praising the WGB's "resolute leader" and his "courageous officers" for playing the principal role in the collapse of Italian resistance in the entire sector.

An achievement worthy of recognition, certainly—but one that brought Rommel for the first time in his career into contact with high-level army politics. When Below and Krafft prepared their attack plans, it became clear that Hill 1114 and Mount Matajur were the major initial geographic objectives. They had to be taken for the attack to progress, and to provide incentive, Below secured authorization to award an immediate *Pour le Mérite* to the officers whose units captured those heights.

The order of the *Pour le Mérite,* created in 1667 by the founder of modern Prussia, the Great Elector, had evolved on its military side into a decoration reserved in practice for senior officers who achieved major victories. The criteria began to change with the development of air-to-air combat. Shooting down enemy planes on a regular basis initially seemed the kind of superhuman achievement that even an Iron Cross was not enough recognition. Max Immelmann, the "Eagle of Lille," Oswald Boelcke, and other fighter-pilot lieutenants in their twenties found themselves sporting an award that acquired a new nickname, the "Blue Max," from Immelman. Similarly, the *Pour le Mérite* was increasingly awarded to junior officers for a major command achievement. It recognized performance, not heroism, which meant an officer could be a good deal more openly interested in winning a PLM than his British or U.S. counterpart a Victoria Cross or a Medal of Honor. It was also why Below could metaphorically place a Blue Max on the peaks in question, for the most skillful, the most courageous, and the luckiest to pick up.

It was not quite that simple. The Blue Max for Hill 1114 went to an officer of the Bavarian Guards—a Lieutenant Theodor Schoenerer, who would finish out a later war as one of Adolf Hitler's Field Marshals. The prize for Matajur was awarded to a Lieutenant Schnieber, of the 12th German Division's 63rd Regiment, who reported in mistaken good faith that his company had reached its summit around 7 A.M. The key in both cases seems to have been that the officers belonged to established organizations, able to make ongoing cases for their candidates. The WGB was a wartime creation, a military mule with indiscriminate ancestry and no hope of progeny, having nothing but its deeds to speak for it to senior officers at higher headquarters.

Rommel was sufficiently aggrieved to complain to Sproesser, and according to some accounts, Below was sufficiently convinced of the lieutenant's claim to request another award, but was refused the authorization. Meanwhile, the WGB pressed forward, improving as it went its cooperation with its neighboring units. Both Sproesser and Rommel were finding that this was a war of divisions, corps, and armies. A battalion was limited in what it could accomplish, no matter how high its quality. So was an officer. Rommel suffered his first defeat on November 7, when his detachment failed to clear the Italians from positions overlooking the German route of advance. By his account, he was coordinating the supporting machine-gun fire on which his attacks usually depended, and the rifle companies held back too long waiting for him to join them. But the Italians abandoned the position during the night. The Austro-German advance continued, crossing the Tagliamento and moving toward the Piave as Krafft and Below defied Ludendorff's original order to halt at the first river in favor of following up a fleeing enemy.

But the rains grew heavier, and the Austrians had neither mounted nor motorized forces to keep the Italians off-balance as the scene shifted from the mountains to the riverine plains of northern Italy. The WGB filled part of that gap in the central powers' order of battle, spearheading the advance to a town called Longarone on the Piave's far side. By that time, the battalion had taken advantage of abandoned material and empty homes and stores along the line of advance to improvise a mixed bag of transport, and to festoon itself with enough gimcrack loot that Sproesser saluted one of his companies with "Good morning, Sarassani," referring to the famous German traveling circus. Just as promptly, his troopers began referring to their commander as "the circus director."

Rommel, ever the pragmatist, was by now using an improvised cyclist detachment on "liberated" vehicles as his vanguard, supplemented by a few mounted staff officers. In a wild ride down a steep road, the Germans shot curves, ran tunnels, and scattered Italian demolition squads and stragglers. Any reference suggesting the foreshadowing of panzer operations in France 1940 or North Africa in 1942 would be redundant. Suffice it to say, Rommel and the WGB reached the valley—again with the machine-gunners somehow keeping pace and holding on to their weapons—improvised a river crossing with men swimming and wading through the Piave's freezing water, and blocked the road south. Then, with Rommel preferring the risks of a night attack to giving the Italians a chance to escape past him in the dark, they marched on Longarone.

Rommel's detachment spent the early hours of the night along the road, repelling increasingly desperate, increasingly disorganized attempts to break out to the south. At the end, it was captured Italian weapons and ammunition that enabled the Germans to hold as their own supplies ran out. Even then the machine guns were down to fifty rounds apiece, and Rommel was holding down one of his flanks with a half-dozen men by the time reinforcements arrived and Rommel took three companies forward.

He was greeted by one of his officers, captured the night before, riding a mule, accompanied by hundreds of cheering Italian soldiers, and bearing a message from the commander of "Fortress Longarone," placing himself at Rommel's disposal in the best eighteenth-century style. This last was in good part the work of Major Sproesser, who the night before, with other elements of the WGB, had advanced to about a thousand yards north of the Piave, then sent a message across the river into Longarone to the effect that the town was surrounded by "elements of" a German-Austrian division, and all resistance was useless. At final count, the bag amounted to more than ten thousand men; two hundred machine guns; three mountain batteries; and the usual accompaniment of horses, mules, and trucks.

Rommel, Sproesser, and the WGB were developing into figures of folklore on both sides of the battle line. On December 13, Major Sproesser announced to the WGB that he and Rommel had both been awarded the *Pour le Mérite*—an unheard-of honor for a single battalion. When, on December 18, the WGB's mail caught up, it included two small packages, each containing one of the coveted medals. It was not exactly a formal award ceremony, but though the record is silent on the subject, it seems a reasonable assumption that the WGB's Christmas celebration was correspondingly enhanced.

The medals were about all the mountaineers had to celebrate. Taken in isolation, the narrative of its exploits in Italy supports a joke told in many versions, to the effect that Italians accepted the Fascist salute because it was easier than putting up both hands. Even when maximum allowances are made for self-congratulation by the Germans and Austrians, the Italian performance at the sharp end of Caporetto was distinctly shabby. When the battle began, the Italian army had sixty-nine divisions in the field. By November 9, that number had shrunk to thirty-three. More than three thousand guns, almost half the army's total, had been lost. Forty thousand Italians were dead or wounded. But 280,000 more were prisoners, and 350,000 more were counted as stragglers or outright deserters.

Even as Below's forward units drove deeper into Italy during the first days of November, he and Krafft were concerned at the corresponding extension of their supply lines. The Germans, true to their tradition of front-loading, had contributed fighting troops, not rear-echelon formations. The Austrian army's logistic system in the Italian theater was geared to support defensive operations. By the end of November, too many of its trucks had broken down. Too many of its draft and pack animals had died of exhaustion, or been converted to ration supplements. The heavy bridging equipment necessary to sustain a full-scale attack across the Piave was finding heavy going through the steep mountain passes. The onset of winter would make bringing up supplies exponentially more difficult. Below's German and Austrian troops were tired—not merely from the previous weeks of constant marching and fighting, but from months and years of shortened rations that told on their strength and endurance. Replacement depots were emptying, even for elite units like the Alpine Corps and the WGB.

On November 21, Below wrote that it was time to call off the operation. Austria's Emperor Karl also urged Below to close down the offensive. On November 26, the German high command reminded their subordinate of the increasing risks generated by the slowdown in the rate of advance. And if Below needed any warnings from the sharp end, he received an unmistakable one on November 25. The WGB had been transferred from the Longarone sector to the Grappa massif, where Below's attack was encountering determined resistance. Given the battalion's reputation, its use as an assault force was a given. The Wuerttembergers, however, were beginning to find their limits. The Italians were no longer the obliging enemy who left gaps in their positions for Rommel's patrols to discover and exploit. Their main defenses were developed enough that two or three understrength companies could no longer break into positions and unravel them from the inside.

To improve his striking power, Sproesser was reinforced, eventually commanding three battalions of elite Austrian *Kaiserschuetzen,* in addition to his own WGB, which he turned over to Rommel. On November 25, the battle group attacked the key Italian position on Monte Salarol. The Austrians were stopped in their tracks, with heavy casualties. Around noon, Sproesser sent in the WGB. But the route Rommel followed brought him into the operational zone of an Austrian division whose commander was not pleased at what he considered interference. The allied attack essentially petered out. Rommel and Sproesser offer different accounts, both exculpatory, of the event. The clearest evaluation was probably Below's. The WGB, he declared, simply lost its way.

The events of November 25 proved Bellona is no man's trull. The WGB had been challenging the law of averages for weeks and months; fog and friction were bound to end its run of success sooner or later. The operation also suffered from planning problems. Sproesser's headquarters, small to begin with, was attempting to control twice as many men as usual, half of them strangers, in a complex attack operation. Sproesser, moreover, had reached a point where he took as given "the tested and brilliant Rommel would find a way to break through," no matter what

the circumstances It was time enough for a rest, and the WGB was pulled
out of the line for two weeks.

Below and Krafft were in any case planning to shut down the offensive—after one more series of efforts to improve their tactical position.
How many men died for that reason between 1914 and 1918? The WGB
returned to action on December 17, its objective again being Monte
Salarol. This time most of the battalion was initially held in reserve, and
the weather was so bad that when the battalion leading the attack was
pinned down, the divisional headquarters directing the operation called
the whole thing off on account of winter.

That was the WGB's last serious fighting on the Italian front. Rommel and Sproesser, after unwrapping and celebrating their medals, returned to Germany on leave. If, at this stage of his career, Rommel came
nowhere near George Patton in his cultivation of friends in high places,
he had been unusually fortunate in his commanding officer. Sproesser recognized Rommel's talent and potential. Professionally ambitious and critical of the orthodoxies of trench warfare, he was sufficiently confident to
cultivate a synergistic relationship with his gifted subordinate instead of
regarding him as a rival. Sproesser allowed Rommel to extend himself
without overextending the battalion, shaping his talents while never letting him forget who was the WGB's commanding officer. Rommel, for his
part, respected and admired his commander, as much as a young man of
Rommel's temperament was capable of admiring a superior who periodically exercised a restraining role.

The WGB was transferred to the Western Front in February and
committed to the German spring offensive, fighting on the Chemin des
Dames. In May, the battalion was renamed a regiment and its detachments retitled battalions. Though a regiment was in principle a colonel's
command, Sproesser, who resumed command in March, remained a major until handing over command on June 3. The regiment fought on the
Western Front, taking heavy losses, rebuilding with whatever men could
be scavenged from nearly empty depots, and earning a Blue Max for its
new commander. Briefly transferred to Macedonia in August and returned, the mountaineers finished the war near where their most famous
member began it—around Verdun and on the Meuse River, and disbanded in the early weeks of 1919.

Rommel never returned to its ranks. When his leave ended, he was assigned to the staff of LXIV Corps, a holding formation on the Western Front. Even that deep into the war, regular officers at Rommel's stage of their careers were regularly shifted from field duty to gain some staff experience and see which of them might have the potential for eventual assignment to the General Staff in Berlin. In the Great War's final weeks, Erwin Rommel was just another junior officer who moved documents around his desk and carried them from room to room. He did some lecturing on his Italian experiences, but in that backwater command, no one seemed particularly interested. His promotion to captain was similarly routine, having nothing to do with his combat career.

In one sense, Rommel's "soldier's luck" nevertheless held: he was far away from both the slow-motion collapse of the German front in the autumn of 1918 and the revolutionary upheavals that accompanied it and eventually brought down what remained of the Second Empire. On December 21, he was administratively reassigned to his old regiment, the 124th, which shortly afterward disappeared like the state it served.

IV

For George Patton, the outbreak of the Great War occasioned one of the more melodramatic gestures of a career studded with them. On August 3, he wrote to Leonard Wood, requesting a year's leave of absence to go to France and participate in the fighting at his own risk. "I will never apply to the United States for help if I get in trouble or am captured," he informed his superior. This was more than braggadocio. During his sojourn at Saumur, Patton had made friends with a French officer who assured him that should war come with Germany and the United States remain neutral, he could procure Patton a commission in his cavalry regiment.

Wood replied matter-of-factly that should Patton go to Europe, it must be as a spectator. His enthusiasm, however, was noted to his credit by his superiors. By the time he graduated from the second-year course, he had also established himself as the Army's leading authority on modern swordsmanship and fathered a second child, a daughter, Ruth Ellen. The only cloud on Patton's immediate horizon was the imminent transfer of his regiment to the Philippines. He traveled to Washington, pulled some strings, and pushed some buttons. He was reassigned to the 8th Cavalry, rotating home from the Philippines to service at Fort Bliss, Texas.

Not too much should be made of Patton's actively seeking a transfer. Regimental loyalty in the U.S. Army was nowhere nearly as strong as in Britain. Applications for exchange when a regiment changed assignments were familiar, and an officer with Patton's credentials and potential was deemed more useful in the States than doing constabulary duty across the Pacific. He successfully passed the examinations for promotion to first lieutenant and patrolled a border increasingly disrupted by the spillover of a Mexican Revolution that transformed into a civil war of near-Hobbesian dimensions.

In March 1916, Pancho Villa crossed the border and attacked the garrison town of Columbus, New Mexico. This culmination of a several months' campaign of reprisal for U.S. support of Villa's rival Venustiano Carranza led President Woodrow Wilson to order a punitive expedition into Mexico. Its commander was Brigadier General John J. Pershing—an officer whose career had benefited even more than Patton's from cultivating personal and political connections in Washington. Patton's regiment was not on the troop list, but Patton was determined to participate. He went unannounced to Pershing's quarters and offered to do any job, even handling correspondents—one step above personally cleaning stables in the minds of most Army officers. "I want to go more than anyone else," he informed the general. When Pershing phoned the next morning and asked how long it would take him to prepare, Patton said he was already packed and ready to go. "I'll be God damned," replied the usually imperturbable Pershing. "You are appointed aide."

A general's aide in that informal era was far more than the proverbial dog robber dedicated to keeping his patron comfortable on campaign. Patton managed the headquarters, arranged Pershing's schedules, assumed administrative responsibilities, and won the favor of a man not easily impressed. Patton, in turn, responded strongly to Pershing's passion for order, established and maintained by personal supervision. An autocrat was arguably necessary in organizing an expedition whose senior subordinates were conditioned to acting on their own responsibility, in an army where staff officers were little more than extensions of the commander's authority. Patton watched, noted, and approved.

President Woodrow Wilson's aim in launching the intervention was to strengthen his influence with the Carranza government while meeting the vociferous demands for security along the border. His orders to Pershing correspondingly established a constabulary mission as opposed to a military one. Mexican soldiers, officials, and citizens responded by conducting a small-scale but comprehensive irregular campaign against U.S. columns that marched futilely across northern Mexico in pursuit of an elusive enemy whose popularity, at a nadir earlier in the year, increased as he and his followers made fools of the *Yanquis* almost at will.

Logistics and communications problems proved far more intractable than had been expected in earlier considerations of military intervention. Patton grew increasingly irascible, venting at least part of his spleen in periodic verbal outbursts against Mexicans of all classes and conditions. Then chance came to his rescue. On May 14, Pershing put him in charge of a foraging expedition: a dozen men sent to obtain corn for the headquarters' horses. But instead of riding out on horseback in traditional fashion, Patton's party took the field in three automobiles. The mission itself proved routine. Most Mexican merchants were quite wiling to take American money while rejecting America's presence. But in the process of making his purchase, Patton decided to investigate a nearby ranch reputed to be sheltering the commander of Villa's bodyguard, the famous *Dorados*.

The upshot of a story often told and retold in later years by Patton himself, his admirers and his critics, was a close-quarters gunfight that left the Dorado captain and two other Mexicans down for no American casualties. Patton's personal score remains debatable; there was a lot of lead flying around the ranch that afternoon. But it was Lieutenant Patton who tied the dead Mexicans across the hoods of his cars and delivered them to Pershing in person. And it was Patton, with the two revolvers he habitually wore low on his hips, who attracted the attention of the increasingly bored contingent of reporters hanging around the expedition's headquarters with no stories to file.

As the Bandit Killer, Patton received national attention, albeit briefly. With the Punitive Expedition winding down into a series of patrols to nowhere, the incident might well have proved his fifteen minutes of fame. He was promoted to first lieutenant. He began writing an article on cavalry tactics and quarreled with Pershing—as much as a lieutenant quarrels with a general—about the continued importance of the saber. He was thirty-two years old, needed reading glasses, and although not exactly at a dead end, seemed in a career position that led nowhere in particular. Becoming a professional general's aide was definitely not part of his career portfolio, even though Pershing, who had overcome the tragic loss of his wife and three children in a fire to become a ladies' man in the best French stereotype, had begun paying assiduous court to Patton's sister.

With Patton in his letters home regularly advocating war with Mexico and denouncing Wilson as a poltroon, in April 1917, the president asked Congress for a declaration of war—against Germany. U.S. entry into the conflict was influenced but not determined by its economic relationship with the Allies. France was the real "arsenal of democracy" in World War I, with America valued as much as a source of raw materials as a supplier of finished weapons. Despite an increasingly sophisticated Allied propaganda campaign, the American people manifested no more than a fan's interest in the Great War for its first two and a half years. The same, however, could not be said for their government. What brought the United States into the war were the calculated policies of President Woodrow Wilson.

Initially sincerely espousing neutrality, Wilson grew committed as the war progressed not only to shaping a peace, but to developing a future world order preventing similar conflicts by making the world safe for democracy and business. The president's conviction was sharpened by an increasing conviction that U.S. security was vitally threatened by German domination of Europe. Steam had made the Atlantic for the United States what the channel had been for Britain: a barrier that could all too easily become a highway. Any expectations that a victorious Reich would prove a benevolent hegemon were challenged by a pattern of direct provocations that were both deliberate and clumsy. The submarine campaign; the Zimermann telegram with its rhetoric of undoing the results of the Mexican War; the heavy-handed contempt with which the German government reacted to U.S. protests—by 1917, these had become impossible to ignore in an international climate offering no institutional means of re-solving such issues and behaviors short of war.

The country's first-line force, the U.S. Navy, was vestigial under the conditions of 1917. Badly unbalanced, emphasizing capital ships at the expense of smaller craft, it was able to provide no more than a token force of destroyers for the convoy work that had become the focal point of the war at sea. To secure Allied victory and establish the postwar posi-tion Wilson desired, the United States required above all an army—a mass army—on the ground in Europe.

Creating such a force was a daunting task, one the Germans dis-missed as impossible and the Allies found difficult to credit. With an au-thorized strength of only 108,000 as late as 1916—half the strength of the British army at the outbreak of war—even the regular Army's poten-tial as a cadre was limited. The National Guard's strength and effective-ness varied wildly among the states that controlled it. To personnel difficulties the United States added a complete lack of infrastructure. Nei-ther the buildings nor the equipment for a mass army existed. As for equipment, as late as January 1918, one division reported itself lacking a third of its allocation of rifles and all of its cartridge belts and haversacks.

The United States became the first modern state to create a mass army from a zero point along industrial lines. Britain's Great War mobilization was artisanal; the work of society's "little platoons." America turned to the factory system. From its beginnings, the new Army was a conscript force, inducted, tested, processed, and trained *en masse*. Between May and September 1917, cantonments were established all over the United States, absorbing as many as fifty thousand men each. The new Army was also homogenized. National Guard units, with their strong local ties, were amalgamated, consolidated, and assigned new roles. Draftees were at first generally organized along regional lines for convenience, but the system broke down as men were transferred *en bloc* to meet the needs of formations with higher priorities for overseas deployment and replaced by others from those lower on the scale.

John J. Pershing was selected as the commander in chief of an Amer-ican Expeditionary Force that eventually included more than two million men and women. His appointment was no surprise. He might not have had any relevant credentials as a battle captain—but neither did anyone else in the Army's senior ranks. But his record indicated he was a first-class administrator and manager, albeit on a small scale—just the man to get the fledgling AEF off the drawing boards and into the field.

The Army that reached Europe by stages was strongly Gallicized. The French army occupied, in Lorraine, the sector of the front best suited initially to introduce the green Americans to the trenches, and eventually to allow the kind of open campaigning the American high command wanted. The ports of southwest France and the railroads running eastward were less burdened than Channel ports and northeastern rail lines already straining to support the British. France was able to supply the high-tech weapons systems the Americans lacked. French training techniques and staff methods proved both reasonably effective and easily assimilated. This was particularly true in the technical combat arms, artillery, engineers, and signals.

Underlying these specifics were questions of affinity. For all their common language, Americans and British simply did not get on well at any level much deeper than the exchange of courtesies. The French had the charm of difference. And if the French among themselves were just as scathing as the British in describing American shortcomings, Gallic courtesy and American ignorance of French usually combined to limit the damage.

Pershing, whose European experience was as limited as his knowledge of French, thus had good reason to take George Patton, newly promoted captain, with him—in charge of his small advance headquarters. It was a long way from the trenches, and a longer way still from glory. For a while, Patton was dazzled at meeting the leaders of France and Britain, enjoying the accolades that greeted the new arrivals, making plans (which eventually fizzled) for his wife to join him. Using her family money, Patton purchased a luxury auto, a twelve-cylinder Packard. He attended the Bastille Day parade. He did a quick tour of the British sector. When Pershing established his headquarters at Chaumont, Patton's responsibilities increased exponentially—but they were all administrative. As a cavalry officer, he was at the end of the queue for assignment to any other combat arms unit. Then a new horizon opened.

"There is a lot of talk," he wrote Beatrice, "about 'Tanks' here now, and I am interested as I can see no future in my present job . . . lots of them get smashed but the people in them are pretty safe. . . . I love you too much to try to get killed but also too much to be willing to sit on my tail and do nothing."

The origins of the tank have been traced back to the armored "war wagons" of the medieval Bohemian Hussites, and to some sketches made by Leonardo da Vinci. In fact, the development of the armored fighting vehicle depended on the internal combustion engine. Even before 1914, speculative military writing had discussed the possibilities of gasoline-powered armored vehicles running on caterpillar tracks. By early 1915, the French and British armies were using increasing numbers of gasoline-driven tractors, originally designed for agricultural purposes, behind their lines to move guns and supplies through the north European mud.

It was nevertheless the Royal Navy, in particular First Lord of the Admiralty Winston Churchill, that began the process of developing "land ships." By the end of 1915, experiments with tracks, transmission, and armor progressed far enough to produce "Little Willie," a metal box with no armament, but a vehicle that ran. The next step was the rhomboid-shaped design still identified with World War I tanks. Dubbed "Big Willie," then "Mother," its transmission was primitive and for steering, it depended on two exposed wooden tail wheels. The noise was such that the crew had to communicate by hand signals. The engine gases alone made the vehicle almost unendurable for any length of time. But "Mother" carried two small cannon. With a bit of luck and some inspired steering, she could cross trenches and climb through shell holes. Within weeks of the first trial, the War Office ordered a hundred fifty like her.

"Mother" was a bit too domestic a designation. (The obvious alternative, "Mother-in-Law," was both too long and politically incorrect even for the time.) The origin of the familiar cognomen reflected concern with keeping the new weapon at least semi-secret. Describing them as mobile water carriers for the Middle East was credible given their appearance. Besides, they looked more like tanks than anything else. They were introduced to battle on September 15, 1916, and played a limited role in the remainder of the Somme campaign and throughout 1917. The British High Command nevertheless sustained faith in tanks' potential. It was the 3rd Army headquarters that came up with the idea for a "tank raid" in a sector where the ground was relatively undisturbed. The Battle of Cambrai, which began on November 20, 1917, was essentially a draw. But the role of tanks in its early stages was prominent and positive.

The French, too, had developed and employed tanks in 1917. Working on their own, they introduced two variants of an armored box on treads. The 13.5-ton Schneider and the 23-ton St. Chamond were originally designed as what a later generation would call assault guns, following attacking infantry and giving it fire support with their 75-millimeter guns, as opposed to leading the advance, smashing down wire entanglements, and crossing trenches like the British heavies. Their hulls overhung their tracks in both front and rear, making them extraordinarily subject to ditching or hanging up. Both also caught fire easily, incinerating their crews in a fashion grisly and spectacular even by Great War standards.

Colonel J. B. Estienne, commanding the tank arm, returned to the drawing board literally and conceptually by sponsoring the development of an entirely different vehicle. The six-ton, two-man Renault FT, mounting a machine gun or a small one-pound cannon in a revolving turret, was also intended as an infantry-accompanying vehicle. But it was more mechanically reliable than its predecessors. Its cross-country capacities were exponentially superior. And its small size and relatively low height made it a less-conspicuous target. The first battalions were organized and equipped in March 1918.

Initial reports filed by U.S. observers of both French and British tanks were generally unenthusiastic. Pershing, who was far from the rifle-and-bayonet tactical troglodyte of general-history myth, nevertheless considered tanks as meriting further study. He established his own board, which—hardly surprisingly—reported that tanks were "destined to become an important element in this war." Patton, meanwhile, was recovering from an attack of jaundice that put him in the hospital, and concluding that his connection with Pershing was eroding his chance to be anything but a glorified caterer. He debated seeking a post as a bayonet instructor and considered requesting a transfer to the infantry. Then one of his former troop commanders, currently in charge of the Tank Department, asked Patton if he was interested in directing an AEF tank school.

Patton vacillated briefly. A few months earlier he had been introduced to a French officer, a tank enthusiast, and came away concluding "the Frenchman was crazy and the tank not worth a damn." Increasingly, however, he saw that he was being offered a unique opportunity. The Great War had rendered regimental officers anonymous. It was a war of administration and management, a war in which even the most heroic deeds were likely to go unobserved and unreported. The AEF, Patton mused, would have hundreds of infantry majors, but only one of light tanks. He would begin by running the school, then move to command the first battalion organized from it. If he and the tanks made good, and the war lasted, he could expect to command a regiment, then a brigade. And Patton would pin on a brigadier general's star. For a professional soldier, the prospect was irresistible.

Writing to Pershing, Patton stressed his familiarity with gas engines and mentioned that he was the only American soldier who had ever made an attack in a motor vehicle. Patton also from the beginning interpreted the missions of tanks in this war as similar to those of cavalry in less-industrialized conflicts. British tanks had been fostered by the Navy. Throughout the war, the spirit of their crews and the tactics they employed invited comparison to gunboats on a cutting-out mission. Estienne was an artilleryman, and French tank units were called *artillerie d'assault*. Patton was the first cavalryman to receive a position of authority in an armored force. On November 10, 1917, he was assigned to the Tank Corps and ordered to establish the First Army Tank School.

This was a patronage appointment: Patton got the job because of connections. That was the way the entire AEF operated. The prewar Army officer corps had been small enough that an officer with a reasonable circle of professional contacts would have access to information about almost anyone he wished. Written evaluations took second place to personal ones in an Army where staff systems were limited and officers, from their cadet days at West Point, were taught to trust their evaluations of "character." That pattern survived even as the Army commissioned tens of thousands of new officers: in a sea of strange faces, familiar ones were correspondingly welcome—and frequently advantaged. The reverse side of patronage was a policy, beginning with Pershing and eventually informing the entire AEF, of ruthless insistence on performance. Especially for regular officers, one mistake was the rule of thumb, third chances were all but nonexistent. Pershing shed generals like a farmer shucking corn. It was a pattern that would persist in the U.S. Army throughout the twentieth century and into the twenty-first.

Captain Patton, in other words, was not being handed a sinecure—particularly because he knew nothing specific whatever about tanks. He toured the French training center for the new Renault battalions, and after Cambrai, he visited Colonel J.F.C. Fuller, already recognized as the British Expeditionary Force's (BEF) leading thinker on tank warfare. The result of a month's work was a lengthy memo Patton later considered the best technical study he ever wrote. Part of it addressed the specifications of the Renault. Another part covered the proposed organization of a tank battalion. A third discussed training methods: an assembly line that could produce two complete battalions in three months.

Of more interest is the section on doctrine and employment. Some of this is derivative: Patton borrowed the French concept of a light tank as an armored infantryman. Some is common sense: the text noted that tanks failed whenever they operated without infantry support. And some is prophetic: when resistance broke, tanks must assume the historic role of cavalry and "ride the enemy to death." This was a glittering generalization, which no tank on the Western front by November 11, 1918, was capable of implementing. It was also a signpost to the future of armor.

A new commanding officer, Colonel Samuel Rockenbach, took over the Tank Corps in November 1917. Like Patton, he was a cavalryman, but the two men were opposites in temperament. Rockenbach was experienced in the ways of Army politics, a conventional thinker content to work within the box—and a good judge of subordinates' talent. Patton once called him "a good hearted windbag," then also, "the most contrary old cuss I ever worked with." But Rockenbach divided the initial labors of the Tank Corps perfectly, assuming responsibility for the heavy lifting in negotiating for men and equipment with the British, the French, and the rest of the AEF, while giving Patton, his energy, and his ambition full scope to bring the institutional framework on line.

Patton from the beginning insisted on a spit-and-polish regime, describing it as a necessary measure to convince men who only weeks ago had been civilians that their status had changed utterly. When officers began to arrive in numbers but there were still no enlisted men, Patton put them to work building barracks, storage facilities, and workshops for the school that had yet to hold its first classes. Like almost every regular officer in the World War I Army, Patton believed in a caste system that separated officers and men. But he was just as firmly convinced that the privileges of an officer depended on performance of duty, whatever it might be. In this case, it was construction work. When the men arrived, the training center was ready.

Patton, now a major, oversaw the details of the operation to a degree inviting characterization as obsessive. In part, this was his legacy from Pershing. But his behavior reflected as well the fact that there was no one in the center to whom major responsibilities could safely be delegated. Patton taught by rhetoric and example, standing in front of classes, then getting his own hands and uniform dirty to demonstrate a point. His embryonic tankers put in twelve-hour days and six-day weeks, spending as much time at drill as they did in the various classrooms, devoting a high proportion of their off-duty hours to cleaning their uniforms and equipment to Patton's exacting standards.

In the first weeks, Patton belonged to a tank corps without any tanks. The French needed every Renault they could manufacture for the battalions they were organizing. The United States was in the initial stages of developing its own version of the Renault. Not until March 23, 1918, would the first real armored fighting vehicles arrive—all ten of them. Their crews were ready. By mid-April, Patton was staging field exercises and inviting the students of the nearby Army General Staff School to attend. The first tank maneuver in the history of the U.S. Army was a major success, showcasing both the potential of the Tank Corps and the capacities of the tank school commandant, newly promoted to lieutenant colonel.

Patton's approach fit well into the insistence of Wilson and Pershing that the United States play an independent role in the Great War. Even the great German offensives of March and April 1918 that shook the BEF to its foundations and brought the German army to the outskirts of Paris did not sway the president and the general from their shared conviction that America and its expeditionary force make an identifiable military statement, not merely for the sake of immediate victory but because of

Wilson's grand plan for the postwar reconstruction of Europe and the world. Wilson was no naïf. He may have put his principal faith in the Fourteen Points and the League of Nations, but he recognized that faith was best accompanied by works—in this case the work of the AEF in demonstrating U.S. military effectiveness beyond reasonable doubt.

In the summer of 1918, Patton got his chance. Allied Supreme Commander Marshal Ferdinand Foch allocated, albeit reluctantly, the newly created U.S. 1st Army its own operational sector, in the region of St. Mihiel, and an independent mission, the reduction of the salient the Germans had established in 1914. This was not a center-ring operation. St. Mihiel had been a quiet zone for years, where divisions exhausted elsewhere on the front came to rest and recuperate. Operations were dominated by an ethic of "live and let live." Allied intelligence, moreover, had considerable evidence that the Germans were preparing to shorten their line by withdrawing from a sector that no longer had any strategic meaning. All in all, the St. Mihiel sector was close to ideal. It provided the Americans with the chance they demanded. Should they prove unequal to the test, there was no possibility of a catastrophe resembling the first day on the Somme, or the French disaster on the Chemin des Dames in 1917. The Germans lacked the strength to do more than bloody the Yanks' noses, hurt their pride, and perhaps make them more receptive to counsel from their elders and betters.

So at least ran the subtexts in French and British headquarters. Pershing, his staffs, and his subordinates correspondingly put forth every effort to make a good showing. That included committing the 1st Brigade, Tank Corps, under Lieutenant Colonel Patton: the 326th and 327th Tank Battalions reinforced by a French battalion of Schneiders. The preparations were a staff officer's nightmare, involving a last-minute change in the divisions to be supported, ongoing battles with the supply services over fuel and lubricants, and elaborate coordination with the French railroads that moved the tanks from their base to the front. To compound Patton's difficulties, most of his tanks did not begin arriving until the last week in August and had to be prepared for the field on the fly.

The men of the brigade were eager to go, brave with the valor of ignorance. Patton issued an appropriate order. "AMERICAN TANKS DO NOT SURRENDER . . . squash the enemy with your tracks . . . This is

our BIG CHANCE." One of his junior officers later said their commander left no doubt that a tank officer was meant to die. If your tank is
disabled, Patton repeatedly insisted, then go forward with the infantry:
"If I find a tank officer behind the lines I will . . ." The threat was left un-
stated; the officer who filled it in as "probably shoot him" was probably
about half serious.

Bloodthirsty rhetoric had no effect on French railway schedules. Not
until two hours before the first waves were scheduled to jump off did the
final tank leave its train. The last units of the brigade moved into position
ten minutes before the ground attack went in. After the challenges of getting where they were supposed to be, the fighting was almost anticlimac-
tic. The major obstacle to the tanks' advance were abandoned trenches in
which tank after tank got stuck. French and American drivers would, in
time, develop and pass on techniques for moving the little Renaults
across trenches often widened for the express purpose of hanging up
tanks. In this first action, drivers frequently either could not see out of
their wildly pitching vehicles, or tried to take trenches at a straight run.

Within the first couple hours, Patton also confronted the fundamental challenge of tactical command on the Western Front. By 1918, both
radio and wire-based communications had been sufficiently improved
that regimental-level headquarters could usually count on maintaining
contact with echelons higher up the chain. Rockenbach had given Patton
a direct order to keep in touch. Instead, Patton went forward—on foot.
Because tanks had no means of communication, the ultimate way for any
senior officers to influence their action was to move from tank to tank
and pound on the hull until someone replied.

It was George Patton's first time under fire, and he freely admitted
wanting to duck. But he soon saw the futility of dodging. If he needed any
encouragement, it was provided by his brief encounter with Brigadier
General Douglas MacArthur, also leading from the front in a style that
became familiar throughout the AEF. In later years, as old roosters, each
spoke at times of a testosterone contest in which neither wanted to be
first to leave. Patton continued forward, crossing a bridge erroneously
reported to be mined, passing through a village recently captured by
the Americans, eventually catching a ride on one of the few tanks still
running.

By this time, the infantrymen, tired and disorganized from their successes, many of their officers and sergeants down, were following the
tanks by reflex, and when the straggling advance reached the next village
on the road, they went to ground. Patton told them the tank would lead
the way. On emerging from the buildings, it came under fire. Patton
jumped off, landing in a shell hole. The tank drove on; the infantry continued to hang back; and Patton found himself in the beaten zones of no
fewer than four German heavy machine guns.

He managed to work his way back to the infantry—itself no mean
feat of fieldcraft—and requested their commander to send a runner to
fetch the tank. The officer, according to Patton, responded, "Hell no, it
ain't my tank." It was a situation in which giving an order was almost
certain to prove embarrassingly futile. Instead, Patton ran after the vehicle at top speed—too busy to be scared, as he later confided. He overtook
the tank, and when the sergeant commanding it asked him what he
wanted now, Patton led the way back to the main American position.

During the balance of the day, Patton got the advance moving,
walked cross-country to contact his other American battalion, found its
tanks out of gas, struck out for the rear in search of fuel, was bombed
from the air, and received a monumental reprimand from Rockenbach
for abandoning his post. There was no room in this war, Rockenbach informed his subordinate, for personal courage. It was a business proposition—a place for everyone and everyone in his place.

By the time the reports arrived and were sorted out, however, it was
nevertheless conceded that the American tanks had done well. Certainly
there had been no reluctance to go forward and take risks. If anything,
the willingness of the brigade's rear echelons to replace casualties contributed significantly to the logistical breakdown that limited the tankers'
effectiveness after St. Mihiel's first day. The mechanics, truck drivers, and
cooks were scattered all over the sector instead of fueling and repairing
the tanks and feeding their crews. That was part of why Rockenbach tore
into Patton—and part of why a new set of brigade orders threatened
court-martial to anyone leaving his post for any reason in the next action.

By September 16, Patton reported 131 tanks on line from or an official establishment of 150. That was a substantial administrative achievement in a war where one of the major problems confronting Allied armor

was attrition due to tactical and mechanical losses. It was significant as well because of Pershing's determination to follow St. Mihiel closely with an even larger offensive against German positions in the Meuse-Argonne—the same sector where Erwin Rommel met his baptism of fire four years earlier.

Pershing's original plan had a whiff of blitzkrieg. It involved smashing through the German front, making a deep penetration on each side of the high ground around Montfaucon, then combining for a massive single thrust through the main defensive system, the Kriemhilde Line. Success depended on an advance of ten miles on the first day—this in a war where gains were measured in hundreds of yards. In contrast to St. Mihiel, the Meuse-Argonne incorporated some of the best defensive terrain in Europe: hilly and heavily wooded, its trails, rides, and clearings overgrown with underbrush after years of neglect. Also in contrast to St. Mihiel, the Germans proposed to fight for it.

The French high command believed their ally was most likely to stall in front of the Kriemhilde Line and bog down in a winter campaign. Pershing believed the risks were worth taking. Given the terrain, the AEF could have used the WGB or a counterpart. Lacking such specialized formations, Pershing and his staff proposed to combine surprise with mass: nine of the large AEF divisions, deployed in depth and under strict orders to keep moving. Patton's brigade was assigned to support two divisions of I Corps, on Pershing's right. The 35th, National Guardsmen from Kansas and Missouri, was to attack across the open ground between the villages of Varennes and Cheppy. The Pennsylvania Guardsmen of the 28th would go in on the 35th's left, along the Argonne Forest's eastern edge.

Patton undertook a detailed reconnaissance of the terrain and concluded the most favorable ground for tanks was the mile and a half or so between the Ardennes and the Bois de Cheppy, the communal woods east of the village. Instead of assigning one battalion to each of the divisions, he decided to use two companies of the 326th, now renumbered the 344th because two of the battalions organized in the United States had the same numbers as Patton's, to support the 35th's initial advance, with the third company going to the 28th. On the second day, the 327th, now the 345th, would take over, using the same disposition. The French

Schneiders, which Patton seems to have regarded as a liability in the early going, would be committed when the 345th was expended.

This was neither a sophisticated deployment nor one embodying the principle of concentration of armor. It is a corresponding warning against seeing Patton as a tank-warfare genius from his early days in command. Patton's dispositions nevertheless reflected the terrain over which he had to operate, the general intentions of 1st Army, and not least the material with which he had to work. This time he devoted even more effort to providing reserve stocks of fuel and ordered each tank to carry two full cans despite the heightened risk of fire. At the suggestion of a Tank Corps private, a repair tank followed the advance of each company to handle emergency maintenance. That the idea came from the ranks, in passing, was not unusual. Patton, recognizing that he had not ever taken a tank into combat himself, began going beyond the old Army caste system by encouraging suggestions from subordinates who had. He further announced his intention to move forward from his headquarters (code-named Bonehead—an unsubtle statement of his opinions of Rockenbach's approach to command) an hour after the attack began: "The brigade commander . . . will be up with the leading tanks at H+3½ hours."

This time, Patton went forward accompanied by two officers, a dozen runners, several carrier pigeons, and a supply of field telephones with extra wire. It was a foggy morning, and the American artillery was using a large number of smoke shells. This may have blinded the German machine gunners; it did reduce the attackers' visibility to a point where Patton and his staff first began following the tank tracks, then to navigating by compass, and finally advancing well ahead of their own tanks.

The American attack had achieved initial surprise, with the tanks in particular generating alarm and confusion. But as the fog lifted, German resistance stiffened. The Renault's small size made it a difficult target for field guns, but the ten-pound shell of a light trench mortar firing at flat trajectory was quite sufficient to destroy or cripple a tank at medium range. German heavy machine guns were issued armor-piercing ammunition, which, depending on the range and the angle of fire, could turn a tank into a colander. German infantry were trained in the use of *geballte Ladungen*: the heads of a half-dozen stick grenades unscrewed from their handles and tied together in an improvised forerunner of the World War II satchel charge. For the very brave or the very desperate, there was the antitank rifle: an enlarged version of the standard Mauser, a single-shot weapon firing a 13-millimeter armor-piercing round with a shoulder-breaking recoil but a devastating effect if it struck home in a fighting compartment.

The British and the French had developed an obvious solution to the problem of close-quarters antitank defense: tank-infantry cooperation. This was particularly important for the Renaults. The heavy tanks, especially the British rhomboids with their multiple machine guns, were small fortresses, capable even when disabled of all-round self-defense, at least for a while. The two-man Renault, whose commander was also entirely responsible for handling the armament and spotting threats, depended heavily on infantry support in everything from ground guiding to avoid the worst of the shell holes and other obstacles, to taking advantage of the tanks' gunfire to knock out machine-gun positions.

All that was—and is—easier described than done. Infantry advances by using ground; tanks by overcoming it: a fundamental difference. To men whose only protection was the cloth of their uniforms, the sight of machine-gun bullets sparking off a tank's armor created a feeling that the machines were able to take care of business on their own. Tank crews, conscious of their limited vision and relative vulnerability, tended to use their vehicles' mobility to evade trouble, as opposed to seeking and tackling it. Patton's tankers and the infantry of the 35th Division had no opportunity to work together before going into action. Few of the infantrymen had even seen a tank, much less had any idea of what they could and could not do. The 35th, like many of the U.S. divisions in the first assault wave, had no previous combat experience. Shortly before going into the line, the division commander made a clean sweep of his senior subordinates. Both of the infantry brigade commanders and three of the regimental colonels, the chief of staff, and the commander of one of the three artillery regiments were replaced—a purge unprecedented and unmatched in the history of the U.S. army.

It did not take long for everything to go simultaneously wrong. The tanks pushed ahead of infantry that suffered heavy casualties among officers and NCOs who led from the front until shot down. German artillery found the range as the fog lifted; German machine guns savaged doughboys, who increasingly lost direction and purpose. American artillery, firing blind according to preestablished schedules, began shelling its own men. After-action accounts determined that there were at least twenty-five machine-gun positions in the village of Cheppy alone, and the prompt capture of Cheppy was crucial to the 35th's mission.

Into the growing confusion came George Patton. He rallied straggling infantrymen, men without officers, some inspired or intimidated by his leadership and others reluctant to risk the machine-gun fire cutting across the way to the rear. Spotting a platoon of tanks held up by two wide trenches, he got the crews out of their vehicles and set them to work making passageways as he supervised, fully exposed to German fire. Urged to take cover, he answered "To Hell with them—they can't hit me." After the tanks got started, Patton returned to the infantry and led them forward, waving his ash plant and shouting "Let's go get them."

It was leadership by example at its best. And when his ragtag force crossed the crest of a small hill into even heavier machine-gun fire, Patton led by going to ground. Even experienced machine-gunners firing uphill were likely to set their sights a bit high. Even so, as bullets whizzed through the grass, Patton thought of a lawn mower back home. He was afraid. His hands were sweating; his mouth was dry; he felt a great desire to run. Then, by his own account, he thought of his ancestors and seemed to see them looking down on him. "I became calm at once, and saying aloud 'It is time for another Patton to die,' called for volunteers." No more than a half-dozen men accompanied him—a rational response to a gesture even Patton's principal academic admirer places in the context of Don Quixote. The outskirts of Cheppy on that day were no place for a walk in the sun. "Come on anyway," was Patton's answer. Only his orderly was with him when he found his bullet.

The shot was fired at battle range—about fifty yards. It hit him in the upper left thigh and exited "just at the crack of my bottom, about two inches to the left of my rectum"—close enough to give even an unimaginative man castration anxieties. Patton made the cover of a shell hole, where his orderly bandaged him. By that time, German infantry had filtered back to within forty yards or so and took the shell hole under fire every time one of the occupants moved. Twice Patton sent his orderly out to inform passing tanks of nearby machine-gun positions. An infantry medic stopped to check and rebandage Patton's wound. By about 1:30, the advance had progressed far enough to bring a stretcher forward. When in an ambulance, Patton ordered the driver to take him to the command post of the 35th Division, where he reported to one of the staff officers before continuing to a field hospital.

Patton's tankers had managed to join forces with what was left of one of the 35th's infantry battalions to outflank and capture Chieppy around 1:30 P.M., but that was their last notable achievement. Forty-three tanks were lost to enemy fire and mechanical failure the first day. By the 29th, the brigade's two light battalions had only 55 runners. More than half the officers and a quarter of the enlisted men had been killed or wounded. Even after a few days of rest and reorganization, Rockenbach informed Pershing that the brigade had no more than a week's combat effectiveness remaining.

George Patton's war was over, but the Americans in the Meuse-Argonne continued to claw their way forward at a high price in casualties and a higher one in straggling. Individual AEF divisions had generally high learning curves, responding quickly and effectively to shortcomings once perceived. But the policy-driven demands for a rapid increase in American numbers meant that fewer and fewer of the divisions committed to active operations had even the time to become effectively second-rate. The familiar cliché that the valor of ignorance may compensate for the absence of expertise was less applicable in 1918 than it had been earlier in the war. The AEF learned its craft against an enemy that overlooked few mistakes and charged high tuition. With winter approaching, and the influenza pandemic beginning to spread among the millions of debilitated men in uniform, would the AEF have been quite as formidable as everyone expected had the war gone into 1919?

3

PREPARATIONS

S T. Mihiel and the Meuse-Argonne were part of a series of coordinated Allied offensives, the "Advance to Victory" during the "Hundred Days" of autumn 1918. They were limited victories. The internal-combustion engine was too undeveloped to convert tactical successes to operational ones. Tanks were essentially one-shot, throwaway weapons. Aircraft were vulnerable to ground fire. Radios were bulky, fragile, and short-ranged. Nevertheless, as its casualties mounted and its morale declined, the German army was no longer able to mount the ripostes its operational doctrine demanded. Instead, it fell back, covering and counterpunching like an overmatched boxer inexorably forced into a corner of the ring.

Between July and November, the German army lost almost a million men dead, wounded, and missing. Hundreds of thousands more were prostrated by influenza. For the survivors, getting home alive became the primary objective. On October 1, Ludendorff declared the war lost. On October 8, Germany officially became a constitutional monarchy: a case of too little, far too late. On November 9, the Kaiser fled to Holland, and a republic was proclaimed in Berlin. That republic was granted an armistice. On November 11, 1918, the guns of August finally fell silent.

I

The end of the war left Patton at loose ends. He was able to write Bea in early October that he "was missing half my bottom but otherwise all right." As the senior casualty in an officer's ward, he could count on unobtrusive preferential treatment. He had several fellow tankers with whom to discuss experiences and tactics. He had hopes of a decoration—the Medal of Honor danced in his head—and enjoyed the honor of what amounted to a battlefield promotion to colonel. At the end of the month, he returned to command of the tank center, with a towel plugging a still-bleeding exit wound that would have kept him off the line for a long time had the war not ended on November 11.

Once back on duty, Patton began by issuing a new order on "dress, deportment, and discipline." He continued by commencing an essay on "German and Allied Theories of War." The paper argued that the Allies emphasized fire as a means of movement, enabling a final closing with the bayonet. The Germans, on the other hand, saw movement as a means of fire, expecting to maneuver to use fire to erode resistance until the bayonet provided the finishing touch. The direct lessons of the war, however, had limited relevance. Nowhere but in Europe could force to space ratios be so high that armies without flanks would be the norm. Nowhere save in Europe could the infrastructures support and supply the masses of artillery and small arms that defined Great War tactics. Everywhere else it would be possible by using cavalry, armored cars, and light tanks to get behind an enemy and prevent the concentration of guns that in Europe consistently checked infantry advances. Those advances, made more deadly by automatic rifles and machine guns, would, in turn, sustain the mobility restored by cavalry and armor.

In other lectures and memos written about the same time, Patton described tanks as a primary weapon of exploitation (once across the main belts of trenches, tanks "could roam at will and demoralize the enemy"). But they were also a supporting weapon for the infantry whose advance ultimately decided battles "now as in the time of Gustavus Adolphus." The U.S. Army that fought in Northwest Europe in 1944–1945 would have more of its tanks allocated to infantry support than assigned to armored divisions.

Patton looked forward to a return to wife, family, and home. He also saw himself cut off from further chances for professional advancement and self-actualization through the disciplined heroism he had spent his life cultivating. His poem "Peace—November 11, 1918" begins:

> I stood in the flag-decked, cheering crowd
> Where all but I were gay
> And gazing on their extecy,
> My heart shrank in dismay.

"It would be funny," Patton wrote Beatrice, "to be commanding a cavalry troop and be through by noon each day." He asked Pershing to consider awarding him a Distinguished Service Cross, one level below the Medal of Honor, for his encounter with the Villista officer in Mexico, and was bitterly disappointed when it seemed he would receive no medals for his combat service anywhere. "I would rather be a second lieutenant with the DSC," he wrote, "than a general without it." He rejoiced inordinately on learning he had, after all, been awarded that decoration, primarily on the recommendation of General Rockenbach. "I wish I had gotten an M.H. [Medal of Honor]. . . . I will get an M.H. in the next war I hope," he noted.

A later generation may well find Patton's concern with medals at the least unseemly. Prior to World War I, ambition for decorations was accepted among junior officers of all armies. As a British lieutenant, Winston Churchill made no secret of his desire for recognition. His fellow officers stationed in India or Africa pulled strings to be included on frontier expeditions in the hope of receiving even the been-there award of a service medal with an appropriate clasp. A large number of awards, moreover, were made for rescuing men left wounded or otherwise isolated, and facing death probably accompanied by torture at the hands of enemies whose customs of war differed sharply from those of the West. The decorated hero of a French or British expedition was able to do well and do good simultaneously—a Victorian ideal.

II

George Patton had gone to France as a lieutenant, in a staff appointment best described as factotum. Less than two years later, he was a colonel with the "red badge of courage," albeit in an awkward location, decorated for valor by a grateful French government as well as his own. Among his final acts in France was to write Pershing a letter thanking him for his "kindness and consideration" and describing Patton's efforts "in a small way to model my self on you." Pershing's episodic romance with Patton's sister was headed for its final collapse; Patton had no real idea of what awaited him in a reorganized peacetime Army. He shared that uncertainty with dozens and hundreds of other AEF officers who had seen their careers flourish beyond any dreams they might have entertained at West Point, all of them busily contacting superior officers, congressmen, newspaper editors, and anyone else who might possess either knowledge of events or power to influence them.

Patton's transport docked in New York on March 17, 1919. Overwhelmed by reporters eager for firsthand information about the new weapon of war, he proved comprehensively quotable. Noteworthy in the light of his later career is the deft touch he showed handling the reporters: eschewing controversy, sharing credit—and providing useful individual hooks for composing different stories, as opposed to giving one boilerplate account.

Patton's immediate preference seems to have been an assignment to what was then called the School of the Line at Fort Leavenworth, Kansas. He was bubbling with ideas about the shape and nature of war that he sought to share with—or impose on—almost everybody with whom he came into official contact in those first months back home. While still in France, Patton had expressed the desire to stay with armor, and his first post-war assignment nevertheless was Camp George Gordon Meade, the new home of the Tank Corps. Located between Baltimore and Washington, D.C., it was well placed for the lobbying and log-rolling necessary to establish the tanks as a permanent part of the Army.

Though Patton's experience had for practical purposes been restricted to light tanks, the AEF had been no less interested in the heavy

British models. At war's end, an improved heavy tank, the Mark VIII, designed cooperatively with the British, was coming off the assembly lines alongside the American version of the light Renault. While Patton was briefly on detached service in Washington, command of the brigade devolved on its senior heavy tanker. Dwight D. Eisenhower had been commissioned into the infantry in 1915 and spent his war in the United States, most of it training tankers in Pennsylvania. He did well enough to be promoted from lieutenant to lieutenant colonel in seven months—as steep a rise as Patton, without Patton's influence and reputation. Eisenhower's luck ran out when he finally got a tank battalion of his own; the armistice intervened before he got overseas.

The two men formed an odd-couple friendship in the course of 1919. Both Patton and Eisenhower enjoyed riding and hunting. Both were intense, with incandescent tempers that demanded rigid controlling. But Patton was marked as a comer even in the peacetime army; Eisenhower carried the tag of a role player. Patton was wealthy; Eisenhower worried about bills. Patton was effusive and efflorescent; Eisenhower favored self-effacement. Both had reputations as the best of hosts, but the Pattons entertained high society on a lavish scale wherever they went. The Eisenhowers concentrated their socializing on the officer corps of the posts where Ike served.

Both men were also poker players, in an era when skill at the game was widely considered a sign of an officer who combined brains and nerve. Patton, although he did not embarrass himself at the table, seldom came out a big winner. It is a reasonable speculation that he recognized the consequences of a moneyed officer regularly cleaning out his less-favored colleagues and was correspondingly aware of "when to hold and when to fold," no matter what his cards. Eisenhower, by contrast, was good enough to supplement his Army pay with his winnings. He was good enough that wherever he was stationed, officers passing through sought the opportunity to test his reputation. And he was consistently able to retain the friendship and goodwill of those he outplayed. That last tells more about Eisenhower the general and Eisenhower the president than any number of learned treatises on battles and elections.

The taproot of their friendship, which Eisenhower described as a simultaneous source of "delight and dismay," was professionalism. "Both of us were students of current military doctrine. Part of our passion was our belief in tanks . . . George and I had the enthusiasm of zealots." They talked of a spectacular future role for tanks attacking by surprise and in masses. They envisaged new designs incorporating speed, firepower, and reliability. They disassembled a light tank, put it back together, and had the gratification of seeing it run. Twice they almost managed to kill themselves—once when an overstretched cable snapped, then again when a machine gun they were test-firing overheated, "cooked off," and blasted the surrounding landscape at random.

As the brigade conducted route marches and provided vehicles for parades, mechanical reliability was becoming a central issue. Wartime tanks could be treated as expendable. Peacetime budgets demanded durability. Nor did it do the Tank Corps's prospects any good when its men were observed spending most of their time in the field repairing serial breakdowns. Hopes at Fort Meade were raised by a visit from J. Walter Christie. An inventor, a designer, a technician, like Edgar Allan Poe "three fifths of him genius and two-fifths sheer fudge," Christie discussed extensively the officers' ideas of what they wanted in a tank and then produced the first armored fighting vehicle designed to military specifications.

The "Christie tank" remains best known for its convertibility: being able to run on wheels while on roads, then shifting to tracks for cross-country operations. The Fort Meade tankers were at least as enthused by its speed. At sixty miles an hour on tracks, it was ten times faster than anything in the Army's inventory. Christie's design also had an exponentially better obstacle-crossing capacity than anything seen in any army. There were all the flaws and bugs to be expected in a radical new design—notably engine reliability and suspension weakness. But in Patton's words, "We are buying a principle, not a vehicle." By some accounts he put money as well as words behind Christie's work and appears to have been one of the few soldiers able to get on for any length of time with the cranky and contentious designer.

In the spring of 1919, Pershing had culled his most successful senior commanders and staff officers to create the AEF Superior Board on Organization and Tactics. Its stated purpose was to study the AEF's arms and services and recommend how each might best function in a future war. Only two of the final report's 184 pages were devoted to tanks. The committee described them as an infantry-supporting weapon, incapable of independent action, and recommended their normal use as being attached by battalions and companies to corps and divisions as the situation required. Pershing in his comments went further, suggesting the employment of tanks would be increased many times, and recommending that they be concentrated for use at decisive points. He also recommended that tanks for the present remain closely linked to the infantry.

Chief of Staff General Peyton C. March and Secretary of War Newton D. Baker both favored an independent tank corps. But Pershing and March were professional rivals whose clashes had grown increasingly bitter during the war. Baker was a civilian, challenging the recommendations of America's most successful soldier since Ulysses S. Grant. And looming behind them were the killer B's of peacetime: budget and branch.

In the course of the postwar hearings on Army reorganization, a Michigan congressman said he could understand that perhaps in case of war a case could be made for a separate tank corps. He could not, however, see any reason during peacetime to create the overhead necessary to add a new branch of service to an already complex army. That sentiment was echoed by the soldiers. The U.S. Army's historic counterpart to the British regimental system was branch identity. Infantry, cavalry, field artillery and coast artillery, engineers, signal corps, and the rest—each had its own structure of patronage and promotion. The National Defense Act of 1920 wrote practice into law by giving each branch a chief, who in most cases was appointed precisely because he was an archetype, incorporating in his person and his principles the core values, strengths, and weaknesses of his branch.

In the infantry, that meant focus on the rifleman. World War I may have been decided by combined arms, but the infantry saw itself as the core of the combination and saw the individual soldier as the heart of the infantry. The branch nevertheless lobbied strongly for the tank corps's absorption into the infantry, partly for operational reasons—the tanks had proven themselves in direct support of an infantry depending primarily on rifles—partly for reasons of budgets and personnel—the more men in the infantry branch, the higher the funding and the better the promotion possibilities—and partly from a desire to trump the other branches.

That last posed few problems. The artillery, which in France had been the tanks' initial patron, in the U.S. Army was busy refining its role as the purveyor of indirect, long-range scientific gunnery. No interest existed in sponsoring direct-support weapons systems, as the German army's artillery would later do with the assault gun. As for the cavalry, the AEF Superior Board had essentially affirmed its traditional roles: disrupting enemy communications, providing flank and rear security, conducting reconnaissance before battle and pursuit afterward. As yet, however promising the Christie design might be, no tank existed that could contribute significantly to those missions in an American context. It was hardly surprising when the National Defense Act of 1920 abolished the tank corps and assigned its components to the infantry.

Debates on the nature of future tanks continued. But discussion was restricted not merely by budgetary factors—every dollar spent on tank development was one less for the "real" infantry—but by a War Department policy requiring light tanks to weigh no more than five tons, and the medium designs projected to supplant the cumbersome Mark VIII to be kept to a fifteen-ton limit. Those restrictions reflected the carrying capacity of the Army's trucks and pontoon bridges, and the weight limitations of the country's roads, bridges, and railroad cars.

Meanwhile, there was weeding to be done and there were choices to be made. Patton had, for more than a year, been writing on the nature and the prospects of armored war. In the May 1920 *Infantry Journal,* the official branch magazine, he published an article strongly advocating maintaining the independence of the tank corps and allowing it to develop its own doctrines and tactics. Grafted onto another branch—the infantry, for example—it would be "like a third leg to a duck—worthless for control, for combat impotent." In the November issue of the same periodical, Eisenhower advocated a future tank, "speedy, reliable, and efficient," possessing "swift movement and great fire power," and useful in situations other than the trench warfare even tank enthusiasts tended to describe as its principal milieu.

The two junior officers were not exactly isolated in their advocacy. In 1919, J. F. C. Fuller had won the gold medal prize in Britain's Royal

United Services Institute military essay contest for a futuristic argument that tanks could and eventually would replace both infantry and cavalry. The next year, a former infantry officer, Basil Liddell-Hart, delivered a lecture at the RUSI describing an "Expanding Torrent System of Attack" that simultaneously widened and deepened breaches in an enemy front. Eisenhower nevertheless found himself summoned to an interview with the Chief of Infantry, in which his ideas were dismissed as not merely wrong but dangerous. In future, he was to keep his opinions to himself and publish nothing that did not reflect "solid infantry doctrine." The alternative was a court-martial—or more likely in practice, a series of negative fitness reports combined with assignments to the most remote posts on the infantry's list.

Eisenhower believed Patton received the same message. If so, he did not record the conversation. But on August 15, 1920, Patton did request formally to be returned to duty with the cavalry. He described his services to the peacetime tank corps, declared his willingness to work with the tankers in the future, but stated that he had no wish to transfer to the infantry. That at least was a sentiment few of his fellow cavalry officers were likely to challenge. Patton had recently been reduced to his permanent rank of captain and almost immediately re-promoted to major. Given the National Defense Act's reduction of the regular Army's strength to only 17,000 officers and 280,000 men, it was the last step up he could expect for a long time if he depended on the usual processes. Patton had no network in the infantry branch, nor was he likely to develop one as a Johnny-come-lately outsider associated with a marginalized weapons system. Since his return to the States, moreover, Patton had freely indulged his passion for hunting, polo, and horse shows. As a cavalry officer, participation in such activities was expected.

Patton's decision was also a product of reflection on his wartime experiences. Tanks were specialized weapons whose effective use even under the unique conditions of the Western Front had been highly situational. In Germany, Britain, and France, postwar military writers were suggesting that the tank had been a response to particular operational circumstances unlikely to be repeated. Patton disagreed but understood from direct experience both the mechanical limits of existing and projected armored vehicles and the unlikelihood of major technological breakthroughs that could or would be financed in the relevant future.

The prewar cavalry, moreover, was intellectually open. Patton's notorious article had appeared simultaneously in the *Cavalry Journal*—albeit in part from a shortage of other submissions. The next year he published a commentary in the same journal on a piece by a fellow tanker who had also returned to his old branch. Major Bradford Chynoweth described tanks as a natural auxiliary to the horse: an iron steed that should be welcomed to support horses of flesh and blood. Patton replied that he could not picture tanks operating in the mountains of Mexico, the rice paddies of the Philippines, nor—against well-handled artillery—on the sandy, gully-scarred plains of Texas. But properly used, he declared, "the tank will mean the difference between victory or defeat," and he recommended creating a separate tank corps as part of the Army's general reserve.

For a student of war ambitious for distinction in combat, return to the cavalry represented arguably the best in a spectrum of professional options. Cavalry was mobile. Horses were dependable all-terrain transport—and predictable, compared to armored vehicles. The cavalry division as theoretically constructed before the Great War, with nine regiments and a strength of up to 18,000 men, with its own artillery and engineers, an air squadron, and organic supply systems including pack trains, wagons, and trucks, was a legitimate successor to the Civil War mounted forces of Phil Sheridan and James Harrison Wilson, capable of independent operations in cooperation with a main force—arguably even capable of operating entirely on its own under the conditions to be expected, for example, in Mexico. And it was Mexico, and the southern hemisphere generally, that seemed the most realistic theater for the future employment of significant U.S. ground forces.

The prospect of participating in future conflicts on the far side of the world may have appealed to Patton's romantic side. It did nothing at all for his professional half—especially when his return to the cavalry was greeted with the equivalent of the fatted calf: command of the squadron of the 3rd Cavalry now assigned to Fort Myer. From a branch perspective, it was a display assignment. Patton had arguably the best, certainly the best-publicized war record of any officer eligible for the job, while his

family wealth made him able to sustain the social demands accompanying it.

The match proved perfect. The Pattons became recognized among
Washington's premier host couples. Patton spent time "dining and lunch-
ing with Belmonts, Harrimans, Penn Smiths . . . the nicest very rich people
I have ever seen." He honed his skills in cultivating the useful, the great,
and the near-great; his daughter describes it as "terribly exciting to watch
Georgie doing his stuff" at social functions. Patton composed extensive
memoranda on improving Army polo, arguing that encouraging officers
to play cultivated qualities of aggreation and teamwork indispensable in
war. He was a spit-and-polish commander whose squadron never failed
to impress at the parades and ceremonies central to duty in Washington,
and whose barracks and stables were as immaculate as his horses and
men. He continued his tinkering, designing a carrier for the Browning
Automatic Rifles coming into cavalry service as a fire support weapon.
And he began remembering concepts of warmaking that had been temporarily obscured by his three-year involvement with an instrument of
war able to move no faster than five miles an hour.

Patton in his Myer years read widely, spending most of his evenings
absorbed in theorists of war from Clausewitz and Xenophon to J. F. C.
Fuller, the writings of great captains like Frederick and Napoleon, and
histories of the Great War and its antecedents the Russo-Japanese War
and the Wars of German Unification. Like most autodidacts, he had
eclectic study habits, one idea or one book leading him to another without any particular system. It may have been his developing interest in the
work of German military thinkers and commanders, a field he had overlooked before the war, that brought him to assert that even the most inspired strategy might be negated by poor tactics, while good tactics could
compensate for incompetent strategy. With that conclusion, which he
modified but never abandoned, Patton came down squarely on the "operational" side of an enduring debate in U.S. military thinking. Especially
in the twentieth century, the crucial problems of American military planning have been at the levels of policy and strategy: deciding where to send
forces and determining how to keep them there. Operational art and tactical proficiency have been secondary concerns. U.S. ground forces have
as a rule been put to school by their enemies charging disproportionately

high tuition. Patton provided the yin to the yang, arguing that strategy that is not implemented at the cutting edge of battle is worthless.

That mind-set reflected, in turn, Patton's developing concept of command. George Patton and Erwin Rommel had as different combat experiences as it is possible to have in the same war. Yet Rommel the assault infantryman and Patton the displaced cavalryman arrived at essentially the same conclusions about mastering industrial war. Mass and machine triumphed only when men allowed them to—only when commanders reacted to numbers and technology, instead of using them as means to an end. "The Golden Rule of War, Speed-Simplicity-Boldness," he reminded himself in a notebook he kept while at Myer. "YOU ARE NOT BEATEN UNTIL YOU ADMIT IT. Hence DON'T . . ." "War means fighting—fighting means killing, not digging trenches. . . . Try to make fanatics of your men. It is the only way to get great sacrifices." Again and again he repeats in bold and capitals. Lecturing on "The Cavalryman," he ascribed success in war as "getting to the right place at the right time." The cavalry officer, Patton declared, must train himself to possess "a GAMBLER'S courage" and educate himself to say "CHARGE." Educate—because the man is not born who can say it out of hand.

In these words, for the first time it is possible to see clearly the outline of the general in the persona of the major. The commander must keep his twentieth-century clarity of vision: the dominance of the forebrain that was a product of the Age of Reason. Yet at the same time, he must be "a personal LEADER." "You must school yourself to savagery," Patton advised his fellow officers. You must overcome the abhorrence of personal encounter, the brakes on emotions, the denial of anger, that are among the central tenets of modern civilization." "At one and the same time," Patton concludes, "you must be a wise man and a fool." Few great captains have taken their own advice so much to heart.

Patton's gratified superiors sent him in January 1923 to the Field Officers' Course at the Cavalry School. In modern terminology, he aced the five-month curriculum and was an obvious candidate for appointment to the Command and General Staff School at Fort Leavenworth, just down the road. Established in 1881, the school, under several different names, had developed into the single most important educational assignment for an Army officer. The normal pattern involved students being given a series of problems to address, basing their presentation on a set of documents provided in a course handbook. Each problem had an approved answer, in principle based on the Army's general doctrine, and students were graded in terms of their conformity to the "Leavenworth solution" or "school solution." Both terms survive in the Army as synonyms for routine, by-the-book approaches to operational problems.

Patton had his own methods for avoiding collapse. He described himself as studying between 7 and 11 P.M. from Monday to Thursday, then going to bed whether or not he was finished. On Friday afternoon he had "several big drinks" and otherwise avoided alcohol. Success, he declared, depended on technique more than intelligence. Never read or discuss an approved solution before getting marked for your own work. Never look for subtle ramifications in a problem—"there ain't any." Patton's approach, seasoned by large infusions of polo, helped him graduate with honors—twenty-fifth out of a class of 248.

Patton kept an extensive notebook chronicling his Leavenworth year and forwarded it to his old study partner when Dwight Eisenhower was assigned to the school in 1925. Ike finished first in his class, and in responding to his expression of gratitude, Patton made the frequently cited observation that Leavenworth concentrated on tactics and administration but ignored morale ". . . what is it that makes the Poor S.O.B. who constitutes the casualty list fight." In the next war, he opined, victory "will depend on EXECUTION, not PLANS."

Patton's observation probed the core of a major anomaly in the U.S. Army's approach to war between 1918 and at least 1945 or 1950. American military thinkers saw the key to victory as the conduct of mobile offensive operations—"open warfare." Key to the offensive was the "offensive spirit"—in other words, morale. In principle, the human element, men and their will to fight, was at the heart of American doctrine. The "principles of war" on which the Leavenworth system was based were applied in an environment defined by human behavior. U.S. planners believed Americans were aggressive, resourceful, self-reliant. Americans were able to take the initiative in a crisis. Thinkers like General John M. Palmer insisted on the continued effectiveness of the citizen soldier, the National Guardsman and the wartime conscript, even in the circumstances of industrialized, mechanized war. In evaluating the AEF's record, the Army assigned primary credit to the front-line soldiers' high morale and individual fighting power. If those qualities were not obviously manifested, as for example when straggling became endemic during the later stages of the Meuse-Argonne, then the problem lay with the system, with the kind of shortcomings in command and administration the Leavenworth curriculum was designed to overcome. Lectures and articles iterated and reiterated such mantras as "in man we have the essential human factor in war" [sic] and "moral force is the soul of battle." Until well after World War II, the subtext of Army training methods and tactical doctrines was that the ordinary American in uniform was a natural soldier and a natural warrior, whose inherent qualities required only cultivation and polishing. Only a few like George Patton went outside the box to ask Martin Luther's question: "What happens if it is not so?"

To a degree, the Army's faith in the military version of the common man was a product of necessity. The National Defense Act and its successors essentially defined the regular Army's peacetime role as a matrix for national mobilization. Tables of organization became nominal and notional, with regiments being scattered across the country and battalions frequently able to muster less than a company for duty once the housekeeping details were assigned. Equipment was of wartime vintage, on the principle of "waste not, want not." When the Army had last been so dispersed, frontier service and colonial expeditions provided at least a degree of operational focus. After 1918, Caribbean and Asian expeditions became things of the past; Hawaii and the Philippines were garrison assignments with palm trees, where liquor and women were cheaper. For the overwhelming majority of officers, going to war from a standing start would have meant taking the field at the head of a body of uniformed caretakers whose previous service had been focused on the skills of the janitor rather than the warrior.

Patton's post-Leavenworth assignments reflected the Army's circumstances more clearly than he would have preferred. From Leavenworth he went to Boston as a corps staff officer. Eight months later, he was assigned to Hawaii, again on staff duty, which allowed ample time to associate with the islands' elites, haole and native, to sail, and to revitalize the Hawaiian Department's moribund polo program.

Patton's polo-playing was not—at least not entirely—a rich man seeking a sublimated substitute for the medieval tournament and the Napoleonic charge. Polo, especially the national-championship level at which Patton participated, demanded a degree of comprehensive physical fitness surpassing anything in an interwar officer corps not known for its commitment to exercise. As he grew older, Patton owed a fair part of his standing among his fellow officers to his regularly demonstrated toughness on the polo field in a military culture where manliness was too often built around late-night elbow-bending at the officers' club.

Nor did Patton sublimate his military intellect to the Islands' social whirl. In November 1926, he was appointed G-3 of the Hawaiian Division: staff officer responsible for plans and training. He swept into his new post by critiquing the command's dress and discipline and savaging what he considered a botched major training exercise. A flurry of aggrieved complaints from fellow officers resulted in Patton's transfer to G-2, the intelligence department, with the comment that he was too outspoken. This was the first time in Patton's career that his fingertip situational awareness of his professional environment failed him. It would not be the last.

Patton nevertheless continued developing his concepts of motivation. In a 1927 lecture on "Why Men Fight," he insisted on one hand that superiority in war was hereditary, and argued that the United States was handicapped in developing leaders because of its lack of class distinctions. At the same time, he established a case for an aristocracy by ascription, saying that class distinctions could be conferred by achievement and behavior. Such trappings of war as decorations could transform a coward into a brave man. His emerging status as a central intellectual figure in his branch was recognized by his reassignment in 1928 to the Office of the Chief of Cavalry: the mounted service's powerhouse.

Mechanization, the Chief remarked, loomed large among issues the cavalry faced, and Patton's experience in the field was considered valuable. What he did not say was that Patton was considered a patron of the horse, at a time when an increasing weight of opinion considered the horse obsolescent as an instrument of war. For the artillery serving with the AEF, the conditions of autumn 1918 had demonstrated the limitations of the horse beyond debate. Loss rates had been so high that projections for the campaign of 1919 included replacing horses with small tractors in about half the light artillery regiments. The cavalry's eclipse during the Great War combined with the increasing stabilization of Mexico to force the branch into a rear-guard action during the 1920s. Regiments were disbanded; those remaining were reduced in strength to a point where even cavalrymen questioned their operational effectiveness. No money was available for large-scale changes. The tables of organization drawn up in 1928 were still built around the "escort wagon" and its four-mule team.

III

Change began with a civilian. In 1927, Secretary of War Dwight Davis was visiting England and observed the British army's newly created Experimental Mechanized Force maneuver at Aldershot. He was sufficiently impressed that on returning home he ordered the Chief of Staff to create a similar force. In July 1928, it assembled: a battalion each of light and heavy tanks of Great War design, a battalion of infantry and one of artillery carried in trucks, a troop of armored cars provided by the cavalry, and supporting units.

The force staged a series of marches and maneuvers that proved obsolete, broken-down equipment could prove nothing. It was disbanded in September. In October, the War Department authorized a permanent Mechanized Force, but as assembled in 1931, it included no more than a company each of tanks and motorized machine guns from the infantry, a troop of armored cars, and a battery of truck-drawn artillery. Total strength was less than seven hundred men.

The commander was a cavalry officer, Colonel Daniel van Voorhis. Though he was sympathetic to motorization, his appointment reflected the cavalry branch's bureaucratic skills rather than an embracing of mechanization at branch level. George Patton found himself squarely in the middle of the action— and for the first time in his life, he seemed to have wished himself somewhere else. The Office of the Chief of Cavalry was expected to develop the doctrines and weapons systems the cavalry needed to perform effectively. As the new head of the Plans and Training Division,

Patton played a central role in that process. It was the first time since his Tank Corps days at Langres that he had a hand on the levers of power.

On the other hand, branch headquarters during the 1920s had become the focal point of traditionalism within the cavalry. Lobbying and publicity, within the Army or in the halls of Congress, focused on maintaining the place of the horse. One of Patton's early assignments was to consider the disadvantages of mechanization. He replied by stressing the limits imposed on motor vehicles of all kinds by weather and terrain. In a later essay along the same lines, Patton observed that horses required no developmental costs.

Horses did not need spare parts and elaborate repair shops. Writing on the "Value of Cavalry," Patton mobilized authority: contemporary experts from every major army who affirmed the continuing value of the proverbial "well-bred horse." He dismissed JFC Fuller as someone who "during the course of four years' war replete with opportunities attained only the rank of Lieutenant-Colonel," and described "Captain Lyle Hart" as "a hack writer"—which in this case invites a pot-and-kettle comparison.

Patton entertained no doubt that he had been assigned to the branch office because of his reputation as a cavalry intellectual—one of the mounted arm's relatively few—and because of his social and public prominence. His superiors expected him to be a representative figure for his branch, promoting and embodying its interests as they defined them. That raised the vexed question of loyalty. The Army's staff system was—and is—a form of what Communists call "democratic centralism." Debate on a particular point may be free and open, but once a decision is reached, discussion and dissent come to an end. A subordinate unable to follow the program had, of course, a right to ask for a transfer and pay the professional price. Otherwise, an American commander had—and still has—a right to expect that his staff officers implement his policies as though they had originated them. Patton's recent Hawaiian experience had been instructive in that regard, and he was junior enough to be still feeling the shock.

Patton also loved horses. He considered hunting "the sport of kings." He believed contact with horses was a good thing for men who were soldiers, helping them remain grounded in war's physical realities, as opposed to becoming desk men focused on abstractions. "We attempt to make leaders out of a large percentage of [military school] students. [E]ach new invention from the chariot to the airplane—from gunpowder to the gas engine—has been heralded as the final solution, and yet in no instance has the adoption of a new weapon materially affected war."

In that context, the dirty little secret of the traditionalists was their near-complete lack of experience in long-term, large-scale mounted operations away from stables, granaries, and veterinary hospitals. The "well-bred cavalry horse" was in fact among the most fragile of large mammals, requiring regular feedings of grain and large amounts of water, depending on elaborate and systematic physical care to maintain basic conditioning. A vehicle even in the 1930s could be neglected, at least temporarily, with fewer negative consequences than those arising from failing to pamper a horse. The old-time troopers' nostalgic memories of the Indian Wars elided the numerous times when on combined-arms expeditions the cavalry's mounts "played out" and it was up to the infantry, the "walk-a-heaps" in Plains pidgin, to complete the mission.

Patton himself had spent relatively little actual field time as a cavalryman. Even in the Southwest, as the twentieth century progressed the cavalry increasingly operated for short periods from permanent facilities. It was one thing to take a troop on patrol or a squadron for field exercises for a few days, even a week or more. It was quite another to keep the field for months with the same complement of animals, especially under the kind of unfavorable conditions traditionalists argued were the cavalry's enduring milieu.

The British cavalry had learned that lesson during the Great War in the Middle East. By the culmination of the great mounted flank maneuver at the end of the 1917 campaign in Palestine, enough horses were on the edge of collapse from thirst that the only solution was a desperate charge to seize the wells at Beersheba before the Turks could blow them up. In Mesopotamia, the summer temperature grew so high that by 1917, improvised motorized formations using American Model T Fords were taking over the patrolling duties of a cavalry whose horses could not endure the heat. When a Ford overheated, a brief pause and a little water usually brought it back on line. For an overheated troop horse, the only remedy was too often a pistol shot.

In his previous writings, Patton had tended to emphasize the "cavalry spirit" as a metaphor for initiative and flexibility at junior and field officer levels; and more important, for the ferocity he considered necessary for the modern soldier: "The psychology of the bayonet and the saber are identical—you have to get close to use them . . . To charge effectively a man must be in a frenzy; you cannot have controlled frenzy." Now he began cultivating a broader perspective as well. The U.S. Cavalry's heritage and doctrine had a stronger operational focus than those of its tactically oriented, battle-centered European counterparts. The employment of cavalry in small detachments or for indefinite missions was a mistake, Patton argued. When an opportunity for decisive results offered, the cavalry must be used to its limits and "ruthlessly expended." The cavalry was vestigial only for incompetent commanders.

To maintain its position, the cavalry could not remain static. Patton saw a possible takeoff point in the armored car. Even cavalry traditionalists were able to see the uses of a vehicle that could move quickly on roads, that provided armor protection to a machine gun or a light cannon, that could scout and patrol ahead of mounted units, and that could deliver exactly the kind of mobile fire support mounted units could not furnish themselves except at significant cost to the mobility and flexibility that were cavalry's primary *raisons d'être*.

Armored cars had been widely used by cavalry in the Great War. The British employed them in Mesopotamia, in the Western Desert, and in the Palestine Campaign of 1918, where they proved valuable auxiliaries to the horsed regiments. Under the much different conditions of the Western Front, by 1918, each French horsed cavalry division had one or two "groups," each of a dozen armored cars, assigned; and their machine guns and one-pound cannon were consistently welcomed by the horsemen during the Allies' final offensive. After the war, though armored cars were assigned to the Royal Tank Corps, a fair amount of British professional writing was devoted to the future cooperation of cars and horses. In France, the cavalry divisions not only kept their armored cars—which ironically were usually built on the chassis of White trucks built during the war in the USA—but during the 1920s, steadily added to their complement of motor vehicles and motorcycles. This process of "blending gasoline and manure" was regularly and positively featured in professional journals like the *Revue de Cavalerie,* and Patton never lost touch with French military literature.

The U.S. Cavalry's direct contribution to the Mechanized Force had been a handful of what were called armored cars by courtesy: commercial chassis with varying combinations of armor plate and machine guns, none of them developed beyond prototype status, all of them exponentially inferior to the purpose-built armored cars coming into cavalry service in Europe. Patton nevertheless touted the armored car, not as a panacea—they were road-bound and susceptible to even improvised obstacles—but as a complement to the horse as an instrument of maneuver. Armored cars, he argued, must never become merely "a perambulating source of fire power." Instead, they must be given the same freedom of movement as horsed cavalry. Their principal means of combat should be audacity and surprise. Some advocates of armored cars for the cavalry saw them as continuing a prevailing American tradition of the dragoon and mounted rifleman, carrying large crews that would usually dismount to fight. Patton answered that armored cars "will restore the cuirassiers to the cavalry," and spoke of a future when squadrons of them would open a hole "through which our equine squadrons will thunder to victory." Substitute infantry in trucks and half-tracks for the horses, and the scenario is prophetic.

In 1928, Walter Christie returned to the military marketplace with his "National Defense Machine." The M1928 was a prototype of propulsion and suspension. With a powerful engine and combining a track suspension with large road wheels, it offered the practical possibility of an armored vehicle capable of working with horsemen both on roads and across country. Patton successfully urged the purchase of several examples for testing, regularly repeating the argument that mechanical progress could only result from physical experiment.

At the same time, Patton continued to emphasize the "chief characteristic of the cavalry" as "horse-induced mobility." While lecturing the Pennsylvania National Guard on "Cavalry in the Next War," he used his exensive experience with mechanized forces to insist that "machines have defects as great as their advantages." His efforts were recognized by a performance rating in which the Chief of Cavalry recommended him as an ideal commander of a cavalry division in war—not only because he was an outstanding horseman, but because he was also "an outstanding authority on mechanization."

During his time in the cavalry office, Major Patton was the cavalry's house intellectual, the go-to man for a few well-chosen words on any subject relating to the cavalry's welfare—a public relations officer without the title. He combined social and military prominence, a distinguished war record, facility as an after-dinner speaker, and a remarkable ability to write simultaneously in-house memoranda, articles for military journals, and think pieces for the public press. His reputation as an outspoken maverick who was best kept away from typewriters and microphones lay in the future.

It is correspondingly unsurprising that Patton tailored his remarks to his audience frequently and consciously. When Major General Guy V. Henry became Chief of Cavalry in 1930, he turned to Patton to draft his lectures promoting the branch. The commandant of the Tank School submitted a staff study proposing to create on mobilization six tank divisions, one for each Army district, to cover advances and retreats, threaten enemy flanks and rear, exploit breakthroughs, seize key points ahead of a general advance, and fill gaps on one's own line as necessary. Patton countered that such a force could be used in only three areas: Asia, Western Europe, and the United States. No prospects of U.S. involvement in the first two existed, while no country had the capacity to mount a mechanized threat in North America. In the immediate context of 1930, Patton was correct on all three counts. But was it scarcely coincidental that the missions assigned to the projected tank divisions he criticized precisely overlapped those traditionally assigned to the cavalry?

For most people in Patton's position, however, the question eventually becomes one of integrity—professional, intellectual, and personal. In 1930, Patton tried and failed to secure the post of Commandant of Cadets at West Point. It was the kind of escape hatch that combined purpose with nostalgia, offering what seemed a refuge from current high stress—the counterpart to that teaching post at a small liberal arts college for which today's officers with pressure assignments often yearn in theory. Sixty years earlier another frustrated hero of a great war whose current career was tangled had sought appointment as Commandant. George Armstrong Custer was also turned down. First Custer, then Patton, overseeing the discipline and character formation of the Army's future officers! The might-have-beens invite at least a counterfactual-history short story.

Patton's stress levels were reduced to a degree by events outside his control. Facing budget constraints only likely to grow worse as the depression worsened, the Army chose to concentrate on maintaining its numbers as opposed to investing in technology. There were limits below which unit strength could not be reduced and maintain operational efficiency. There were limits on the number of units that could be disbanded without affecting the Army's dual missions of an initial protective force and a nucleus for national mobilization. Personnel factors also determined the fate of the Mechanized Force; none of the Army's branches of service were willing to sacrifice even a few hundred men to a potential new rival.

In 1931, Chief of Staff Douglas MacArthur ordered the force disbanded and declared that in the future, infantry and cavalry would share responsibility for tank development. To avoid rewriting laws and to spare the infantry's feelings, cavalry tanks would be called "combat cars." This was a shrewd decision for two reasons. It gave each branch the opportunity to mechanize according to its perceived needs. And it made mechanization an Army issue rather than a branch issue. If either infantry or cavalry neglected the mechanization issue, it was by default making a major concession to its rival.

Patton meanwhile was winning accolades and publicity in horse shows and on the hunting field. No less important to a man in his forties and increasingly pessimistic about his prospects for seeing active service again, he was assigned to the Army War College in Washington for the 1931–1932 term. The AWC had existed since 1919 as the top Army educational institution. Its purpose was to prepare senior officers for the highest level command and staff appointments. Its curriculum involved preparing reports on the world's major nations, reports emphasizing the study of armed forces but integrating economic, social, physical, and political characteristics. These reports became the basis of war plans for a variety of contingencies. While the planning process was the school's heart, its spirit was seen by many participants to be the "information periods," consisting of lectures, conferences, and student research projects designed to expand students' general knowledge. Unlike Leavenworth, the school integrated external resources. Reserve officers, businessmen, academicians, government experts, and foreign officers attended classes and gave lectures. The AWC and its counterpart the Naval War College were the only national institutions where civilian and military came together to discuss national security issues.

As a rule, the classes incorporated the best and the brightest. Dedicated work for the welfare of a particular branch was seldom enough by itself. In January 1931, Patton had published an article in the *Cavalry Journal*. Titled "Success in War," it brought together a set of ideas he had been developing since before his assignment to the cavalry board. Success, Patton reflected, was not the fruit of knowledge. Defeated generals frequently knew more about war than their conquerors. Planning by itself was not a sovereign prescription. Hooker's plan for Chancellorsville was excellent. Systems ensured nothing. The Germans built in the years before the Great War a mighty machine but neglected the crucial factor. That factor, in Patton's mind, was the commander, the leader. He must be a living presence, linked to his men by outward forms as well as inner connections. Patton saw the "warrior soul" as susceptible of acquisition and cultivation, as opposed to being an inherent quality. But its essential characteristics of courage, enthusiasm, self-confidence—these were not enough by themselves to make a warrior a commander as well. They must be communicated. Thus the leader must be an actor—but "an actor who lives his part," and thus becomes larger than life.

This conclusion helps explain much of Patton's personal and professional behavior over the next decade, as he continued to mold himself into a model of a commander that could become a reality. The essay also helps resolve the issue of Patton's conflicted behavior during his tenure at the cavalry branch. By the time he finished his tour, George Patton was in his own mind neither a trooper nor a tanker. He was becoming a man of war.

IV

Patton's major project during his AWC year was a fifty-six-page essay on "The Probable Characteristics of the Next War." Not the least of its significance was its challenge to a growing body of Army opinion that studying anything but the most recent conflicts was a waste of time because of the "military revolution" brought about by technology. Patton applied twenty years of private reading and reflection to an account that began in 2500 B.C.E., concluded with the South African War of 1898–1902, and classified armies in two general categories: mass and professional. Based on that body of data, he drew a conclusion revolutionary in its implications. Mass armies, the kind of force to which U.S. national policy was committed *de facto* and *de jure,* were socially useful in conveying a sense of security through size, creating a reality of shared obligation, and facilitating the homogenization of complex societies. They were politically useful in that they were considered cheap, and in providing governments with a ready-made explanation for defeat, namely that nothing more could be done. Militarily, however, the best Patton could say about mass armies was that they could fight a multiple-front war.

Professional armies, on the other hand, compensated for their inevitably smaller size by being easier to supply, train, and discipline. Professional armies were less tied to their logistical systems. They were better able than mass armies to disperse without becoming disorganized—a quality demanded by the growing influence of air power on the battlefield. They were more maneuverable and more likely to remain functional under stress. They were more reliable tools in the hands of commanders seeking to exercise the intiative that wins wars. Battles, Patton argued, were primarily fought at their grass roots, by junior leaders who acted without orders. The role of higher commanders was essentially inspirational—an argument Patton extended to the point of supporting the death in battle of senior officers because of its positive moral effect on the rank and file. And professional armies by their nature were more susceptible than mass forces to influence by inspiration, just as the high-bred race horse or polo pony responded in a way impossible for the larger, stronger draft horse. The text concluded by asserting that small professional armies would restore mobility to a next war Patton believed would be shorter and more decisive than its 1914–1918 predecessor.

Patton's essay had a good portion of red institutional meat. He argued that the current U.S. Army of 130,000 men fell 200,000 short of the minimum needed for a professional field army that would be more than a collection of housekeeping details for citizen warriors. He called for increases in the number of trucks and armored vehicles, citing in particular the importance of motorizing the Army's rear echelons. He advocated as well a comprehensive reorganization of the infantry from the division down, including the adoption of a light machine gun on the European model as the basic squad weapon—the latter a fundamental challenge to orthodoxies in the infantry branch.

The wider flaws of history and logic in the presentation are nevertheless so obvious that the paper's forwarding to the War Department and the AWC's commending its author for "work of exceptional merit" at first glance seem incomprehensible by present-day standards. To cite only one obvious example, Patton was too widely read in military history to be unaware of the fact that mass possesses a quality of its own. The wars of the French Revolution and the Franco-Prussian War of 1870–1871 were only the most recent examples of the problems professional armies could face when confronted with mass—especially mass multiplied by enthusiasm. Emory Upton, whose post–Civil War writing on the nature of armies was widely interpreted in the United States as supporting a professional army over a mass conscript force, conceded that there was a point beyond which even the highest quality could not prevail over time against superior numbers.

As for Patton's concept of directly inspirational leadership, its day—if one ever existed—had passed by the time of the Civil War. Patton's own concept of future battle, with small units acting independently, communicating with each other only episodically, the positive impact of a commander's heroic personal sacrifice was likely to be subsumed by the immediate problems of fighting and surviving. One cannot help wonder if Patton's memory cast him back to his own experiences in the Argonne, and whether he would have done anything differently had he learned of General Pershing's dying in the front trenches with a pistol in his hand.

When the two presentations and their matrices are considered together, Patton appears to have followed a pattern of reasoning that moved from the particular to the general to the particular. Based on his initial reading, he developed a master idea in the early 1920s, almost an ideology: a theoretical construction of the kind of leadership needed to win wars. From there, during his Cavalry Office and War College years, he defined the kind of Army for which that leadership style would be most effective and mined the history of war for examples supporting his preconceptions. Such an approach is common among soldier-historians, especially when their ideas do not generate much feedback. And Patton's concept of heroic leadership did not challenge enough myths on levels fundamental enough to inspire the kind of discussion his more practical articles evoked.

Patton left the AWC with a rating of "superior," and a note that he was "an aggressive and capable officer of strong convictions" who also "qualified for duty with any civilian component." His next assignment, executive officer of the 3rd Cavalry at Fort Myer, brought him into direct contact with civilians in a different fashion. Patton's regiment was one of the units called out to deal with the Bonus March of 1932, a desperate effort by unemployed veterans to secure by marching on the Capitol early payment of a small bonus Congress had voted Great War veterans after the Armistice. From a maximum of around twenty-five thousand, their number had shrunk to around ten thousand when the administration, increasingly frightened of civic disorder and red revolution, called out the troops. The cavalry used the flats of their sabers to drive the veterans from downtown Washington into the "Hooverville" on Anacostia Flats. Fires broke out and spread, destroying most of the improvised shelters, and the marchers began leaving Washington that day.

It was scarcely the kind of active service for which Patton yearned. Being hit in the head by a thrown brick was scarcely the kind of heroic sacrifice he described in his War College thesis. Even more ironically, one of the participants in the march was the former corporal who had brought Patton in when he was wounded in the Argonne. When the next morning he asked to see Patton, Patton first denied knowing him, then explained to witnesses of the incident that he had supported his rescuer since the war and would continue taking care of him.

The mixture of anger, embarrassment, and *noblesse oblige* Patton demonstrated was closer to typical of the officers who participated in suppressing the march than was the cautious sympathy manifested by Dwight Eisenhower, then on duty at the War Department. To date, the Pattons had scarcely felt the effects of the depression. Their money was soundly invested, continuing to produce dividends through the worst of the hard times. They continued to co-sponsor a hunt patronized heavily by congressmen and senior officials and officers, opening the 1934 season by treating twenty-five hundred guests to an entire steer roasted over an open grate—an early example of the barbecue coming to Washington. In June, Patton's older daughter was married, predictably if not naturally, to an Army officer. In March, he was promoted to lieutenant colonel: his first step in rank in fourteen years. George Patton was forty-nine rising fifty and beginning to ask if that was all there was going to be.

Terms such as "midlife crisis" and "male menopause" have entered the West's vocabulary with the late-century self-help movement. They correspondingly invite dismissal as what critics call psychobabble. Yet anyone surveying George Patton's personal life in the mid-1930s is likely to find themselves falling back on self-help conventions. There is nothing quite like a daughter's marriage to remind a father of his mortality—assuming Patton needed reminding. Patton's father had died in 1927, a loss not untimely, but for Patton extremely significant. His doting and beloved aunt Nannie died in December 1931, and her half-sister's family contested the will: in Patton's eyes, a betrayal of family loyalties. While his everyday health was sound, when being honest with himself, Patton had to admit that in recent years he had been drinking more than was good for him even though he held it well. He wore a partial plate. His hairline was receding, and his nearsightedness increasing. It was small comfort that Gustavus Adolphus, too, had been myopic. With no war on the horizon, the promises Patton had made to himself in his younger days seemed to be returning now in shades of mediocrity.

British author Robert Graves was a soldier before he became anything else and once described armies as consisting of only three agencies: the Circle Game Department, the Practical Joke Department, and the Fairy Godmother Department that makes the other two bearable. When, in March 1935, the Pattons learned that George was being reassigned to Hawaii, it seemed that the Fairy Godmother was smiling. Instead, the assignment revealed itself as the work of the Practical Joke Department.

Patton bought a small boat, had it shipped to California, and sailed to the islands in style. He arrived just in time to observe and report on the summer maneuvers and dissected his new colleagues for their lack of initiative, flexibility, and imagination. He mocked the concern for comfort in the field, the pattern of commanding from the rear that required unsustainable levels of communication, and—by now predictably—the focus on machines. "The Army exists to kill men," he concluded, "not to groom vehicles."

It was not the most tactful way of making an entrance. As the Department's G-2, Chief of Intelligence, Patton developed an internal security plan for the contingency of war with Japan that involved declaring martial law, suspending habeas corpus, and holding more than a hundred prominent Hawaiian Japanese, citizens as well as aliens, as hostages for the good behavior of the islands' Japanese population. While nothing in the document expressly violated American precedents or existing laws of war, it demonstrated a lack of concern for both the rights and the welfare of Hawaii's Japanese that would arguably have been self-defeating had the plan been implemented. A beleaguered island garrison did not need the additional risks of an uprising behind its lines.

Both the maneuver critique and the internal security plan arguably reflected a deeper crisis. Both at social functions and on the polo field, Patton's behavior rapidly spiraled out of control. As his athleticism declined, he compensated not with technique, like most aging polo players, but with an increased aggressiveness that led to a hard fall on his head. The doctor called it a slight concussion, and Patton continued to function. Three days later he asked, "Where the hell am I?"

That was no bad question. During a later game in the Hawaiian polo championship series, Patton's language and behavior led to the Department's commanding general, Hugh Drum, who was attending the match as a guest, to summon Patton to his box and administer a scathing reprimand that culminated in relieving Patton as captain of the Army team and ordering him to leave the field.

Drum was not officiating the match and, therefore, was acting entirely as Patton's military superior. The captain of the opposing team, one of the richest, most powerful men in the islands and a close friend of Patton's, informed the general that if his order stood, his team would refuse to continue to play. The captain of another team in the tournament asserted that he had never heard "Georgie" use foul language—making him either hearing-impaired or the biggest liar in Hawaii. Drum backed down, told Patton to watch his language, and left the grounds.

More was involved here than Hawaii's horsy set rallying behind one of its own. Since the U.S. annexation of the islands after the Spanish-American War, a struggle for precedence had existed between the civilian plantation owners and businessmen, most of them Hawaiian-born, and the senior Army and Navy officers who represented mainland authority. Drum was a dour man of humble origins, accepted only by courtesy in circles where the Pattons moved by virtue of their wealth. The chance to show him, and by extension the rest of the uniforms, his place was too good to miss—not least because Drum himself had gone over the line and knew it.

At the same time, Patton's polo-playing friends acted as enablers. The Patton of a few years earlier possessed too much situational awareness to become involved in a public altercation with a two-star general over a polo game. Now his mood swings and temper outbursts grew more extreme, less balanced by the effervescent bursts of kindness and good cheer that previously compensated for them.

It is possible to speculate that the polo accident resulted in an undiagnosed head injury that affected Patton's ability to control his behavior. The accident certainly diminished his tolerance for alcohol. Where he had been a hard social drinker nevertheless able to hold his liquor, he became alternately a mean and a sentimental drunk, with an unpleasant sideline of verbally abusing Bea when she tried to warn him off, and another of playing humiliating practical jokes on friends and family. An even clearer—and professionally far more serious—indication of his loss of control was a pattern of getting stumbling drunk in the company of junior officers. The interwar Army had a good number of colonels who had to be walked back to their quarters after a long night at the club. Most of the time the youngsters found it amusing. The bill came due on duty, when the boozy superior found himself encysted and sidetracked by subordinates who no longer trusted his judgment.

Patton's children still at home, his younger daughter Ruth Ellen and his son George IV, born on Christmas Eve 1923, began avoiding him systematically. His wife cultivated separate friends and activities—including writing a romance novel that even in another century remains readable. Patton himself noted that he had too much time on his hands—"too much alcohol and too little persperation."

Bea eventually had a deeper reason for withdrawing. Her niece Jean Gordon stopped off in Hawaii on her way to the Far East. Twenty-one, attractive, and unmarried, "she found herself a husband—but he wasn't hers." That a battered fiftysomething, already believing himself a back number, did in public every stupid thing possible for a middle-aged man besotted by a young woman is unremarkable. What remains obscure— and of corresponding interest—is why Jean made the initial running. Patton was by no stretch of the imagination the suave older gentleman of a Bette Davis movie. The family money was Bea's. Jean's mother was Bea's half-sister—a situation offering ample room for speculation about rivalries and grudges in which Patton was a mere pawn. But the family kept silent on that topic. In the end, Jean continued her travels, with Patton waving farewell from the end of the pier. Bea, as recorded by her daughter, based her behavior on the Yiddish proverb that an erection has no brains: "even the best and truest of men can be be-dazzled . . . I stuck with [your father] cause I am all that he really has, and I love him and he loves me."

Left unsaid was the fact that Patton seems to have been a first offender. He had a consistent eye for the ladies but enjoyed shocking women rather than seducing them. He might offer to display his wound at parties. But on one occasion he had begged his wife to save him from a would-be temptress seeking to take advantage of a moonlight swimming party. Now, behind the closed doors of the marriage, he bent every effort to atone for his lapse, and whatever he did, it worked.

More was involved here than middle-aged folly and adult forgiveness. The armed forces of the 1930s was still strongly conventional in matters of scandal. Womanizing was by no means uncommon in the officer corps. A future Chief of Naval Operations was allegedly admonished by his dinner partner to "remove your hand from my thigh, Admiral King! This is a tablecloth, not a bedsheet!" Ultimate power usually rested with the wife in the case. It was possible for the career of an officer of low rank and low profile to survive an unpleasant martial breakup. The Pattons were too well known outside the Army for a divorce to be kept quiet. When the third party was Bea's close relative, the result was sure to be the kind of compound scandal that would sufficiently embarrass everyone involved to encourage the alternative of Bea's playing what a later generation might call the Hillary Clinton card and assume the persona of a good-hearted woman in love with a good-timin' man.

Noblesse oblige has its own forms of payback. Patton worked to clean up his public act as well as his private one. When he left Hawaii in June 1937 for his new assignment to the Cavalry School at Fort Riley, he was surrounded by a nimbus of high ratings—including a significant comment from General Drum: "Heretofore I have noted on this officer's Efficiency Report a weakness in 'Tact.' In the last year he has overcome this weakness in a satisfactory manner" and demonstrated "those qualities so essential for a superior combat leader." The point here was not whether Patton had, in fact, reconfigured his personality. It was that Drum unmistakably acknowledged that his altercation with Patton was resolved.

Irony, if not karma, defined the next stage of Patton's progress. Before reporting to Fort Riley, he took some accumulated leave at the family estate in Massachusetts. He was riding with Beatrice and their son-in-law when a kick from Bea's horse broke his leg. Complications included a near-fatal embolism. The only treatment was immobilization, and Patton sank into a depression his daughter, at least, considered suicidal. It was Bea who held him together, and she lost patience about the time he tried to beat to death with his crutch the horse he considered the author of his misery.

Few people who have spent any time involved with a depressive have not entertained the question of just how unable the person is to control their behavior, and to what extent they are throwing a long-term adult temper tantrum and getting away with it. Certainly Patton was able to control himself in the presence of outsiders. His over-the-top high spirits kept the hospital in turmoil during his initial recovery: his room was christened the "Hula-Hula Night Club." As a convalescent, he donned a facade of good cheer that sent away friends, relatives, and fellow officers of higher rank laughing and shaking their heads. But on one occasion when Bea asked her daughters to try to cheer up their father temporarily, they drew straws. The loser baby-sat Dad.

Patton's psyche improved as it became clear that he would not have to retire on disability. In February 1938, he reported to the Cavalry School as a member of its faculty and Executive Officer of the 9th Cavalry. The black troopers of this segregated regiment had won fame on the Plains and in the Spanish-American War, earning the cognomen of "buffalo soldiers" for their courage and endurance. In a postwar Army that denied blacks possessed the qualities of fighting men, the 9th and its sister regiment the 10th had been relegated to housekeeping duties at places like Riley. The title of "school troops" deceived no one, and Patton's command assignment was understood to be nominal.

Patton's tour at Riley acted as a tonic. Recovering his physical strength and coordination rapidly, he was soon able to ride again. Feeling himself among kindred spirits, he began dealing with the black moods that had so contributed to his bizarre behavior, to the relief and delight of the family, Bea in particular. Fort Riley in those months was overflowing with middle-aged cavalrymen believing they would never have their own war, and Patton found corresponding resonance for his anxieties in that regard. He began once more to take a consequent interest in his career—by sending three models of a heavily redesigned cavalry saber to the new branch chief, Major General John Herr.

There was a long story behind the blades. When General MacArthur made mechanization a joint responsibility of the infantry and cavalry, the mounted branch responded by converting the 1st Cavalry to a mechanized regiment stationed at Fort Knox, Kentucky. In 1936 the force was increased to a two-regiment brigade. Though its missions were defined in traditional cavalry terms as reconnaissance, pursuit, and exploitation, its status was that of an unwelcome stepchild. Certainly Patton made no effort to secure an appointment to Fort Knox on his return from Hawaii.

In contrast, Colonel Adna Romanza Chaffee, who stood alongside—and arguably ahead of—Patton as the cavalry's branch intellectual, did two tours at Knox in the 1930s. Like Patton, Chaffee was extroverted and charismatic. He argued eloquently in print, in lecture halls, and not least in officers' clubs, that the cavalry's future depended on acculturating to the internal-combustion engine. Chaffee and his supporters initially proposed to use mechanized regiments as part of horse cavalry divisions, following the infantry pattern of using armored vehicles to support the branch's dominant element. What was needed in that context above all were light tanks.

That requirement was not branch-specific. Infantry and cavalry alike in the late 1930s regarded mobility and reliability more important than gunpower and protection in a tank—or a combat car, if one prefers. Between 1936 and 1938, the Spanish Civil War had highlighted the sovereign importance of durability. In the broken terrain of the Iberian Peninsula a stalled tank was an easy kill no matter what its armament and armor. A light vehicle placed less of a burden on engines and suspensions.

As much to the point, at this stage, neither the U.S. government nor the U.S. Army had any concrete sense that substantial U.S. forces would be deployed overseas in a high-tech, high-risk environment. Should expeditionary forces be necessary, shipping space would be at a premium. So would maintenance facilities on arrival. Heavy armored vehicles seemed a correspondingly dubious investment. The same criteria applied in reverse to any possible invasion of the United States. No enemy in the Western Hemisphere had any tanks to speak of. Armored forces deployed from Europe were hardly likely to reach North America in strength. The correspondingly probable missions for U.S. tankers, no matter whether they wore cavalry yellow or infantry blue, would depend for success on two abilities: "float like a butterfly; sting like a bee," and "take a licking and keep on ticking."

These criteria above all defined the M-2 light tank. The first armored vehicle put into serial production since the old Mark VIII, more than a hundred of them were acquired in the mid-1930s. At 7.5 tons, they carried only machine guns. The most familiar infantry variant sported a pair of fixed turrets that earned it the nickname "Mae West," in tribute to the buxom movie star. The cavalry's "combat car," confusingly titled the M1, carried its weapons in a single rotating turret. Mechanically, the designs were essentially the same.

The new M-1's posed tactical problems from their arrival at Fort Knox. The mechanized regiment, on paper, consisted of a troop of armored cars, two squadrons of tanks, fifty-four altogether, and a machine-gun troop that included only a single rifle platoon. The original premise of mechanizing the cavalry had been that the trooper and his rifle remained the primary combat unit, whether riding a horse or a truck. Patton's tentative concept of tanks as successor to Napoleon's cuirassiers and the "all tank" theories of Fuller and Liddell-Hart found little acceptance in a branch with the U.S. Cavalry's strong dragoon heritage. Mechanization's critics and supporters instead agreed mechanized cavalry regiments needed more riflemen to serve as holding and support elements for the armored vehicles.

Some officers recommended increasing the strength of the mechanized regiments. Others favored creating a mechanized cavalry division, incorporating the Knox Brigade, and combining tanks and infantry in light-armored scout cars. Chaffee spoke and wrote of a mobile army, built around light, fast tanks and able to maneuver in enemy flanks and rear. Branch-conscious pragmatists looked with concern to Germany, where the once-strong cavalry arm was being dismembered, absorbed by the new armored force on one hand and the increasing number of "straight-leg" infantry divisions on the other.

The principal stumbling block to change in any direction was the branch chief. Herr's commitment to preserving the horse in the U.S. Army bordered on the irrational. In January 1942, with Hitler's Panzer divisions at the gates of Moscow, he published an article in *Cavalry Journal* that attacked "motor-mad advocates . . . obsessed with a mania for excluding the horse from war" and that advocated replacing trucks with animals in half the Army's divisions. In 1953, he co-authored a book advocating the *remounting* of the 1st Cavalry Division, which he alleged "still longs for its horses"!

Patton had not lost his situational awareness. Clearly this was the right man to offer a redesigned saber despite the fact that the U.S. Cavalry had not carried them since 1934. The cavalry branch was running low on competent field officers who shared Patton's apparent belief in horsed cavalry's future. In May 1938, Herr informed the Army's adjutant general that he wanted Patton promoted so he could be assigned to command the 5th Cavalry at Fort Clark, Texas—a historic post and a horsed regiment, part of the 1st Cavalry Division.

In June, Colonel Patton, eagles fresh on his shoulders, took up his new assignment. The 5th partied hard, but Patton took pains to report to Bea that he confined himself to beer, which he drank "till my teeth floated." He took the regiment in hand, starred in the annual maneuvers by penetrating the "enemy's" rear unobserved, and hoped for war with Mexico.

Perhaps his greatest interwar disappointment came in November, when he was transferred back to Fort Myer as commander of the post and its garrison regiment, still the 3rd Cavalry.

It was an economic decision. Patton's predecessor, with no income but his pay, had gone into debt keeping pace with the social requirements of the job. Despite the recommendation for promotion to brigadier general that accompanied the transfer, a disgruntled Patton blamed Bea and her money for ruining his career by taking him away from troop duty! Bea, too well bred or by then too fed up to throw a lamp at him, retired to her room—initially, one hopes, with a long-term headache, but eventually with a debilitating kidney ailment. Part of her recovery involved cultivating a horseback-riding friendship with Eleanor Roosevelt. Patton left no record of his reaction to the relationship.

Change winds were blowing in the Army as war spread through Asia and approached in Europe. When, in 1939, President Franklin Delano Roosevelt dipped deep into the pool to select George C. Marshall as the new chief of staff, it was a surprise to Army insiders: the smart money was on Hugh Drum. Marshall took office determined to create an Army large enough and modern enough to balance the threat he saw developing from the Rome-Berlin-Tokyo Axis. Word had it that a major part of the process involved clearing out the dead wood in an officer corps with too many old men and too many back numbers.

Patton made plain in correspondence and conversation his immediate availability for a higher command. What he wanted, he declared, was to be part of testing the weapons and developing the doctrines the Army would take into a next war that suddenly seemed closer than Patton— and many of his military contemporaries—had believed possible. Patton may have restored sabers to the 3rd for parade and exhibition purposes. He also built, while building on the 3rd Cavalry's reputation as spit-and-polish show troops, to introduce realistic training programs featuring live ammunition that developed the regiment into a formidable field force. Yet whenever he looked into a mirror, he saw more past than future. The erratic behavior and the black moods returned with a vengeance— arguably even worse than during his last tour in Washington. When Ruth Ellen married, her father enlivened the newlyweds' departure by jumping onto the roof of their car, emptying two pistols into the air, and walking nonchalantly away.

V

Shifting focus from Patton to Rommel in the interwar years involves shifting perspective from the stage center occupied by *Othello*'s title character to *Henry V*, with its warriors for the working day. Patton was the star of his personal psychodrama. Rommel was glad enough to have a place in the chorus. If Patton was thrown off-balance by the armistice, Rommel was cut adrift. He was twenty-seven, married, and knew nothing except soldiering. But whether Germany would even have an army was an open question in the last days of 1918. What kind of army it would be and what kind of officers it would want or need were matters far beyond the purview of a mere captain. Rommel had a distinguished combat record—but so did dozens and hundreds of other junior officers. He had done his greatest deeds in a specialist formation that no longer existed—he could not count on the old boys networks that began to function in the officer corps almost as soon as the war ended. Would even the Blue Max Rommel wore with such pride count against him in a revolutionary environment where officers were deprived of their insignia on streets and in railway stations by bands of disgruntled soldiers?

Rommel helped supervise the demobilization and disbanding of his old regiment. He was then sent to Lake Constance as commander of an "Internal Security Company," an ad hoc organization dominated by soldiers and sailors who had nowhere else to go. As far as they were concerned, the government, whoever might be in charge of it, owed them "three squares and a sack," and they were determined neither to drill nor to fight. Rommel turned the full force of his personality on the recalcitrants. When they commented sarcastically on his medals, he answered that he wore them now to remind himself of those days in combat when he prayed to God to save the German fleet—"and my prayers were answered, because here you are."

German humor has its own unique flavor. Perhaps one had to have been there to appreciate the impact of Rommel's speech and the others that accompanied it. It represents no denigration of Rommel's charisma and command power to suggest that his men for a while may have welcomed more than they admitted a daily routine that had structure and purpose, at a time when whirl seemed to have become king in the Reich.

David Irving says that the few existing photos of Rommel in civilian clothes show "an awkward shambling misfit . . . somewhat reminiscent of a small-time hoodlum." They certainly show a man whose appearance could have been significantly improved by a reasonably competent tailor. They show a man whose carriage is a far cry from the front-line officer, cap cocked at a jaunty angle and eyes bright with confidence. They also suggest someone who, all of a sudden, has no tools to defend himself against his limitations. Without the uniform, without the army, without his position as an officer—who exactly was Erwin Rommel?

Patton from his adolescence was intensely self-aware. From VMI and West Point to the Argonne Forest, he was the conscious central figure of his own psychodrama. Rommel, by contrast, was a creature of circumstances. He had found by the random processes of war something he did superlatively, and increasingly defined himself in that context. But contexts can be changed. They can even be removed. And Germany in the Great War's aftermath was not a promising environment for a man lacking a gyroscope.

The twin shocks of defeat and revolution had an impact more surface than seismic. The Allies never attempted to change Germany's identity by direct application of superior force. The German Revolution of 1918 was thus completed on German terms. It was more a turnout than a turnover, more the removal of a discredited government than the reconstruction of a society rejected as dysfunctional. The Weimar Republic established a new political order, which its founders considered a necessary beginning for deeper social and economic reforms. The Versailles Treaty affirmed Germany's continued existence as a power, partly in an effort to establish the new republic as a bulwark against the tide of chaos that seemed to be swamping central Europe and partly from recognition that a prostrate, bankrupt country would be unable to pay the reparations French and British politicians alike promised their people as some compensation for their wartime sacrifices.

The reduction of the German army to a force of 100,000 long-service volunteers without aircraft, armored vehicles, or heavy artillery was a stunning blow to a sovereign state—and to the soldiers who contributed so much to its definition and image. Even without Versailles, however, the German army would have faced a comprehensive overhauling. Total war and industrial war generated new styles of combat and new methods of leadership. The officer no longer stood above his unit but functioned as an integral part of it. The patriarchal/hegemonial approach of the "old army," with professional officers and NCOs parenting youthful conscripts and initiating them into adult society, was giving way to a collegial/affective pattern, emphasizing cooperation and consensus in mission performance. "Mass man" was a positive danger in the trenches, argued Germany's military futurologists. What was necessary was "extrordinary man": the combination of fighter and technician who understood combat both as a skilled craft and an inner experience.

The Prussian army had historically regarded itself as a transmutator of national effort into military effectiveness. The Great War seemed to indicate that the army must become part of an even wider synthesis, incorporating and coordinating businessmen, politicians, and intellectuals in a total enterprise. At General Staff levels, the paradigm of professionalism as focused reason began expanding to incorporate ideological elements foreign to what was generally understood as the Prussian tradition. Officers like Max Bauer began developing expanded definitions of national spiritual mobilization, with the *Volk,* the community, replacing both Kaiser and state as the focus of loyalty and identity.

The emerging Weimar Republic thus confronted not the "old army" but rather an institution whose identity had been significantly modified by the Great War. Generals like Wilhelm Groener and Walther Reinhardt had little use for even the trappings of a traditional system they regarded as having failed Germany in its ultimate test. Their initial responsibility was to create an army out of the fragments of defeat and the provisions of Versailles. Officer procurement was a particular problem. The Versailles Treaty limited the number of officers to 4,000. That was just about one-sixth the number of wartime officers who had stayed with a demobilizing army in hopes of gaining a permanent commission.

They were a mixed bag. On one hand, prewar professional officers who had begun the war in batteries or companies were increasingly assigned to duties increasingly remote from the front lines, sometimes while recovering from wounds or shell shock, sometimes because their administrative skills were needed. In their own minds, these men were hardly shirkers. Their current service was honorable. Most of them worked hard at their jobs. Besides, their absence from combat was temporary. Soon, they told themselves and each other, they would request return to the front. Some may even have believed it. At the other end of the spectrum, the wartime "trench officers" posed problems as well. Not since the days of Frederick the Great had Germany possessed such a crop of battle-tested hard cases, muddy-boots soldiers with authentic combat credentials, who believed a soldier needed nothing else. Toughness, charisma, readiness to stake one's life in battle—such qualities far outweighed professional education, and often self-discipline as well.

Erwin Rommel had peacetime training and wartime staff experience. His front-line credentials were impeccable. If he had any ideas of re-ordering German society, he kept them to himself. He spent eighteen months on a variety of internal security duties that grew easier as time passed. Domestic disorder subsided to a point where riots could be handled with fire hoses instead of machine guns. The Reichswehr's senior leadership continued massaging the force's structure and reducing its numbers to conform with the Treaty standards. The forlorn and the feckless, the traumatized and the indifferent left the barracks and faded back into civilian life—like the Austrian-born private first class who had fought the war in a German uniform and now decided his future lay in the politics of his adopted country. New recruits were beginning to present themselves: youngsters who had been just too young for the trenches but were enthralled by the war stories in the popular press; older men willing to accept a twelve-year term of service in return for the security and the promises of army life. In January 1921, Rommel received his permanent Reichswehr assignment as commander of a rifle company in the 13th Regiment, 5th Division: two officers in addition to himself, one hundred sixty-one enlisted men at a full strength seldom reached, and only God knew how many years to make major. It was a long way from the physical and professional heights of Italy. It was also better than nothing.

The biggest institutional change in Rommel's early postwar career came in 1924, when he was transferred to command a machine-gun company in the same regiment. His personal life was no less ordinary. He dabbled in peacetime pastimes, trying his hand at stamp collecting and resuming, at intervals, a prewar interest in the violin. He helped organize an Old Comrades' Association of the WGB and participated actively without becoming a professional veteran. He studied engines, dismantling a motorcycle and reassembling it much as Patton stripped down old tanks, riding it around the Wuerttemberg countryside in his free time.

In 1927, he took the bike, and his wife, on a trip to his old hunting grounds in Italy for the purposes of refreshing his memory and collecting photographs to supplement the recollections. That excursion terminated unpleasantly in Longarone, when he was asked with more force than courtesy to take himself and his camera elsewhere. Longarone was a frontier zone, and Germans were unpopular in Benito Mussolini's Italy: there was much about the Great War that government and people alike were trying to forget.

Rommel also remained an enthusiastic outdoorsman. His attempts to share that passion with his wife foundered on Lu's sedentary nature—plus a stubbornness that on one occasion kept her sitting in the snow of a mountainside until her husband relented and abandoned the planned climbing expedition. Lu had a more acceptable excuse to keep close to easy chairs and warm fires after 1928, when their only child Manfred was born. The younger Rommel eventually became Lord Mayor of Stuttgart, a prominent figure in the post–World War II Christian Democratic Union and an eloquent voice for the "decent Germans" who had been caught in the meshes of Hitler's Reich. That combination colored his stories of childhood—stories that in any case were naturally shaped by incomplete memory and frequent repetition. What emerges from his recollections, and those of other family members and friends, is a paint-by-numbers presentation of a conventional German family from the cultivated professional class, with some sharper edges eroded by the wartime experience.

The Rommels' circle was neither wide nor prominent. They associated almost exclusively with soldiers, and Rommel's off-duty relationships were more likely to be *Korrekt* than warm. Lu set the domestic tone. By prewar standards, she did not quite fit the template of a "typical" officer's wife, but four years of war had expanded the army's conventions to a point where she was not an anomaly. Lu fit well into the routines of garrison-town life, though she did determine the family's guest lists and social agenda with perhaps a bit more freedom and authority than most of the regiment's ladies.

Captain Rommel was not a hands-on father, but most of the time he had time for Manfred and interest in his enthusiasms. He brought his work home to a degree, as any successful man does, but was not obsessed with his career in Patton's fashion. The house was not dominated by military symbols and trophies, nor did Rommel speak much of his wartime experiences. When Manfred did ask him what he had done in the war, the reply was a set of verbal images conveying a sense of devastation that left Manfred, at least, completely uninterested in following his father's career path. In short, the kitschy domestic conventions so often associated with bourgeois Germany, *Geborgenheit, "Trautes Heim/Glueck allein,"* and the rest, suited Rommel well. He loved his wife, enjoyed his son, and seems to have been seriously plagued neither by nightmares from his past nor by a sense of unfulfilled destiny. One might almost call him boring.

The concept of the Reichswehr as an "army of leaders" has been worn threadbare with repetition. It is worth emphasizing the relative modesty of much of the Reichswehr's practical approach to rearmament and the revision of Versailles, even by those who expected revision to require force. Its institutional vision of the force required to restore the Reich's position seldom went beyond twenty or thirty divisions, with proportionate amounts of tanks, aircraft, and heavy artillery. In such an expansion, most of the officers would still be performing duty at regimental levels.

Thinking about war at its higher levels was considered the province of the General Staff. Forbidden by Versailles, the institution had survived with only the thinnest camouflage, as the Troop Office (*Truppenamt*). The training program for admission to that body emphasized grand tactics and operational art, staff rides, and war games, rather than strategic theory and policy formation. The final year, spent in Berlin, included lectures on political, economic, and diplomatic issues. After 1927, selected officers were also assigned to an extra year at the University of Berlin, taking liberal arts courses with a military emphasis. The Reichswehr's institutional intellectual climate was nevertheless not calculated in general to encourage its officers to extend themselves.

At the same time, the Versailles Treaty was putting an essentially new set of demands on the German army. Its peacetime heritage was as cadre for a mass army of short-service draftees: citizen soldiers to be taught the rudiments, then cycled back into civilian life and replaced by a new batch of recruits. The concept of a professional army was so emotionally alien that military German did not even have a developed vocabulary for it. What the British or Americans called a "regular" was likely in German to receive the appellation "*Soeldner*," which meant something entirely different: a mercenary who served only for pay, eschewing any higher considerations. In the same context, much of the everyday process of maintaining the Reichswehr's institutional effectiveness reflected the importance of preventing its personnel from stagnating as a consequence of too many years of doing the same things in the same places with the same people.

The Reichswehr shared attitudes and value systems to a degree impossible in a conscript force drawing on the entire spectrum of Germany's population. Liberal and Marxist critics frequently charged recruiters with discriminating against urban applicants and those with left-wing sympathies in favor of rural youths with nationalist orientations. There is truth in the accusation. It seldom hurt a candidate for enlistment to have the endorsement, written or verbal, of a veterans' organization like the *Stahlhelm*, or a retired officer, or the village pastor. At the same time, the Reichswehr was deeply committed to preventing the development of partisan politics in its ranks; and a record of political activism on the right as well as the left could render a prospective recruit unsuitable.

The Reichswehr's formal and informal personnel criteria were scarcely secret, and to that extent, the pool of volunteers was self-screening and self-selected. They were disproportionately children of farmers, craftsmen, and lower-ranking officials. Their background usually included fathers, uncles, or brothers who considered their experiences in the army as positive. A fair percentage of them had at least some secondary education, and Reichswehr soldiers as a rule took full advantage of the opportunities for training in civilian occupations, and the accompanying veterans' preference connections, offered to enlisted men. The food was good: ample, well prepared, and served on china plates in clean dining halls. New barracks, comfortable and spacious, began replacing Imperial mausoleums. The Reichswehr was popular everywhere it was stationed and almost everywhere it went. It was small enough to be unobtrusive, and its men were well behaved. That made it easy for them to attend dances, patronize the better restaurants and bars, and meet respectable girls. It was a good life by comparison to many of the Weimar Republic's available alternatives.

Men committed to a minimum of twelve years' service could no longer be expected to regard their time in the army as a rite of passage, with discomfort and disorientation only enhancing the mythic aspect of the transition to adulthood. One of the best ways of preventing it was held to be the systematic involvement of officers with their men. The barriers existing in the mass conscript army of the Second Reich had been eroded by the Great War. Now officers and enlisted men, close to the same age, sharing a common ethos, were expected to form a community. Training methods sought a dialectic between understanding and obedience. In the field, everyone ate from the same kitchens and used the same latrines. Captains and lieutenants took their men on hikes, on swimming expeditions, on cultural excursions—a pattern borrowed from the prewar youth movement and from the *Vereinsleben,* the proliferating number of associations, characteristic of Weimar society. The Imperial army had paid little attention to athletics apart from gymnastics. The Reichswehr emphasized every form of sport. In contrast to the U.S. Army's tendency to replicate varsity and professional athletics by emphasizing a star system and regimental teams, Reichswehr sports were structured intramurally—though a particularly talented individual usually received a chance to develop his skills, especially if they were applicable in the Olympics and similar competitions. Officers, NCOs, and men participated together, and ability rather than rank determined playing time and status—though no sensible recruit deliberately embarrassed a sergeant who had lost a few more steps than he realized.

Rommel adapted readily to the conditions of everyday service in the new Germany. Team sports were not his forte, but he did everything else, including organize dances for the men of his company, taking the opportunity to provide as well instruction in current middle-class social courtesies and table manners. He continued to command respect for his unusual physical fitness. Qualifying as an instructor in mountain warfare, he also regularly took his own men on climbing and skiing expeditions. His superiors consistently rated him highly as a company officer, highly praising his tactical skill, his eye for ground, and his management methods. Rommel occasionally complained that his *Pour le mérite* was a handicap in peacetime service because it aroused the jealousy of his colleagues. His official records offer no indication that Rommel was medal-proud. They describe a tactful, modest man, measured in speech and behavior, who let his deeds speak for him.

That Rommel was never assigned to attend the War Academy or given an opportunity to serve in the *Truppenamt* is frequently noted by his British and American biographers. German students of his career seldom find it surprising. That he was not a nobleman made no difference, though there were in fact higher proportions of aristocrats at the army's higher levels. More likely, determinants were Rommel's wartime record and his peacetime development as a regimental officer. He showed no interest in studying the craft of war in any but limited, practical contexts. Nor did he demonstrate any particular aptitude in abstract theories. His persona was of a hands-on, uncomplicated battle captain who was happy in that role: what you got was what you saw. The Reichswehr of the 1920s had dozens of officers cut from similar cloth. Few had Rommel's combat achievements to their credit—but among the 250 or so commanders of infantry companies, Rommel stood above his colleagues rather than apart from them.

That evaluation was by no means a dismissal. By 1923, the new Reichswehr proved that it could provide for Germany's internal security. The *Freikorps* and similar paramilitary groups on the right and the left were losing their appeal. The neighborhood gangs and local self-defense associations that had stockpiled weapons in the aftermath of the army's collapse were turning them in. Social relations generally tended to demilitarize; political intercourse took a less belligerent tone.

Those developments, in turn, highlighted the Reichswehr's effort to develop into a military instrument capable of defending the German Republic against external threats. The process had begun almost as soon as the Armistice was signed, with systematic evaluation of the Great War. The initial fault line lay between those officers who took their cues from the experiences of the Western Front and those believing that the experiences in France and Belgium had been anomalous. Initially "Westerners" predominated—natural enough given the wartime distribution of forces and talent. The problem they faced was that on "Western" terms, those established in the trenches, Germany's security situation was prima facie hopeless: the Reichswehr as organized by Versailles lacked the human and material resources to put up even a token fight for its own territory.

General Hans von Seeckt, appointed chief of the High Command in March 1920, was an aristocrat and a Prussian Guardsman who fit few of the stereotypes associate with either background. In an officer corps whose reading tended to be confined to professional journals, Seeckt was well up on contemporary English literature. Educated at a civilian secondary school rather than a cadet academy, he spoke several languages and had traveled widely in Europe and visited Egypt and India before the war. More to the point, he had made his wartime reputation on the Eastern Front instead of in the trenches of the West. As a staff officer, he planned the 1915 breakthrough of the Russian front from which the Tsar's army and empire never recovered. That fall, he orchestrated the overrunning of Serbia. In 1916, he structured the German/Austro-Hungarian overrunning of Rumania in which Rommel and the WGB participated.

Untarred by the brush of disaster on the Western Front, Seeckt was the logical choice to succeed national hero Paul von Hindenburg as chief of the General Staff in the summer of 1919. He brought to his new appointment a healthy skepticism regarding the "lessons" of the war of positions fought by the German armies in France and Flanders. As early as February, he broke decisively with recent German military experience by calling for a small, elite professional army recruited voluntarily instead of by conscription. That was three months before the Treaty of Versailles required Germany to create such a force. Though the rumor mills in Paris were making it clear that something like it was a virtual certainty, Seeckt was not merely making the best of a situation. He even accepted the forbidden word *mercenary* for the force he was proposing. Its tentative structure was a minimum of 200,000 men, enlisted for two-year terms and backed by a militia based on three months' compulsory training for all eighteen-year-old males.

For Seeckt, however, form took second place to concept. For a century, he argued, Germany and Europe had striven for numerical superiority. This "universal levy in mass" had outlived its usefulness by being taken to its logical development in 1914–1918. Instead of decision, it produced attrition: a sequence of mutually exhausting struggles until one of the combatants collapsed materially, then morally. Mass, Seeckt argued, is able only to crush by sheer weight and, therefore, cannot win victories except at costs rendering them meaningless. For Seeckt, the touchstone of future war was mobility. But in an age of firepower, mobility was a function of quality. The modern army must be better than its opponents—not bigger. The Reichswehr needed force multipliers, and in the Weimar years, it concentrated on two in particular: technology and leadership.

In December 1919, Seeckt instructed the *Truppenamt* to produce a series of position papers addressing the experiences of the war, structuring them around the questions of what entirely new situations had developed, how effective were prewar doctrines in dealing with those situations, and what new problems remained unsolved. He next presented a list of fifty-seven specific aspects of the war to be analyzed—everything from leadership to correct use of the weather service. By 1920, more than four hundred officers were at work studying Germany's military experiences in the Great War. Their reports became the basis for a new operational doctrine: a doctrine based on the infantry.

That approach was not a consequence of the Treaty of Versailles. In the immediate aftermath of the Great War, infantry was the only tactically mobile arm. The cavalry's vulnerability to terrain and firepower meant its mobility was at best operational. Not until the mid-1920s would the technology of the internal combustion engine develop the qualities of speed and reliability beyond the embryonic stages that for practical purposes still restricted tanks to a supporting role. Aircraft as well were limited in their direct, sustained contributions to a ground offensive. Wire-and-strut, fabric-covered planes with fragile engines, even the specialized ground-attack versions developed by the Germans, were terribly vulnerable to even random ground fire. Artillery, despite the so-

phisticated fire-control methods of 1918, was a mass weapon of mass destruction. And because the Reichswehr possessed neither tanks nor aircraft, and only light field artillery, that left victory in the hands of the
infantry—which had been the heart and core of Germany's armies since
the days of Tilly and Frederick the Great.

The foot soldier's central position in the Reichswehr was as far as can
be imagined from the contemporary French mantra "the artillery con-
quers; the infantry occupies." Nor was that perspective confined to
France. Sir John Monash was widely regarded as the best British battle
commander on the Western Front by November 11, 1918. His Australian
Corps included five divisions of the fiercest warriors and finest soldiers
ever to dominate a battlefield. Yet Monash, in evaluating the Australian
victories in France, concluded that "the true role of the infantry was . . .
to advance with as little impediment as possible; to be relieved as far as
possible of the obligation to fight their way forward; to march . . . to the
appointed goal and there to hold and defend the territory gained . . ."
Germany was going its own military way well before it discovered the
tank, and the path had been marked out by officers like Rommel. On
October 1, 1929, he was assigned to the Infantry School as a junior
instructor.

That post was in the same category as service in the *Truppenamt*. The
Reichswehr considered every officer an infantryman somewhat in the
way the U.S. Marines consider every Marine a rifleman, and cadets spent
a year at the Infantry School before transferring to their own branch
schools. The school was originally established in Munich in 1920. Twice
relocated after some of the students joined Adolf Hitler's 1923 Putsch, it
wound up in Dresden in 1926. The developed curriculum included
courses in civics and foreign languages, as well as specifically military
subjects such as aerial warfare, motor technology, and communications,
and battalion-level tactics. Halfway through the year, a rigorous comprehensive examination separated future officers from those returned to
their regiments for discharge.

Rommel taught his own experiences. His lessons were built around
the problems of conducting small-scale independent operations in difficult terrain—lectures that formed the basis of his later book *Infantry Attacks (Infanterie greift an)*. It has been said that inside every German

officer there lurks a historian seeking to break free. Rommel insisted on a practical orientation. Unlike a number of his colleagues, and in sharp contrast to Patton, he did not use case studies as a springboard for speculation on such military generalities as the nature and future of war. He made no secret of his belief that he was there to teach cadets how to be good company commanders. Because that was what all of them needed to learn and most of them wanted to know, Captain Rommel's classes were among the most popular in the curriculum.

Rommel favored modern classroom technology, making constant use of sketch maps displayed on screens by the projectors just coming into use. Then as now, a major challenge of such visual aids involved keeping students awake in a dark room. Rommel, with his energy and his charisma, never found it a problem. As a fellow instructor later observed, Rommel remained eternally a lieutenant, eagerly making instant decisions and acting on the spur of the moment. At the same time, he established himself as a mentor who may have taught the past but did not live in it, whose presentations stressed moral as well as technical aspects of small-unit combat leadership and emphasized the importance of character to command at all levels. His efficiency reports described "a towering personality," "a genuine leader," "a first-rate infantry and combat instructor . . . Respected by his colleagues, worshipped by his cadets."

If there was a hair in Rommel's soup during his tour at Dresden, it was the presence of Ferdinand Schoenerer, who had also stayed in the peacetime army and was assigned as an instructor during the same time. The professional rivalry between the two officers on the whole remained in professional bounds. But Schoenerer, a Bavarian, had a Bavarian's sense of humor: direct rather than subtle. One of his favorite jokes involved surreptitiously placing silverware in the pockets of his colleagues on formal occasions in the officers' mess. Sooner or later it fell out, usually to the victim's embarrassment. Rommel was among his victims; he did not appreciate being the butt of schoolboy humor. On the other hand, a practical joke, especially one played on others as well, was scarcely an appropriate justification for a personal feud.

In October 1931, when his Dresden tour ended, Rommel received command of the 3rd Battalion of the 17th Infantry Regiment. In April

1932, he was promoted to major—his first permanent advance in rank in fifteen years. The assignment was something more than routine. Each division of the Reichswehr had one of its battalions designated as *Jaeger*. Wearing the green facings and preserving the traditions of Germany's elite light infantry, those stationed in high country also emphasized training in ski and mountain warfare. Rommel's new battalion was garrisoned in Goslar, in the Harz Mountains. Its ancestors had served in the army of the Electorate of Hanover, fighting in the ranks of the King's German Legion in the Peninsular War and at Waterloo. As the 10th, the *Goslarer Jaeger*, it had suffered more than three thousand casualties in the Great War, when its reserve battalion had served in the Alpine Corps alongside the WGB. It was as close to a homecoming as Rommel was likely to find.

Battalion legend has it that on the day of his arrival, the officers tested their new commander by asking him to join them climbing and skiing down a nearby mountain. After three up-and-down cycles, Rommel invited them to a fourth. They respectfully declined. If the story is not true, it deserves to be. Certainly Rommel impressed all ranks with his physical fitness, and the accompanying strength of will that time and again drove a forty-ish major forward on exercises that left young lieutenants and veteran sergeants alike longing for the sound of *"das Ganze halt"* that signaled the day's end. The woodsmen and farmboys from Lower Saxony who made up the bulk of the rank and file performed so well for their major that the 17th's regimental commander, who would himself rise to general's rank and have a distinguished career in World War II, described his third battalion as "the Rommel Battalion"—an accolade rare in a Reichswehr that, as a rule, shrank from that kind of personalization, and unusual, too, from an immediate superior conceding his subordinate's superior charisma and influence.

Rommel's colorful attacks during World War II on what he considered Germany's military "establishment," the Prussians, the noblemen, and the General Staff, has led to a certain exaggeration of his "outsider" status. He was anything but marginalized during his Reichswehr years. Nor was he encysted and dismissed as a throat-slitting hard charger, anomalous in a modern, scientific military establishment. In October 1933, the Army High Command issued Part I of *Truppenfuehrung* (unit command). This document, and its second half issued a year later, distilled fifteen years' worth of considerations on the nature of modern war. It began by defining war as "a free and creative activity founded on scientific principles." That Hegelian paradox, in turn, placed "the very highest demands on the human personality." *Truppenfuehrung* from its first page to its last stressed the centrality of leadership. Throughout the text, officers were exhorted to believe in themselves and trust subordinates molded by instruction and example. War's defining characteristics were risk and uncertainty; the best means of overcoming them were intellectual energy and strength of character.

Erwin Rommel was not the only field officer in the Reichswehr who fitted that template—but he fitted it as though it was made for him. Promoted to lieutenant colonel in 1935, he had every reason to expect to advance to regimental, and in due course, division command. Higher appointments were probably beyond his reach given his lack of advanced staff experience. But as suggested earlier, that lack was in good part a career choice as opposed to a caste-based exclusion. It made small sense to waste a staff appointment on an officer who made no secret of his dislike for desk work and was at the same time a gifted trainer and leader of troops.

VI

The infantry centering of the Reichswehr that directly shaped Rommel's postwar career was only part of the army's reconstruction. A major weakness of the German army of the Great War—arguably its fatal weakness—had been its failure to develop an exploitation capability. The High Command concluded early that mounted warfare was obsolete on the Western Front, and eventually converted most of the cavalry divisions in that theater to infantry formations. Germany did far less than the western allies to integrate the internal-combustion engine into its land-war effort except for using heavy trucks to transport personnel and supplies and haul guns well behind the lines. The notion of developing vehicles able to move men and weapons forward of the main lines of advance, in poor terrain and against opposition, never got beyond the remote planning stages.

Exploitation remained the task of infantry, specifically the special assault battalions, the storm troopers, who proved so effective cracking open enemy positions in the first stages of German offensives during the war's final year. But eventually casualties and fatigue wore down the assault forces. Eventually, as enemy reserves arrived, the survivors ran out of weak spots to probe and penetrate. And the following waves crested behind them, exhausting their own momentum as the Allies prepared to counterattack.

As early as spring 1919, a series of articles in *Militaer-Wochenblatt,* the army's leading professional journal, dealing with the army's projected reconstruction included two on cavalry. General Maximilian von Poseck, Inspector-General of the arm, argued that in the east, large mounted units had been effective for both reconnaissance and combat, and mobile war was likely to be more typical of future conflict than the high-tech stalemate of the Western Front. Seeckt strongly agreed. Charges on the grand scale might be a thing of the past, but cavalry still had a crucial role to play as the central element of mobile divisions, including armored cars and motorized infantry and artillery. These light divisions, in Seeckt's vision of the future, would retain traditional cavalry functions of scouting and screening. A new mission, no less important, would involve completing the work of the infantry, taking up pursuit of a defeated enemy, conducting both tactical and operational-level envelopments of exposed or emerging flanks.

Seeckt's concept of the cavalry's role antedated the structures imposed by the Versailles Treaty, which required Germany to maintain the highest proportion of mounted troops of any army in Europe: eighteen regiments, more than half as much again as the authorized strength of the artillery, a force structure hearkening back to the days of Frederick the Great. The army was correspondingly impelled to take its horse soldiers seriously, to consider how they could participate directly and effectively in preserving Germany's frontiers and guaranteeing its sovereignty.

The postwar cavalry's regimental officers initially included a high percentage of men without experience in the new ways of war—men who had spent their active service in staffs or on dismounted service, and now were anxious to get back to "real cavalry soldiering." In the early 1920s, Seeckt consistently and scathingly criticized the mounted army's tactical sluggishness, its poor horsemastership, its inaccurate shooting both dis-mounted and on horseback. Too much training was devoted to riding in formation—a skill worse than useless in the field, where dispersion was required—and in training with the lance and saber. Not until 1927 was the lance abolished, over the opposition of all eighteen of the regimental commanders.

The Reichswehr high command entertained an entirely different ap-proach. The "modern cavalry division" proposed in *Leadership and Battle* as early as 1923 was an all-arms force, including cyclist and machine-gun battalions, and an infantry battalion capable of being carried in trucks, an armored car battalion of twelve vehicles, and an air squadron of twelve observation planes. The artillery incorporated a horsed and a motorized battalion and an anti-aircraft battalion. With signal, supply, and medical troops, horsed and motorized, this division on paper com-bined mobility, firepower, and sustainability to a greater extent than any of its predecessors or counterparts in Europe. On the defense, it could hold ground against a superior enemy by virtue of its flexibility, with its three cavalry brigades controlling combinations of forces in the pattern of the combat commands of a World War II U.S. armored division. Of-fensively, the division could operate independently behind a fixed enemy front, disturbing movements with "shoot and scoot" operations while creating and exploiting opportunities for more comprehensive penetra-tions. Given a bit of luck, the modern cavalry division with its own re-sources had the potential even to break through thinly defended sectors of a front.

This was the kind of cavalry division the Reichswehr deployed in its annual maneuvers, testing the structure as far as possible by making tem-porary attachments although most of the elements had to be stipulated, or represented by flags and other symbols. Standard accounts of German violations of the Treaty of Versailles focus on small-scale cooperation with Russia in testing tanks and aircraft, or on purely theoretical specu-lations on the nature of possible future mechanized operations. Arguably the pattern of directly subverting the treaty began with the combinations of mobile forces the Germans presented openly and regularly for attaches and observers to evaluate.

The institutional result was the development of a modernizing urge from below. A new generation of cavalry officers increasingly accepted motorization and mechanization as essential for their branch in a Reichswehr that had no surplus to spare for nostalgia. While as a group they still saw the horse as important, they did not remain committed to the extent of their U.S. counterparts. They acquired increasing influence as the wartime veterans retired. They profited from the absence of institutional rivals. There was no air force to lure free spirits and forward thinkers. Unlike France and Britain, even the United States, Germany had no tank corps to claim technical expertise, to challenge the cavalry's position, and to encourage the branch loyalties that absorbed so much of the latter armies' energy on the mechanization question. To a degree as well, Germany's cavalrymen were likely to find motor vehicles attractive because their branch was deprived of them.

Ironically, the Versailles Treaty itself created what became a major institutional loophole for motorization and mechanization. The Treaty allocated to every Reichswehr infantry division a motor transport battalion. This was intended as a logistics formation, but its men and vehicles were likely to be significantly underemployed for most of the year once the peacetime garrison system was in place. The first inspector-general of the branch correspondingly requested an officer with General Staff training to work with him in considering the motor troops' future development. He was assigned a man who had attended the War Academy just before the outbreak of war in 1914 and spent most of the next four years alternating field service in signals with troop staff appointments.

Captain Heinz Guderian knew just enough about motor vehicles to be able to start an engine. But he was intelligent, hard-driving, and ambitious. Some branch officers may have agreed with the general who allegedly told Guderian that army trucks were there to haul flour. But a century earlier, advocates of railroads had depicted a Germany made invulnerable by troops shuttled behind steam engines. Now a new potential form of strategic/operational mobility was attracting notice. The Reich's steadily improving road system had even the state railway service investing in busses to supplement its locomotives. Even conservative officers saw the prospects—and career advantages—of eventually establishing a transport force that could shift regiments, perhaps divisions, quickly to threatened sectors and regions.

The hundred-odd men of a motor company had access to two dozen heavy trucks and eleven smaller ones; six passenger cars; four busses; seventeen motorcycles, including five with sidecars; and two tractors. Treaty interpretation even allowed a complement of five wheeled armored personnel carriers like those used by the civil police. With that kind of vehicle pool on call, small wonder that as early as 1924, units conducted on their own responsibility small-scale experiments with organizing motorcycle formations, and provided dummy tanks for maneuvers. The motor transport battalions rapidly became foci of practical support for operational motorization

Initial Reichswehr theory on the use of tanks closely followed contemporary French concepts in projecting a first wave of heavy tanks, followed by a second wave of lighter vehicles maintaining close contact with the infantry. Evaluations of the best way of using tanks were, however, shaped strongly by their technical limitations. In particular, they were considered too slow and too unreliable to play a central role in the fast-paced offensive operations central to Reichswehr tactics. In contrast to the French, who saw tanks as the backbone of an attack, Seeckt in particular warned against the infantry laming its offensive spirit by becoming too dependant on armor.

At the same time, German thinkers, Seeckt included, recognized that even with their current limitations, tanks were general-service systems, able to engage any objective and move in many different formations. In that they were like the infantry and essentially different from other arms. Their future correspondingly seemed to lie with emphasizing their essential characteristics—speed, reliability, and range—rather than developing them as supporting weapons built around armor and armament.

Heinz Guderian eventually did such a good job exaggerating his role in the development of Reichswehr thinking on armor that those who correct his overstatements run a certain risk of going too far in the opposite direction. Guderian's fondness for the first person singular should not obscure his early investigations of armored vehicles' possibilities at a time when even his progressive colleagues were thinking of mobility in terms of trucks and motorcycles. Guderian was also, at this stage of his career at any rate, willing to learn. Lieutenant Ernst Volckheim, a wartime tank officer who found himself in the motor transport *faute de mieux,* specialized in studying the use of tanks in foreign armies, introduced Guderian to French and British literature, and made him aware of the practical tests going on in those countries and elsewhere in Europe.

Guderian responded by writing articles for the military press—not on armored forces as such, but on the potential of increasing the army's mobility as a whole, through motorization. He attracted enough notice to be appointed in 1924 as an instructor in the staff training school at Stettin—a three-year tour that, in the same way as Dresden did for Rommel, enabled him to bring together his ideas, general and specific, on the possibilities of motorized warmaking. In 1928, he was assigned to the Transport Department of the General Staff to study the question of large-scale troop transport by motor vehicle. He continued as well to discuss and lecture on tank tactics. In 1929, he finally even got to test-drive one of the vehicles for the first time during a trip to Sweden.

At the same time the Reichswehr continued field testing. In the winter of 1923–1924, maneuvers incorporated cooperation between motorized ground troops and simulated air forces. In 1925, the 1st Division in East Prussia included armored cars, motorized artillery, and dummy tanks in its maneuver orders of battle. Such exercises highlighted the Reichswehr's limited achievements in motorization. They also offered opportunities to consider problems as they arose—and foreign observers noted the Germans seemed well able to correct mistakes involving motor vehicles.

Design work on tanks in Germany began in 1925, when specifications for a "large tractor" of twenty tons and a "small tractor" of half that weight were established. In 1928–1929, the firms of Krupp, Rhenmetall, and Daimler-Benz built two "large tractors" each as test beds. In 1926, work commenced as well on a new generation of radios, small and reliable enough to be mounted in vehicles. These would provide the basis for the communications system panzer generals like Rommel were to use to such devastating advantage in the early years of World War II.

The Germans paid increasing attention to foreign models. Guderian, Werner von Blomberg, Walther von Reichenau, and their colleagues read and translated the works of Liddell-Hart and Fuller. They followed assiduously the British maneuvers of 1927 and 1928, with their emphasis on armor-heavy combined-arms mobile forces. The *Truppenamt* was beginning to argue that tanks employed in brigade strength, 300 to 350 vehicles, would be the offensive weapon deciding future battles. It was beginning as well to develop theoretical training schedules for tank regiments.

Motorization and mechanization alike received a major institutional boost when, in 1926, Colonel Alfred von Vollard-Bockelburg took over as Inspector General of Motor Troops. He expanded and transformed the branch officers' course from a focus on technical details of maintenance to a program incorporating, then emphasizing tactical studies. It would eventually become the Armored Forces School. In 1929, a motorized "Reconnaissance and Security" Battalion, drawn primarily from the 6th Battalion, took the field for maneuvers. In 1930, the 3rd Battalion was completely reorganized as a fighting formation, including mock-up tanks, improvised armored cars, and antitank guns as well as the more orthodox mix of trucks, cars, and motorcycles. The battalion also received a new commander: Major Heinz Guderian.

Decisive as well was the appointment in 1931, when Bockelburg's term expired, of Colonel Oswald Lutz as his successor. Lutz had begun his career as a military railroader, served as director of motor transport for the 6th Army in the Great War, and spent much of his early postwar career in the *Truppenamt* as a technical specialist with a focus on mechanization. Transferred back to the Motor Transport Troops in 1928, he fostered enthusiastically the branch's development as a combat force. As Inspector, he appointed Guderian his chief of staff and conducted a series of exercises centering around the dummy tanks, which were widely disliked at unit level because they were so obviously "toys." Based on the results, Lutz nevertheless argued eloquently that technological developments currently feasible would exponentially enhance tanks' value as a mobile arm.

The Reichswehr's focus on motorization reached its first plateau in the maneuvers of September 1932. Held in the area of Frankfurt an der Oder, they were designed to stress mobility at all levels. The defending force, designated Blue, had two cavalry divisions and only a single infantry division. The Red invaders included an entire cavalry corps, with motorized artillery, cyclists and motorcyclists, and motorized reconnaissance elements. Although the combat vehicles were almost all simulated, radios were liberally supplied. Results were mixed, particularly when horses and motor vehicles attempted to cooperate. But the speed and scope of the exercises impressed all observers. Some motorized units advanced 300 kilometers in three days—a pace unmatched since the Mongol invasions of the Middle Ages. These last maneuvers before the National Socialist rise to power set the Wehrmacht's operational course beyond alteration. Its moral and political development in the emerging Third Reich would prove quite another matter.

The preceding pages may seem surreal. A German army expressly forbidden the use of aircraft and armored vehicles nevertheless systematically investigates, analyzes, and begins to implement in exercises the techniques of modern mechanized war. No mention is made of the Treaty of Versailles. Instead, the text repeatedly refers to foreign observers taking notes at Reichswehr maneuvers. Just what was going on?

Weimar Germany was a sovereign state. Its soldiers could not reasonably be prevented from speculating on the nature of the wars they might have to fight. When the issue came up, German spokesmen made a convincing case that the very circumstances of German disarmament required the Reichswehr to be highly cognizant of possible threats it could not match directly. In practical terms, moreover, the Germans kept well to the Treaty's terms. The few dozen imitations and improvisations that took the field for a few days each autumn were hardly fear-inspiring and were quickly dismantled. The collaboration with the Soviet Union, the tank school at Kazan, and the air school at Lipetsk were likewise known to the Allied agencies responsible for enforcing the armistice terms. Their combined contributions to Germany's military system was correctly judged as marginal.

From the perspectives of France and Britain, and from the perspective of the League of Nations as well, standing on details was considered counterproductive when compared with the prospects of drawing Weimar Germany into a general program of European disarmament. In 1927, the Foreign Office successfully negotiated the withdrawal of the Inter Allied Control Commission, which since 1919 had supervised the nuts and bolts of disarmament. The diplomats saw this as a step toward national security in an international context. The Reichswehr considered it an opportunity to pursue and expand its programs of preparing for a bigger future. By April 1931, a plan was in place for assembling material for a twenty-one-division army. By 1933, about two-thirds of the basic weapons for that force were in hand. The immediate problem involved personnel, and it was on this subject that the army began finding common ground with Adolf Hitler and the National Socialists.

The Nazi Party has been compared by scholars to almost every possible human organization, even medieval feudalism. The one adjective that cannot be applied is "patriarchal." Hitler's public persona was that of leader, elder brother, perhaps even erotic symbol, but never a father. Change, progress, was the movement's flywheel. Nazi nostalgia found its essential expression in domestic kitsch. It had no place in military matters. The Reichswehr and the "Movement," *Die Bewegung* as the Nazis preferred to be known, thus had the common ground of emphasizing a commitment to the future rather than a vision of the past. Hitler's initially enthusiastic wooing of the soldiers was based on his intention of using them first to consolidate his hold over both the Nazi Party and the German people, then as the standard-bearers of territorial and ideological expansion until they could safely be replaced by the party's own Waffen-SS. The Reichswehr, for its part, also saw the Nazis as a means to an end, albeit the more pedestrian one of increasing the armed forces' resources.

National Socialist views of war were different in important, arguably essential respects from those of the Reichswehr. But on such subjects as anti-Marxism, antipacifism, and hostility to the Treaty of Versailles, the military's values were not incongruent with those avowed by Nazi theorists and propagandists. Those positions were also respectable across a broad spectrum of Weimar politics. Germany wanted normalcy in the years after 1918 but was unable to achieve it at the price of abandoning the illusions and delusions of the Great War. The gradual turn to Nazism that began in the late 1920s represented a "flight forward," an effort to escape that cognitive dissonance, as much as a belief in the Nazis' promises to make things better.

The concept of a nonpolitical Reichswehr has been so frequently critiqued that there is a certain risk of overcompensation. The army was not a Fascist coup or a right-wing conspiracy waiting to happen. From its inception, the Reichswehr had regarded itself not as an independent player, but a participant in a common national enterprise based on rearmament and revision. Refusal to identify the armed forces directly with the Republic facilitated the transfer of loyalties from the Empire. It enabled avoiding on one hand the problems of a Soviet model of military professionals reduced to technicians while commissars wielded real power, and on the other the risks of saddling Germany with an officer corps of mercenary technocrats out of touch with state and society.

Yet as the gulf between soldiers and politicians widened, as the Republic's crisis deepened during the Great Depression, few officers saw their responsibilities to the state in any but the narrowest terms. The war game of December 1932, with its predictions of domestic disaster should Nazis and Communists combine against an overextended, outnumbered, and probably outgunned Reichswehr, were presented with a kind of malicious pleasure that reflected more than simple anti-republican sentiment. It suggested instead a fundamental detachment from the processes of governance that had been alien to a Prussian army with its comprehensive ties to state and society.

The Reichswehr's everyday emphasis on focused professionalism offered limited guidance, particularly below the levels of high command. Erwin Rommel, for example, encouraged his wife to vote for "centrist" parties: the German Democrats and their successors—at least according to their son's account. Other versions have Rommel taking "socialist" positions, at least when it came to an aristocratic class he often criticized as dangerously narrow in its perspectives. His first systematic exposure to National Socialism seems to have occurred during his tour at Dresden. The school drew students and faculty from the entire Reichswehr. Its atmosphere was more free-wheeling and permissive than the average unit mess; and newspapers everywhere on the political and cultural spectrum were running stories on the court-martial of three lieutenants alleged to identify more closely with National Socialism than regulations permitted. It would have been unusual for a respected faculty member such as Rommel not to be solicited, informally and unofficially, for his position. It would have been even more unusual for Rommel to take the professional risk of strongly affirming or denouncing any political development.

Rommel's reaction to the Nazi assumption of power in 1933 was similarly conventional. In the most basic terms, as a serving officer, there was no reason for him to do anything at all. The "pseudolegality" of what academicians like to call the "seizure of power" (*Machtergreifung*) was as lost on Rommel as it was on most Germans. The National Socialists represented a significant plurality of the voters. Combined with their allies the German Nationalists, they had a majority in Parliament. Hitler had been appointed Chancellor by legal processes and affirmed by Germany's president, the respected national hero Paul von Hindenburg. The public euphoria that spread across Germany in the next six months or so may have been largely orchestrated by the Nazis themselves. It nevertheless encouraged the keeping of doubts and questions to oneself. The train to the future was leaving the station: board it or miss the opportunity Germans had been saying they longed for ever since November 1918.

Rommel, it must also be noted, was not what the Germans call an "intellectual deep-sea diver." He was no complex, self-searching character out of Henry James, able to see the fourth side of every three-sided question. Indeed, it might be said that one could walk through Erwin Rommel's deepest thoughts on any subject outside of soldiering and emerge with dry ankles. He saw the public impression Hitler made and the public enthusiasm with which he was received. He approved the Nazi program of militarizing German youth and their promise to remilitarize the Reich despite the Treaty of Versailles. Rommel supported the breaking of the Stormtroopers, the SA, in June 1934 both for their radical image as a possible focal point for a "second revolution" and because of the organization's apparent challenge to the army's monopoly on armed force in Germany. Though he privately criticized the massacre of SA leaders and their families as excessive and unnecessary, it seemed the kind of one-off occurrence that could be processed as an unfortunate lapse of judgment on an otherwise promising administration.

None of that, however, added up to a belief that National Socialism offered a quick ticket to accelerated promotion through political means. Selling out, moreover, or even changing patrons, is a two-way street. Rommel, who was nothing more than one promising field-grade officer among many, initially did not have much to bring to the table. His first direct encounter with Hitler was while commanding an honor guard when the Fuehrer visited Goslar in 1934: an entirely official occasion.

More significant was his transfer in October 1935 back to the Infantry School, now located at Potsdam. In March, Hitler had ordered the reintroduction of conscription to support a projected army of thirty-six infantry divisions plus specialized formations. The new Wehrmacht, in contrast to an Imperial predecessor that in peacetime had places for only about half those eligible, now drafted virtually every fit man. As a consequence, it was a people's force in ways foreign to Moltke or Frederick II. Its officers, especially the lieutenants, were drawn from a broad spectrum of the educated male population. The 4,000 regulars of 1933 grew to 24,000 in 1939, and the number of reserve commissions increased proportionally.

Rommel had lost none of his classroom skills. On this tour, he memorized the logarithmic table and was correspondingly able to do math tricks impressive even to students with engineering specialties. Rommel was a master of triangulation in another way as well. He took no pains to conceal his intellectual and professional distance from the "theorists" of the General Staff who predominated in the school's faculty and administration. He was impatient of any reference to doctrine or authority at the expense of a student's own mental processes. At the same time, he completed the process of turning his lectures and experiences into a book, making him one of the relatively few instructors who did any major publication in their military fields.

Infanterie greift an (*Infantry Attacks*), published in 1937, stands with Heinz Guderian's *Achtung-Panzer* as the best-known military work published in interwar Germany. It stands alone in terms of its quality. While Rommel was writing for a professional readership, the book possessed two prerequisites for general-audience success that endure today in military writing. It told an exciting story, and it had a personal dimension. Nor did it hurt that Rommel was honest. He had his critics, and he had his enemies. No one ever succeeded in demonstrating mendacity in the combat narratives that are the work's substance. Appearing at a time when Great War narratives were undergoing a resurgence in popularity, Rommel won critical praise for avoiding the heroic-pathetic tone, the "high diction" present in so many of the newer works. His matter-of-fact approach combined with an unusual clarity of style to produce a work that even at seven decades' distance leaves the taste of cordite on its read-ers' tongues. It also made so much money that Rommel wound up seeking to balance his taxes by having his publisher defer most of the royalty payments—which on balance were in any case more windfall than wealth. Although he may have occasionally expressed dislike of making money by describing how other men died, Rommel was too much the Swabian to donate his profits to the WGB's regimental fund, and none of his old comrades went on record as grudging him his new and modest affluence. He had paid his dues in advance.

The broader question was whether Rommel's painstaking analysis of the dynamics of small-unit infantry tactics would have anything beyond specialist interest in the new Wehrmacht. Even before Hitler's rearma-ment, the army was institutionalizing the concept that future campaigns would be decided at neither tactical nor strategic levels, but in that inter-mediate zone called "operations" or "operational art." Mobility, surprise, and concentration, originally developed as keys to tactical survival, now became the basis of operational power projection. In the late 1920s, sev-eral private automobile manufacturers developed models of half-tracked vehicles for towing artillery. In 1933, the Reichswehr ordered the design of a light tank that by the end of 1934 was entering service in some numbers.

The Mark I was never regarded as anything but a stopgap. Its small size, weak armor, and an armament of only two rifle-caliber machine guns put it well below the standards of other nations' flagship tanks. But the Mark I was able to do twenty-five miles an hour on level ground. It had a long range. Its relatively spacious turret facilitated command by providing room for two crewmen. And it could mount a radio. The Mark I set the technical parameters of the armored vehicles with which Ger-many would fight World War II.

In 1933, some German cavalry officers affirmed the concept of linking motorized and horsed units in orders of battle. Some infantrymen still re-garded that tank's principal task as facilitating the advance of the infantry. They were outflanked on the political front. The advocates of motorization and mechanization wasted no time after March 1933 in showing their wares to the new chancellor. Hitler was impressed. Though unwilling to plunge forward immediately with a full-blown mechanization program, he recognized its potential and supported, by not interfering with, the decision to organize three Panzer divisions as part of the rearmament program.

These formations were from the beginning conceived in combined-arms terms. Built around a tank brigade with no fewer than 560 Mark I's organized in four battalions, the division also included three infantry battalions, two truck-borne and one on motorcycles, a motorized artillery regiment, a reconnaissance battalion, and a full complement of supporting troops. Their component units came from every branch of the army; their personnel was largely composed of new draftees. It said much for the Reichswehr's heritage that the divisions were ready for the 1936 maneuvers, and more that they showed so well in the field.

In 1937, four infantry divisions were motorized as well. The cavalry, hemorrhaging its best and most energetic officers to the new armored force, began in 1938 reorganizing into "light" divisions with four battalions of infantry and one of tanks, intended to perform traditional cavalry missions of screening and exploitation. Even the "ordinary" infantry benefited—at least in the active divisions. While the majority of its guns and vehicles remained horse drawn, and the new reconnaissance battalions had only a few armored cars, each regiment was allocated a motorized company of antitank guns, and each division a full battalion—a total of seventy-two pieces. The artillery became a player indirectly, responding to a growing awareness of the gap between its fire-power and the weight of metal the arm could throw in 1918, and to concern that the German infantry of World War I had at seventh and last become excessively dependant on mass artillery support. When General Erich von Manstein of the General Staff's Operations Section in 1935 suggested instead developing a direct-fire, close-support vehicle, an infantry gun mounted on an armored chassis, the artillery responded positively. The eventual result was the turretless assault gun, which made its operational appearance in the spring of 1940.

What began as rearmament rapidly developed into peacetime mobilization. By 1936, the army was projecting a war footing of 102 "divisional units"; a force profile comparing favorably to France's mobilized strength. That projection heralded the takeoff of a growth that rapidly became its own justification and increasingly outran available resources.

The German army that took the field in 1939 was the product of comprehensive improvisation.

Since the 18th century, the Prussian/German army had stressed the desirability of a high average. One regiment, corps, or division had been considered as capable as any other of performing a specific mission. That concept had been shaken to a degree during the Great War. Ludwig Beck, Chief of Staff from 1935 to 1938, sought to combat it by saturating the army with tanks and armored vehicles. The Reich's industrial capacity and industrial policies made that impossible—particularly in a political environment where Hitler's clock was perpetually set at five minutes to midnight. Instead, the army was constrained to develop a full-blown hierarchy of reliability, with the mobile divisions created from peacetime formations at the apex. Most of the new divisions were formed by "waves," each wave with differing scales of equipment and levels of training. All of them were infantry. Few had even the full theoretical complement of motorized antitank guns, while the new assault guns took the field only in 1940, and then only in token numbers.

That put increasing emphasis on personnel. In the context of an emphasis on motorization and mechanization, the quality of the ordinary infantryman must be as high as at any time in the German army's history. That was the aspect of National Socialism that most appealed to military professionals from the general staff to the rifle companies. As the Wehrmacht expanded and rearmed, its conscripts were motivated, alert, and physically fit to degrees inconceivable in all but the best formations of the Kaiser's day. Thanks to the eighteen months of compulsory labor service required of all seventeen-year-olds since 1935, they required a minimum of socializing into barracks life and were more than casually acquainted with the elements of close-order drill.

The soldiers were confident that once Germany's young men changed their brown shirts for army *Feldgrau*, their socialization away from any superficial influences of National Socialism would be relatively easy. The relevant virtues the Nazis preached—comradeship, self-sacrifice, courage, community—had been borrowed from the army's ethos. The army knew well how to cultivate them from its own resources. The new Wehrmacht had new facilities. Barracks with showers and athletic fields, plenty of windows and ample space between bunks, were a seven days' wonder to fathers and uncles who had worn a uniform under the Empire. Food was still well cooked and ample. As in the Reichswehr, officers were expected to bond with their men, leading by example on a daily basis. One anecdote may stand for many experiences. A squad of recruits was at rifle practice. The platoon leader asked who was the best shot among them and offered a challenge: "Beat my score, and you can have an early furlough." At the end of three rounds, the private won by a single point—by grace of a lieutenant who knew how to lose without making it obvious. When the wheels came off in a combat situation, such officers seldom had to order "Follow me!"

The backdrop of this situation was an increasing tug of war between the army and the party for influence over German youth—a tension neither side wished to boil to the surface. The mid-1930s were the golden age, at least in public, of Hitler's "two pillars" rhetoric: the argument that the Wehrmacht and National Socialism were the "two pillars" of a reborn Germany. Rommel's *Infantry Attacks* was a popular Christmas, confirmation, and graduation gift for teenage Nazis and a popular guidebook for Hitler Youth field exercises. Rommel had an unusually high reputation for working with young officers, and his freshly burnished image as a front-line warrior set him apart from the "General Staff Prussians" against whom the Fuehrer so often railed in private. He was a logical choice when the War Ministry sought a liaison officer to Baldur von Schirach, head of the Hitler Youth, and assumed the post in February 1937.

Von Schirach argued that Rommel—and by extension the army—sought to introduce too much direct paramilitary training of the hut-two-three-four variety into the Hitler Youth program. Rommel's proposal to require unmarried lieutenants to devote part of their weekends to Hitler Youth activity set even less well with Schirach and his subordinates, who disliked the notion of that kind of competition. Rommel, for his part, was a schoolmaster's son and a German paterfamilias whose relationship to his own son had included some spectacular clashes over the appropriate exercise of parental authority. To his military associates, he increasingly criticized the Hitler Youth for incorporating too much "military education" of the wrong kind: the sort of ruffles and flourishes that involved adolescents playing soldier: saluting each other and conducting inspections. The Hitler Youth's leaders, he said, knew nothing of soldiering and less of war.

Professional differences were exacerbated by personal dislike. Schirach, a decade younger than Rommel, with an American mother, had been a Nazi youth organizer since the mid-1920s and had a legitimately high opinion of his qualifications and talents in the field. He did not take kindly to what he considered Rommel's categorizing of him as a promising junior officer who needed have his bark removed. Rommel took little time to decide that Schirach was the kind of arrogant ignoramus who gave the Third Reich a bad name. The two clashed over everything from Rommel's war stories to seating precedence at a theater function.

The failure of Schirach and Rommel to find common ground in youth training arguably had longer-term significance for the Wehrmacht's Nazification. Rommel's final judgment that the army was better advised to train its recruits as soldiers once they were sworn in gave the party a free hand over adolescents it was quick to exercise in later years. But whatever his low opinion of von Schirach, Rommel had been impressed by his direct exposure to the New Order at its highest levels. There was no question either that he was Hitler's kind of army officer: a blunt-spoken man of action, uncontaminated by aristocratic social origins and unreflective on matters outside his professional sphere.

Those qualities made him particularly useful to the army in the autumn of 1938. Senior army officers, including Chief of Staff Beck, had grown sufficiently dubious about the risks of Hitler's free-wheeling foreign policy in the context of Germany's still uncompleted rearmament that they had developed plans for a "housecleaning." These involved eliminating Nazi Party radicals, restoring traditional "Prussian" standards in justice and administration, and putting Hitler firmly under the thumb of the military leadership. Should that last prove impossible and the Fuehrer suffer a fatal accident—well, no plan survives application, and the state funeral would be spectacular.

In March 1938, Hitler bullied the right-wing government of Austria into accepting *Anschluss*, or union, with the Third Reich—a more fundamental violation of the Versailles settlement than rearmament had been. He convinced the rest of Europe to accept it through the application of diplomatic smoke and mirrors. Diplomacy, however, is always a credit operation. States unable to settle the bill in the hard cash of war face bankruptcy. And the military aspects of the German takeover were farcical. In particular the Panzer division ordered to march on Vienna left behind it a trail of broken-down vehicles that reduced its commander, Heinz Guderian, to an unusual condition of silence.

It was poor preparation for the propaganda and diplomatic offensive against Czechoslovakia that Hitler mounted almost immediately. Czechoslovakia had a large army supported by one of Europe's leading arms industries. It had a formidable system of frontier fortifications. It had an even more formidable diplomatic network of allies and supporters. The possibility of disrupting Czechoslovakia without initiating a general war Germany had small chance of winning seemed so limited that Beck resigned in August. His successor, Franz Halder, inherited the outlines of a generals' plot to seize Hitler's person as soon as he issued orders for an invasion of Czechoslovakia.

Whether anything would have come of it remains a subject of speculation. The agreements secured from Britain and France at the Munich conference of September 1938 left Czechoslovakia twisting in the wind, and hung any potential military conspirators out to dry. Czechoslovakia's western provinces, the Sudetenland, were ceded to the Reich without a shot fired. Those who had urged caution on the Fuehrer were correspondingly discredited, despite Hitler's private rage as being cheated of the war he wanted by the "poor little worms" in Paris and London. Then Hitler decided to celebrate by touring the newly annexed region. Responsibility for his security fell to the army. And the War Ministry had just the officer to take charge of security.

Rommel was no stranger to the Fuehrer. He had been attached to Hitler's escort during the 1936 Party rally in Nuremberg and won favorable notice for preventing a traffic jam of followers on a day when Hitler wanted to take a drive relatively unaccompanied by only a half dozen cars. Hitler, who at this stage made much of his own experiences as a front-line infantryman, had read—or at least paged through—Rommel's book. The conflict with Schirach, far from being an obstacle, was the kind of thing Hitler liked to see at all levels of the Reich: personal antagonisms that left him free to act as he saw fit. Rommel's assignment, in short, was politic at all levels, a gesture of goodwill and reconciliation at a time when the army's stock with its government was arguably lower than at any time since the aftermath of Jena.

All went well—well enough that in November 1938, Rommel was assigned as commandant of the new officer cadet school at Wiener Neustadt in Vienna. The appointment—accompanied by promotion to colonel—was by no means a political reward, but the position was recognized as highly political. Austria had its own army, now in the process of being assimilated into its larger compatriot; and its own long military heritage—much of it a sharp contrast to Prussian practice and experience. While cadets from all over the Reich would be assigned to the school, the institution would inevitably have a strong Austrian savor. The commandant bore a heavy responsibility for setting the new institution's tone.

Here again Rommel was the right man in the right spot. He was a walking counterpoint to the stereotypical rigid, humorless Prussian officer. He had extensive Great War service with the Austro-Hungarian army and left a positive image behind. And he was sufficiently wired into the regime's power structure and value system that he could be expected to make Wiener Neustadt an integral part of both Reich and Wehrmacht. Rommel had taken to signing personal correspondence with *Heil Hitler*—not a usual step for a senior officer at that stage of the Reich's history, but not necessarily a statement of principle, either. Like most of his military colleagues, Rommel he had serious reservations about the developing military pretensions of Heinrich Himmler's SS. Expansion and rearmament, however, offered not merely promotion, but challenging and responsible work in his chosen field. He had been impressed by the enthusiastic reception accorded the Fuehrer by the German population of the Sudetenland: the flowers, the tears, the unforced cheering. Rommel seems as well to have decided that most of the members of Hitler's personal entourage were not all that bad on closer acquaintance. On balance, his behavior offers a case study in what party ideologues called "working toward the Fuehrer": doing things in ways Hitler would approve.

Certainly that would have included his plans for making Wiener Neustadt a model institution, combining intellectual and physical elements of education, practical and theoretical aspects of war. He was to have, however, no real opportunity to institutionalize his theories. In March 1939, he was again temporarily transferred to command Hitler's field headquarters. This time Hitler was spearheading the occupation of what remained of the Czech lands after Munich and the subsequent breakaway of Slovakia. Rommel met him at the frontier. A snowstorm had delayed the SS troops who were supposed to be Hitler's personal bodyguard. A senior army general, Erich Hoepner, suggested that the army was perfectly capable of guaranteeing the Fuehrer's safety. Himmler disliked the idea. Then, according to his own account, Rommel took charge, telling Hitler he had no real choice but to enter the waiting car and drive through Prague to the Hradcany Castle, symbol of sovereignty and government. "To a certain extent," he boasted later to a friend, "I made him come with me. He put himself in my hands . . ." The story no doubt improved with the telling: colonels are seldom inclined to give unsolicited and unsupported recommendations to a head of state. But Rommel's words did influence Hitler—who was no coward—to follow the bolder course of action, and when it proved successful, to mark the officer in his memory.

With Czechoslovakia gone, Hitler's attention turned to Poland—guaranteed now by a treaty with France and Britain, but no less tempting a next step. Rommel did not follow closely the complex negotiations that produced the Nazi-Soviet Non-Aggression Pact and cleared the way for the outbreak of the Second World War. He expected a war whatever the diplomatic circumstances, and like a high proportion of the officer corps, found the prospect welcome. Poland was seen as a country that through the Versailles Treaty had profited from a victory it had not earned, severing East Prussia from the Reich by the infamous "Polish Corridor," using its protected status to detach as well the city of Danzig and seek to make it a Polish dependency. Poland had been the Reichswehr's favorite "designated enemy" during the Weimar years. Now was the time to settle accounts.

4

RUNUPS

ROMMEL expected a short war, and expected to spend it somewhere in the rear echelons. Instead, on August 22, he was summoned to Berlin and informed that he was to command Hitler's field headquarters in Poland. Never unconcerned with career advancement, Rommel had already become far more of a "player" than he might have thought possible in 1930. Now he was serving a personalized regime under the very eyes of the Presence. All he needed to do was avoid stumbling. And Erwin Rommel would prove true to the sure-footed heritage of a mountain soldier.

I

A head of state with Hitlers's aspirations to become "The Greatest Warlord of All Time" could scarcely have his security overseen by a mere field-grade officer. Rommel was promoted to brigadier-general, with date of rank from June 1, 1939. His new command was, however, a throwback to his lieutenant's days. Eventually the Fuehrer's escort would become an entire division. In 1939, it amounted to a rifle company and another company on motorcycles, plus a few light antitank and antiaircraft guns. Its job was to secure Hitler and his entourage from small-scale air attacks, snipers, stragglers, and partisans. Headquarters was a train: a dozen coaches fitted as sleeping, living, and conference rooms. Quarters were close, and Rommel was frequently in Hitler's company, including meals—the latter a traditional courtesy extended to the captains of households since medieval times, but no less gratifying to Rommel for that.

II

Rommel's respect for Hitler grew as he saw the Fuehrer's willingness to go forward into newly conquered territory, flying over broken ground, driving through sniper country, visiting headquarters and formations exposed to Polish artillery fire. Hitler, in turn, reverted to his Great War days as a rifleman and runner, reminiscing and swapping stories with an officer he felt understood from his own experience what it was like "out there." He began inviting Rommel to staff meetings, soliciting his opinion on operational decisions.

This chance to look over the supreme commander's shoulder was as eye-opening to Rommel as a formal General Staff short course might have been. The technological and doctrinal backwardness of the Polish army has been grossly exaggerated. Polish cavalry never charged German tanks with lances. They did surprise several small motorized columns and achieved some local defensive successes against the Panzer divisions—which were duly noted by the Chief of Cavalry's office in Washington. The Polish government, however, had been constrained by a mixture of political and strategic considerations to deploy the bulk of its forces in a cordon along its lengthy frontier with the Third Reich. After the Germans broke through the initial positions, little stood in their way except an air force rapidly reduced to ineffectiveness by a numerically and materially superior Luftwaffe. German tactics, training, and technology decided the campaign's outcome well before the Soviet Union sent its armies across Poland's eastern frontier on September 17.

From Rommel's perspective, the Polish operation illustrated the continuing validity of his belief in shock, speed, and surprise. For twenty years he had been telling cadets, junior officers, and any superiors willing to listen that boldness, readiness to risk, brought gains out of all proportion to the original investment of forces. Rommel was an infantryman, but the principles he derived from his infantry experience were not restricted to men moving on their feet through broken country. Geographically, the plains and marshes of Poland could not be farther apart from the high mountains and narrow valleys of Northern Italy. The tactical and operational imperative was nevertheless the same: get inside the enemy's loop of initiative, and unravel his forces from the center outward. As he grew more confident in their personal association, Rommel lost no opportunity to make those points to Hitler, who, in turn, responded positively to an officer he seems increasingly to have regarded even at this early stage as a model for the fusion of Germany's old and new orders. Rommel excitedly informed his wife that he did not expect to return to Wiener Neustadt as a schoolmaster in uniform after the campaign was over.

Beginning with the Franco-Prussian War of 1870–1871, the German army had developed a doctrine of controlling occupied territory by immediate harsh repression of all forms of resistance. In 1914, this policy had generated widespread atrocities against civilians in France and Belgium. The resulting damage done to the German image, especially among neutrals like the United States, would lead to a commitment on the part of both the armed forces and the political leadership to avoid a repetition in 1940.

Poland was another matter. Well before the outbreak of hostilities, generalized concepts of the "east" as an object of German manifest destiny, long present in the nation's culture, were integrated with National Socialist conceptions of the east as "living space." Soldiers were informed that they were the vanguard of Germany's destiny, with the missions of conquering the new territory, settling it as "soldier-farmers" (*Wehrbauern*) and ruling over the primitives who inhabited it.

To an average draftee, the first task might seem dangerous and the second far-fetched. The third proved congenial from the early days of September 1939. Negative, derogatory attitudes toward Polish and Jewish cultures informed the army's official reports, its private correspondence, and its public behavior. Troops used Nazi jargon to describe the people: "subhuman" or "inhuman." From the war's first days, the army showed consistent willingness to initiate reprisals; to implement terror; to translate vague authorizations into fists, boots, and firing squads. It stood beside the SS rather than apart from it as an instrument of repression.

Rommel did not go out of his way to encourage harsh occupation policies. That those policies would be harsh he considered a matter of course, noting during the campaign, for example, that all able-bodied Polish men were being rounded up for forced labor. Rommel was kind to his family, a genial social companion, and not inclined to indiscriminate rank-pulling and decoration-flashing. None of those characteristics made him any less a hard man, who had matured in circumstances and institutions that were anything but nurseries for finer feelings and nuanced moral speculation.

Rommel's attitude may have been influenced by his absence from the combat zone. By the end of the campaign, he was consistently in Hitler's company, not only eating lunch and dinner with him, but frequently seated next to him. Given the importance of mealtimes in Hitler's Byzantine court protocols, a newcomer could scarcely enjoy greater favor. Envy mounted among more permanent members of the entourage. But Rommel had not gone to war to be a headquarters paladin or a carpet-knight. When the headquarters went into suspended animation after the final victory parade in Warsaw, he knew what he wanted: a division command.

Rommel was one step short of the usual rank for the job: major general. His peacetime record and his wartime connections suggested, however, that was a shortcoming to be soon remedied. The High Command agreed, and the personnel office knew just the thing. The army had three specialized mountain divisions, one Bavarian and two based on units from the old Austrian army. Given Rommel's experience, one of them seemed a perfect fit.

Rommel balked politely. He wanted a Panzer division. The personnel office in effect responded, "So does everyone else." Rommel was an infantry officer—more than that, he was widely considered the model of a modern infantry general. He had never served with tanks, or with any other mobile branch barring a few weeks with the artillery in 1914. Rommel, in contrast, saw himself embodying a long-standing Prussian/German tradition in his firm belief that understanding *principles* was preferable to understanding *particulars*. His experience suggested specific expertise could be developed more or less at need, the way he had studied logarithms. The time Rommel spent in Hitler's headquarters seems to have played a significant role in moving his perspective from the tactical/operational level of his Great War and Reichswehr service to the operational/strategic plane. The maps on Hitler's table were of a different scale than those to which Rommel was accustomed—a larger scale, one that encompassed not sectors of a front, not even theaters of war, but entire countries.

A Panzer command, moreover, offered the best opportunity to implement the synergy between technology and vitalism Rommel's experience with the WGB had convinced him was the key to waging modern war at any level. Weapons by themselves were cold iron. Courage by itself was wasted sacrifice. The challenge lay in bringing the two together: recognizing and creating situations where warrior qualities were multiplied by speed and firepower to produce irresistible shock.

Did Rommel ask Hitler for the plum command he wanted? Did Hitler intervene directly, whether to oblige a favorite, because he recognized Rommel's potential, or simply to spite the army's establishment? Things seldom are that obvious in such matters, particularly in the Third Reich at that stage of its history. Rommel had no interest in being stereotyped as the Fuehrer's *Protektionskind,* his protégé. A senior general such as Walther von Reichenau could embrace Nazi principles and manifest Nazi sympathies and be understood as acting from conviction. A mere brigadier was likely to be stamped an opportunist, with all the professional drawbacks that implied. Hitler, for his part, still sought to win over or co-opt the officer corps so far as either might be possible, Rommel was potentially a means to that end, and too valuable a tool to risk breaking by such clumsiness as overt interference in mid-level command appointments.

The most promising explanation involves a delicate web of hints dropped and responses comprehended, leading to the personnel office deciding that Erwin Rommel was after all the man to take over a Panzer division—especially the one they had in mind. On February 15, 1940, Rommel received command of the 7th Panzer Division. It had started life as one of four light divisions based on converted cavalry units. Renumbered and converted in October 1939, it still possessed a strong cavalry ethos. Its officers and senior NCOs had not taken all too kindly to their new mechanized role. Rommel had a reputation as a man who could galvanize subordinates. The assignment thus saved face at higher levels and put Rommel squarely on the spot and in the spotlight—which was where he wished to be in the first place.

The division included a tank regiment of three battalions, two two-battalion motorized regiments, a motorcycle battalion, and a reconnaissance battalion of motorcycles and armored cars. This structure eventually became the standard for the army's Panzer divisions until nearly the end of the war and shaped the armored divisions of other armies as well. As yet no armored personnel carriers were available. The tank regiment, however, was in the process of replacing its Mark I's. The Mark II was another stopgap design pending the production of heavier models. At ten tons, with a single turret-mounted twenty-millimeter cannon, it relied on speed and endurance. More useful was the Panzer 38(t). This was a Czech model taken over by the Wehrmacht after the occupation in 1939 and kept in production. Also weighing in at about ten tons, it was as reliable and robust as its German stablemate and carried a more powerful 37-millimeter gun in its turret, giving it a significant antitank capacity. By May 10, 1940, the 7th Panzer Division had 68 Mark II's and 91 38(t)s in its inventory. Only 34 Mark I's remained, most of them as command vehicles. The division also had two dozen Mark IV close-support tanks, whose short-barreled 75-millimeter cannon were primarily intended to provide high-explosive supporting fire to the lighter vehicles.

The 7th's new commander retained his emphasis on physical fitness as a prerequisite for modern mobile warfare, and set an example with early morning runs—never a staple of the cavalry, which like its counterparts in all armies, rather prided itself on an insouciant approach to sweat. He spent his days absorbing details. A dismissal or two for effect nailed down the point that he would not tolerate inefficiency or excuses, and Rommel had lost nothing of his ability to galvanize through personal contact. Within a few weeks, he was taking his division on cross-country exercises in the teeth of a hard winter, relocating from the comfortable resort environment of Bad Kissingen, the 7th's official headquarters, to the Rhoen Mountains.

To a degree unusual, arguably unprecedented, in a victorious force, the German army in the aftermath of the Polish campaign undertook a major reassessment of its practices, judging even the spectacular results gained to be insufficient and inadequate. Above all, the "lessons learned" disseminated to all formations insisted on an aggressive spirit. Caution and circumspection were discounted as leading to the overlooking of opportunities while giving the enemy time to recognize and frustrate German intentions. Commanders of mobile troops in particular were exhorted to lead from the front. Orders and practice emphasized combined-arms cooperation in an all-arms battle coordinated by radio communication at all levels.

Throughout World War I, the officer in the front ranks had no way of keeping in touch with anyone outside reach of his voice and line of sight. In the 1930s, what seemed a magic-bullet solution to the problem emerged: the radio revolution. The bulky, fragile radio sets of World War I were being replaced by smaller, more reliable versions, crystal-tuned and operating in the high-frequency range. Instead of requiring Morse code, the new designs enabled direct voice communication, facilitating the transmission of real-time information and concise orders. Beginning with the production versions of the Mark I, every German tank carried its own radio.

Events in Poland demonstrated the practical limits of radio communication under operational conditions and highlighted another problem. "Leading from the front" invited the dispersion of effort as commanders seeking to exploit presumed opportunities wound up directing isolated actions that eventually devolved to skirmishes with limited tactical results. How could the commander of a mobile formation built around the internal-combustion engine be at the critical point of a battle while at the same time continuing to command his whole force effectively?

That challenge led to Heinz Guderian's familiar phrase *klotzen, nicht kleckern* ("slug, don't fumble"): keep focused on an objective. Rommel addressed it on three levels. One was technological. It involved developing a mobile headquarters whose core was an electronic command system mounted in a cross-country vehicle: a network of radios allowing him to contact both subordinate formations and his own main headquarters, operated and maintained by selected signal officers and NCOs. A second was professional. Rommel made clear to his senior staff officers that he depended essentially on them to process and evaluate information that arrived at headquarters in his absence, and to act on it should that seem necessary. By later American standards, Wehrmacht divisions had small headquarters whose officers were relatively low ranking. The Versailles Treaty had been successful in limiting the number of General Staff officers and restricting the scope of their training; the Wehrmacht after 1933 was never able to keep pace with its own expanding need for troop staff officers. The Operations Officer of the 7th Panzer, Major Otto Heidekaemper, performed most of a chief of staff's duties. On paper, the rough counterpart of a U.S. G-3, Heidekaempfer was responsible for far more: coordinating the division's external relations, maintaining its internal balance, and acting as principal adviser on combat operations. His chief assistants were the intelligence officer and the quartermaster, a major and a captain respectively.

The "lean and mean" German structure meant everyone worked constantly. Vital information could be overlooked by busy men. Fatigue and stress led to errors of judgment and to problems of communication, as tired men snapped at each other. Especially in a mobile division, success depended heavily on a commanding general willing to support the decisions of even junior staff officers in whose ability, toughness, and loyalty he had confidence.

Success depended as well on a system that functioned as close to automatically as possible. The third leg of Rommel's command triangle was training. Rommel shared Helmuth von Moltke the Elder's conviction that no plan survived first contact with an enemy. It was correspondingly necessary for commanders at all levels to exercise independent judgment. Independent did not mean random. Rommel proposed to act as a kind of *deus ex machina* using his sense of the battle and the information provided by his headquarters to select points of intervention, ideally to refine and complete the efforts of the men on the spot. He bent every effort to develop a common way of doing things in the 7th Panzer—not as a straitjacket, but rather a framework for structuring the behavior of subordinates in the constant emergency that was the modern mobile battlefield.

The genesis of the German strategic plan against the Western allies is familiar. The High Command was reluctant to mount a western offensive under any circumstances. Its foot-dragging produced an initial concept for "Case Yellow" that involved sending seventy-five divisions, including most of the army's mobile formations, into the low countries to engage the main Anglo-French strength in what was expected to be an encounter battle in central Belgium. Even before Hitler became directly involved in the planning process, this unpromisingly conventional proposal was generating increasing criticism as owing more to Ludendorff's abortive 1918 offensive than the Schlieffen Plan to which it has often been compared. The High Command's thinking seemed to go no further than punching a hole and seeing what developed. It anticipated the kind of hard fighting that made decisions dependent on contingencies. And it incorporated no proposals for destroying enemy armed forces.

The alternative proposal put forward by Erich von Manstein, then chief of staff to Army Group A, was intended as much to provide a central role for his commanding general Gerd von Rundstedt as to furnish a program for victory. His projected thrust through the Ardennes would transform Rundstedt's army group from a secondary mission to the campaign's focal point. Broken terrain made the option a risk—but a calculated risk, taking maximum advantage of the force multipliers of the Reichswehr become Wehrmacht: leadership and technology. Hitler, disgruntled by his generals' conventionality and angered by a security breach that put copies of the original plan in Allied hands, took advantage of Manstein's temporary presence in Berlin to discuss his ideas. A few days later, he issued a new operational plan, putting seven of Germany's ten Panzer divisions under Army Group A for a "scythe cut" (*Sichelschnitt*) through northern France.

Rommel's 7th Panzer was teamed with the 5th in the XV Panzer Corps. Commanded by Lieutenant General Hermann Hoth, it was on the right flank of Rundstedt's main attack, with the mission of crossing the Meuse River at Dinant and pushing forward into the Ardennes. The Belgian Ardennes was a nightmare of hills and valleys, unimproved regional roads, and local tracks leading nowhere in particular. The Belgians, however, chose to defend only a few of their obstacles, making the advance that began on May 10 more of an engineering and traffic control problem than a tactical one. The French and British air forces, unexpectedly slow to react to the German onslaught, devoted most of their efforts to the central Belgian plain and the German bridgeheads over the Meuse around Sedan. Rommel's division was left undisturbed from the air as it rolled forward against uncoordinated, though occasionally fierce, opposition.

Rommel spent most of his time with his advance guard. Occasionally, he took advantage of the division's aviation element: light Fieseler Storch aircraft, counterparts of the American Piper Cub and capable of landing and taking off from even rougher terrain. The still-unfamiliar spectacle of a plane landing in a combat zone and the "old man" climbing out was a predictable morale-booster, and the stories of Rommel's omnipresence lost nothing in the telling.

Beginning on May 11, the 7th Panzer encountered the French: elements of the 1st and 4th Cavalry Divisions, which combined mounted and motorized units plus a few tanks. They were tailored for screening missions against mobile forces. Rommel responded along lines tested in Italy. He sent his reconnaissance and motorcycle battalions forward in small elements and multiple directions to discover and report enemy presence. He deluged the 7th Panzer's routes of advance with fire from every weapon from howitzers to machine guns as soon as a shot was heard or a movement observed. Saturation was more important than accuracy, he insisted. Even against dug-in antitank guns, armored formations that opened fire immediately were likely to have the advantage.

Make them keep their heads down; go through them and past them; mop up what remains: this was blitzkrieg *pur*. In three days, Rommel advanced almost sixty miles. Hoth, following the German pattern of reinforcing success, temporarily put the 5th's advance units under Rommel's command and told him to get across the Meuse and keep going. The bridges at Houx and Dinant went up almost in the face of 7th Panzer's leading elements. But motorcyclists, from the 5th Panzer Division's advance guard and not, as usually stated, Rommel's 7th Motorcycle Battalion, crossed an abandoned weir to an island in the middle of the river, and from there a lock gate to the west bank. They took some fire, but the main French positions were on high ground away from the river. The Germans had a foothold, and the commanders of the 7th Panzer's rifle brigade and its pioneer battalion were no less quick off the mark. Rubber boats rowed by the pioneers began moving infantry across the Meuse— about a company's worth by the time the defenders came fully alert a little before daybreak.

In a short time, French machine-gun fire cut off the possibility of either evacuating or reinforcing the men on the far bank. French artillery began disrupting movement on the German side of the river. As casualties mounted and morale declined, Rommel arrived on the scene sometime after 4 A.M. and took little time deciding it made no sense to continue dribbling his forces into battle. He returned briefly to division headquarters, where he met and reassured Hoth and Hoth's superior, 4th Army commander Gunther von Kluge, then drove back to the river. Ordering the available tanks and artillery pieces to shell the French side as long as their ammunition lasted, he started a fresh wave of reinforcements across the Meuse—and took a place in one of the leading rubber boats.

For the next couple hours, the verifiable record reads like something from a comic book. Rommel almost immediately found himself caught up in a French tank attack. The men on the far bank had no antitank weapons. Rommel ordered them to open up on the tanks with rifles and machine guns. Bullets glancing off their armor, sparks and fragments ricocheting through firing ports, the tanks, unsupported by infantry, fell back. Rommel returned across the river and drove to a new crossing site established by the division's 6th Rifle Regiment. There infantry and antitank guns were being boated across without direct opposition. The pioneers were working on a pontoon bridge. Rommel ordered a heavier one, able to bear the weight of tanks. Then he got into the waist-deep water and lent a hand, heaving timbers under fire and taking his command vehicle across to the west bank only "as soon as the first pontoon was ready."

By that time, French counterattacks were coming in greater force; French artillery was finding the range on all the crossing points. German casualties were mounting. Ammunition in the forward positions was running low. Rommel had spent the whole day under fire. He seemed to have been at every vital spot exactly when he was needed; and to the officers and men of the 7th Panzer, who had seen just enough combat in Poland to be impressed, he seemed as well to be bulletproof. Now he took charge of ferrying tanks across the Meuse to the original bridgehead—a slow and frustrating process. At daybreak, he received word that elements of the 7th Rifle Regiment had infiltrated French positions, reached the village of Onhaye, and were now surrounded by a French counterattack.

Rommel promptly mounted a rescue mission, built around the thirty tanks that by then had crossed the Meuse. On his way, he discovered that the 7th was not *surrounded* in Onhaye, but had *arrived* there—Rommel's radio operator had mistranscribed the message: *eingeschlossen* for *eingetroffen*. Well enough: instead of rescuing the infantry, the tanks would use them as a base for further operations. Just outside Onhaye, the Germans came under artillery and antitank fire. The tank Rommel had commandeered took two hits and skidded down a hill. Rommel, bleeding from a splinter in the cheek, bailed out, sought his command vehicle, and found it immobilized from a hit in the engine. He later noted his belief that if the German tanks had been more willing to fire on the move, the French gunners would probably have decamped altogether. In fact, the French continued to mount counterattacks against Onhaye as 7th Panzer developed its bridgehead. By evening, however, the 25th Panzer Regiment and the riflemen had secured the crossing and Rommel issued orders for the next day: keep moving and shoot up anything in the way.

At this stage of the war, the Panzer division's tanks and infantry did not practice the near-symbiotic close association that later characterized their tactics. The 25th led out, followed by the infantry and supported by the division's artillery and any dive-bombers Rommel might be able to scare up over the radio. That last was not automatic. The Luftwaffe, contrary to many accounts, was not organized and configured for ground support. Its primary missions were air superiority and interdiction, or battlefield isolation. Its main elements were heavily engaged to the south, in the Sedan sector, where the Panzers were converting another river crossing to a breakout on an even larger scale. Rommel considered himself correspondingly fortunate when a Luftwaffe major informed him that yes, he could count on Stukas being available at intervals.

Once again Rommel rode with the leading elements—a tribute to his excellent working relationship with the Panzer regiment's commander. Colonel Karl von Rothenburg, like Rommel, held a Blue Max from the Great War, had seen enough combat to be perfectly willing to share its risks, and believed four eyes were better than two on a fast-moving battlefield. Rommel's tactical innovation for the day was a "thrust line" established on the division's maps and divided into sectors. To call in air support or artillery fire, all Rommel needed to do was refer to one of the sectors. The recipient's job was to note the target area, bring it in, and keep it coming. By the elaborate standards of the Great War, the system was crude: a back-of-the envelope improvisation. The division's artillery commander was nevertheless "delighted" to be able to provide the kind of instant support artillery had been able to deliver in its salad days a hundred years earlier, when guns galloped into battle behind six-horse teams.

The French front-line forces, from the 9th Army of General André Corap, were in the process of falling back for reorganization. The French high command had, however, ordered a counterattack toward Dinant by two of its best divisions, the 1st Armored and the 4th North African. The armored division included two battalions of B-1s, each mounting two guns heavier than any in Rommel's vehicles: a 47-millimeter antitank gun in the turret and a 75-millimeter cannon in the hull. The North Africans included a large number of long-service professional soldiers, some of the best fighting men in France.

The situation offered corresponding possibilities for the 7th Panzer to become enmeshed in 9th Army's stop line and then face a stand-up fight against heavier metal and superior numbers. Instead, Rommel bounced the designated French position before it was occupied, the tanks taking every possible target under fire on the move; the artillery firing in support along Rommel's thrust line; and headquarters kept in the picture by radio messages sent in German but composed in a stark, almost cryptic "battle language," meaningless even if it should be intercepted. With his Panzers on their initial objective, Rommel drove back to bring up the infantry, which in its unarmored, wheeled trucks, had lagged behind. He found dozens, then hundreds of French soldiers streaming out of the woods on either side of the main road, surrendering even to the crews of broken-down tanks. As he had done in Italy, Rommel sought out the senior officers, promising them quick delivery of their baggage and any other small perquisite that might encourage further surrenders.

The still-advancing 25th Panzer Regiment had in the meantime encountered the leading elements of the 1st Armored Division. The French had had a long, hard day on the 14th. Advancing through swarms of their own people, constrained to move at slow speeds and in low gear, their fuel tanks were nearly empty and their crews tired. For convenience, their commanders bivouacked in the open to await the gasoline trucks. No one bothered to dispatch even a few motorcyclists to screen the roads to the east. The French were displayed on a serving dish for the 66th Panzer Battalion, an original element of the 2nd Light Division, now assigned to the 25th Panzer as its third battalion and bringing up the regiment's rear. Its commander deployed in what Rommel called a "sea battle formation," two companies charging forward and firing "broadsides" into the French while the third covered the battalion's flanks.

The 66th had about two dozen Mark II's and the same number of 38(t)s. Even at ranges of two hundred yards and less, their light shells ricocheted off the French armor. But the gunners shifted their fire to the thinner sides of the French tanks, to ventilators, tracks, and suspension systems. The Mark IV's of the 3rd Company used their high-explosive shells on crews caught in the open and against the fuel trucks that began arriving just as the German attack started. Coordinated resistance foundered as French tank commanders found their radio batteries had been run flat. Crew after crew ceased fire, waving rags and handkerchiefs from their turrets to indicate surrender. Thirty-five tanks, including nineteen heavy Char B's, went under in a matter of minutes.

Rommel left the rest of the 1st Armored to the 5th Panzer Division's just-arriving 31st Regiment, and led his own 25th barreling westward at forty kilometers an hour. Surprised French motorcyclists going in the opposite direction drove off the road into the ditches. By the end of the day, the 25th's tanks were at Cerfontaine, on the edge of the northern extension of the Maginot line that had been constructed in the late 1930s. Tank officers were taking masses of prisoners at pistol point: officers and men of rear-echelon units without a clue responding to any orders they received, even if the language was German and the content was "Drop your weapons! Hands up!"

As the long lines of trucks and halftracks carrying riflemen and towing guns came up to flesh out the position, Rommel was ready to repeat his performance beginning the next morning. He had no intention of treating the vaunted Maginot Line like a set of improvised field defenses. He took enough preparation time that Kluge paid him an unscheduled visit around 9:30 A.M. to express his surprise at the delay. Rommel explained the 25th Panzer Regiment was to advance on the main French position in extended order, supported by every gun in the division. The rifle brigade would pass through and crack open the defenses under covering fire from the tanks. Then the 25th would resume the lead, and the division would go forward.

It was a plan showing Rommel as more than a head-down tactical opportunist. As the tanks moved into the fortified zone, they once again took under fire everything that seemed a likely target as pioneers attacked bunkers with flamethrowers and grenades and infantrymen took out machine-gun nests and antitank positions. Here was no slashing blitz, but a steady grind forward against stubborn resistance that seemed to intensify as the day waned. The moon was up, the long European twilight had set in by the time the last roadblocks were cleared, and Rommel saw his chance. There was still enough light for the Panzers to drive forward and break out. A risk, yes—but preferable to a night's delay and an enemy further reinforced. "Turn your people loose," he ordered Rothenburg. "Blast anything resembling a French position—and don't spare the tracer." That last was another case of making lemons from lemonade. The 20-millimeter cannon of the Mark II was not much in a stand-up fight with heavier French tanks, but its tracer rounds could be terrifying to inexperienced men.

The tanks rolled forward in a long column, impelled by the hammering of their own guns, picking up speed as the confidence of the lead drivers increased. French soldiers and refugees abandoned the road for its ditches. No time for prisoners—just fire a few bursts as warning and deterrent. An occasional brief position report to his increasingly confused, increasingly anxious division headquarters was Rommel's only contact with the rear. Still no resistance—and then it was clear that 25th Panzer was through the Maginot Line. "It was not just a beautiful dream," Rommel later recorded. "It was reality."

By now the operational situation had dissolved into chaos. Rommel's lead elements were through the town of Avesnes, but the balance of his division was strung out behind him, its men and vehicles intermingled with refugees and soldiers, some anxious to surrender and others looking for a chance to fight. Sixteen tanks, the remnants of 1st Armored Division, stumbled into Avesnes, blocked the main road, and held out most of the night, the three survivors withdrawing around 4 A.M. Tank after German tank exhausted its ammunition, turning to its hull-mounted machine gun instead. Radio communication was at best episodic—partly, it seems, by Rommel's design. Certainly, the corps order authorizing an advance on Avesnes only for the next morning did not reach him until long after it had become irrelevant.

Rommel drove forward in the style he developed with the WGB. He had most of a Panzer battalion and part of the Motorcycle Battalion in hand. He was confident his division would clear the way and follow him to Landrieces, where a bridge over the Sambre River pointed the way deep into the rear of the Allied forces in Belgium. At 4 A.M., the Germans moved out. Rommel broadcast a simple order over every frequency his radios could cover: get to Landriecies as fast as possible, any way possible. With ammunition dangerously low, the advance now depended on speed rather than shock. Again the Germans bypassed long columns of refugees and re-treating soldiers. In contrast to the previous day, however, the French sim-ply dropped their rifles and about-faced, marching east into captivity. One lieutenant colonel seemed too hostile to leave behind. When ordered to get into a tank, he refused three times. Rommel ordered him shot.

The sun was well up as the lead tanks rolled into Landrieces and across a bridge still intact. The town was full of trucks and wagons, ani-mals from horses to house pets, terrified civilians, confused soldiers, and officers so demoralized that some of them obeyed German orders to fall in with their men and march them east. Rommel kept the advance going. It was a quarter past six when he finally halted—by coincidence in the vil-lage of Le Cateau, site of a memorable rear-guard fight by the British Ex-peditionary Force in 1914. Leaving Rothenberg to set up a perimeter defense with his tankers and a few motorcyclists, Rommel drove back through Landreices toward Avesnes in his command vehicle, accompa-nied by a single tank, which soon broke down. He raced past hundreds of French troops who seemed deliberately to ignore him, eventually taking charge of a stray column of trucks, some full of troops and others mount-ing machine guns, and leading them into Avesnes to support the Germans still fighting in the town. It was the stuff of melodrama—but substanti-ated at every turn by eyewitnesses.

By around 4 P.M., Rommel's headquarters and the rest of the division began arriving. One of the artillery battalions captured in the process most of a French tank battalion, an indication of how rapidly and completely French morale and command had eroded. Rommel pushed his combat elements across the Sambre toward Le Cateau, then took an hour and a half rest. His division had advanced more than fifty miles, made a night march unprecedented in the history of armor, captured ten thousand prisoners and a hundred tanks—and recorded losses of thirty-five dead and fifty-nine wounded.

III

By the standards of the campaigns of Frederick the Great, the Wars of German Unification, and the trenches of 1914–1918, the achievement was almost beyond comprehension—but not beyond exploitation. At midnight, orders came through from Hoth: continue the attack, direction Cambrai. One observer credits Rommel with assembling his senior officers and informing them the division's axis of advance was "Le Cateau-Arras-Amiens-Rouen-Le Havre." If the story sounds a little pat, it is true enough as metaphor. On May 18, the 25th Panzer Regiment, fuel and ammunition replenished and most breakdowns repaired, shot its way into Cambrai across country where during the Great War advances had been calculated in hundreds of yards and casualties counted in tens of thousands.

By that time, even Rommel saw the need to pause for reorganization. His division was deep in hostile country, strung out along a hundred miles of a road network crowded with refugees, stragglers, and organized bodies of French soldiers. To seek phone contact with friendly forces was to risk hearing "Bonjour monsieur" at the other end of the line. Rommel nevertheless planned to resume his advance late the next day. When the corps commander paid him a visit and ordered a second day's rest, Rommel replied that his division would have been twenty hours in the same place—time enough for the Allies to draw a bead on it. By this time, the 7th Panzer was attracting war correspondents, and Rommel was the best kind of copy. This, he declared, was war as Frederick the Great's cavalry generals had waged it. Seydlitz and Ziethen had led from the front and exploited fleeting opportunities to win tactical victories. Modern generals must do the same thing at the operational level, with tanks replacing horses. A night advance, he argued to Hoth, only appeared risky. It would cost less and gain more than conventional daylight operations.

Hoth's caution was more than conditioned reflex. Rommel's was not the only Panzer division running miles ahead of the rest of the army. The three divisions of Guderian's corps, breaking out of the Sedan bridgehead to the south, were even deeper into France than was the 7th, though their advance in miles had not been as far. Seen on a map, the Panzer spearheads looked like fingers thrust out from a hand—and correspondingly vulnerable to being seized and broken one by one. Rundstedt as early as the 15th considered halting the motorized forces rather than risk even a local defeat that might throw the German advance off-balance. He had his staff prepare a stop order just in case. Then the army group commander received a call from the Wehrmacht High Command, Hitler's mouthpiece: shut down the Panzers.

Hitler may not have given that order personally, but during a visit to Rundstedt's headquarters on May 17, he emphatically supported it. A successful counterattack, he declared, might encourage both the Allied generals and their politicians. Not a helter-skelter push to the English Channel, but a solid defensive shoulder in the south should be the next step.

The Fuehrer, for the first time since assuming power, encountered overt, coherent, and cohesive resistance among the soldiers. Early on May 17, General Ewald von Kleist, Guderian's immediate superior, delivered the halt order in person. Guderian's reply, more expressive than polite, concluded with a request to be relieved. Kleist wisely left before someone said something that could not be overlooked. The halt order stood—until Chief of Staff Franz Halder executed a neat political flanking maneuver, first convincing the army's Commander in Chief Walther von Brauchitsch to order the offensive renewed, then confronting Hitler to insist the Panzers' southern flank was not a problem. Hitler, according to Halder's diary, raged and screamed in one of the virtuoso emotional performances that had earned him the nickname of "carpet-biter." In the end, however, he, too, acquiesced.

Hermann Hoth was no gambler, but he recognized hot dice when he saw them. At 1:40 A.M. on May 20, the 7th Panzer's lead elements broke out of Cambrai heading north to Arras—the next bead on Rommel's projected string. His primary opposition was the French 1st Army, hammered hard in Belgium, now withdrawn to face a greater threat. But Arras was also the original headquarters and a major administrative area of the British Expeditionary Force. The region was saturated with detachments theoretically completing their infantry training while they worked on constructing defenses. Green troops with few heavy weapons, they were led by Great War veterans who frequently had fought on the same ground and did not propose to yield it tamely now. North of the city were also two good divisions, the BEF's reserve, as yet uncommitted.

Hoth's orders to his division commanders were to avoid direct engagement, instead swing around Arras and move toward Bethune, threatening the French and British where they had proved most vulnerable: on their flanks. Seventh Panzer on the corps left spearheaded the advance; Rommel rode as usual with the leading company of the 25th Panzer Regiment. At 3 A.M., the armored spearhead reached the *Canal du Nord,* only to have the bridge blown up almost under its treads. Two hours later, the tanks found and seized another bridge a few kilometers south. Driving across the canal, they advanced almost twenty miles in less than two hours. But less than two miles from Arras, Rommel ordered a halt. The infantry had failed to follow. With daylight upon them, the tanks would have no chance penetrating Arras by themselves.

Rommel, leaving Rothenberg to set up a perimeter defense, set out in search of his errant riflemen accompanied by a tank and an armored car. He promptly encountered French tanks, which knocked out both of the German vehicles. Rommel and the rest of his escort took cover as French troops moved randomly in their neighborhood. Only later in the morning did elements of the 7th Panzer's infantry arrive to give a lift to their embarrassed commander, who remained on the defensive in the context of reports that several Allied divisions were massing around Arras for a counterattack.

Nothing of any size materialized, and on the morning of the 21st, 7th Panzer rolled forward again. This time, in tribute to the previous day's close call, Rommel inserted his reconnaissance battalion between the tank regiment and the rifle brigade to maintain communications and rear security. His orders were again simple: bypass Arras to the west and head for the English Channel. Again the 25th Panzer Regiment got off to a fast start against scattered resistance. Again the infantry fell behind. Around 3 P.M. Rommel decided it was safe to drive back and put the fear of their commander into the slower-moving rifle regiments. By the time he returned at the head of the trucks, the 25th's rear echelons were under artillery fire, and one of his own howitzer batteries was engaging tanks advancing south from Arras.

French commander in chief General Maurice Gamelin had been pressing since the beginning of the German attack for a counteroffensive against the armored columns. BEF commanding general Viscount Edward Gort was under similar pressure from his government, now headed by the aggressive Winston Churchill. Hoth's corps offered a target of opportunity. The end result was the concentration of two British tank battalions, a couple infantry battalions, and some field and antitank guns on the old World War I battlefield of Vimy Ridge, with promises of French support and orders to strike the Germans when they came within range.

Planning was random; air support nonexistent. Maps, radios, and the other less-obvious trappings of twentieth-century war had long since been lost or broken. The infantry reached their staging areas at the last minute, exhausted after an all-night march. The British, however, had a trump card: British tank design between the wars had followed two paths. One concentrated on developing light, fast-moving vehicles for independent armored formations. The other focused on designing tanks for the direct support of infantry, and the two tank battalions that were the core of the counterattack had around seventy-five Infantry Tanks Mark I and II between them.

They were not exactly awe-inspiring. Their cross-country progress was so simultaneously stately and ungainly that their crews called them "Matildas"—after Matilda the Duck, a well known comic-strip character. The Mark I's best speed was eight miles an hour. It was armed with nothing more formidable than rifle-caliber machine guns. The Mark II was a bit faster, and its high-velocity two-pound turret gun was effective against all models of German tanks from any angle. More importantly, the Matildas carried up to three inches and more of armor, most of it frontal.

As they came down the roads from Arras, the Germans they first encountered were not Rothenberg's Panzers, able to seek positions for flank shots, but elements of the reconnaissance battalion and the rifle brigade, supported by 37-millimeter antitank guns. The 37 was a good weapon, mobile, fast-firing, and accurate. A Rheinmetall design widely licensed and copied in Europe and the world, it had been in Wehrmacht service since 1936. Its crews knew the gun; the infantry they supported were correspondingly confident they could see off this attack as they had so many others in the past week.

What they experienced instead was a fireworks display as the small armor-piercing rounds skidded off the Matildas' armor. Because the well-trained Germans held their fire until the range closed, the Matildas were able to use their machine guns with devastating effect, first on the anti-tank crews, then on the unarmored vehicles crowding the German rear area. Fear was not a French monopoly in May 1940. As the Matildas crawled on, infantrymen discovered urgent personal business out of the line of fire; truck drivers sought to get out of range; and the German position seemed on the verge of unraveling. A simple radio message reached division headquarters: "Strong enemy tank attack from direction Arras. Help. Help."

Better coordination and control, a little more artillery support, a few hundred fresh infantrymen, and 7th Panzer might have been in deeper trouble than its commander could match. But none of those things were forthcoming. The advancing British tanks increasingly lost touch first with their infantry, then with each other. Rommel reached the scene in his command car and ordered his remaining antitank guns and the howitzers of the division artillery to take the tanks under fire, overriding the gunners' protests that that the ranges were still too long. The howitzers' thirty-pound high-explosive shells did damage to treads and suspensions, but the Matildas were designed to withstand heavier metal than the 7th Panzer could provide. Rommel turned to the Wehrmacht's junior service, the Luftwaffe.

In contrast to British and U.S. practice, antiaircraft defense was primarily an air force responsibility in the Third Reich. With Allied strategic air activity virtually nonexistent, Goering and his generals had provided a large number of guns to cover the ground offensive, and the young captains commanding the batteries and battalions kept pace with the mobile divisions whether or not they had any flying targets. Twenty-millimeter cannon hammered the Matildas with tracer rounds. Then the heavies joined in. The 88-millimeter gun had first seen action in the Spanish Civil War, where its high velocity and pinpoint accuracy made it a valuable ground-support weapon. An 88 round could crack open even a Matilda II like a hard-boiled egg. The attack slowed, then stopped, then fell back.

Seventh Panzer benefited as well from the fierce fight made on its flank by elements of the *Waffen SS*. The *Schutzstaffel*, Heinrich Himmler's private army had been given the cutting nickname "asphalt soldiers," good only for parades, by a Wehrmacht jealous and protective of its self-proclaimed role as the Reich's sole bearer of arms. Himmler nevertheless found men and equipment to organize three SS motorized divisions for the campaign of 1940. The 3rd, the *Totenkopf*, was originally formed primarily from concentration camp personnel and bore the death's head of the camp guards as its designation. Poor company for honorable men—but the SS troopers recovered from their initial attack of "tank fear" to tackle the Matildas with grenades at close range and artillery over open sights until a Stuka strike forced the survivors back toward their start lines.

Rommel had been in the front lines throughout the long late afternoon, directing fire and encouraging men in a style not seen on German battlefields since the Wars of Unification. His cold-blooded courage might well have averted a disaster. In the process, Rommel temporarily forgot about his Panzer regiment. The 25th had long since reached its assigned objectives, but even the intrepid Rothenberg was reluctant to go forward into the blue without some infantry for support and a few armored cars for reconnaissance. Instead, around 7 P.M., he received Rommel's orders to turn around and take the Allied armored attackers in flank and rear.

By that time, the 25th was becoming accustomed to moving in twilight. Its leading elements nevertheless took heavy losses breaking through a screen of British antitank guns supported by French SOMUAS and light tanks The final bill was twenty tanks—almost 10 percent of the 25th's original strength. When company *feldwebels* finished calling the rolls, the 7th Panzer's personnel casualties amounted to 89 dead, 110 wounded, and 173 "missing." Most of those would later rejoin, but the figure was no less an indication of the force and impact of the Allied attack on May 21.

Rommel recovered his equilibrium almost immediately—at least on the surface. He was complacent when the 7th Panzer was stood down for a couple days to sort itself out. "The war will be won in a fortnight," he wrote to Lu. "There's little prospect of any more hard fighting." The division's movements around Arras on the 23rd and 24th were nevertheless almost cautious. Nor did Rommel complain when, on May 24, Rundstedt ordered the Panzers to halt once more, this time giving the Allies three invaluable days to prepare for the evacuation of Dunkirk. Ironically, Rommel may have contributed to the anxiety that infected the High Command. He believed he had taken on five full-strength divisions on the 24th instead of elements from three, and made great play in his reports with the "hundreds of tanks" his division had confronted. He wrote Lu that the 7th Panzer had suffered around 1,600 casualties since the start of the campaign: more than twice as many as in reality. Rommel was pushing fifty—a fit, hard fifty to be sure—but for two weeks he had put himself under a captain's level of physical stress and sleep deprivation. One of his aides had been wounded and another killed, both literally at his side. Not for more than twenty years had Rommel literally smelled blood and felt the bitter, coppery bite deep in his throat. The familiar metaphor of courage as a bank account invites consideration. Rommel might not have drained his, but he had written some substantial checks and might well have needed some time to rebalance his books.

Certainly he showed no signs of low balance when the 7th Panzer was sent on the move once more. Elements of its rifle brigade crossed the La Bassee Canal on the evening of the 26th (Rundstedt's orders said nothing about infantry!), and Rommel was at the main crossing point early on the 27th, supervising the construction of a heavy bridge under British sniper fire, directing 20-millimeter and tank fire against the snipers, finally moving armor and guns across the bridge in force. Hoping for a Rommel-type breakout, Hoth put the 5th Division's Panzer brigade under Rommel's command. Instead, he succeeded in inhibiting his subordinate, who found controlling seven tank battalions from the front line a different matter from handling three—especially in the broken, built-up country outside of Lille.

Rommel's opponents, moreover, were not those to which he had become accustomed. The French, elements of the 1st Army, survivors of defeat and retreat in Belgium, had shed their summer soldiers. They were learning that tanks were vulnerable. The 75-millimeter guns that remained the backbone of the field artillery may have been obsolescent as artillery pieces, but their high velocity and flat trajectory put them in the same category as the German 88 when it came to knocking out tanks. Rommel contented himself with establishing defensive positions south and west of Lille during the night of the 27th, then spending the next day thwarting French efforts to break through them while the British elements of the garrison withdrew toward what was becoming the Dunkirk perimeter.

Relieved on the line by infantry who took the garrison's surrender on June 1, 7th Panzer stood down for a much needed six-day rest. It had a nickname now: the *Gespenster-Division,* the Ghost Division, bestowed for its elusive unpredictability by the correspondents made welcome at its headquarters. From his first days with 7th Panzer Division, Rommel had been criticized as a publicity seeker. He carried a personal camera, a gift from Josef Goebbels himself, and enjoyed taking candid shots—frequently asking someone else to take a snapshot that showed Rommel as part of the action.

This involved more than vanity. Rommel's style of command depended on the control exercised by a general who appeared from nowhere and took charge of critical situations. With the WGB, and as a small-unit commander in a long-service professional army, Rommel could put his personal stamp on his officers and men by direct contact. At division level, the thing could not be done entirely in the same way. It required an image. To present that image involved working with the Ministry of Propaganda and its head, Josef Goebbels, who assigned the journalists and the photographers and passed their work for publication and broadcasting.

Earlier in May, Goebbels had attached one of his officials, Karl-August Hanke, to Rommel's headquarters with a lieutenant's rank. An outspoken Nazi and an abrasive personality even by Third Reich standards, Hanke was unpopular from the beginning, regarded as a party plant and a potential informer. Ironically, Goebbels had sent him to the field in part to be rid of him. Hanke was, however, too useful as a conduit and a contact to be wasted. Nor did it hurt that he had a full measure of "the right stuff," knocking out a pillbox during the division's crossing of the Meuse, then single-handedly disarming a group of Frenchmen in Rommel's presence. When Hitler approved the High Command's recommendation and awarded Rommel the Knight's Cross of the Iron Cross, the opportunity to demonstrate the symbiosis between party and army was too good to miss. He designated Hanke to make the presentation, and Hanke played it to the hilt, conferring the award almost on the front line on August 27.

Rommel was the first division commander to receive the decoration. And lest there be any doubt of his place in the Reich's order of merit, Hitler himself paid a visit to 7th Panzer's headquarters on June 3 during a flying tour of the front and requested Rommel's company for the balance of the afternoon. "The Fuehrer's visit was wonderful," Rommel informed his wife. "He greeted me with the words 'Rommel, we were very worried about you during the attack.'" Since the days of Frederick the Great, the Prussian/German general officer corps had never been exactly a band of brothers. A more apt comparison might be with a group of streetwalkers competing for the most profitable corner. Rommel's success was likely to make him enemies no matter how he played it. At this stage, he saw no reason not to take pleasure in what he considered the well-earned favor of his commander in chief and the plaudits of a grateful nation. "Would you cut out all the newspaper articles about me, please?" Rommel requested to Lu. ". . . it will be fun to look at them later."

Since 1933, German public culture had been saturated with an ethnically based blend of pride, hope, and fear, whose primary emphasis was an appeal to the collective virtue and moral righteousness of the German folk community. For more than a century, the army had considered itself the primary embodiment of that virtue and righteouness. Now the soldiers were winning the kind of victory that even the great Frederick could do no more than imagine. Places that symbolized a generation's sacrifice a quarter-century earlier—Ypres, Amiens, Arras—had fallen into German hands so easily that they scarcely rated a line in the daily communiqués. The British were fleeing across the channel with no more than the uniforms on their backs and the rifles in their hands. The French were falling back into their own country, awaiting an end game whose outcome could hardly be doubted.

Rommel understood the "two pillars theory" popular in military circles at least as well as most of his contemporaries. He understood as well that a true sharing of power in the Reich was highly unlikely. A barely concealed subtext of senior-officer discourse in the 1930s had been that the Wehrmacht would win Germany's wars and then teach the "Bohemian corporal" some badly needed manners. Rommel did not consider himself one of the army's insiders, either the "Potsdam set" drawn from the traditional aristocracy or the "learned gentlemen," the general staff and its wannabes. But he believed he was establishing a new paradigm of military leadership, one embodying the national warrior spirit evoked by National Socialism and institutionalized in the army. And he had spent enough time at the center of Reich politics to understand the value of public relations in contexts wider than those a division.

At the end of the campaign, Rommel would make his own statement on that point by getting rid of Hanke after a messy incident when (probably more or less drunk), he allegedly declared his party rank was higher than Rommel's military rank and then withdrew his recommendation for a Knight's Cross Hanke had well earned. Not every Nazi official at that stage of the war was a hack primarily interested in preserving his own skin. The question was who would be was using whom in the long run.

IV

Those events lay in the future as the 7th Panzer Division turned south to close accounts with France. It was still part of Hoth's corps, and that formation had been transferred to Army Group B, deployed along the Somme River and north to the Channel. At 4:30 A.M. on June 5, the 6th Rifle Regiment captured a road/railroad bridge that the French had failed to demolish. Rommel walked across under fire, followed by his command vehicle. He spent most of the morning under machine-gun fire as his forward units struggled with French defenses that reflected earlier lessons learned against the Panzers. Instead of manning continuous lines, the forward units were deployed in strong points based on villages and small

woods, organized for all-round defense, with orders to hold until relieved. French artillery had recovered much of its equilibrium, keeping
roads and trails under harassing fire and zeroing in promptly to support
threatened "hedgehogs" to its front. Not until mid-afternoon did Rommel feel comfortable ordering Rothenberg to flank the principal strong
point at Le Quesnoy and drive forward while the riflemen cleared the village and followed the Panzers into France.

He later described the maneuver as going as smoothly as a peacetime
exercise. In fact, the garrison of Le Quesnoy, most of them Senegalese,
took heavy toll of the German infantry in house-to-house fighting. Unlike
other occasions in 1940, when Germans and Africans met, there was no
deliberate massacre of survivors. Nevertheless, the riflemen took few
prisoners, and the delay imposed by the *tirailleurs* forced the Panzers to
advance unsupported until Rommel was ordered to halt for fear of coming under attack by Stukas, whose target-acquisition skills were still developing.

The rest of the day and night 7th Panzer had all it could handle
against French artillery and tank-led counterattacks, whose repulses
owed an increasing amount to Luftwaffe-manned 88s pushed almost into
the forward positions. Rommel shared the near-universal German army
prejudice against using Africans against "Europeans" and was at pains to
mention that a large number of the "colored" prisoners taken by his division were drunk. But he was soldier enough to credit the Senegalese
with taking their share of the night fighting that belied his report of "All
quiet forward. Enemy in shreds."

The next day Rommel pulled another experimental formation from
the list the division had practiced before the campaign. The *Flachen-
marsch,* or area march, was designed to cope with the loss of contact between tanks and supporting arms that had been plaguing the 7th Panzer
since first encountering the more determined Allied defenses around Arras. It involved deploying the entire division on a two-thousand-yard front
with a twelve-mile depth, then advancing cross-country. There were usually tanks to the front and on the immediate flanks: an armored sheathing
that could be supported by infantry, pioneers, artillery, or antitank guns as
needed, depending on the opposition. The tanks still shot up any potential
strongpoint, but in contrast to Rommel's previous handling of his Panzers,

this massive formation moved more deliberately—partly so the infantry could keep pace, partly to spare the suspensions of the vast majority of the division's vehicles that was not designed for cross-country work.

On June 6 and 7, the division nevertheless made around thirty miles, straight across to the open country of Picardy: over grain fields, through hedges and fences, bypassing villages that might be fortified, avoiding major roads blocked with refugees and French rear-echelon elements—and cutting the French 10th Army in half before its command quite understood what had happened. In the absence of air reconnaissance, and with communications disrupted, it was surprisingly easy for even a large force, moving in a single, mass formation, virtually to disappear.

By late afternoon on the 7th, Rommel's armored spearheads were outrunning the refugees, occupying farms as their inhabitants were packing to leave. His armored cars and motorcycles had cut the Paris-Dieppe Road, and Hoth, still riding his subordinate's dice, was talking about getting as far as Rouen. That proved overoptimistic, but Rommel had high hopes for adding Rouen to his bag on the 8th, swinging southwest to seize the bridges over the Seine, and take the city from the flank and rear. Instead, his lead elements were slowed by masses of refugees and checked by elements of the British 1st Armored Division, deployed to Brittany as a goodwill gesture by the new British prime minister, Winston Churchill. The close, hilly terrain disrupted the radio contact on which Rommel so depended. By nightfall, the 7th Panzer was still on the wrong side of the Seine, and Rommel pushed forward to rectify the situation. The closest usable bridges were in Elbeuf. By the time Rommel reached the town and began pushing his vanguards toward the river, French engineers set off the prepared demolition charges.

Rommel was not pleased with the commander of his motorcycle battalion, who had failed to push through the refugees and bounce the bridges in the confusion. Nor did he exactly rejoice when Rouen fell to the 5th Panzer Division, which had been Rommel's attendant lord since the beginning of the campaign. But, as he wrote to Lu, more than forty miles gained in a day was no bagatelle. The French and British, whose improvised "Second BEF" also included the 51st Highland Division and the 1st Canadian Division, were falling back on the fortress harbor of Le

Havre, but it was a fair question whether they could run faster than the 7th Panzer could chase them.

Rommel spent June 9 pulling together his still-scattered division and cleaning up the area it had overrun—that latter amounting to disarming French POWs and moving refugees into holding areas. "It looks to me inevitable," he wrote Lu, "that the other side will soon collapse . . . We never imagined war in the west would be like this." On June 11, he was ordered to finish the job by capturing Le Havre. The division's tanks and armored cars went all out against collapsing resistance, reaching an average speed as high as forty miles an hour by the time the lead elements reached the sea and cut off the Allies' last line of retreat.

Rothenberg drove his command tank through the beach wall and down to the edge of the English Channel as Rommel and some of his staff waded in to their boot tops like schoolboys on an excursion. The mood of exuberant relaxation lasted until Rommel remounted his command vehicle and led his division along the coast to St. Valery en Caux, a projected evacuation port crowded with French and British troops, both organized units and stragglers. As Rothenberg's tanks shot up the harbor, Rommel sent a white flag into the city and summoned the garrison's surrender. Met with a refusal, he responded by taking St. Valery under fire during the night with every weapon in the 7th Panzer's inventory. The next morning, tanks and riflemen pushed into the town against scattered resistance. The senior French officer agreed to surrender while insisting that his decision was motivated solely by lack of ammunition. The Highlanders went into the bag alongside the French, albeit far less willingly. A corps commander, four division commanders, and their staffs, a dozen generals altogether, presented themselves before Rommel in the marketplace as correspondents and photographers recorded the scene from every angle. "The Ghost Division again!" one French staff officer marveled when told whom he had been facing.

That evening, the 7th Panzer's band gave a concert on the promenade in the nearby seaside town of Fecamp. Le Havre fell without serious fighting. Civilians relieved the shooting had stopped, and even more relieved at the good discipline and relative goodwill shown by their new conquerors, responded with flowers in a few instances.

That relative breathing spell lasted until June 17. The remnants of the Second BEF and a gaggle of second-line administrative troops were falling back into Brittany and the port of Cherbourg, where their government and High Command hoped to stage a mini-Dunkirk before the imminent French collapse carried them down in its wake. Rommel was ordered to take his division, plus an additional motorized brigade, and take Cherbourg. This time, the 7th Panzer covered a hundred fifty miles in twenty-four hours, two hundred more on the 18th. Word of an armistice had spread among the French troops in Rommel's path, and he heard news of it himself over the radio. It was a perfect opportunity to turn the Panzers loose one last time, confident that the French troops strung out in the division's rear would make no further trouble.

Cherbourg was a strong fortress, with a developed system of defenses against land attack. Rommel counted again on speed and shock. On the morning of June 19, he entered the city with the rifle brigade as the division's artillery took the main forts and individual centers of resistance under fire. In by-now typical fashion, he spent time bringing a dilatory platoon commander into action, moving an antiaircraft battery off a road it was blocking, and acting as a forward observation officer against one of the forts. He disposed of an unmanned roadblock by having his communications truck push it out of the way.

Cherbourg was large enough to absorb Rommel's few thousand infantrymen like a sponge despite his heroics, but in addition to shells the Germans had been throwing in canisters of surrender leaflets. Around noon, the Prefect of Police and a local member of the Chamber of Deputies offered to act as go-betweens. By 5 P.M., it was all over, and the Ghost Division's troops began materializing in the streets of their latest conquest. The British had made good their escape, as at Dunkirk at the price of abandoning most equipment heavier than rifles. But the acres of burning vehicles, the miles of demoralized prisoners, and the swastika flags springing up like poppies made it seem no more than a matter of time before that little detail would be seen to by the Wehrmacht and its Fuehrer.

From Cherbourg, the 7th Panzer Division moved south toward the Spanish frontier at what seemed a stately pace while armistice negotiations proceeded. Rommel found time to inform his wife of a brief digestive problem and to complain of quarters he described as "middling." He found time as well to consider statistics. In absolute terms, 7th Panzer's losses had not been light during the campaign: approximately 700 killed, 1,650 wounded, and 300 missing out of an initial strength of 15,000. But in the Great War, divisions had regularly paid twice that price in a day or two for a few lines of trenches—or for nothing at all. Seventh Panzer's bag included almost 100,000 prisoners, 450 tanks, more than 300 field and antitank guns, 4,000 trucks—and 1,500 horse-drawn vehicles, in case anyone needed concrete proof that a new day had dawned in warmaking.

Erwin Rommel and the 7th Panzer had done something more than win a series of tactical victories that remain unprecedented in terms of time, space, and numbers. They had established an archetype of blitzkrieg. Ever since May 1940, "lightning war" in military mythology is more than just quick, lethal, aseptic conflict; something other than the "shock and awe" of paralyzing aerial bombardment, or massive artillery barrages anonymously delivered, or even of hundreds of tanks rolling forward in an irresistible mass. What the 7th Panzer Division did was set a pace that transformed each enemy it faced into an obliging enemy, whose decisions and behaviors seemed to fit German requirements as closely as though Rommel himself had drawn up the plans and issued the orders. It was a virtuoso performance, after a half-century when war had become an endurance test.

Rommel was not an easy superior, and even while the division was winning its battles, slight rumblings of dissent were audible in the staff and at the regimental headquarters. Rommel's senior staff officer, whose position combined roughly the functions of an American G-2 and G-3, went so far as to submit shortly after St. Valery a memorandum criticizing his chief's methods. Rommel's flair for publicity exacerbated the friction. He had the game, he had the name, and he enjoyed his developing mystique. What in a more restrained personality and a more conscious team player might have been processed as initiative and aggressiveness came was frequently described as showmanship. His connections with Hitler—which included being ordered to provide the Fuehrer a map of his division's advance—acquired an aura of careerism.

Rommel responded to the downside of his growing reputation by reflecting that a longer time in command before the beginning of the campaign would have given his subordinates a better chance to internalize his methods. And if he had regularly shown his rough side in the field, he manifested unusual generosity afterward. Rothenberg, Colonel von Bismarck of the 7th Rifle Regiment, and several other field officers received the Knight's Cross on Rommel's recommendation. For the fighting on May 13 alone, sixteen junior officers and NCOs were awarded the Iron Cross, First Class, and the lists grew with each victory. Rommel might be ambitious, but he had long coattails.

Rommel's front-line presence, moreover, manifested an unself-conscious intensity shone through whatever he did. From building a bridge to sighting a gun, from stopping a tank attack to getting an infantry platoon moving, Rommel was a soldier—the best soldier in the whole division. And the men who fought under him remembered. Long before "doing a Rommel" became a British phrase for a battlefield coup, "to Rommel" meant the same thing in the 7th Panzer despite Rommel's half-irritated, half-gratified disclaimer.

On July 7, Hoth submitted his official report. General Rommel, Hoth declared, had "explored new paths in the command of Panzer divisions." He especially praised Rommel's drive to be at the front and his instinct for the decisive point of even a fast-paced battle. Blitzkrieg at seventh and last means convincing participants and observers—one's own side and the home front included—that enemies face inevitable and humiliating defeat. In a technological age, that no longer meant man-to-man physical superiority, as in the Middle Ages, or even at times in the trenches of the Western Front. It spoke rather to the ability to use the means at one's disposal so effectively that resistance seemed not merely futile but pathetic, without even the heroic element that traditionally informs last stands and forlorn hopes in Western military mythology.

Lightning war as practiced by the 7th Panzer Division meant Rommel could ride, essentially alone and defenseless, through thousands of trained, armed French soldiers. Not a shot was fired at him, even when his senior rank was obvious. Instead, French officers and men flocked around him as someone to show them what to do next. Prisoners usually look frightened and shabby compared to their captors—one reason why the current laws of war forbid showing their pictures. Prisoners of blitzkrieg appear shocked out of their higher cognitive abilities. Their conquerors seem from another dimension, unmarked physically and psychologically—"overmen" in the original sense of Friedrich Nietzsche.

The German generals in 1940 were as surprised as their enemies by the overwhelming nature of their combined physical and psychological triumph. The disaster that overtook the French army in May and June 1940 has been ascribed to the erosion of national will and morale during the interwar years. It has been presented as the fruit of strategic and tactical doctrines inadequate to meet the German challenge. It has been described as reflecting shortcomings of organization, training, and intelligence. In the same context, the German victory is presented as a *faute de mieux* improvisation, a combination of unpredictable chance, Allied mistakes, and the behavior of a few hard-driving Panzer generals who presented their own High Command with a series of *faits accomplis*. Far from prefiguring a new way of war, the successes of 1940 led Germany down a dead-end road of "operative Hubris," emphasizing combat at the expense of strategy. In an age of industrialized war, critics argue, the lightning victories Rommel embodied would prove a fatal anachronism.

Blitzkrieg's real victor was National Socialism. Hitler, ever the opportunist, celebrated the successes of May and June 1940 in a National Socialist context: a triumph of will, infused with a consciousness of martial superiority that in turn depended on the racial superiority evoked and refined by the Third Reich. In that context, blitzkrieg in the months between the fall of France and the stagnation of Operation Barbarossa played a central, arguably an essential, role in the "exterminatory warfare" that was Nazi Germany's true contribution to modern warmaking. That, however, was a story still to unfold.

V

Genius has been described as an ability to seize even unlikely opportunities. We left George Patton tall in the saddle at Fort Myer, orchestrating Army ceremonies with his expected flair, bending every effort to secure a field command, and periodically generating doubts regarding his stability if not his sanity. But Patton, like Hamlet, was mad only when the wind was in certain quarters. Otherwise, he knew a hawk from a handsaw. When, in July 1939, newly appointed Chief of Staff George C. Marshall found his quarters temporarily unready. Patton jumped in with an offer of hospitality and chortled in a letter to Bea that "once he got his 'natural charm' working, he would need no more recommendations from Pershing or anyone else."

Although Bea's reaction is unrecorded, it seems reasonable to speculate that it included a fervent prayer or two. Marshall took office with a policy of weeding out a senior officer corps that he regarded as too long in the tooth for the kind of war the Germans were pioneering on the plains of Poland. As a rule of thumb, no one over fifty would be seriously considered for high command in an army that by now everyone knew was in line to expand exponentially. Patton, at fifty-four, was exactly in the zone for blighted hopes, and he knew it. Morning after morning, when Marshall appeared at the Fort Myer stables for his daily ride, Patton was there first, saddled and eager to be invited along. Marshall enjoyed greeting his subordinate courteously and leaving him cold—partly from a reluctance to play Army politics during the one period of relaxation he allowed himself, but partly as well from a barbed sense of humor that took pleasure in Patton's obvious frustration.

Patton had little cause to worry. Whether or not Marshall kept a literal black book in which he recorded the names of promising officers, for almost twenty years he had been keeping systematic track of the sheep and the goats among his contemporaries and his juniors. He had formed a good opinion of Patton in France and kept track of him afterward largely through his writings. And Patton, who in private vitriolically disparaged almost every officer he served with when the mood was on him, never recorded a single negative comment about Marshall.

Some insight into the relationship comes from Marshall's family. After the death of his first wife in 1927, he had remarried in 1930. His stepdaughter liked Patton and found him amusing, "like a little boy." His wife was part of the audience for one of Patton's patented off-color remarks at a Fort Myers party. According to Marshall, she responded with, "George, you mustn't talk like that. You say these outrageous things and then you look at me to see if I'm gong to smile. Now you could do that as a captain or a major, but you aspire to be a general, and a general cannot talk in any such way."

According to Marshall, Patton laughed off the incident, "but she hit the nail on the head." At least she did so as far as Marshall was concerned, by articulating an acceptable reason for not reacting to Patton's behavior. The new chief of staff was committed to seeking out unusual talent in an environment that fostered high averages. In a perceptive analysis of the general officers who served in the V Corps during the European campaign, Charles Kirkpatrick notes both a pattern of competence as opposed to excellence, and the difficulty of determining what factors nurtured that competence. No single factor or combination of factors seems decisive. Kilpatrick offers a baseball metaphor of an interwar environment encouraging average batters to develop their swings, and thereby producing lineups of reliable singles hitters. Marshall recognized better than most that Patton possessed many of a singles hitter's attributes. For all his obvious ambition, Patton had time and again proven himself a team player, loyal to his branch and his superiors, willing to lay down intellectual bunts when called upon. At the same time, in his published writing and his advanced schooling, Patton had demonstrated that he could swing for the military fences. His flame and color and ardor had consistently translated into success as a commander. Marshall had to decide whether Patton was merely a 2 o'clock performer, good in the batting practice of parades and maneuvers.

In the end, it came down to the slippery concept of character—and to an old Army officer corps that resembled sufficiently the extended family it prided itself on being to make room for a difficult uncle: the kind who is invited to holiday dinners with a prayer that this time he can be kept away from the Manischewitz at least until the meal is over. Total institutions and closed communities such as prisons, asylums, religious orders, academic faculties, and officer corps frequently contain a few licensed taboo-breakers. Sometimes cast as jesters and sometimes as lords of misrule, they perform the function of relieving collective stress, and occasionally as well of speaking truth to power. Had Patton been less obnoxious, less of a strain on his colleagues, he might have been defined as a boor, socially and professionally encysted, and retired a major. His behavior, however, was so often so far over the top that the only way to justify overlooking it was by a usually unspoken agreement that it was an unfortunate manifestation of a still-undisciplined talent that just might cross the line into a genius for war. In practice, it meant a rueful shrug, a shaken head, and a "that's Georgie"—accompanied occasionally by a half-smothered grin.

Though Patton was the only officer the reserved, punctilious chief of staff regularly called by his first name, that was arguably less of a compliment than a half-conscious reflection of Marshall's belief that Patton had never quite grown up. Marshall saw Patton as a difficult man, one needing "a tight rope round his neck," but believed he knew how to handle him. What counted for the chief of staff was Patton's consistently successful performance of his assigned duties and his conviction that "George will take a unit through hell and high water." In 1936, Marshall used the same phrase when telling Patton that should he reach high command he wanted Patton's services. Marshall interpreted what seemed Patton's retrograde affirmations of horse cavalry as a defensible manifestation of branch loyalty in difficult times. He told one of his staff officers that Patton was the best tank man in the Army and proposed to give him command of a corps—an armored corps—when one became available. At a time when even its infantry divisions were paper formations, Marshall's vision of the Army's future is as striking as his affirmation of Patton's ability.

Although its primary European connection remained with France, during the interwar years, the U.S. Army also maintained close and cordial contacts with the reorganized Reichswehr. The experiences of a small professional army had an everyday relevance not present in a French system of mass conscription for total war. U.S. officers studied at German academies and observed German maneuvers, acquiring in the process a comprehensive respect for the professional abilities of their German counterparts that would endure for most of the century.

The replacement of the Weimar Republic by Hitler's Third Reich did not disturb the U.S. Army's German connection. On one level, Germany's rearmament offered a new set of comparisons and benchmarks for American officers expecting to have to do something similar in a national emergency. The new regime's structural anti-Semitism was not particularly off-putting to an officer corps itself significantly influenced by anti-

Jewish attitudes ranging from country-club prejudice to systematic, intellectually sophisticated racism. The Wehrmacht's officer corps, moreover, tended to put its best foot forward in such matters, taking pains to present an urbane face to its transatlantic comrades in arms, dismissing the party's Jewish policies as something for the gutter and not to be taken seriously.

German officers continued to be valued speakers at Army schools, particularly for their ideas on mobility. U.S. attachés and observers in turn reported the fundamental changes taking place in the cavalry, the creation of the Panzer arm, and the development of a doctrine of maneuver war that combined traditional concepts with the innovations of mechanization. Those associating totalitarianism with obsessive secrecy will find few obvious examples in the Germany of the late 1930s. Instead, the Americans found open doors wherever they went—and wagging tongues as well, in a broad spectrum of informal situations involving military matters.

This openness was one manifestation of Hitler's deliberate display of Germany's reborn military might for purposes of deterrence and intimidation. It reflected as well the Germans' professional pride in their achievements, combined with the belief that it was safe to boast to representatives of an army posing no threat. Americans were uniquely welcome in the field even during the Polish campaign, if for no other reason than they were about the only neutrals remaining.

Where armored warfare was concerned, U.S. officers were as a rule impressed. The Germans, reported their observers and interlocutors, emphasized simplicity, aggressiveness, common sense—the same virtues American soldiers enjoyed ascribing to themselves. They paid less attention to underlying values, whether professional ones like mission tactics or ideological ones such as the influence of National Socialism on military behaviors.

The comments of visiting German officers on the utility of having mechanization controlled by a single authority did not impress branch chiefs determined to maintain their autonomies and boundaries. Infantry branch Chief Major General George Lynch went on record as late as October 1939 that the infantry did not want any Panzer divisions. Under Lynch, the infantry concentrated instead on developing the light triangular division with which it would fight World War II. Like many other infantrymen, Lynch believed the use of tanks independently, or in large numbers, had been discredited during the Spanish Civil War, and in 1938, he ordered the Army's tank manual rewritten accordingly, emphasizing antitank defense. The basic antimechanized weapon was a 37-millimeter gun, obsolescent when it was introduced in 1937 and unsupported by tactical or operational doctrines much more sophisticated than taking under fire any AFV that came into its sights.

Cavalry Chief Herr as late as 1938 insisted that mechanized cavalry had not yet reached the stage of development where it could be considered equal to horse cavalry, much less displace mounted formations. Herr's mind changed a bit in the aftermath of the German invasion of Poland. On September 15, 1939, with the Panzers on the outskirts of Warsaw, Chaffee called for the immediate organization of a mechanized cavalry division and the authorization of men and equipment for the cadres of two more. Herr agreed in principle that the Knox Brigade be expanded to a full division—but insisted that the horse cavalry must be strengthened as well.

The question became moot when the "Limited National Emergency" declared by President Roosevelt on September 8, 1939, resulted in an Army increase of only 17,000 men. For the second year in a row, Patton was certified eligible for promotion to brigadier general, and for the second time, nothing happened. He presented a set of solid silver stars to Marshall on the latter's promotion to full general. He did the same for old friend and patron Kenyon Joyce when the 1st Cavalry Division's commander put on his second star. General Herr placed Patton first among twenty cavalry colonels and lieutenant colonels who merited promotion to brigadier. But Patton's step to general's rank proved more complicated than he hoped.

It began with the planning of the annual maneuvers for 1940. Their designated commanding general, Major General Stanley Embeck, had worked closely with Chaffee and was eager to test the prospects of mechanization. Under Marshall's auspices, Embick and Chaffee organized a provisional mechanized division by attaching a regiment of infantry in trucks to the Knox Brigade. In January, the infantry had organized its own Provisional Tank Brigade by combining almost all the modern tanks in its inventory and assigning them to Fort Benning. To complete the picture, the 1st Cavalry Division was ordered to participate. Patton was so far out of the loop he saw no ethical problem in passing to Joyce some insider's information on the 1st Cavalry Division's mission, and some advice on how best to accomplish it. A month later, ironically, he received an assignment to the maneuvers himself, as an umpire.

Almost all the tanks involved in the 1940 maneuvers belonged to the same family of M-2 light tanks and M-1 combat cars. An improved version, with a 37-millimeter gun turret replacing machine guns as the main armament and enough additional armor to raise the weight to about 12 tons and cut the speed to 25 miles per hour, was ordered in 1939. By May 1940, a total of ten were in unit service, and they spent most of their early careers posing for photographs. The unimpressive inventory was sufficient to dominate the maneuvers held in April and May 1940. In the second stage, the cavalry and infantry tanks were combined in a provisional armored division that ran literal rings around the horse cavalry despite Patton's earlier tips, and despite the terrain advantages offered the troopers by the roadless, broken country of western Louisiana.

As a counterpoint impossible to overlook, on May 10, the Wehrmacht launched its offensive in the West. The unexpectedly rapid German success and the unexpectedly smooth cooperation of the infantry tanks and the mechanized cavalry generated increasing discussion among maneuver participants of the advantages of forming a new force, separate from the existing branches and combining the combat and support elements needed to implement mechanized war. On May 25, the last day of the official maneuvers, a group of officers met in the basement of a Louisiana high school, concluded that the Army must proceed with mechanization under a unified command independent of both infantry and cavalry, and communicated their position to the chief of staff.

On June 10, Marshall called a second meeting including the branch chiefs, representatives of the General Staff, and senior officers of the mechanized units. Its purpose was to outline plans for a new, separate armored force. When Lynch and Herr objected, Marshall replied that his decision was already made, and it was final. The chief of staff's recommendation rolled through the Army bureaucracy smoothly, its progress eased by headlines and broadcasts depicting a German victory unprecedented in speed, scope, and consequences. Against that back-drop, it was impossible to deny that the U.S. Army needed to expand both the strength of its mechanized forces and the scale of its thinking on mechanized warmaking.

An example lay to hand in the Army Air Corps. Originally no more than a branch like the rest, it had evolved during the 1930s into a semi-independent entity incorporating operational, administrative, and main-tenance elements under a unified command. On July 10, 1940, the War Department created an Armored Force also comprehensively responsible for doctrine, training, command, and procurement for armored corps and divisions intended to act independently, and for independent tank battalions whose primary mission was seen as the direct support of in-fantry divisions. Its distinctive insignia, an equilateral triangle incorpo-rating infantry blue, cavalry yellow, and artillery red, still endures. Its commander was Adna Chaffee.

The revolutionary implications of the new force should not be exag-gerated. Neither the U.S. government nor the U.S. Army still had any rea-son to believe substantial American forces would be deployed overseas in a high-tech, high-risk environment. An administration seeking an un-precedented third term was unlikely to advocate creating a force specifi-cally configured to fight Nazi Germany. President Roosevelt's election campaign in 1940, and his own principles, were predicated on keeping America out of the war if at all possible, and in any case not committing large ground forces anywhere. In January 1941, Patton put the issue in a nutshell to a colleague in the War Plans Division: "If you are ever in a po-sition to tell us who we may be expected to fight, I will appreciate it . . ."

The armored division that took shape in 1940 included a division headquarters, a brigade, and no fewer than five subordinate regiments. That was a large number of senior officers in an Army that still counted time in grade by decades. Marshall ordered Lynch and Chaffee to make experienced personnel available for reassignment. Chaffee had repeatedly requested Herr to take point on the issue, to convert horsed cavalry to create the first armored divisions, and been as repeatedly rebuffed. Now the cavalry chief denounced recreant conspirators who set up an inde-pendent arm so they could get promotion.

Colonel George Patton had long regarded mobility, maneuver, and firepower were the keys to victory. "Grab the enemy by the nose," he stated in an article published in 1940, "and kick him in the pants." In other words, find, fix, envelop, and destroy. The article was written for the benefit of horse cavalry. But Patton had been one of the officers who met in the by-now famous—or notorious—basement; one of the de facto supporters of the new Armored Force. On June 26, he wrote to Chaffee, congratulating him on his new appointment and inviting him to stay with the Pattons whenever he found himself in Washington. From Chaffee's perspective, much was to be gained in terms of service politics by recognizing and affirming supporting the new orientation of one of the Army's "horsiest" cavalrymen and better-known officers. Far more to the point, he had a job: command of the armored brigade of the 2nd Armored Division. Chaffee submitted Patton's name to division commander Brigadier General C. L. Scott, an old cavalryman who immediately placed Patton at the head of the list of prospects. On July 26, Patton, still a colonel, received the appointment. He assumed command the next month.

The 2nd Armored Division, in the process of being organized at Fort Benning, was built around the infantry's Provisional Tank Brigade. Chaffee assigned a number of former horse soldiers to its senior commands in an effort to break down previous branch loyalties. He did it as well to expand the horizons of a formation whose tanks had been rigidly restricted to the role of close support for infantry. Deviating from that line resulted in significant career penalties. Lieutenant Colonel Bradford Chynoweth, while commanding a tank battalion, stressed mobility to the point where he was transferred to an infantry regiment in the Philippines—and he was the branch chief's brother-in-law!

Second Armored's original strength had been slightly more than 2,000 out of a table of organization calling for almost 10,000. The division benefited from June 26, 1940, legislation expanding the Army from the token size of 227,000 to the still-token 375,000. All volunteers, most of the new recruits came from the South and gave the outfit a flavor it never quite lost, even after the introduction of the peacetime draft in September brought in men from all over the United States. Patton's contemporary praise of Southern boys with "light hair and eyes—the old fighting breed—" as superior to "subway soldiers" from Pennsylvania and New York need not be taken too seriously as an example of his prejudices. Patton would have praised his division's makeup had it been recruited from Eskimos. To balance the discussion, Major General John Wood, whose crack 4th Armored Division was originally chiefly recruited from Pennsylvania, New York, and New Jersey, ascribed its effectiveness in good part to its personnel—especially the high percentage of Jews, whose drive and aggressiveness Wood said made them natural mechanized warriors.

Many of the new draftees were anything but eager soldiers. Expecting to be part of a cutting-edge, high-tech force, they found the few tanks in the 2nd Armored's inventory to be a long step down from what they saw in the newsreels from Europe. Equipment of every kind was in short supply. Hastily constructed barracks leaked at every angle. Food tasted as if the cooks had taken special Army courses in how to ruin it. Tensions developed between privates from the East and Midwest and freshly promoted NCOs from the deep south. Too many officers were reservists, products of college ROTC programs and similar peacetime systems. Some had been little more than correspondence courses; few had been taken seriously by either supervisors or participants; none had paid any serious attention to armored warfare.

Patton floundered. He began by applying the methods that had worked in his previous commands from France to Texas. He worked to improve the military appearance of both officers and men, following his familiar axiom that men who looked like soldiers would act like soldiers. He sought to establish his personal presence, going so far as to use a siren-carrying tank to travel among his units. He added a light plane to his transport pool. He continued and expanded his reading on armored operations.

None of it quite worked. Neither Patton's enthusiastic letters to Pershing, Herr, and other senior officers nor his formal promotion to brigadier general in October hid the fact that the 2nd Armored Brigade was not progressing as hoped, and its commander was not moving it along as expected. Questions began to circulate within and outside the Armored Force—only from the most professional of motives, of course. Was Patton past his best? Were the responsibilities of this new type of command too much for an old polo player who may have suffered one head injury too many?

Patton's performance was not helped by the state of his marriage. Bea did not accompany him to Georgia, and Patton, alone in a way he had not been in years, seems to have had as much of an epiphany as he was capable of experiencing. His letters embodied not merely the apologetic tone of previous correspondence designed to get him off the hook, but a deeper recognition that the marriage was on the edge of collapse because of his long-term behavior and attitude. It is impossible to say with certainty that Bea left Georgie twisting in the wind during the summer of 1940, but he was on a visibly ragged personal edge.

The consequence of failure was—promotion. Chaffee had broken his health creating the Armored Force. He was suffering from cancer, and in September, Scott was transferred to Fort Knox and temporary command of the I Armored Corps. Patton took over as acting division commander; in December, the assignment became permanent. Despite the problems he was having, no one on the Armored Force's immediate horizon seemed remotely likely to do any better. And in a classic example of challenge and response, Patton found his footing and hit his stride.

He benefited from Bea's decision to relocate to Benning and resume both the marriage and the social round that helped define it. He profited as well from the discovery of the 2nd Armored Division by the country's journalistic and political communities. Fort Benning was an obvious destination for opinion-makers seeking to observe the new Army in action, and Patton had lost none of his ability to put on a good show. His personal tank was ringed with red, white, and blue stripes—with a yellow one added for the cavalry and the Armored Force. He designed a special uniform for tankers—dark green with brass buttons, and a plastic, football-style helmet. Then he modeled it for photographers, his fiercely martial expression contrasting with a sartorial effect Carlo D'Este appropriately describes as a combination of football player and bellboy.

The costume promptly won its wearer nicknames like "Flash Gordon" and "Green Hornet" and was eventually relegated to the list of might-have-beens. But 2nd Armored Division was anything but a military circus. As the division's internal economy improved, as tanks and vehicles arrived to fill out its orders of battle, Patton's officers and men began realizing their new commander was more than the sum of his public relations. Thirty years of study and reflection translated on one level into a set of practical ideas for getting things done that no American for-mation had ever attempted, much less accomplished. Where a couple hundred men had conducted road marches under carefully regulated con-ditions, now two thousand routinely motored from here to there, prac-ticing road discipline, learning how to refuel on the move, and studying camouflage techniques. Where a few improvised armored cars had tested methods of reconnaissance and communication, an entire battalion exer-cised techniques of acquiring and communicating information to main-force units themselves widely dispersed. New soldiers learned the difference between tinkering with a secondhand Ford and maintaining a light tank. They discovered the limits of their civilian drivers' skills be-hind the wheels of a hot little utility car just coming into service that the armored force called a peep, but the rest of the Army dubbed "jeep."

Patton's long-standing belief that citizen soldiers required fundamen-tal enlightenment on the nature of war led him to make a practice of lec-turing to his junior officers and enlisted men—a practice also reflecting his delight in having a mass captive audience. These speeches blended in-spiration and professional insight. A warning to the division officer school that in combat they must expect to be "up to their necks in blood and guts" was the origin of a nickname Patton never liked and never shed. His description of the salute as a sign of mutual respect probably made few converts. On the other hand, his assertion that brave but undis-ciplined men had no chance against disciplined valor, and his insistence that maneuvers must be taken seriously, which meant no slacking and no umpire-baiting, were commonsense points whose Army-wide inculcation eventually saved thousands of American casualties.

Patton was consistently on the spot, personally addressing every problem from bogged-down tanks to traffic jams. Where in his early days on the job he fussed and fumed, now he solved problems, and solved them in ways leaving positive impressions. Because he did solve prob-lems, the spectacular—often deliberately spectacular—explosions of ef-florescent profanity that accompanied his interventions generated as much admiration as resentment.

Carlo d' Este makes a good deal of Patton's readiness to apologize for his impulsive outbursts, particularly when junior officers or enlisted men were the targets. In 1940, American males were not expected to show their softer sides in male communities. Employment structures were hierarchic. Most jobs, whether in factory or office, on farms or behind counters, involved taking the rough side of the bossman's tongue as a matter of course. A fair number of the 2nd Armored's junior officers and enlisted men had some experience of team sports at a time when coaching styles tended toward the abrasive.

That did not make Patton's persona universally appealing. Some of his subordinates, both commissioned and enlisted, were not impressed by what they regarded as bogus posturing. Others found his vulgarity inappropriate or embarrassing. Yet the 2nd Armored was nevertheless rapidly becoming Patton's division, taking collective pride in its personal appearance and unit drill, responding—albeit at times in spite of itself—to its commander's insistence that well-led, courageous soldiers were the ultimate arbiters of war, and coming to believe Patton's insistence that he would ask no man to undergo risks he was unwilling to face himself.

Nineteen forty-one was the year of maneuvers, the year when the draftee army, its new formations, and its rapidly promoted commanders grappled with each other in search of strengths and weak spots. The Armored Force's initial manual, issued shortly after the Force's organization, emphasized the objective of armored attack as the destruction of the enemy. In that, it reflected the tone of the Army's provisional 1939 Field Service Regulations, which depicted the direct application of combat power along the lines of the French "managed battle." Tanks were not primarily intended for independent action on the battlefield itself, or in pursuit and exploitation.

The updated version of FSR issued two years later took a significantly different tone. While still focusing on battle, its concept of the offensive implied greater flexibility, including operations against enemy rear echelons and lines of communication. Envelopment took its place alongside penetration as a tactical option. The Armored Force received a chapter of its own, and the armored division was given decisive missions against enemy rear areas. These attacks were described not in tactical, but operational terms, as directed against movement routes, reserves, and vital areas. The division was expected to operate independently for an extended period of time—another indication of a growing sense of war's operational level.

In tactical situations, tanks were expected to seek an enemy's flanks and rear, avoiding where possible direct engagement with other tank forces. This was not unusual. None of Europe's armies intended to pit tanks against tanks as a matter of course. Such tactics made no more sense than a chess player seeking to exchange queens as an opening gambit. The doctrinally favored counter was the antitank gun. High-velocity weapons usually between 37 millimeters and 50 millimeters, with low silhouettes, shields for their crews, and motor traction, they were intended to move quickly to threatened points in company or battalion strength and knock out tanks as they came into range. Antitank guns were cost-effective compared to tanks: so easy to mass-produce and so simple to operate, they might well be considered expendable, and often were.

The U.S. Army was adding an entirely new version of the weapon to its order of battle. In 1940, the War Department accepted the argument of then Lieutenant Colonel A. D. Bruce that attacking tanks were best countered by not mere battalions, but entire groups and brigades of fast-moving, lightly armored vehicles relying on speed and gun power against better-armored adversaries. To emphasize their mission of "seek, strike, and destroy," the new units were called tank destroyers. They received their own training center, and what amounted to status as a separate arm that at peak strength had more than a hundred battalions. When the M-10 Tank Destroyer based on a Sherman chassis appeared in 1942, its 3-inch gun was as good as any armor-piercing weapon on tracks, even the 76-millimeter gun of the Russian T-34, and was expected to be used against much smaller numbers of attacking German tanks.

The tank destroyer concept has been so often and so sharply criticized in tactical and operational contexts that its relationship to American industrial mobilization is correspondingly neglected. The tank destroyer in its developed form was unique to the United States. No other combatant could afford to distribute state-of-the-art tank chassis so casually. German self-propelled antitank guns were for most of the war improvisations. Britain depended for such vehicles on U.S. allocations.

The development of the tank destroyer also allowed the Armored Force to concentrate on developing its offensive capabilities. Its new field manual, developed during 1941 and published in March 1942, defined armor's role as conducting highly mobile, primarily offensive warfare. The manual emphasized surprise, speed, shock, pursuit, and exploitation: independent action deep in the enemy rear, striking at logistics and communication centers, not stopping even for nightfall. The text favored terms like "demoralization," as opposed to "destruction." It stressed as well the decentralization of control to commanders who would be guided only by the general plans of higher headquarters: "mission tactics" with a vengeance, strongly reflecting American perceptions of German experience in 1940.

For Patton and the 2nd Armored, it began in June, with Army-level maneuvers in Tennessee. Patton addressed the entire division, emphasizing two maxims. The first was tactical. "Hold the enemy by the nose and kick him in the pants": in orthodox soldierspeak, find out where the enemy is, fix him in position by fire, and go around him. The second mantra was moral. Remember, Patton insisted that "one of our greatest qualities is the ability to produce in our enemy the fear of the unknown . . . keep on, see what else you can do to raise the devil . . ."

For a first-time commander of an untried formation, the maneuvers were a remarkable successs. Patton's aggressive leadership and the drive of his subordinates consistently made nonsense of timetables schedules set to the pace of infantry. Each phase of the exercise ended the same day the 2nd Armored entered the scene—as many as twenty-four hours ahead of schedule. On one occasion, elements of the 2nd Armored "captured" an enemy division commander and his whole headquarters; the men involved each receiving a $25 bounty from their jubilant division commander.

Some idea of Patton's impact on the maneuvers can be gained from the official evaluations. The division was criticized for a high loss of tanks in one phase, for inadequate reconnaissance in another, for poor security and a disorganized river crossing at other times. Patton was faulted for spending too much time away from his headquarters. But the negatives were far outweighed by the umpires' consistent praise for the 2nd Armored as an aggressive, exceptionally well-commanded division.

The Tennessee maneuvers were a warm-up. The real test of the developing U.S. Army would come in the autumn, when the 2nd and 3rd Armies, twenty-seven divisions, took the field against each other in a mock war of a scale seldom matched in history. Intended in good part as a test of the new armored force, the Louisiana maneuvers were held in some of the Southwest's least promising tank country, a mix of swamps, rice fields, and second-growth pine forests. Second Armored was burned by well-sited antitank guns in a preliminary exercise. Patton set himself up for a fall in the second stage of the maneuver by overextending his division in an effort to gain the enemy rear. He was able to extract himself only by bending to the breaking point key rules involving the time needed to repair bridges and the lethality of antitank mine fields.

When the main maneuvers began on September 15, Patton, serving with the 2nd Army, suffered a third tactical blow when his division trains were overrun—by, let it be noted, the 1st Cavalry Division—and the 2nd Armored hopelessly pinned against the Red River. In 1940, Patton had offered his old friend Dwight Eisenhower a job as his chief of staff. Instead, Eisenhower received the same appointment with the 3rd Army, and his quick work contributed significantly to Patton's discomfiture.

It was the Louisiana maneuvers' final exercise, however, that carried forward the Patton legend. His division, now under the 3rd Army, executed a 400-mile flanking maneuver that brought him out on the 2nd Army's rear. Sidestepping antitank screens, overcoming flooded terrain and the collapse (real, not simulated) of a key bridge, and buying gas from small-town filling stations, the 2nd Armored put the rest of the 3rd Army into a position to win a victory so decisive that Army Chief of Ground Forces Lesley McNair ended the exercise five days ahead of schedule.

McNair, a firm proponent of antitank weapons, denied that Patton's performance had anything to do with his decision. Critics complained that Patton's enveloping maneuver had taken him well out of the maneuver area. One umpire noted that Patton's political connections made him impossible to handle. The War Department censured him for turning in dirty tanks when the maneuver ended. It added up to a laundry list of trivia.

Adhering to limits and scenarios was important; maneuvers were designed to test doctrine and equipment under controlled conditions, not provide opportunity for displays of personal *virtu*. Yet at seventh and last, Patton had underwritten his insouciant insistence that winning was all that mattered with a level of daring and initiative not seen in the U.S. Army since the Civil War. Patton had shown understanding of the operational and tactical importance of surprise. He had overcome unexpected challenges of weather and terrain. He had succeeded in intimidating his opponents to a degree not experienced since the days of Robert E. Lee; some said Patton's name alone was worth a full division.

For Chief of Staff George Marshall, what stood out was Patton's aggressiveness. Considered as an exercise in higher command, the Louisiana maneuvers had been a disappointment. Too many division and corps commanders, both regulars and National Guardsmen, lacked the physical vigor and the intellectual flexibility to keep pace with the kind of wide-open mobile operations in which Patton specialized. Three-fourths of the forty-two senior officers who went into Louisiana were relieved or transferred in the succeeding weeks. Patton and his division were also transferred—to the Carolinas, their third stage setting of the year.

The Carolina maneuvers held in mid-November pitted the 1st Army under Hugh Drum against a smaller force including both the Army's armored divisions. These maneuvers had a more specific agenda than their predecessors. The supporters of antitank weapons and doctrine argued that tank killers properly employed could neutralize armor, if not drive it from the field altogether. Drum, frustrated at having been bested by Marshall in the contest for Chief of Staff, both handled his command competently and fudged the rules to a degree that impressed even Patton. Nevertheless, Patton's divison showed to consistent advantage despite McNair–mandated instructions stacked artificially in favor of the antitank elements. Patton's reconnaissance battalion even "captured" Drum himself, and McNair was constrained to order the seething general's release so the exercise could continue.

More important than those kinds of bragging rights was the favorable impression Patton continued to make on the man who counted most: Marshall. A generation of young majors and colonels were beginning to emerge: Isaac White of the 2nd Armored's reconnaissance battalion; Robert Grow, who would move from staff work to division command; John "P." Wood, arguably the best of them all. But their places would be with the divisions now being activated. Patton, for the moment, stood alone among the senior officers not merely as a tactician but as a trainer and motivator of citizen soldiers. His 2nd Armored was obviously one of the best divisions in an Army still struggling for identity. When Patton thanked Marshall for his subsequent promotion to corps command, the Chief of Staff replied, "I had nothing to do with your selection; the 2nd Armored selected you."

Wider factors were involved as well. The Army's current planning for national mobilization projected an eventual force of around two hundred divisions. But even at this early stage, Marshall questioned whether America's manpower resources could sustain anywhere near such a force in the context of the requirements of the Navy and the developing Army Air Force, plus the demands of an economy that would be responsible for sustaining not only the United States, but its major allies. In the end, Marshall would accept what became known as the "ninety-division gamble": going to war with a bare minimum of ground combat forces, making up for mass with shock—the kind of shock George Patton seemed to be a developing master at delivering.

Patton's growing reputation did not mean he had a free hand. General Chaffee's death in August left command of the Armored Force vacant. Marshall replaced him with a West Point classmate of Patton's: Jacob L. Devers. Devers, a Marshall protégé currently commanding an infantry division, was an artilleryman by branch, and something of an outside choice. His selection correspondingly affirmed the "joint" nature of the armored force, demonstrating its senior positions were not merely to be divided between former infantrymen and former troopers.

Devers's appointment also marked a break with the force's prewar roots. Scott and the 1st Armored Division's John Magruder were soon retired. Of the seniors, only Patton remained, and in the summer of 1941, Devers paid him a visit. Years later, Devers described an after-dinner discussion on Armored Force policy that he initiated to make a point. When he asked, "Are you going to play ball or aren't you?" Patton stood up, saluted, and said "Yes, boss." "And that was the end of it," reflected Devers. "He was a good soldier—always was."

Patton was also not a loose cannon when it counted. In January

1942, in the aftermath of Pearl Harbor, he was assigned to command the I Armored Corps. Division command represents about the limit of most general officers' personal and professional capacities: their ability to influence large bodies of men and command complex organizations. Corps command has been another situation altogether, especially in Western armies where the corps in both world wars was usually a tactical unit with divisions assigned as needed.

Changing composition and larger scale adversely affected two key elements of Patton's effectiveness: his hands-on approach to problem-solving and his cultivated idiosyncratic style. The usual response involved rounding off, toning down, and playing it safe. The avoidance of risk-taking so frequently ascribed to U.S. senior officers was arguably less a question of limited capacities than of a command style designed to confuse or irritate subordinates as little as possible. For Patton, the challenge involved translating his approach to a higher level. He continued to read comprehensively, assimilating virtually everything available in English on the subject of mobile warfare, whether in books or newspapers. He also benefited from a decision to create a new training ground for the Armored Force. One of the obvious conclusions of the 1941 maneuvers was that even relatively unsettled areas east of the Mississippi could not be adapted for optimal training in the kinds of maneuver and exploitation operations expected of armored divisions. That left the West—specifically the Southwest, where the federal government controlled much of the land and the local population was more likely to welcome Army payrolls than denounce ecosystem damage. Ordered to evaluate possible training sites, Patton recommended a desolate section of southern California with nothing but open ground and far horizons. In March 1942, the first units of the I Armored Corps left for their new home.

Given the actual conditions under which most of the Armored Force engaged in Northwest Europe, the War Department might have been better advised to keep its training areas in more built-up areas. Patton's selection of a training site reflected his emphasis on toughening troops physically and mentally. To his officers he said, "If you can work successfully here . . . it will be no difficulty at all to kill the assorted sons of bitches you meet in any other country." He continued to maintain high visibility, living in the base camp alongside his men, participating in every exercise, and using every kind of vehicle in the corps' inventory to maintain contact with units in the field. He rode all ranks hard and put them away wet. Junior officers in particular felt his lash, usually for a lack of the initiative Patton more and more regarded as the key to successful armored operations.

Patton in the desert regularly wore what he called his "war face," a near-perpetual scowl, to make the point that war was not a subject for laughter. His language grew more sulfurous—a teaching device, he explained. Swearing "helped to get the point across" in preparing American young men to be killers, and wars were only won by killing the enemy. A more developed justification might have discussed the value of taboo-breaking: men raised in closed, respectable societies frequently found the language of war, its profanity and obscenity, a threshold whose crossing brings them into an entirely different world—one where the killer, in another of Patton's phrases, can be "the noblest work of God," and where the Scriptural injunction "thou shalt not kill" was dismissed with a reference to David slaying Goliath.

American soldiers during World War II responded to battle in a broad spectrum of ways, but few—very few—developed into heroic warriors on the Patton model. Those who did were frequently regarded by their fellows in the same way feral dogs shrink from the half-wolf that joins their pack. Never in history has so relatively and absolutely large an armed force, citizen or professional, fought so far from its own borders, in a war that was not obviously its fight. Whatever its desires, Japan could not seriously threaten, much less invade, the U.S. mainland. The danger incorporated in Nazi Germany's "Z Plan" for a huge ocean-going navy could only be manifested in a later conflict. The U-boat campaign in U.S. waters during the "Happy Time" of 1942 did not arouse enough public concern to secure a comprehensive blackout of the coastline cities.

The war waged by the United States was also characterized by its absence of ideology. Nazi Germany had race and the Soviet Union, class. Great Britain, the weary titan, had fear; and Japan had nationalism. America had—the Four Freedoms? Few knew what they were. The Holocaust? A story on the back pages of a *New York Times* even fewer read. Americans' collective indifference to high causes was the bane of the Office of War Information and the burden of German POW interrogators.

To the extent that Americans in uniform had a "world-view" of the war, it was as a job to be done, as quickly and completely as possible.

From the beginning of the great Allied counterattacks of 1942, U.S. battle casualties overall may have been risibly low by German or Soviet standards. But American rifle companies in the European Theater of Operations (ETO) consistently took casualties of 200, 300 percent, and kept coming. The Army Air Forces never aborted a bombardment mission because of risk or loss. Marines climbed the cliffs of Peleliu when it was clear that the operation's purpose had evaporated. The records show desertion, straggling, hanging back—but no refusals of duty. Even the much-abused 5307th Composite Unit (Provisional), better known as Merrill's Marauders, as jerked around and as far from home a formation as any the United States fielded, staggered forward as long as its survivors could stand up.

As many as fifty thousand Germans were executed for "military" offenses by the Wehrmacht during World War II. The Red Army shot ten thousand of its soldiers at Stalingrad alone. Throughout the war, one—one—U.S. serviceman was executed for desertion—not because desertion did not exist, and certainly not because of the armed forces' principled hostility to capital punishment, but because the ultimate deterrent was considered unneeded. The typical American serviceman quit only when he broke and wound up in a hospital or a psychiatric ward.

The U.S. Army's steepest learning curves nevertheless involved hardening. Arguably the hardest lesson American soldiers had to learn was that they were in the war for the duration, and the only way home was through the enemy. To most Americans, even those in uniform, the Germans remained throughout the war an abstract adversary. After Pearl Harbor and Bataan, American hatred was focused eastward, against Japan. Germans fighting Americans, moreover, as a rule did not behave like Nazis were supposed to. They followed most of the conventional rules on such crucial issues as respecting the Red Cross and treatment of POWs enough of the time to enable the processing of violations as part of the "filth of war."

Considered in these wider contexts, Patton's copybook maxims were useful rules of thumb for developing the toughness essential for coping with battle. Do not fear being killed, Patton urged. Your chances are

worse driving a car. Make the mind dominate a body that always demands submission to its weaknesses. Never give up; never defend; never
worry about defeat. Attack always; keep moving and never let the enemy
rest. Words, yes—but not empty words for a green Army that would, in
a matter of months, face action against an enemy far more unforgiving of
mistakes than was General George Patton.

VI

In the summer of 1940, the Third Reich's public relations apparatus em-
braced Erwin Rommel with an enthusiasm hitherto denied any senior
Army officer. Rommel's tanks "carve long bloodstained trails across the
map of Europe like the scalpel of a surgeon," wrote one commentator—
exactly the metaphor sought in a Third Reich at the zenith of its power
and prestige. Rommel and the 7th Panzer were summoned to re-create
their crossing of the Somme for the major propaganda film *Victory in the
West*, with French Senegalese POWs temporarily released to act as extras.
Rommel enjoyed playing the role of director and discussing his plans to
write a tanker's counterpart to *Infantry Attacks*. He basked in the admiration of junior officers who took advantage of temporary peace to make
a pilgrimage to the 7th Panzer's headquarters. Invited to report personally to Hitler, he hoped in vain for a higher grade of the Knight's Cross and
settled for a briefing on the success of the air campaign against Britain.

   The Ghost Division was scheduled to play a major role in Operation
Sea Lion, the projected cross-channel invasion. Rommel spent an increasing amount of time training his men in embarkation and debarka-
tion techniques and was correspondingly frustrated when the operation
was cancelled and the 7th Panzer sent south to Bordeaux. He was overlooked in the spate of promotions made in that summer of victory; not
until January 1941 did he become a major general. His public response
was to complain of the continuing influence of a General Staff clique that
understood better how to further its own interests than to wage modern
war. He also prepared an elaborate illustrated version of the 7th Panzer's
war diary and sent it to Hitler directly. "You can be proud of your
achievements," the Fuehrer responded.

Although unlikely to be influenced at any time during his career by souvenir photo albums, Hitler nevertheless was developing plans for his ambitious outsider. Italian dictator Benito Mussolini had remained neutral in the war's early stages, entering the conflict only in June 1940. An Italian army spectacularly ill prepared for modern warfare suffered a humiliating defeat against France's Alpine defenses. The Italian air contingent dispatched to the Battle of Britain performed so poorly it had to be withdrawn. Mussolini, however, was primarily concerned with establishing an independent imperium in the Mediterranean. Refusing Hitler's offers of assistance, he embarked on a disastrous campaign against Greece, an air offensive against the island of Malta that the Royal Air Force managed to stand off with a few obsolescent fighters, and an invasion of British-ruled Egypt that stuck fast only a few miles from the border.

Churchill responded by committing an increasing amount of the scarce resources Britain possessed after Dunkirk to the Mediterranean. He was desperate for a victory, both for the sake of domestic morale and to improve America's confidence in British capacity to endure and prevail. Churchill's initial refusal to consider negotiations with Hitler had in good part reflected his belief in the prospect of rapid, large-scale U.S. help for his beleaguered island. That illusion died hard, and Churchill eagerly seized upon the Mediterranean as a theater where Britain might confront its enemies at relatively favorable odds. In December 1940, a carefully prepared attack commanded by Major General Richard O'Connor overran and destroyed the Italian forward positions, captured the port city of Tobruk, and sent what remained of Italy's North African forces flying in rout westward along the coast, toward Tripoli.

In the autumn of 1940, Admiral Erich Raeder had urged breaking Britain's power in the Mediterranean immediately, before initiating war with Russia. Hitler initially was attracted by the prospects of beginning his conquest of world empire cheaply, with a detour through the Middle Sea. Now the disproportionate successes the British gained on their military shoestring encouraged his thinking first, that Britain was Germany's real and most dangerous enemy; and second, that the best way of convincing Britain to conclude peace was through a strategy of the indirect approach: striking Britain's "continental sword" from her hand by overrunning the Soviet Union.

Attacking Russia played to German strengths. Waging mobile war against a continental enemy was something the army and the Luftwaffe knew how to do. The insouciance with which Germany's armed forces approached the Russian campaign has frequently been exaggerated. The generals were well aware of the size of Russian armies, the abundance of her natural resources, and the vastness of her spaces. They were also confident that they had developed a way of war that would neutralize these advantages, forcing the Red Army and the Soviet state into a paradigm they could not match.

The metaphor of bringing a gun to a knife fight was dominant in German planning for Barbarossa. The Mediterranean, on the other hand, was unfamiliar and uncongenial ground, especially to the soldiers. Whatever their limits as strategists, German generals understood that Mediterranean operations must be joint operations, with air and sea elements playing cooperative rather than subordinate roles. Warmaking there would require thinking out of the box to a far greater degree than had the 1940 campaign. When the two theaters were compared, Russia seemed the better bet because it was emotionally and intellectually familiar—the challenge involved scale, not concepts.

Hitler reacted to the Italian debacle with a degree of that malice the Germans call *Schadenfreude*. His immediate diplomatic interests in the region involved encouraging support for Germany's Atlantic ambitions on the part of Vichy France and Falangist Spain and attracting Balkan support for the developing attack on the Soviet Union that was the core of his strategic planning. Neither end was best served by Italian-initiated upheavals that challenged the status quo by open-ended claims to enlarged spheres of influence.

They were served even worse by open-ended military catastrophes. The Italian defeat in Greece created opportunities for Britain to negotiate a Balkan front and support it with a minimum investment of stationing planes on Greek bases. The oil fields of Rumania were only the most obvious potential target. If the Italians were driven from North Africa, the stresses on British shipping would be reduced by the resulting opening of the Mediterranean. The French North African colonies might reconsider their allegiance to Vichy. Italy would be subject to air and naval strikes of the kind that had recently crippled its battle fleet in Taranto, and face the consequences of a loss of prestige that could potentially lead to the collapse of the Fascist system itself. German diplomats and generals already had no illusions and little optimism where their ally was concerned; they saw few prospects for an unaided recovery. Hitler, who never forgot that Italy's adherence to the Axis depended on Mussolini's continuation in power, grew correspondingly determined to take action.

As early as July 1940, the High Command had suggested assigning a Panzer division to North Africa and sent a top armored expert, Major General Wilhelm Ritter von Thoma, to evaluate the situation. Thoma, who had worked extensively with the Italians in Spain, reported that any serious mobile operations in North Africa were best carried out by Germans alone and would require at least four Panzer divisions. Even though the German armored force was in the process of being increased from ten divisions to twenty by converting infantry divisions and reducing the number of tanks in each formation, such a proposal had no chance even had the Italians supported it enthusiastically.

Germany's initial Mediterranean commitment instead involved a minimum ante: transferring the antishipping specialists of the X Air Corps from Norway to the Mediterranean. As the Italian situation continued to deteriorate, the commitment of ground forces seemed necessary. The Wehrmacht High Command projected the main relief effort for the Balkans: a large-scale mechanized offensive to be mounted in the spring of 1941. The buildup would take time, but the operation offered three advantages: taking Greece out of the war once for all, intimidating the other Balkan states into supporting Germany, and keeping the forces involved close enough to the Soviet Union to be available for the projected invasion later in the year.

German intervention in North Africa was originally intended as no more than a minimum-scale holding operation. On January 11, 1941, Hitler ordered the organizing under the code name Operation Sunflower (*Sonnenblume*) of a *Sperrveband,* a blocking force, for dispatch to Tripoli with the mission of containing the British while the Balkan offensive took shape. This was a far cry from even the single Panzer division suggested earlier. Its title, the 5th Light Division, was more hope than reality; the formation resembled nothing so much as a scratch brigade. The continuing, rapid deterioration of Italy's position in the theater indicated to both

Hitler and his generals that something more was needed. Sunflower's order of battle was increased by a full Panzer division, the 15th, still in the process of organization, and the African Special Service Division (Division z. b. V. Afrika). The latter formation was later retitled the 90th Light Division; for convenience and clarity, it will be referred to by that designation.

The "Blocking Force" also rejoiced in a new title: the *Deutsches Afrika Korps* (German Africa Corps). And a corps needed a corps commander. Major General Hans von Funck, sent to Libya in January 1941 to reassess the situation, was the initial choice, but his reports were too pessimistic for that kind of mission. The Panzer arm's tested senior division and corps commanders were penciled in for assignments in the forthcoming invasion of Russia. Hitler briefly considered Erich von Manstein for the African adventure, but rejected him in favor of another general, junior to most of his contemporaries but with a proven ability to inspire his men—an ability Hitler considered essential in demanding climatic conditions. On February 12, 1941, Erwin Rommel was summoned to Berlin. He left with an appointment as commander in chief of German troops in Libya.

Seen from the perspective of the Axis alliance, it seemed a bad joke. Rommel had made most of his initial reputation not merely defeating but humiliating Italians. His ego and his tactlessness were remarkable even by German army standards. Yet on other grounds, Rommel and North Africa were an ideal match. Rommel had proven himself an outsider even in the young and flexible community of the armored forces. His ability and his potential were alike subjects of debate. No one suggested his services might eventually be more valuable against the Soviet Union; no one put in a particular bid for him as a subordinate. If he proved a flash in the pan, the Italians could pay any military bills he might run up. Hitler himself seems initially to have made his choice as much on grounds of Rommel's availability as from any intuitive sense that he was giving a wider stage to an unacknowledged genius. He would proclaim Rommel as the Third Reich's "hero in the sun" only in the aftermath of one of history's most spectacular runs of battlefield victories.

5

ENCOUNTERS

THE Mediterranean theater is generally dismissed by students of World War II as having little value to either the Allies or the Axis. Conventional wisdom describes its importance as having been exaggerated because the Mediterranean was the last opportunity for a declining British empire to play an independent, leading role; because its complexity invites speculation about alternative solutions; and not least because of the dramatic element generated by the presence and performance of Erwin Rommel.

I

Rommel, as surprised as everyone else in the army by his appointment, landed in Tripoli on February 12, 1941. On the way, he stopped in Rome to meet with the Italian chief of staff, and in Sicily to discuss plans with the Luftwaffe commander. Hitler insisted that the Italians be treated as equals, and Rommel understood the central importance of air support in the kind of operation he proposed to begin. The second meeting was prophetic in another way. When informed that the Luftwaffe had been asked not to bomb Benghazi because so much of the city was Italian property, Rommel appealed directly to Hitler. A telephone call, and the bombers were authorized to take off. It was by no means the last time Rommel would stage an end run around obstacles, political or military.

Rommel was initially a general without troops. Not until mid-March would the 5th Light Division arrive; the balance of the corps would take even longer. He seemed as well a general without opportunities. The Italian theater command made clear that the Germans were welcome, but as backup to their own reorganizing and reequipping forces. These were unwitting beneficiaries of one of Churchill's most controversial strategic decisions: to shut down operations in that theater temporarily in favor of dispatching an expeditionary force to Greece. O'Connor, not pleased at losing most of his desert-experienced units, nevertheless recognized that his forces were at the end of their logistical tether and believed his enemies sufficiently disorganized that he would have time to season white-kneed replacements arriving from all over the empire.

Rommel had an entirely different set of ideas. Studying maps and intelligence reports, observing the zone of operations from a light airplane, he was convinced the best defense was a deployment not around Tripoli but forward, on the Gulf of Sirte. When his first German battalion arrived in Tripoli, Rommel paraded it through the city and sent it east. Two days later, its armored cars tangled with a patrol of the King's Dragoon Guards. They were followed by the rest of their division, then eventually the balance of the DAK, as ships arrived and unloaded. "The desert awaits us!" Rommel greeted one group of newcomers. "We are about to embark on a great safari." "Heya safari!" someone shouted in response. Others took it up, and the Afrika Korps had its slogan and its war cry. Uttered with enthusiasm, irony, and every emotion in between, it remains the signature of Germany's war in Africa.

The spectacular early successes of the Afrika Korps led many Allied journalists to describe it as an elite formation, specially trained and equipped for desert conditions. The closest the men of the Afrika Korps came to being specially screened was a fairly cursory physical examination evaluating whether their level of fitness was suitable for service in Africa. Not surprisingly, most of them passed. The men of the 5th Light and 15th Panzer did not even have the screening. Their medical preparation consisted of cholera and typhus inoculations. Their equipment was Wehrmacht standard, with the addition of a few hundred sun helmets—

most of them soon discarded in favor of field caps—and a few thousand gallons of camouflage paint in varying shades of brown. Their standing orders prescribed which of Tripoli's many brothels they were to use. Their order of battle represented a near-random cross-section of the army's mobile forces.

The 15th Panzer Division was the most conventional, organized to 1941 standards of two tank and four motorized battalions, a motorcycle battalion, and a reconnaissance battalion plus divisional troops. Its 8th Panzer Regiment had been transferred in as part of the general reorganization of the mobile forces. The rest of the division was new to armored service, having begun converting from the 33rd Infantry Divison only in November. The 5th Light, later retitled the 21st Panzer, drew its mechanized elements primarily from the 3rd Panzer Division: a two-battalion tank regiment an antitank battalion, a reconnaissance battalion, a motorized artillery battalion, and some support elements. Fifth Light also included a rifle regiment headquarters controlling two motorized machinegun battalions, assigned from army troops. From army troops came as well another antitank battalion, with French guns on self-propelled mounts, and a couple antiaircraft battalions, including a dozen 88s. The 90th Light was a mixed bag of independent infantry and antitank battalions that evolved into a pivot and support force for the Panzers, whose mobility and firepower made it formidable alike in attack and defense. The 90th was also the most colorful of Rommel's outfits, unconventional in dress and easygoing in discipline by German standards and eventually including a regiment of men transferred (willingly or not) from a French Foreign Legion anxious to be rid of its German elements. Thee three divisions would remain the heart of the Afrika Korps until its destruction.

By this time, the basic German tank was the Mark III, the backbone of the armored force in 1941–1942. At slightly more than twenty tons, it was classified as a medium. Like its stablemates, it was fast, mechanically reliable, and carried a radio—the last proving indispensable in North African conditions. An original and inadequate 37-millimeter gun had by the time of deployment to Africa been replaced by a 5-centimeter, 42-caliber weapon, which later gave way to a 60-caliber mount, essentially the same weapon as the 5-centimeter antitank gun that proved such a formidable long-term enemy to British armor. Each of the Afrika Korps's original Panzer regiments had a theoretical strength of 71 Mark III's, 20 Mark IV close-support tanks with the short 75-millimeter "cigar butt," and still no fewer than 45 Mark II's useful primarily for scouting.

On paper, the DAK resembled the kind of ad hoc mix of men and units that British commanders in the desert constantly complained of over the next two years. But the Germans were riding the crest of a wave of victories. They had confidence in themselves and their officers, their training, and their doctrine. Their divisions were teams of specialist experts trained to fight together, combining and recombining as the situation changed. This system of "battle groups" was enhanced by the German practice of providing every unit, down to companies, with the organic specialists and supporting weapons needed to perform routine missions independently. Assembling them was like working with a child's set of Leggos: individual pieces once fastened together would hold even if the final construction was awkward.

The British regimental system by contrast encouraged compartmentalization, with not merely infantry, armor, and artillery, but different units of the same arm of service going their own ways. Desert humor had it that the only way two British regiments could be sure of cooperating was if their commanders had slept with each other's wives. Relatively few of the officers and men who faced Rommel's rapidly assembling force had had any experience of the German way of war. Most of the veterans of the 1940 campaign were in England. Most of the pamphlets and manuals describing how the Germans fought were still being written; the doctrines to counter them were in the process of development. Not until 1944 would the British army emerge from behind the tactical curve and be in a position to fight the German enemy that existed, as opposed to the one in the field a year earlier.

The DAK had one further advantage: its commander. Rommel did not take long to decide that something had happened, that the rhythm of British operations had been interrupted. He proposed to disrupt that rhythm even further. On March 11, the 5th Light Division's Panzer regiment disembarked and started toward the front. Rommel benefited unwittingly from an apparent success on the part of British intelligence. ULTRA, the decoding service that for most of the war read most of the important German electronic mail, intercepted a direct order not to undertake any significant offensive action until the 15th Panzer Division became available in May. The British at the front drew a long breath while Rommel flew back to Germany, where he received the Oak Leaves to his Knight's Cross and confirmation that the Afrika Korps was a blocking force, intended to boost Italian morale for a minimum investment of resources.

Ordered to play it safe, instead, on March 31, Rommel opened a general offensive. His Italian superiors had given him two of their infantry divisions, Brescia and Pavia. In theory, these and their counterparts that would later serve under Rommel had enough organic motor vehicles to move about half their men at one time. In practice, the number was always small enough to restrict mobility to a foot pace. Rommel also had the Ariete Armored Division, with an assigned strength of around a hundred light and medium tanks that so far had proved vulnerable to almost anything the British threw at them. The Italian contribution nevertheless enabled Rommel to attack in three sectors: on the left a drive down the coast road; on the right a sweep into the desert aimed at cutting the British line of retreat; and in the center the *Schwerpunkt,* with most of the German armor driving for Msus and Mechili.

Rommel's blow caught the British between wind and water, with neither a developed system of forward positions, enough reserves to organize a defense in depth, nor a doctrine for managing large-scale retreats. Rommel projected the same demonic energy he had shown in France, taking frequent advantage of Axis air superiority to keep in touch with his leading elements by light plane. When told that the 5th Light would have to suspend operations for four days, he ordered the division to devote its entire truck fleet to bringing fuel to the forward units. The improvisation worked—not least because of one of the Wehrmacht's humbler artifacts, the robust five-gallon gasoline cans that could be stacked and jostled without springing the leaks endemic to their smaller British counterparts.

When O'Connor and his field commander Lieutenant General Sir Philip Neame were captured, theater commander Sir Archibald Wavell took over the conduct of operations from his Cairo headquarters. German senior officers were able to lead from the front, thanks to the elaborate radio networks they enjoyed. German mobile formations were all-arms groups—Mark III's and IV's, artillery, antitank guns, and motorized infantry—able to support each other as needed, sometimes weaving battle tapestries that baffled their counterparts, more often bypassing pockets of resistance and driving on into the British rear.

It was deep penetration on a level not seen even in France. All did not go well. Columns became lost in broken, poorly mapped terrain, or deceived by mirages. Engines overheated in 120-degree temperatures. Sandstorms slowed rates of march. Rommel himself nearly landed next to a British column by mistake. But Benghazi fell on April 3. The British reeled back, survivors and stragglers threatening to swamp still-organized units. Rommel had returned to Africa with the intention of mounting a limited attack. On April 10, he issued an order setting the Axis objective as the Suez Canal.

The vision of a great captain or the vainglory of a shortsighted one? A month earlier, Rommel had hosted a gala performance of "Victory in the West" and told his guests that he hoped the day would come for a showing of "Victory in Africa"—with the unspoken addition that the second lead would move up to a star's role. There was no question that within weeks, Rommel had imprinted the Afrika Korps just as he had the 7th Panzer Division. He had demonstrated the same omnipresence, the same unconcern for danger, the same physical hardness, the same interest in his men's welfare, that he had in France. Rommel was hard in other ways as well: a ruthless driver free with threats of court-martial or relief from command. At the same time, he was constantly teaching, showing officers from lieutenants to colonels better ways of getting it done.

Even more than in Europe, Rommel manifested a situational awareness, both geographic and tactical, so finely honed that men spoke of a sixth sense. A soldier of his escort describes Rommel as time after time arriving without warning in some crucial sector, standing up in his car, shouting "Attack! Attack!" and inspiring even more desperate efforts. Perhaps more than anything else, this confirmed his place as leader of the Afriksa Korps as well as its commander. To the Germans, born in a country where everything was always green, used to clear landmarks and short distances, North Africa was a completely alien environment in every way. Someone who seemed to master it with Rommel's ease would attract followers instead of subordinates apart from any military qualities he might possess.

Tanks and trucks, however, did not respond to charismatic leadership. The Panzers' air filters were a weak spot, unable to block the fine desert sand with the result that engines seized up and had to be replaced. Sprints and shock absorbers gave way on the rough and roadless going. As maintenance personnel complained, Rommel began acquiring his reputation as a general either ignorant in principle of logistics or culpably careless in supervising them. In a wider context, the German officer corps's tactical and operational proficiency becomes a manifestation of tunnel vision, with caste pride or misunderstood professionalism relegating administration to those unfit to command troops in combat.

Rommel, in fact, was at the center of a paradox. The development of the internal-combustion engine made offensives in depth possible and improved the flexibility of supply systems. But the dependence of motor vehicles on fuel and maintenance imposed a limit of around three hundred kilometers on gasoline-powered advances. Nor had the Wehrmacht achieved anything like full conversion to motorization. For most of its operational life, the army depended heavily on railroads at the strategic end, horses at the tactical, with trucks more or less filling the operational gap.

A cursory examination of the Afrika Korps's order of battle shows an emphasis on motor vehicles and motorized weapons at the expense of manpower and horsepower that was unique even in the German army's mobile forces. Even before Rommel's first offensive, the motor transport capactiy required by the Afrika Korps was proportionally ten times that allocated for the projected invasion of Russia. Rommel saw as well as anyone on either side of the war that victory in the desert depended on supply. He also believed that if every subordinate shared his sense of urgency, then problems of any kind were more likely to be favorably resolved. Those who did not accept and internalize that attitude seldom remained long in key positions. Rommel, perhaps reflecting his own lack of staff training, believed staffs were by definition cautious: prone to address operational questions with sharp pencils, prone to see difficulties instead of opportunities. Instead of accepting the estimates of the administrators, Rommel argued that a commander should form his own evaluations of the logistically feasible and couch his demands accordingly. There would be grumbling and complaint—but what else was new? When the 5th Light Division reported it required a two-day halt for what its commander called essential maintenance, Rommel replied that "every man and vehicle that can move, must move"—with the strong implication that if necessary, they would do so under a new CO.

The clearest expression of Rommel's position came when, at the end of a long discussion emphasizing the need for caution in North Africa, Chief of Staff Franz Halder asked Rommel how many troops he would need to conquer Egypt and the Suez Canal. Rommel replied that another two Panzer corps should do. Halder than asked how Rommel proposed to supply that force. Rommel replied that was Halder's problem.

Rommel and Halder did not care for each other. Yet Rommel was expressing the mentality of the German army as reorganized after 1933. The General Staff system in the Third Reich resembled a "troop staff" (*Truppenstab*) much more closely than the institution of the days of Moltke and Schlieffen. The army's rapid expansion encouraged a more pragmatic, hands-on ethic than had been the case prior to the Great War. The pace Hitler demanded encouraged emphasis on the operational side of war. Planning, in turn, revolved around operational considerations; the logisticians were called in afterward. The material, Halder declared after the war, must serve the spiritual; quartermaster must never hamper the operational concept.

The development of the Reichswehr's motor transport service into a fighting branch had removed the institution most concerned with developing a modern approach to logistics. Throughout the war, supply officers remained the "red-headed stepchildren" of staffs at all levels. Frequently reservists, their rank and status placed them lower on the scale of authority than their colleagues charged with operational matters. Indeed, the very term "logistics" was a Western importation into the West German Bundeswehr. During the war, the terms used were *Versorgung* and *Nachschub,* both meaning "supply," and both with the narrow context of keeping forward units haversacks, ammunition pouches, nosebags, and gas tanks reasonably full.

Rommel, in short, was well within the World War II German army's paradigm in his approach to supply matters. He also understood from the campaign's beginning that he had relatively little control of his logistics. Germany was a guest in the theater, depending on Italian goodwill and Italian abilities to sustain a small expeditionary force. Particularly in the months before his legend took hold, Rommel's influence on his allies was marginal. He might be able to influence tactical-level issues, as he did with fuel shortages, where he proved a master at making gasoline from captured British dumps. Otherwise, he was constrained to rely on his German superiors—and the best way to get their attention was to remind them forcibly and constantly of their own axiom that administrations must never impede operations.

The operational side of the campaign was giving Rommel enough cause for concern. Despite his alleged indifference to logistics, he wanted Tobruk—a port that would provide an ideal advance base for that drive on the Suez Canal Rommel had proclaimed as his ultimate objective. Rommel proposed to "bounce" Tobruk, capturing it by a *coup de main*— or rather a *coup de Panzer.* That decision was, in turn, based on his knowledge that Tobruk's fixed defenses were as formidable as anything he had encountered in France. The alternative to a siege was to take advantage of the presumed British disorganization and demoralization and overrun the place in one quick rush.

On April 12, Rommel sent in the Afrika Korps. The garrison at that stage was mostly Australian. The 9th Division began life as a scratch formation of leftover brigades and battalions. Its training was incomplete when it withdrew into Tobruk's somewhat dilapidated defenses. But its mission did not require tactical sophistication. The Aussies put the Germans to school at close quarters, containing their initial break-ins and inflicting heavy casualties on tanks and infantry. Rommel, who believed the Australians were fighting a rear-guard action as a preliminary to evacuation by sea, clashed again with the 5th Light's CO, who said—correctly— that the ships in the aerial photos were bringing in reinforcements. Rommel responded by taking personal command of a full-scale attack on the 14th. He came away with a bloody nose. Coordination among armor, infantry, and artillery collapsed, with the tanks running into a nest of field guns and losing half of the three dozen vehicles committed to the assault.

The 8th Machine Gun Battalion, spearhead of a half-dozen victorious attacks, was cut off and almost wiped out, losing four hundred of the five hundred men who crossed the line of departure.

Rommel described himself as "furious," blaming the tank commanders for leaving the infantry in the lurch and blaming the Italians for failing to advance at all. A staff officer on a fact-finding tour reported privately to the army High Command that the Afrika Korps could not take further head-down attacks against the Australians: ". . . tough and hard opponents as individual fighters, highly skilled in defence . . . cold-blooded and skilled in in-fighting . . . and capable of standing hardships of all kinds."

On April 16, Rommel directed another abortive attack with elements of the Trento and Ariete Divisions. It proved a fiasco, with many of the Italian tanks breaking down before they could be knocked out and large numbers of the infantrymen surrendering to the Austrailians without a fight. A few days later, the Italians provided plans of the defenses they had constructed around Tobruk. Rommel decided the better part of valor after all was to blockade the fortress with Italian infantry while withdrawing his mechanized troops for mobile operations. During the changeover, on April 27, a High Command representative arrived to evaluate the situation.

General Friedrich Paulus was close to Rommel's personal and professional opposite as could be found in the German army. Cultivated, urbane, and polite, he was a quintessential staff officer who played a key role in planning Operation Barbarossa. He spent two weeks in North Africa and reported that Rommel was a headstrong field soldier whose limited perspective might well encourage the High Command to divert forces from the decisive campaign against Russia. Instead, Paulus recommended shortening the Afrika Korps's supply lines by withdrawing—a move that would also improve the lot of the soldiers, which Paulus found appalling.

Pending a decision, Paulus authorized Rommel to try for Tobruk again, this time using elements of the newly arrived 15th Panzer in an attack that began on April 30. German engineers made a breach in the wire, and infantry followed on foot, in a classic example of the soft-spot infiltration tactics developed in the Great War and cultivated by the Reichswehr. Bypassing strong points, the forward elements advanced quickly. But the Australians kept their nerve and their heads, pinning down the supports with heavy and accurate fire. The tanks, advancing on their own, got as far as three miles into the defenses before running into mine-fields that blew the tracks off all but two of the two dozen that were still running.

In an example of the small-unit leadership that made the Afrika Korps what it was, the tank company commander ordered his disabled vehicles to keep firing, brought up infantry and engineers in support, and managed to salvage all but five of his tanks. Another wave of tanks and infantry got even farther before running into a line of twenty-five-pounder field guns and an armored counterattack. By the end of the day, half of the seventy tanks the 15th Panzer sent into the fight had been knocked out. More than 1,200 infantry were down. And the 15th Panzer needed a new commander. Major General Heinrich von Prittwitz und Gaffron died in the front line when his command vehicle took a direct hit from an antitank gun.

It took several more days of heavy fighting before Rommel decided that the Afrika Korps and its Italian allies lacked the strength to carry To-bruk by assault and would have to resort to a siege. At least that would give the large number of unmotorized Italian troops a useful mission. Rommel described himself as "extremely annoyed"—not least because Paulus, before returning to Berlin, forbade any more attacks until sup-plies and reinforcements could be brought up. But Rommel was not merely suffering from bruised ego. The losses of the German infantry par-ticularly disturbed him. "The finest fighting man," he wrote, "has no value in mobile warfare without tanks, guns, and vehicles . . . This is not the case with position warfare, . . . which is always a struggle for the de-struction of men."

In analyzing his defeat, Rommel noted the inadequate training of many of his infantry, who had been sent to the front from depot forma-tions. He noted the collective inferiority complex of the Italians—a logi-cal consequence of poor armament, training, and leadership. He noted the negative effects of the separation of command between the army and the air force. He even commented on the shortage of necessary supplies. He did not refer to his own ill-advised stubbornness in pursuing an objective that, if it was not gained in the first attempt, was unlikely to be achieved at all.

As Paulus had reported to the army High Command, the central Axis problem in North Africa was logistics. Each month the Afrika Korps needed 24,000 tons of supplies to maintain itself, and double that for an offensive. The Luftwaffe needed 9,000 tons, the Italians 63,000 tons. The port of Tripoli could only handle 45,000 tons a month under optimal conditions—assuming the Italian merchant marine could bring it across the Mediterranean and the Italian navy could protect the cargo ships and tankers. Neither was certain. The Italians refused to send ships forward to Benghazi because of the threat of British air attacks, which cut the port's theoretical capacity of 2,700 tons a day to less than 800. Coastal convoys were vulnerable for the same reason. That left the land route from Tripoli—an eleven-hundred-mile stretch of dubious-quality highway that the Germans and the Italians together lacked the trucks to exploit. Apart from limited numbers, European vehicles were not designed for the kind of long-haul work in demanding environments that was the norm in the United States. Breakdown figures were correspondingly high as suplies piled up on the docks.

On May 11, Halder noted in his diary that Rommel, through his disobedience of orders, had created circumstances that ignored the possibilities of supply. "Rommel,"the chief of staff concluded, "is not equal to the situation." Rommel was aware of his superiors' lack of confidence and knew the British would not remain passive indefinitely. By now his men were subsisting on Italian rations whose principal component was poorly preserved beef in cans labeled "AM." The Afrika Korps Landsers promptly translated this as "Alter Mann" (old man) or "Asinus Mussolini" (Mussolini's donkey, in the polite version). It was hot enough that on one occasion Rommel sought—as a publicity stunt, and vainly—to fry eggs on a tank. He also tightened his grip on the Afrika Korps's command. Fifth Light Division in particular underwent a purge. The division CO, the commander of its Panzer regiment, and a number of junior officers were relieved, both for cause and *pour encourager les autres*.

The 5th Light's Brigadier General Johannes Streich later claimed Rommel told him he was too concerned for his troops and was rendered speechless by Streich's reply that he could think of no higher compliment. The exchange, like most reports of such encounters, probably owed something to the narrator's self-protective memory. Rommel did not judge victory by casualty lists. He was, however, convinced that speed and shock might cost lives in the beginning but would ultimately save them in the long run. Any subordinate who failed to act accordingly was at corresponding risk of his job.

Doubted by superiors not at all sorry to see Hitler's protégé fall on his face, coping with an uncertain supply system, and adjusting to new commanders in both of his principal formations (Prittwitz's replacement was wounded shortly after taking over and had to be replaced), Rommel was not in the best position to launch a new offensive. Nevertheless, as the fight for Tobruk died down, he began shifting German and Italian elements of his command eastward, to the Italian-Egyptian frontier. And as the Germans butted heads with Tobruk and Rommel with his subordinates, Wavell prepared to relieve the fortress and deal with the threat posed by the new Axis commander.

He was under heavy pressure from Churchill who, informed of Paulus's reports to Berlin by ULTRA, was convinced the Axis troops were vulnerable to a full-scale counterattack. So convinced was the prime minister that he dispatched a convoy, codenamed "Tiger," through the Mediterranean in defiance of the threat from aircraft and submarines, instead of the longer but safer route around South Africa. Its principal cargo was three hundred tanks—which Churchill delighted to refer to as "tiger cubs"—and fifty Hurricane fighters.

Front-line levels of confidence were high when Operation Battleaxe began on June 15. Wavell's plan was to move across the frontier south of the main Axis positions, then swing north and drive on Tobruk. He had a clear numerical superiority in men and tanks. But the tanks from Britain were a new model that proved seriously unreliable. The armor and the infantry kept losing contact. British tanks that did not break down encountered an enemy that did not fight by the books of the Royal Armored Corps. British tank officers in the initial stages of Battleaxe stormed forward seeking the Panzers with an enthusiam worthy of a better outcome. Instead, they encountered screens of dug-in antitank guns, many of them second-generation: high-velocity 50-millimeter pieces brought over by the 15th Panzer Division as replacements for the 37-millimeter popguns that had proven so ineffective in France.

Rommel had brought forward a Luftwaffe anti-aircraft battalion with three batteries of 88s. The high silhouette and complex mount of the Flak-88 was anything but ideal against ground targets. Nor could the heavy gun be moved readily. But their crews had dug them in solidly at a place called Halfaya Pass, key to the coast road to Tobruk, and they tore the heart out of the initial British attack. Even the Matildas, whose armor had been impervious to anything in the theater, went up like torches, at ranges beyond any their own supporting arms could reach.

Farther south, British tankers pushed forward despite losses of fifty percent and higher in the attacking units. A Suth African–born officer serving with the Royal Tank Regiment observed that British tank design and British tactical doctrines alike reflected a mentality that wanted to make a tank that was as much like a horse as possible, then use them as horses had been used in the Charge of the Light Brigade. As an obliging enemy impaled himself on the German antitank guns, Rommel ordered the 15th Panzer to counterattack while the 5th Light swung around and enveloped the British left.

Throughout June 16, the armored forces savaged each other at gun-barrel range. By nightfall, despite heavy German tank losses, Rommel was convinced the fight was turning in Afrika Korps's favor. He ordered his two Panzer divisions to push east, then swing north with the dual objective of relieving Halfaya Pass and cutting off what remained of the British armor. Around 4 P.M. on June 17, the first German tanks rolled into Halfaya. But the British had escaped Rommel's net, by some accounts executing a fighting withdrawal and by others retreating faster than the Germans could chase them. They left behind almost a hundred tanks. Permanent German losses totaled a dozen, half of them the expendable light models.

On one hand, Rommel was pleased. A three-day head-to-head battle had resulted in a complete tactical victory despite British air superiority, which meant heavy losses for the "soft-skinned" supply vehicles. Morale in the German units soared. Rommel might be a man with rough edges, but his professionalism struck positive chords wherever he went. The Italians under his command had also fought well, particularly at what the British now were calling "Hellfire" Pass, and Germany had a new hero: Major Wilhelm Bach, a reserve officer and an Evangelical pastor in civilian life, who commanded at Halfaya with a skill and courage that attracted the prompt notice of a propaganda apparatus that made the defeat of Battleaxe the stuff of headlines and newsreels throughout the Reich.

Hitler urged Rommel's promotion. Halder grumbled about Rommel's "pathological" ambition and proposed subordinating him to a "Commander of German Troops in North Africa." The final decision was to send a liaison staff to North Africa to "coordinate" operations with the Italians. The Italian commander in North Africa said neither he nor Rommel had requested such a body and warned Mussolini it could become a stalking horse for German control of the theater. Then Rommel entered the discussion with a demonstration that he could speak General Staff perfectly and play a sophisticated game of army politics when he wanted to. The Italians, he declared, intended to create two corps headquarters for the six divisions they had placed under his command. That meant he would be commanding a minimum of eight full divisions and three corps: too many for his present small headquarters. Rommel, therefore, requested the staff officers be assigned to him temporarily—until a commander could be named for the German army necessary to command the expanded organization. Modesty forbade suggesting who the commander of that army should be.

The Italians were reluctant to accept the expansion of German authority—but if it were to be done, then only with Rommel in command. His obvious arm's-length relationship with his own high command made him that much more acceptable to the Italians. Since his arrival in North Africa, moreover, Rommel had both successfully cultivated the Italian senior officers and gained the confidence of the fighting troops, who, after months of humiliation, cared more about winning than about the nationality of the general who led them to victory.

The High Command was unwilling to hand Rommel an army command—something no armored officer had yet received. Instead, Halder and Paulus suggested a compromise. At this stage of the war, the German mechanized divisions and corps were organized in "Groups," which stood one step below field armies in the command structure. Why not create a "Panzer Group Rommel" and place it under Italian command? Brigadier General Alfred Gause, the senior German liaiaon officer in North Africa, concurred. According to Gause, Rommel's "character flaws" and "inordinate ambition" combined with his support in "the highest quarters" had created a situation best met by creating a Panzer Group whose staff, composed primarily of officers assigned by the High Command, would act as a governor and a brake on its tempestuous commander. On June 1, Rommel was promoted to lieutenant-general (*General der Panzertruppen*), and on July 31, the liaison staff became the headquarters of Panzer Group Africa with Gause the chief of staff. Following the German pattern, the Group was under a higher headquarters: the Italian commander in chief in Libya, Marshal Ettore Bastico. Rommel could also receive orders directly from the army High Command. His chief of staff was to report to both the Italian commander in North Africa and the representative of the German supreme Command (*Oberkommando der Wehrmacht*) assigned to the Italian High Command. It was a structure reflecting the mutual commitment of Nazi Germany and Fascist Italy to wage parallel, as opposed to coalition, war. It was also a structure that allowed Rommel to disregard any particular chain of command by claiming to respond to an alternate one.

Rommel had won a political victory that far exceeded the scope of his triumph in the field. At seventh and last, there was no doubt that the British had escaped. Rommel noted the continuing problem of coordinating the movements of two Panzer divisions under new commanders with no desert experience. His decision to exercise command from Tobruk represented a departure from his previous practice and proved an anomaly he did not repeat. But a Panzer group had higher priorities for supply and reinforcement than a mere corps. And his new staff proved an asset from the first.

Following the German pattern, it was small relative to its British and U.S. counterparts—no more than twenty officers all told. German economy in headquarters staffs has been so widely praised that it is useful to repeat a counterpoint. Small numbers meant no relief. Everyone had to work long hours under high stress, and the resulting fatigue led to errors in judgment, exaggerated personal friction, and problems falling through cracks. All three would plague Panzer Group Africa later in the campaign.

For now, Rommel could count himself fortunate in his subordinates. Gause, whose opinion of Rommel greatly improved with exposure, exemplified the axiom that a hard-charging commander is well paired with a low-key chief of staff. More troop officer than military intellectual, Gause was easy-going by German standards and possessed—again by German standards— a sense of humor that was welcome in a headquarters where intensity was the norm. Among the junior officers, Operations Officer (Ia) Lieutenant Colonel Siegfried Westphal stood out for his character and intellect. "The best horse in the stable," a later superior called him. Karl von Mellinthin is best known for his postwar writing on armored war, but in the desert, he handled the Panzer Group's intelligence admirably. The rest as a group were well above the curve.

It is also significant that they came in with a collective distance from Rommel, as opposed to being his men, and within weeks gave him a rational loyalty that served far better than simple devotion would have. Their subsequent accounts reveal high levels of respect for Rommel's military talent and for the energy he brought to his task. Rommel, in turn, made no secret of his appreciation for his smooth-working staff that also functioned increasingly as a military family—a source of relaxation for a man who spent most of his time at center stage under bright lights.

As Rommel and his staff adjusted to each other, Winston Churchill cleaned house. Wavell, who never lost his dignity while he was losing battles, was replaced by Sir Claude Auchinleck. "The Auk" was an Indian Army officer who had made a favorable impression on Churchill, and who had something of a prewar reputation as being interested in armored warfare—not much, perhaps, but the best Britain could do in the trying days of mid-1941. The same might well be said for Auchinleck's choice as field commander for what was now designated the 8th Army. Lieutenant General Sir Alan Cunningham had presided over the British conquest of Italian East Africa the previous year and had a correspondingly stronger sense of space-time factors than someone fresh from England. He was, however, inexperienced in higher command and tended to think at a foot pace rather than tank speed. With a bit of seasoning and a bit of luck, he might have done well enough. Rommel was not the kind of opponent, however, to offer on-the-job training.

German intelligence was aware the British were planning a new offensive, on a far larger scale than Battleaxe. So much has been written about the importance of intelligence, ULTRA in particular, to the Allies' victory in the Mediterranean that the contributions of German intelligence to Rommel's planning tends to be overlooked. Its core was reconnaissance, whose air and ground elements were unusually well coordinated. If the German patrols never matched the effectiveness of the 8th Army's Long Range Desert Group, the heavy armored cars of the reconnaissance battalions, frequently guided by local Arabs, nevertheless managed to put together reasonable data on British forward movements.

This material was enhanced by capture of prisoners and of paper, ranging from personal letters taken from casualties and POWs to orders and reports left in overrun command posts. The British army was strong on paperwork, especially on its administrative side; and the Germans were more likely than their opponents to control captured headquarters long enough to take advantage of the raw intelligence data they provided. As for prisoners, British soldiers were ordered to reveal nothing under interrogation beyond name, rank, age, and home. It was, however, usually possible for a skilled and sympathetic interlocutor to tease out more from men disoriented by capture and all too aware that they had suddenly become totally dependant on their enemy for such mundane benefits as a cigarette.

From the desert campaign's beginning, both sides consciously sought to wage a "clean" war—war without hate, as Rommel put it in his reflections. Explanations include the absence of civilians and the relative absence of Nazis; the nature of the environment, which conveyed a "moral simplicity and transparency"; and the control of command on both sides by prewar professionals, producing a British tendency to depict war in the imagery of a game, and the corresponding German pattern of seeing it as a test of skill and a proof of *virtu*. The nature of the fighting as well diminished the last-ditch, close-quarter actions that are primary nurturers of mutual bitterness. A battalion overrun by tanks usually had its resistance broken so completely that nothing was to be gained by a broken-backed final stand. The result, at least in the war's classic period before El Alamein, was a mutual goodwill that German interrogators exploited to their advantage.

Third on the list, but by no means last in importance, was signal intelligence. Rommel's 621st Radio Company under Lieutenant Alfred Seebohm grew so good at its job that it was able to identify individual operators—a valuable aid to unit identification—and frequently translated and forwarded British messages faster than the intended recipients. British radio security was in general poor, with messages broadcast in clear or in slang. This was not mere fecklessness. As a British staff officer noted, time was everything in desert war. Speak in code, and everything slows down. Send ciphers, and hours are lost coding and decoding. Speak in clear, and make the enemy a present of your plans. "You pay your penny, and you choose your inconvenience."

The challenge involved keeping far enough ahead of the enemy that even information gained by direct interception was useless when it was applied. And that was a skill beyond the 8th Army that launched Operation Crusader on November 18. The British had air superiority. They had more than 800 guns and as many tanks, a number of them provided by lend-lease: M-3 developments of the U.S. light tank that had been the backbone of the 1941 maneuvers. The Axis could count only around four hundred tanks in their orders of battle, and fewer than half were the combat-worthy Mark III's and IV's. The rest were German lights or Italian models, useful at best for reconnaissance and intimidation.

II

The British also had developed their intelligence service, complementing ULTRA with theater and local systems that combined to indicate Rommel was preparing to try once more for Tobruk. That shaped the British plan and its timing. A flanking attack in the south, with most of the armor, would turn northeast as though it were aiming for Tobruk. This was expected to draw Rommel's armor into an encounter battle and onto British guns: Battleaxe in reverse. After the Panzers were engaged, a second, infantry-heavy corps would attack on the right flank of the armor, advance north to the sea around Sollum, then turn west and link up with the Tobruk garrison while the armor finished off the Panzers. As the garnish on the recipe, the 8th Army dispatched a commando raid to decapitate Panzer Group Africa.

Not for centuries had a Western army included in its battle plan the targeted killing of the enemy general. That the highly conventional British High Command approved the project speaks volumes for the respect in which Rommel was held even in these early stages. Downplayed today as unsporting in most standard histories of the commandos, it deserves remembering for its audacious planning and professional implementation. The raiders, transported by sea, reached the targeted building—more than two hundred miles behind the front—inflicted casualties and withdrew successfully. Rommel changed locations shortly before the strike, making it all for nothing.

Rommel had also apparently obliged his enemy by once again fixing his attention on Tobruk. Its capture, he declared, was essential to the successful conduct of mobile operations in North Africa—positively, by opening a supply route closer to the front, negatively by removing the substantial British forces in his rear. By this time the Australians had been replaced, mostly by British and Free Polish troops no less stubborn in defense. More serious was the loss between June and October of a quarter-million tons of Axis shipping—most of it Italian, on the North African run. Malta, far from being neutralized, was developing into a major base, with the British taking full advantage of ULTRA to savage Italian convoys by sea and air. In November, as British surface activity engaged increasing numbers of ships from a navy unable to replace losses readily, the Italians stopped running convoys into Tripoli and used only the limited capacity of Bengazi.

Rommel faced as well a set of difficulties codenamed Operation Barbarossa. On June 28, the High Command requested Rommel to prepare a draft plan for an offensive against Egypt—but only in autumn, after the Soviet Union should be destroyed. Rommel opted for two additional German divisions, then on July 3, he was told he must carry out the operation with the resources on hand. And as the pace of the German offensive slowed, Rommel expected the British to feel more comfortable mounting an offensive because they need no longer fear German tanks pouring through the Caucasus.

Seen in these contexts, Rommel's continued focus on capturing To-bruk as soon as possible emerges as more than narrowly focused bloody-mindedness. Operating on a shoestring, able to expect no significant reinforcement in the foreseeable future, Rommel was correspondingly unwilling to resign initiative to a British force exponentially superior in armor and artillery. That alternative meant that his own already-slender resources would be eroded to no purpose, like a small-stakes player in a poker game who sees his pile of chips sinking every time he antes and does not bet. Better to use proactively the tanks, the gasoline, the ammu-nition on hand. Rommel planned to attack on Tobruk in the third week of November. The 15th Panzer and 90th Light—the latter just coming onto line—would do the heavy lifting, supported by four Italian divi-sions. The 5th Light, now rebaptized the 21st Panzer Division and bene-fiting from such christening gifts as a motorcycle battalion, a rifle regiment, and enough new guns to make an artillery regiment, was to keep an eye on the British, supported by Ariete and the newly arrived Tri-este Motorized Division, organized as XX Corps.

Tobruk's fall might be enough to deter the British attack German and Italian senor intelligence agencies were by now predicting. If the British came anyway, Rommel was confident in the strength of his fixed defenses in the north around Halfaya Pass, and in the striking power of the 21st Panzer and the skill of its new commander Major General Johannes von Ravenstein to buy him enough time to deal with Tobruk, then turn on the would-be relief force.

As an army commander, Rommel could not expect to intervene in the field with the effect he had obtained at lower echelons. He saw his role in the coming battle as demanding judgment, will, and strength, and his bat-teries badly needed recharging. He spent the first two weeks of Novem-ber in Italy on furlough with Lu and in the company of the von Ravensteins, returning on November 18. The day before, signal intelli-gence had reported radio silence across the British front.

The British plans for Crusader have been generally criticized for re-signing too much of the initiative to Rommel. If he did not oblige by launching the expected all-out attack on the armored spearhead, the 8th Army would have to improvise—not its particular strength. Tactically as well, the notion of waiting for the Germans to drive onto British tank guns seems in hindsight excessively optimistic, despite the 8th Army's two-to-one advantage in armored vehicles. The British attack nevertheless gave the 21st Panzer in particular a very bad day before the Germans were able to regroup and counterattack. That was in good part the work of Lieutenant General Johannes Cruewell, who had succeeded Rommel in command of the Afrika Korps. Rommel initially was both reluctant to accept the British attack as the real thing and uncertain of its directions. Cruewell, intelligent and persuasive, helped the *Chef* make up his mind—another first. Rommel gave him the 15th Panzer and a free hand to "destroy" the British forces on his front—in other words, to see them off wherever he found them. By the evening of November 20, however, Rommel understood that this was no raid and no diversion. The British were determined to relieve Tobruk, and Rommel ordered Cruewell to begin swinging the Panzers north to choke off what he considered a threat to the entire Panzer group.

For four days, beginning on the 19th, German and British armor grappled around the airfield at Sidi Rezegh. The details of the swirling fight remain obscure and confusing after more than a half-century. At the cutting edge, German combined-arms tactics again proved superior to the British tendency to fight in compartments. Two of the 90th Light's infantry regiments brought south by Rommel as emergency reinforcements did particular damage to the 7th Armored Division, which failed by an eyelash to crack open a way into Tobruk. The British further obliged by, as a rule, committing their armored units piecemeal by brigades, reacting to real and perceived German initiatives as opposed to concentrating and seeking to take control of the battle. In Rommel's words to a captured British officer, "What does it matter if you have two tanks to my one, when you spread them out and let me smash them in detail?"

Rommel, issuing his orders in clear, and Cruewell, disobeying those orders when it seemed necessary, were able to keep a jump ahead operationally. Von Ravenstein proved an ace in his first test as a division commander, his veteran 21st Panzer hammering the British away from Sidi Rezegh in an all-day battle on November 22. German artillery and anti-tank guns inflicted tank losses whose catastrophic scope remained unclear to headquarters depending on increasingly fragmentary radio reports from the front. The British nevertheless gave the Afrika Korps all the fighting it could handle. A reinforced Royal Air Force inflicted heavy losses on German units who had never before had to worry about dispersion and camouflage. When losses were tallied, the 8th Army still had numerical superiority in the sector.

The Germans were down to about a hundred fighting tanks in their two Panzer regiments. The other arm of the British offensive, moreover, was wearing down Axis defenses in the Sollum sector, prefiguring its move toward Tobruk, whose garrison had begun its own sortie on the 21st. Rommel's decision was to go for what remained of the British armor even if that meant turning away temporarily from the fighting around Tobruk. November 23 was Sunday, and the last Sunday in November is Protestant Germany's day of remembrance for the dead: *Totensonnntag*. The night before, Rommel ordered Cruewell to take what remained of the German tanks and encircle and destroy the British armor south of Sidi Rezegh.

That began one of the most daring and controversial moves of Rommel's career: the "dash to the wire." The reference is to the barbed wire entanglements marking the Libyan-Egyptian frontier. Cruewell protested that regroupment and consolidation were wiser options, but there was no blind-eyeing the long, coded order from Panzer Group headquarters. Cruewell's own headquarters was overrun early in the morning, but he escaped to lead his armor into, over, and through a tangle of British supply columns that reacted by starting a headlong flight across the desert. Joining forces with Ariete, which though not part of the Afrika Korps had been "invited" to participate, Cruewell put both his tank regiments under the 15th Panzer and sent them forward, each followed by a regiment of motorized infantry. There was no time to send the infantry ahead to clear the British defenses; no time to form smaller, more flexible tank-infantry battle groups. The price paid to die-hard British tankers and antitank crews was heavy as the Boar's Head (*Saukopf*) ground its way forward. But once the Germans broke through, the panic begun that morning in the rear echelons developed and spread, as men and vehicles fled in all directions before the German machine guns.

Totensonntag was Cruewell's battle. Rommel spent the day away from his headquarters, accompanied only by the Panzer group staff and his escort force, about five hundred men, calculating the time and the

place for a decisive strike that would turn the tide by personal intervention. On the evening of the 23rd, he wrote to Lu that he was "in good
humor and full of confidence." The Tobruk sortie was progressing at a
foot pace; the British advance toward the coast was slowing down. On
the morning of the 24th, he briefed his subordinates. Speed is vital, he insisted. The Panzer Group must make the most of the shocks already administered to the enemy. He proposed to use what remained of his mobile
forces to advance southeast to the Egyptian frontier, relieving the Sollum
front, encircle its attackers, and finish the staggering British once and for
all. Captured supply dumps would keep the forward units moving. Rommel intended to lead the Afrika Korps and the Ariete in person—literally
lead them, from the front as he had done in France—for the first day, at
any rate. He expected to be back next morning at the latest; until then
Westphal would command the Tobruk front.

The West German official history, noting that Rommel himself did
not write the part of his memoirs dealing with "Crusader," questions
whether he really believed a day-long excursion to the frontier would
sever the 8th Army's supply lines and cut off its retreat. The volume
comes closer to the truth when it states that the "dash to the wire" had
little in common with a typical General Staff exercise. Rommel's decision
certainly had few supporters in his headquarters. The situation already
seemed hopelessly confused, with British troops likely to appear almost
anywhere from out of the fog of war and Rommel now proposed to add
to the chaos. Cruewell advocated cleaning up the opposition in his immediate sector—a formidable task in itself. Fritz Bayerlein, Afrika Korps
chief of staff since September 1941, called the operation a raid and
seemed to think he was being generous to an old friend.

Rommel did not see it so. When the 15th Panzer was delayed, he
broke out around 10:30 at the head of the 21st Panzer alone. As the 15th
caught up, a German column forty miles long slashed into the British
rear, overrunning headquarters, and spreading alarm, despondency, and
panic despite taking fire on its flanks from less shaken enemy units. Rommel forced the pace and came close to adding another set of generals to
his POW collection: Cunningham was visiting a corps headquarters at
what seemed a safe distance behind the front when the unexpected appearance of German tanks led to an undignified race for safety in what

humorists dubbed the Matruh Stakes. He came even closer to being "put in the bag" himself when he and Gause crossed the wire in an unescorted command car, then could not find a way back. To add to the low comedy of the affair, Cruewell, driving by in his headquarters vehicle, offered a lift—but no one in the combined party could find the gap in the wire that led back to Libya, perhaps not least because Rommel insisted on driving. The senior officers of Panzer Group Africa spent the night in as meat on the table for any wandering British patrol.

Over the next two days, the German counterattack dissolved into a series of poorly coordinated actions, in good part due to Rommel's insistence not only on remaining at the front with only brief stops at subordinate headquarters, but on abandoning his radio truck when it bogged down. He considered being cut off from current intelligence an acceptable risk in the context of the fluid battle he sought to force: if the Afrika Korps could set the pace, information was something for the British to worry about. "Fog and friction," however, increasingly asserted themselves. Corps and division headquarters had their own internal communications problems, consistently losing touch with each other and their subordinate units. The Panzer divisions found resupply increasingly difficult, with captured British material only partly able to make up shortages. Ironically, the Germans bypassed the two major supply centers supporting the advance, in one case driving through the water point on the northern edge of one of them.

Above all, however, Auchinleck kept his head when most of his subordinates were losing theirs. He replaced Cunningham with Major General Neil Ritchie, took more direct control of the operation, and turned Rommel's methods against him by pressing on with the relief of Tobruk despite the continuing havoc on his left flank. The advance was spearheaded by the 2nd New Zealand Division, arguably the best citizen-soldier division of any army in World War II. The Panzer Group staff and Marshal Bastico shared the fear that Rommel was off chasing shadows instead of concentrating against the real threat. On November 26, Westphal acted. Unable to reach his superior, he ordered the 21st Panzer back toward Tobruk and sent Rommel a signal explaining his decision.

Rommel received the message the same day. Initially furious, his considered reaction shows both the power of the German commitment to delegating authority and Rommel's self-command. Instead of losing his temper in public, he announced he was going to lie down. The next morning, he confirmed Westphal's decicion and turned the balance of his mobile forces against the New Zealanders.

Whatever temptations he might have had to follow his original plan dissipated in the course of the next few days. The 15th Panzer was burned by a counterattack of a British armored brigade, reequipped with whatever tanks remained available. The 21st Panzer lost its commander when Ravenstein drove into a New Zealand outpost and was captured. And the New Zealanders overran Sidi Rezegh and established contact with Tobruk during the night of November 26–27.

Rommel threw the whole Afrika Korps—what remained of it— against Sidi Rezegh. By this time, everyone on both sides was stumbling from exhaustion—everyone but Rommel, who reported to Lu that he was fresh and felt enormously fit. It was that driving energy that kept the hard-hammered Afrika Korps going around Sidi Rezegh: standing off British armor that still seemed unable to mount coordinated, large-scale attacks while simultaneously inflicting casualties on the New Zealanders that were devastating to a small country where so many people knew each other. The survivors finally drew off, escaping encirclement by a hair. If Rommel lost his focus during the dash to the wire, he had recovered it with remarkable speed. But the Panzer Group had fought itself to exhaustion. On November 30, it counted 31 Mark III's and only nine Mark IV's, forty fighting tanks, plus thirty "sardine boxes" in the ranks of Ariete.

In the first week of December, Rommel continued to seek the relief of his frontier garrisons and the restoration of the Tobruk envelopment. But a staff officer sent by Mussolini himself informed Rommel that no reinforcements and nothing but basic supplies could be expected until early January. With German intelligence figures showing British strength in North Africa rapidly recovering, Rommel could see it was time to cut his losses.

Essentially dependant on the Italians for supply, Rommel needed the best relations possible with the Italian High Command. With the small, almost token, force of Germans at his disposal, Rommel needed to make

the best possible use of Italian troops.The Italian army was not as retrograde in its understanding of mobile war as is frequently assumend. By
1940, Italian theorists had studied German successes in Poland and
France and developed a doctrine of "fast-moving war" (*Guerra di rapido
corso*). Their defeats at the hands of O'Connor led them to reinforce their
North African forces with increasing numbers of armored and motorized
formations. Their standard medium tank, the M13/40, had a useful high-
velocity 47-millimeter gun, and its inadequate armor was not a mortal
shortcoming given Rommel's principle of eschewing tank-on-tank combat. The Ariete Division performed as well as its German stablemates in
the initial stages of Crusader. Communications was Ariete's principal
weakness: the lack of reliable radios to coordinate movements. That, and
an excess of courage that too often led regimental officers to make the
kind of unsupported frontal attacks against the British that the British
were prone to make against the Germans.

Given German shortages in those arms, the Italian infantry and artillery were more important. The overwhelmingly Italian blocking force
at Tobruk restricted the British breakout despite its superior firepower
and armored strength. The Bersagliere, Italy's elite light infantry did well
at Halfaya Pass in May and June even though the Germans reaped most
of the publicity; while dug-in Italian 100-millimeter guns contributed
along with the 88s to the defeat of British armor in that sector. A battalion of the Young Fascists Motorized Division held off an Indian brigade
for four days in the final stages of the Sidi Rezegh fight.

Rommel publicly recognized enough of these achievements to balance the acerbic remarks about Italian effectiveness with which his papers are seasoned. Some of his criticism invites interpretation as a
manifestation of frustration: a simple blowing off of steam. Italian weaknesses were at higher levels. A centralized supply service controlled from
the rear found it difficult to keep pace with those units that did adjust to
Rommel's pace. Too many senior officers were unwilling to take chances
and seize initiative.Too many juniors confused professionalism with careerism and scorned or ignored their conscript enlisted men. Brave
enough at the front, they looked to their own comfort out of battle to a
degree that shocked even British regulars accustomed to a caste system at

regimental levels. The Germans, who prided themselves on sharing misery equally, were even more appalled.

For all its military shortcomings, Italy in the spring of 1942 was reaching the peak of its contribution to the Axis war effort, assuming a significant share of the burdens of Balkan occupation, increasing its naval effort—successfully sinking two British battleships in a daring raid by naval commandos—and committing an entire army to the Russian campaign. That last absorbed most of the new weapons and the best of Italy's divisions. It remains a minor question of counterfactual history what the consequences might have been if Mussolini had taken his often-proclaimed *sacro egoismo* seriously enough to send to North Africa even part of the force that was to disappear in the early stages of the Red Army's Stalingrad offensive.

Rommel's nominal superior General Bastico regarded Rommel's commanding from the front as bizarre and ultimately unproductive. Rommel considered Bastico a "decent man with a sober military understanding and considerable moral stamina." Bastico needed that stamina when he confronted Rommel about his proposed retreat from Cyrenaiaca. This was an Italian colony; its abandonment meant another blow to the prestige of an Italy with too many already on its war record.

Bastico's criticism was echoed by the Italian chief of staff, General Ugo Cavallero, and by an unexpected arrival from Germany. Field Marshal Albert Kesselring had begun his career in the army, transferred to the Luftwaffe on its formation, and Wehrmacht High Command had sent him to the Mediterranean in December 1941 as commander of all German forces in the theater—except for Rommel, who officially at least came directly under Italian command. It was that independent status, and not the often-implied collusion between Rommel and Hitler, that gave Rommel the continuing right to communicate directly with the Wehrmacht High Command.

Kesselring's nickname of "Smiling Albert" reflected his optimistic character. His glass was always half full, which made him particularly attractive to Hitler. It was also typical of the Fuehrer that he sent two men with roughly equal responsibilities and roughly equal authority at the same difficult task. One could be expected to watch the other; both would complain to Hitler, who thereby held the whip hand without seeming to. Kesselring, while no desk hero—he made more than two hundred flights across enemy lines, and his Storch alone was shot down five times—considered Rommel an example of the lowest type of German senior officer: a combat commander without general staff experience, and correspondingly limited in perspective. Kesselring saw the most urgent need in the theater to be the restoring of a steady flow of supplies, and was committed to cultivating the best possible relations with the Italians. His relationship to Rommel, whom he saw as an obstacle to that policy, was correspondingly chilly.

On December 12, Bastico called on Rommel to be informed that if he interfered with any of the Italian divisions under Rommel's command, the Germans would retreat alone and leave the Italians to their fate. Because most of these formations were infantry, without enough trucks to carry the men, even if all equipment were abandoned, this was the same as making them a present to the British. The next day, or rather night, at 11:30 P.M., Bastico returned accompanied by another Italian general and Kesselring. Bastico demanded the retreat be cancelled; Rommel refused. To remain was to sacrifice the entire Panzer Group, while ground could always be regained.

In the end, the generals left and Rommel initiated a neatly executed series of retrograde movements—generalspeak for retreats. No one was more surprised than the British, who on the basis of intercepted signals, expected the Panzer Group to remain in place. As British advance guards stumbled around abandoned positions, Rommel's forces took advantage of bad weather to break contact, turn, and give their pursuers a bloody nose at a place called Agedabia. They celebrated the Christmas season by knocking out sixty tanks for a loss of fourteen, and in mid-January, settled into a defensive line anchored in the north on Mersa el Brega—not too far from where it had all begun so many months and lives ago.

From first to last Crusader cost the Axis 340 tanks, more than 300 aircraft, 8,300 dead and wounded, and more than 30,000 prisoners, including the frontier garrisons around Sollum and Halfaya, who had fought so bravely in Battleaxe and now held until water and ammunition were exhausted. Major Bach was among the prisoners. Tobruk had been relieved, with corresponding comprehensive effects on British morale and status. All three of Afrika Korps's division commanders were gone: von

Ravenstein a prisoner, Neumann-Silkow of the 15th Panzer mortally wounded by a shell burst, the 90th Light's Max Suemmerman killed in an air attack. Losses among officers and senior NCOs at regimental levels had also been heavy. The German pattern of leading from the front, a near-fetish in Rommel's command, levied disproportionate tolls on increasingly irreplaceable leaders wherever the enemy made a fight of it. And no one in Panzer Group Africa ever questioned British courage.

There are fashions in generalship as there are in clothing. Robert E. Lee, for example, is currently on a down cycle, while Ulysses Grant's stock is high. For a quarter-century after World War II, Rommel was considered a paragon of mobile war at the tactical and operational levels. In the next quarter-century, military historians and professional soldiers have judged him with a sharper pencil. Rommel's handling of Crusader and its aftermath has been generally criticized along three lines. The first is operational: Rommel failed to maintain the objective. Initially focused on Tobruk to a point where he refused to consider the probability of a British attack, he then sought to draw off his adversary by the "dash to the wire." Facing another Rommel, the plan might have worked. Given the rigidity of British planning and command, the prospects of such a dramatic response were as slim as they proved in fact. Frustrated at the frontier, Rommel then turned and fought a straight-on encounter battle that for all its tactical successes used up most of his remaining German tanks and cost him qualitative losses he could not easily replace.

Rommel's second mistake was institutional. His organization of the Panzer Group did not reflect an operational situation with three distinct sectors: the ring around Tobruk; the fixed defenses at Sollum/Halfaya; and the mobile reserve, the Afrika Korps, and the Trieste and Ariete divisions of the XX Italian Corps. Instead of responding with the German "mission system," appointing three subordinates and supervising them as they fought their battles, Rommel established no clear lines of authority. The problems this caused with the Afrika Korps have been highlighted, but the Italian generals, more used than their German counterparts to precise orders, were also left adrift too often for their effectiveness.

That problem led in turn to a third: the psychological. Rommel under stress sought to control the entire situation by putting himself at one decisive point after another. What was just possible at division level, in a developed command structure and with reliable formations on his flanks, could not be done at army level. The distances were too great; there were too many emergencies at once. Rommel was still learning how best to use his very competent staff. In Crusader, he barely used it at all, and within days, the battle spun to the limits of his control. The problem was exacerbated by fatigue. Rommel was a fitness fetishist, with more endurance than many soldiers thirty years his junior. But he was fifty, and even his admirably toned body could only be pushed so far. Believing fatigue was a matter of will, Rommel refused to deal with getting tired. By the end of the fighting, his mental edge was becoming dulled, and no one on his staff had the moral authority to tell him he needed sleep.

Rommel, on the other hand, gets as a rule high marks for a command presence that never failed him and consistently enhanced his image with his subordinates, German and Italian alike. His tactical sense was unmatched on either side: when he was involved in a battle, he appeared to sense its flow, becoming part of the action in a near-literal sense. He knew when to cut his losses and was able to switch from advance to retreat with an easy smoothness that boded well for future operations.

Crusader developed Rommel's moral ascendancy over an 8th Army that had failed to win a clear victory despite odds heavy in its favor. The relief of Tobruk, although welcome, was in no way a decisive blow against the Germans and Italians. The memories that remained in the 8th Army's collective memory were of the Panzers' daring and virtuosity around Sidi Rezegh, and in the dash to the wire. And out there beyond the horizon, Rommel was still waiting.

The structural discrepancy between the combatants was also significant. Despite the myths enveloping it, the Desert War was never a gladitorial contest. North Africa was Britain's primary land theater, normally exercising first call on weapons, supplies, and talent—a situation, paradoxically, in good part due to Rommel's developing mystique on the British side, from Churchill downward. Rommel, by contrast, was at the low end of German priority lists for everything. He was making war with pocket change, especially as the Russian invasion did not become the walkover the High Command was expecting.

Rommel was also caught in the most difficult form of allied command: the sandwich. Exercising authority over Italian divisions and corps, he was himself subject to Italian superiors. Italy's priorities differed from those of Germany. So did its armed forces. As a point of comparison, even as late as the Northwest European campaign, British and U.S. formations served under each other's command were seldom integrated below army level, and then usually only in emergencies. And while a player at the top levels of allied politics, Rommel was only a three-star general constrained to negotiate with field marshals on a regular basis. An assertive, in-your-face approach was his only practical option. Whether he could develop situational awareness in conferences to match his battlefield instincts was still an open question as the year turned.

That Rommel could have done a better job in his first command at army level is clear. The same thing can be said of virtually every commander in a large-scale action: perfect battles, like perfect storms, are few and far between. The common thread of his problem was a tendency to revert to playing a division commander's role when addressing emergencies. This was more than regression to a comfort zone. Rommel believed in a hands-on style of command, characterized by direct, personal intervention. Like any approach, it has its strengths and shortcomings. During Crusader, Rommel experienced the shortcomings for the first time. The text mentioned earlier that division command is about the practical limit of most generals' predictable capacities. Success at higher levels is in large part a product of trial and error, of learning on the job. Could Rommel make the transition from a battle captain to a *Feldherr*? The jury was out as Crusader spasmed to a final halt.

III

Erwin Rommel might have been a work in progress, but he never lost confidence in Erwin Rommel. As soon as his troops reached their new positions, he began planning a second attack. Kesselring did not come empty-handed. Hitler sent substantial Luftwaffe reinforcements along with him, and though the Axis air forces never succeeded in neutralizing Malta, they did ease British pressure on the convoys. On December 16–17, four ships, escorted by much of what remained of the Italian surface fleet covered the route from Italy to North Africa. On January 5, six more heavily escorted transports reached Tripoli. In addition to material for the Italian forces, they landed 51 Mark III's and IV's, 16 armored cars, and a number of antitank guns for the Afrika Korps.

It was as good as winning a battle—especially when Rommel and Westphal made separate flights over the Panzer Group's positions and saw how thinly manned they really were. Westphal, who by no means shared his chief's risk-taking propensities, confirmed the impossibility of stopping a major British offensive. That left one solution: attack. Logistics remained a problem. The prospects for constructing a railroad east from Tripoli were highly remote given the limited Italian resources. Rommel's compensatory request for eight thousand trucks was turned down flat by a High Command seeking desperately to replace the swinging losses inflicted by the Russian winter.

Rommel was nevertheless encouraged by intelligence provided by intercepted messages from the U.S. military attaché in Cairo, Major Bonner Fellers. Axis cryptographers had cracked the U.S. diplomatic code and fully appreciated the extensive information on British plans and force structures Fellers provided to Washington. Not till the end of June would the leak be plugged. Meantime, its information combined with data from other sources to indicate the British were undertaking a major buildup for a new offensive. When Mellenthin reported January 25 as the bench date for a decisive shift of the balance of forces in Britsh favor, Rommel calculated he had a window of opportunity. With he reinforcements he had 120 German and 80 Italian tanks—the latter by now mostly M-13/ 40s. The British had about 150, but their senior armored headquarters was green, sent to the desert to gain experience. Rommel proposed to provide all the experience the newbies could handle.

The plan of attack depended on absolute surprise. Rommel did not trust Italian security and had no intention of being restrained by careful superiors. Nothing, therefore, was said to any of the Italian higher headquarters—or to Kesselring. Only Bastico's chief of staff was made party to Rommel's intentions, and then only because he was needed to provide the fuel and trucks the Afrika Korps lacked. On January 18, Rommel issued orders whose final version consisted of twenty-one paragraphs, each averaging no more than seven lines—a model of compact staff work. The 90th Light Division, reinforced by a detachment of motorized infantry and antitank guns called "Battle Group Marcks" for its commander, would punch up the coast road. On the Panzer Group's right, Cruewell's Afrika Korps would swing northeast to complete the encirclement. The Italians were to fill gaps and provide blocking forces.

Rommel accompanied Battle Group Marcks, and this time made certain his headquarters knew of his whereabouts. An indication that he was aware of what was at stake, for his troops and for him personally, is his letter to Lu describing his faith in "God's protective hand." Rommel was no more than conventionally religious and turned to a Higher Power primarily when he was worried! On July 19, covered by a sandstorm, the assault formations moved into position. The next day, Hitler, also unaware of Rommel's intentions, awarded him the Swords to his Knight's Cross.

On January 21 at 8:30 A.M., Panzer Group Africa rolled forward. Rommel, in a tribute to British front-line intercept services, had ordered radio silence in the motorized units. Initially slowed by loose sand, the attack took the British completely by surprise at all levels. The senior officers were planning their own offensive in the more comfortable environments of Cairo and Palestine. The foward units were caught flat-footed. German records complain of having achieved smaller successes than appeared possible, but that reflected primarily the British ability to run faster than the Panzers could chase them.

On January 23, Cavallero arrived at Rommel's headquarters expressing Mussolini's concern at the risks Rommel was accepting, and bearing an order to fall back toward his start line. Kesselring supported the Italians. Rommel refused, stating that only Hitler could order him to retreat because most of the troops engaged in the fighting were German. Because Hitler had upgraded the Panzer Group to a Panzer Army the previous day and would soon promote Rommel to full general (Colonel General or *Generaloberst*), he was playing from a stacked deck. It should be noted that this was part of a general, long-term redesignating of Panzer Groups. For example, Panzer Group 1, in Russia, was retitled in October 1941; Panzer Group 4 on January 1, 1942; and the normal rank of an army commander was full general.

Late on January 24, Rommel decided to keep pushing cross-country toward Msus. His fuel was running out, but his feel for the battle suggested that a move that looked like the beginning of a drive across the bulge of Cyrenaica, in the direction of Tobruk, might encourage the British to keep retreating. And although Mussolini's order grounded the Italian infantry, it did allow the mobile forces to pursue offensives with limited objectives. That was all the loophole Rommel needed. His two Panzer divisions, supported by Ariete and the recently arrived Trieste Motorized, stormed forward at speeds reaching twenty-five miles an hour, overtaking and scattering what remained of the British armor, slowing and halting only as fuel tanks emptied. On January 26, Mussolini telephoned his congratulations. On January 29, Benghazi fell, making the Axis a gift of its extensive fuel and supply dumps, and of a forward port.

In eight days, Rommel had retaken the territory lost during Crusader. He did so in spite of continuous British air superiority; the RAF consistently failed to find or strike effectively either his spearheads or his supply lines. The reeling 8th Army fell back to the Gazala line, a network of strong points extending from the coast to Bir Hachiem in the south. By February 5, the front had stabilized. The British, confronted with the stunningly unexpected Japanese victories in the Far East, were juggling strategic reserves and reconsidering strategic priorities. Rommel was aware through reconnaissance reports of the strength of the British position, believed it would take six or eight weeks to restore their offensive capability, and understood refitting his own army would take only slightly less long. As congratulations poured in, he flew to Rome on February 16, went from there to Hitler's field headquarters at Rastenburg to receive his Swords from the hand of Hitler, then took a month's leave at home.

Fritz Bayerlein, talking after the war with British military writer B. H. Liddell Hart, said a desert soldier needed "physical capacity, intelligence, mobility, nerve, pugnacity, daring and stoicism." In a commander, these qualities must be even greater, and to them must be added ". . . toughness, devotion to his men, instinctive judgment of terrain and enemy, speed of reaction, and spirit." Rommel, Bayerlein declared, combined these traits to a greater degree than any officer he knew. Rommel had also focused his energy, keeping his staff reasonably informed of his whereabouts and spending most of his forward time with one unit, Battle Group Marcks, as opposed to dashing about among his divisions as he had done during Crusader.

The withdrawal to Gazala was not an unmitigated disaster for the British. Auchinleck, like Rommel, understood that ground in North Africa seldom possessed much intrinsic value. As early as January 19, he was considering a retreat to the Egyptian frontier rather than try to rally too far forward and be caught again by the Axis advance. The balance of casualties favored the British: since the beginning of Crusader, 18,000 as opposed to 15,000 Germans and 22,000 Italians. When it came to armor, the figures shifted drastically: 220 German and 120 Italian tanks to more than 1,600 British. In both cases, however, it was easier for the British to replace their losses—particularly as American lend-lease material began pouring into North Africa in late 1941.

The significance of Crusader and Rommel's counterattack for the Axis did not involve losses that were bagatelles compared to those being suffered in Russia. In view of their other commitments, the Italians were increasingly considering using reconquered Cyrenaica as a glacis for defending Tripolitania. Kesselring believed the Mediterranean theater's strategic function was to cover the German southern flank during the decisive struggle in Russia. From his perspective, North Africa was an outpost, best secured by the commitment of limited German forces to a flexible defense.

Rommel believed, especially given the growing imbalance in material resources between Germany and its opponents, the best solution involved launching economy-of-force offensives taking advantage of German leadership and German fighting power to demoralize the enemy, keep him off balance, and eventually create the opportunity for a decisive blow. This was a common mind-set among Germany's Panzer generals as the war reached its middle stages: Rommel realized British strength would continue to be renewed as long as North Africa remained the primary theater where Britain could deploy modern ground forces. He understood as well that Malta was the bone in his logistical throat, though he had no idea of the effects of ULTRA in improving the overall effectiveness of the British war in the Mediterranean. He took corresponding advantage of his "face time" with Hitler to discuss the long-term prospects of a grand-strategic initiative in North Africa. Rommel was convinced that with the capture of Malta as a prerequisite, and with a limited increase in his Panzer forces, he could conquer Egypt and eventually move northeast toward the Caucasus, providing the southern pincer of a double envelopment that would secure the oil fields of south Russia and drive across Iraq and Persia, breaking permanently Britain's power in the Middle East.

Hitler, for his part, had been reappraising Germany's strategic prospects since the day of Pearl Harbor. The navy was calling for systematic cooperation with Japan in a campaign designed to produce a junction in the Indian Ocean that would bring about the final collapse of the British empire. Hitler, absorbed in the operational situation on the Russian front, considered this vision unrealistic. For him, victory over the Soviet Union was the linchpin of future operations, both for its own sake and as the best means of bringing Britain to reason and to the conference table. As early as October 1941, he had projected his intentions for a 1942 campaign directed against the Caucasian oil fields. The globalization of the war only confirmed that decision. Hitler at this stage still hoped Britain would negotiate or surrender in the face of a hopeless situation. He saw the Japanese conquests in Asia as weakening Britain's imperial position sufficiently that the presence of Axis troops in the southern foothills of the Caucasus would produce the attitude adjustment he sought and leave Russia to be finished off before the industrial potential of a United States Hitler admitted he had no idea how to defeat could be developed and deployed.

If Hitler and Rommel had anything in common, it was that their military clocks were both set at five minutes to midnight. Like Rommel, Hitler perceived time as an enemy if wasted. America's entry into the war threatened the Reich with a grand-strategic encirclement, while the military situation provided a window of opportunity—six to eight months, perhaps—for consolidating Germany's position not merely in a Fortress Europe, but in a continental redoubt of the kind depicted by geopoliticians such as Halford Mackinder and Karl Haushofer. Mastery of what they called the "Heartland"—the Eurasian land mass—would set the stage for eventual mastery of the world.

As far as the Mediterranean was concerned, Hitler had been consistently skeptical of plans from any quarter for an invasion of Malta. He had little faith in the Italians, who would of necessity provide the bulk of the land and all the naval resources. After the swingeing losses suffered by German airborne forces in Crete, he was reluctant to risk them a second time in what promised to be a death ride. Nor did Hitler and the High Command consider the Luftwaffe's increasingly limited strength best expended on bombarding an island fortress that showed no signs of capitulating to air power alone. At the end of April, the air offensive would be curtailed, the planes distributed to meet more pressing operational requirements. After flirting with various alternatives during the spring of 1942, Hitler would essentially scuttle the Malta operation on May 20 in a stormy interview with paratroop commander Kurt Student.

The Fuehrer was more sanguine about an extended operation against the Suez Canal—an operational victory sufficient to bring down a Churchill whose domestic position Hitler believed vulnerable. That was enough for Rommel, whose intention in any case was to create conditions on the ground that would compel support from Axis higher echelons. He had received an "all is forgiven" phone call from Mussolini even before capturing Benghazi. If he took Cairo, who then might be on the line?

The prospect of Rommel at the head of a full-blooded Axis drive into the Middle East continues to engage counterfactual historians. It is a staple chapter in the alternative histories that show Germany winning the war—usually by some means that involve Hitler's not being Hitler and the Wehrmacht being something essentially different from the Wehrmacht. Reality is less dramatic. A prerequisite for large-scale offensive operations in the Middle East was Axis maritime superiority in the Mediterranean—enough sea power not merely to capture Malta, but to prevent any significant Allied intervention in the theater. The Germans could make no significant contribution to surface forces above the small-ship level, and the average of twenty U-boats the *Kriegsmarine* maintained in the Mediterranean was not enough to do more than harass the Royal Navy and British merchant shipping. The Italian navy had suffered heavy losses in the war's early years. Neither its construction nor its repair facilities were in a position to replace them. The fleet's increasing success at converting to convoy operations and its efforts to prepare for an amphibious attack on Malta correspondingly diminished its effectiveness as a ship-to-ship combat force.

Air power was vital for control of the Mediterranean, and here, too, the burden would have fallen on an Italian air force whose material and logistics proved consistently inferior to its allies and enemies throughout the war. Although improved designs were on the drawing boards in 1942, production facilities failed to keep pace. Test models do not fight. Nor were the Germans able or willing to deliver the more powerful engines required to improve aircraft performance. While the courage of Italy's airmen could never be questioned, the quality of their training steadily declined because of lack of fuel, and from indifference at senior levels. As for the Luftwaffe, those human and material resources not deployed to Russia were increasingly being reassigned to home defense.

Diplomacy might have compensated for military shortcomings. Spanish and Vichy French participation in the war would have facilitated sealing the Mediterranean's western end, if only by providing base facilities and operational flexibility to the Germn and Italian forces that would still have been tasked with most of the real fighting. But the possibility of bringing in either state in 1942 was for practical purposes nonexistent. Neither Franco's nor Petain's governments had seen any reason to join the Axis when it was riding high. Why participate in a gamble two years later?

Logistics, too, worked against an Axis Middle East offensive mounted from the Mediterranean. That operation would require a port. Alexandria was sure to have been at least damaged by the British. Transporting material, repairing demolitions, and clearing blocked channels would have strained a semi-industrialized Italy to the limit even with no other major responsibilities. Should Rommel somehow succeed in "bouncing" Alexandria, that would do no more than provide the starting point for an increasingly long line of communication over terrain even more formidable, and less developed, than Russia. The survivability of German and Italian trucks in the mountains of Syria and the deserts of Iraq was likely to be less than on the *Rollbahns* of the Soviet Union. The Middle East lacked even a partially developed railway network to compensate. And the problem of securing a thousand miles and more of natural guerrilla/ bandit country would have daunted the most brutal of Himmler's specialists in genocide.

The final damping factor on a Middle East campaign was its dependance on a successful drive through southern Russia to the Caucasus. Should Rommel's Panzer strength be doubled, without regard for the demands of the Russian front, or for how the additional tanks and trucks would be supplied, the offensive through Egypt would nevertheless be a secondary operation. If German tanks did not appear in the southern passages of the Caucasus by early winter, any successes Rommel might achieve were likely to prove all too ephemeral.

Rommel nevertheless returned to Africa in mid-March with his mood improved. Halder may have informed him that he was fighting a losing battle in trying to compete with the seemingly endless demands of the Russian Front. The Afrika Korps might still be close to the bottom of the Reich's priority lists. But at the turn of the year, Kesselring had opened a major air campaign against Malta. In February, the Luftwaffe and the Regia Aeronautica combined for three thousand sorties. From March 30 to April 28, Kesselring increased the pressure to levels comparable with the Battle of Britain at its height. The island's defenses might not be collapsing under the pounding, but Malta's ability to intercept convoys steadily diminished. Italian and German figures on losses and deliveries vary, but the best available statistics indicate that the tonnage arriving in Libya doubled after December 1941 and almost tripled during February as sinking rates dropped close to zero. In March, tonnage declined by a third, but in April reached the campaign's highest absolute figure: 56,700 tons.

This was the only month when deliveries came near matching the Panzer army's requirement of sixty thousand tons. Moving that amount of material forward on bad roads with worn-out trucks, as Rommel observed, was as much of a headache as getting it to North Africa in the first place. Benghazi, however, was by now working up to full capacity, reducing the distance for about a third of the Panzer army's supplies to about three hundred miles. By the end of March Rommel was convinced that within two months his force would be ready to mount another offensive. This one would be no mere raid, no riposte. It would be systematically prepared and supported by a built-up reserve of fuel and ammunition. Its immediate objectives would be the port of Tobruk and the airfields of Cyrenaica. The first would provide a forward staging point for continued operations; the second would contribute to Malta's isolation.

Rommel's relative restraint reflected his respect for the British Gazala

Line. The 8th Army had constructed a layered network of defended positions, or "boxes," each holding a reinforced brigade; each supplied with ample food, water, and ammunition; each surrounded by barbed wire and overlapping minefields. The areas between the forward boxes were screened by more minefields and by tanks—elements of two full armored brigades were assigned that mission by the time of Rommel's offensive. Bir Hachiem at the southern apex, the most vulnerable point of any North African defensive system, was manned by the best infantry brigade in the 8th Army: the Free French; the bulk of the armor, two divisions, was deployed in reserve behind the boxes in the south.

The British idea was that the brigade boxes would channel the Germans into frontal attacks against superior armored forces. Should they try to maneuver, British tanks would force them into the minefields. Had Auchinleck and his subordinates been able to concentrate on what the British army in World War II did better than anything else, that is, hold ground, the next few weeks might have told a different story. Instead, Churchill insisted on an offensive as soon as possible, both for prestige reasons and to reoccupy airfields that could be used to relieve pressure on Malta. Auchinleck temporized, then in response to a direct order, fixed the date for an offensive in early June.

Rommel struck first. His intelligence was not as good as it had been, due largely to improved British radio discipline. He nevertheless possessed a sufficiently accurate understanding of British strength and dispositions to produce a characteristically bold plan. His Army Order of May 20 set the objectives as the destruction of the British army in its forward positions, followed by the capture of Tobruk. Two Italian corps would mount a series of frontal diversionary attacks in the northern sector. The mobile forces, with Trieste and Ariete on the left, Afrika Korps's Panzers in the center, and the 90th Light covering the desert flank would envelop the British in the south with a short right hook, then roll them up from the rear. Rommel assumed command of the mechanized sweep and placed Cruewell in charge of the feints—a sign of respect for his subordinate's ability. If the British were not held in place, the offensive was likely to achieve little, and Rommel's time frame was tight, allowing only four days for the capture of Tobruk.

Both the German and the Italian High Commands saw this as a limited operation, a spoiling attack to disrupt British timetables. Rommel's Order of the Day for the 26th, with its references to a decisive assault, suggested much wider objectives. Its concluding salutes were given to the King of Italy, Mussolini, and Hitler, in that order. Rommel might never be a military politician, but he knew where his supplies came from. The Axis enjoyed air superiority, four hundred operational aircraft against two hundred, with the Me 109f still the best fighter in North Africa. Rommel knew the British had more tanks—850, including 170 of the latest U.S. M-3 Grants, with 75-millimeter guns. Rommel's 565 tanks included only 240 Mark III's and 40 Mark IV's. More than 200 of the rest were Italian: M-13/40s and the slightly improved M-14/41s, still not very good. Rommel counted on his 48 88-millimeter long-barrels to redress the balance. He counted even more on the skill of his desert veterans of both armies in the kind of maneuver battle he planned to fight.

By now, Rommel's fame had spread across Germany: the rough-tongued, warm-hearted general who led from the front and did not bother with General Staff subtleties. Josef Goebbels honestly admired Rommel and threw the power of the Reich's propaganda machine into promulgating his legend. Rommel had simultaneously achieved near-mythic status in the 8th Army. Auchinleck finally issued an army order warning against making Rommel a "magician or bogeyman" and describing him as an "ordinary German general." As might be expected, this document had an opposite effect from that intended.

The British were taken by surprise and caught off-balance. Tank for tank, any two of the three British armored brigades in the south were capable of matching the whole Afrika Korps. Give the Germans the initiative and put Rommel at their head, and the story unfolded quite differently. The initial German advance overran an Indian motorized brigade south of Bir Hachiem, drove another brigade into confused retreat, and scattered the headquarters of the 7th Armoured Division, before encountering the main British armored force.

The Afrika Korps's Panzers nevertheless lost heavily to the Grants despite their awkward configuration. The M-3's sponson-mounted main gun outranged anything the German tanks carried, while even the shells of the Mark IVs did no more than dent the Grants' armor at battle ranges. About a third of the German tanks were knocked out in the first day's fighting alone. Had the British concentrated their armor instead of employing the three brigades separately, Gazala might have had a different outcome. Had the British armor deployed closer to the forward boxes, enabling direct cooperation between position and mobile operations, things might also have been different. As it was, the Axis tanks drove upward like a knife beneath a rib cage. By the evening of the 27th, Rommel had the 15th and 21st Panzer Divisions concentrated in an area called the Cauldron, a depression in the sand a few miles south of the Knightsbridge Box, manned as the name suggests by a brigade of Guardsmen. His supply lines, ranging far into the desert, were wide open to strikes from Bir Hachiem. Its garrison, Foreign Legionnaires and Senegalese, men from Tahiti and New Caledonia, would give the Italians and the Afrika Korps elements that subsequently joined the battle for the box all the fighting they wanted for two blazing weeks.

To anyone able to read a map, Panzer Army Africa's mobile forces were in a pocket. Rommel's staff expected a concentrated armored counterattack against the Afrika Korps on the 28th. It was what they would have planned. As a counter, Rommel ordered the 21st Panzer, the only division that had managed to resupply, north in a spoiling attack. The 15th Panzer was literally stalled in its tracks for want of fuel. Rommel and Gause set out to find a safe supply route, and on May 29, Rommel personally led a convoy through to the 15th.

Kesselring criticized the "hussar's trick." Mellenthin praised it. The Afrika Korps expected it. Rommel always seemed able to pull a rabbit out of his hat when needed, and in the succeeding hours, he handled his depleted Afrika Korps like a rapier, rallying the 21st Panzer, 90th Light, and Ariete on the 15th Panzer, always just ahead of British attacks characterized more by courage than coordination. The 8th Army's tank losses mounted. When Cruewell's light plane was shot down and the general captured, Rommel turned command of his northern sector over to Kesselring, who was making a tour of inspection. The generals agreed the original plan of a sweep north was no longer feasible. Instead, Rommel desperately needed to open a secure supply line through the minefields that were taking an unobtrusive but heavy toll on his trucks.

He did so in reverse—from the east side, overrunning a box held by the 150th Brigade. Rommel personally reconnoitered the attack routes and oversaw the assault. The British, "as usual," Rommel observed, fought to the last round and surrendered with their arms in their hands, but the convoys could move through, and in Rommel's mind, the crisis of the battle was over. It had not gone the way he planned, but he was in a position to strike north or east and keep either effort supplied. The British had shown no ability to coordinate their superior numbers, but if they did launch a counterattack, the Axis armor and antitank guns were in position to chew it up. Panzer Army Africa was setting the pace and determining the agenda, and once again Rommel seemed everywhere he was needed. He paid for leading from the front with the loss of Westphal and Gause, both wounded. But the latter's replacement, Fritz Bayerlein from the Afrika Korps, was a step upward in ability and energy. The two would make a first-rate team in the weeks ahead.

Rommel's next move was to finish off Bir Hachiem. The box had lost its earlier tactical importance, but he was unwilling to leave its aggressive garrison in his rear and wanted its water and supplies. The attack began on the night of June 1, and despite substantial air support, made slow and costly progress against a network of trenches and bunkers defended to the last man. Rommel frequently took direct command of the attack himself, and "seldom in Africa was I given such a hard-fought struggle." Three times he summoned the position to surrender; three times General Pierre Koenig refused. Not until June 10 did the garrison stage a daring breakout, 2,700 of them making it back to the British lines and only the rear guards, a thousand in all and many of them walking wounded, going into captivity. Hitler ordered the execution of any German nationals, political refugees, or Foreign Legionnaires. Rommel destroyed the order.

Rommel's decision to deal personally with Bir Hachiem was facilitated by the slow pace with which the British concentrated their forces for the attack on the Cauldron Rommel knew was sure to come. An initial offensive on June 5 was shattered with a loss of sixty of the seventy tanks committed. Rommel led the counterattack that annihilated a brigade of Indian infantry, overran the headquarters of an armored brigade, and captured four thousand prisoners. With Bir Hachiem's fall, the 8th Army's time was out. Now the Panzer Army could resume the maneuver war at which it excelled. In a desperate effort to forestall disaster, the British threw in their last two armored brigades. Rommel caught them between his two veteran Panzer divisions, and took personal command of a head-on fight that on June 11–12 accounted for no fewer than 140 British tanks. On the morning of June 14, Ritchie, overmatched from the first, ordered the 8th Army—what remained of it—to retreat to Egypt. That night, the lead elements of the Afrika Korps reached the sea.

Tobruk remained. Auchinleck would have preferred to evacuate it. Churchill refused to consider abandoning such a potent symbol of the Empire's resistance. Auchinleck complied, leaving an assortment of British and Indian battalions and a green South African division under an inexperienced commander as sacrifices to the power of hope. Rommel convinced Kesselring to shift the Luftwaffe's focus temporarily from Malta to Tobruk and recycled his plan of the previous year to hit the fortress from the southeast. On June 17, his spearheads took the Gambut airfield and its fuel depots. For the next three days, Rommel drew an Axis ring around Tobruk, and on June 20, the Afrika Korps and the Italian motorized corps rolled forward behind the heaviest air and artillery bombardment Rommel had yet employed. Again he was in the forefront of the attack, his headquarters detachment directly accounting for a British strong point. By nightfall, two-thirds of the fortress had fallen. Its commander surrendered the next morning.

Hindsight argues that Tobruk's fall had little effect on the military balance in North Africa. It may have been a blessing in disguise, encouraging as it did both Roosevelt's willingness to commit major U.S. resources to the Mediterranean, and a scalding out of the amateurism that had so long characterized British efforts in the desert war. Such projections were at best cold comfort at the time. Thirty-three thousand prisoners, five thousand tons of supplies, fourteen hundred tons of fuel, a hundred tanks—even these statistics fail to convey the moral impact of Tobruk's capitulation, from the 8th Army's forward slit trenches to the British Parliament, which on June 25 tabled a censure motion Churchll regarded as a "serious challenge." Vehicles streamed toward Egypt in what came to be known as the "Gazala Gallop." In Cairo, plans were discussed for a retreat to Palestine, and the smoke of burning documents filled the air. In Britain, newspapers speculated on Rommel's imminent capture of the Suez Canal and his probable drive for the oil fields of the

Middle East. Egyptian nationalists cheered Rommel's forthcoming arrival. Rumor even had it that a suite awaited him in Cairo's flagship Shepheard's Hotel, and many would have been unsurprised to see Rommel and his headquarters guard roll into the city at any moment.

Gazala was the apogee of Rommel's style of command. Reflecting, he made the case for micromangement, concern with details of command and frequent visits to the front, under four headings. First, he argued, it was a mistake to assume every officer would make the most possible of every situation. Most "soon succumb to a certain inertia." The commander's physical presence was the best antidote. Second, the commander must keep his troops abreast of the latest tactical developments. Third, it was in the commander's own interest to have a personal perspective of conditions at the front. Success came most freely to the general whose ideas developed from the circumstances. Finally, the commander must be able to feel and think with his men. The one basic rule was to avoid artifice and posturing. The ordinary soldier has "a surprisingly good nose" for true and false.

All this was a far cry from the command environment in the 8th Army, where senior officers routinely disliked and distrusted each other to a point where orders became starting points for discussions and cooperation was at best ad hoc. The Panzer Army was not exactly a band of brothers, but its officers knew what their general expected, and if they could not always internalize those expectations, they soon learned how to vamp them.

Rommel, whose euphoria never overcame his eye for the next chance and the main chance, sent one of his public relations officers to Berlin to tell the Panzer Army's story. Congratulations poured in from everywhere in the German empire. Hitler responded by promoting Rommel to Field Marshal—the youngest of his rank in the army. He responded as well by begging Mussolini to exploit "a chance that will never recur a second time" and support an attack "into the heart of Egypt." Its conquest would have global repercussions; combined with the German drive toward the Caucasus, it would demolish "the whole oriental edifice of the British Empire."

Mussolini's senior military commanders were less sanguine, arguing for the continued importance of Malta and warning that an advance into

Egypt might open the door to an Allied landing in French North Africa. But an invasion of Malta posed a spectrum of concrete difficulties for the Italian armed forces who would bear the brunt of the operation. An attack on Egypt offered nothing but promise. There was little doubt which alternative Mussolini preferred, especially because by now he was fully under the spell of Rommel's spectacular victories.

Roosevelt had responded to the fall of Tobruk by asking, "What can we do to help?" Churchill requested three hundred tanks. Within days, they were on their way; M-4 Shermans, the latest design, pulled from the inventories of America's still-embryonic armored divisions. U.S. air groups began supplementing a British air force already on its way to achieving permanent superiority over a thinly stretched Luftwaffe. Rommel was more than ever convinced that his choice lay between an advance that offered at least a hope of victory and a shift to the defensive that promised only defeat.

On June 22, the newly minted field marshal requested that current limitations on his freedom of movement be removed. Four days later, he assured Kesselring and Cavallero that a breakthrough on the frontier should have the Panzer Army in Cairo and Alexandria by the end of the month. Bold words—but even as Tobruk fell, the 90th Light Division was advancing toward Egypt, meeting no resistance. The Afrika Korps and the Italian motorized corps followed, their rest days cancelled, the Panzer divisions taking heavy losses from British air attacks but reporting their men in an "aggressive and confident" mood. The Italians were running on shoestrings—Ariete was down to 10 tanks and 1,500 infantry—but their morale was high as well. Rommel had taken pains to make them feel part of the team and was generous in his praise of performances, which from the beginning of the offensive, had matched the best of the Afrika Korps when relative strengths are considered.

Ritchie and Auchinleck proposed to defend Egypt along a line based on Mersa Matruh. The position's center was weak: minefields covered by what remained of an Indian infantry division. The 90th Light hit the Indians on the afternoon of June 26 and broke through, with the 15th and 21st Panzer following. Auchinleck, who replaced Ritchie in direct command on the same day, proposed to conduct a mobile defense built around ad hoc battle groups, sometimes cynically described as brigade groups that had been twice overrun by tanks. The Germans, even as their numbers shrank, continued to fight—and win—as divisions. The New Zealand Division was encircled, almost overrun, then cut its way out at bayonet point, partly through Rommel's battle headquarters, which by now predictably was in the thick of the action. For the first time, credible accounts surfaced of wounded and medical personnel killed in the confused night fighting. The British corps holding the southern sector fell back in disorder—an official euphemism for blank confusion at headquarters levels and panic-stricken rout in the rear echelons. Most of the garrison of Matruh, the better part of another corps, broke out before that position was overrun on June 29, with Italian bersaglieri playing a leading role in a close-quarters fight resulting in the capture of six thousand prisoners and a division's worth of equipment.

"Less than a hundred miles to Alexandria," Rommel exultantly reported to Lu. He joked with a captain in the 21st Panzer that the next day they would drive together into Cairo for coffee. He noted as well that five weeks of campaigning against superior numbers had brought the Panzer Army to the brink of exhaustion. By now, most of the Germans and Italians were riding British trucks using British fuel. The Afrika Korps was down to forty operating tanks. The 21st Panzer had a day's worth of water remaining. The Italians had long insisted that the Panzer Army could not be supported as far forward as Rommel wished without Tobruk and Matruh. Now they complained of the captured ports' limited unloading capacity, and the effects of constant British air raids. Rommel in turn excoriated the peacetime atmosphere, the general absence of urgency, he described as prevalent in Rome. He denounced Italian bureaucracy and Fascist corruption. He went so far as to suggest defeatist elements in the Italian navy were dragging their anchors when it came to supplying North Africa.

In fact the Navy was so short of fuel oil that its big ships were operating with half-empty bunkers. The port of Tobruk was intact but could handle at best 20,000 tons a month. With ULTRA continuing to supply information on convoy routes and schedules, British air strikes made the Tobruk run a particular killing zone. The situation grew worse as shipping losses compelled the use of slower, smaller vessels on the African run. Shifting the center of gravity back to Tripoli meant increasing time required to move supplies to the front, well past the operational danger point, especially given the increasing shortage of gasoline imposed by the demands of the Russian front.

For logistic and stragetic reasons, therefore, the Italian High Command still intended the Panzer Army at most to close up to the Egyptian frontier and establish a defensive line roughly along that of 1941. Rommel still insisted no less strongly that defensive operations were a high-risk option under North African conditions, especially given the fundamental, by Hitler's decision unalterable, imbalance of forces in the theater. Should the attack on Malta succeed—and Rommel by this time was convinced the project was mostly moonshine—the Panzer Army would remain for weeks exposed to the relentless hammering of superior Allied air power, confronting a ground buildup that would face no significant challenge. Even with Malta's fall, transporting fuel, weapons, and reinforcements to North Africa would take time. And because the Naples-to-Tripoli route would be the shortest and safest, fuel would be used and vehicles worn out in the process of reaching the front.

Rommel's insistence that a weaker force could counter quantity with quality, balancing numbers with leadership, tactics, and surprise, came close to epitomizing the German way of war as it had developed since Frederick the Great. In a sense, Rommel was the victim of his own successes: he had dome so much with so little that his current requests for men, tanks, and supplies tended to be filed under "R" for "Routine." But with the British arguably in fundamental disarray since the fall of Tobruk, allowing them time to regroup violated military wisdom and common sense. Based on previous events and present circumstances, Rommel was hardly indulging in wishful thinking to believe the momentum of his victories and his reputation would carry the Panzer Army at least to the Suez Canal. Questions of the ultimate objectives and prospects of a successful overrunning of Egypt could be postponed for future consideration.

Mussolini concurred, expressing a willingness to go to Africa himself, and issuing detailed orders on how his troops should conduct themselves in conquered Egypt. A still-reluctant Italian High Command climbed on the bandwagon, defining the Suez Canal as the operational goal. On July 1, Rommel launched his first attack on what would become known as the Alamein Line. He had two options. One was to drive across the open desert in the south, directly toward the Suez Canal. That, however, meant accepting the risk of leaving the entire 8th Army in his rear, ready to slash across lines of communication that would be vulnerable at bet. He chose the second alternative.

Auchinleck had deployed the 8th Army on what has been called the only position in the North African desert with a top—the Mediterranean coast—and a bottom—the Quattara Depression, a salt marsh whose surface was more than two hundred feet below sea level, and the Great Sand Sea below it. The "Alamein Line" also possessed something like a defensible southern flank: the Ruweisat/Alam el Halfa ridge line running east/west just above the Depression. This resembled its counterparts in World War I Flanders: a ridge line by courtesy, consisting of little more than folds in the ground that nevertheless offered favorable terrain to hull down tanks and dig in antitank guns.

Deprived by geography of tactical flexibility, Rommel opted for a direct thrust by the Afrika Korps against the Ruweisat Ridge. He expected to achieve a quick breakthrough, then turn north toward the coast and bring on the mobile battle in which he and the Afrika Korps excelled. Instead, the British stopped all three of his German divisions almost in their tracks, and Rommel found himself caught in a battle of attrition. The Germans were down to fifty tanks when the attack began, and the Panzer divisions suffered increasing losses among infantry constrained to operate without the armored cooperation to which they were accustomed. The British had not merely air superiority but air supremacy, as the Luftwaffe suffered from a lack of forward bases.

Despite these handicaps, the offensive ground forward until July 4, when Rommel finally began replacing his exhausted Panzer divisions with Italian infantry. The 8th Army, taking a leaf from the Afrika Korps's book, promptly mounted a counterattack that just as promptly fell victim to dug-in antitank guns. As Rommel sought to rebuild the Afrika Korps and shift it southward, the 8th Army concentrated on whittling down the Italians holding the north sector of the line. On July 10 and 11, the 9th Australian Division destroyed one division and crippled two more. Rommel's intelligence system also took a serious blow when the Australians overran and destroyed his radio interception company, its vital codebooks falling into the hands of the 8th Army. On July 15, a combined-arms attack spearheaded by the New Zealand Division eviscerated two more Italian divisions. Held in place by their lack of transport, without the antitank capacity and firepower to hold independently, the Italians fought courageously but vainly as the Panzer divisions burned themselves out plugging the worst holes.

By mid-July, it was the 8th Army that held the initiative despite continuing weaknesses on coordinating both its combat arms and its operational planning. In a meeting with Kesselring, Bastico, and Cavallero on July 17, Rommel, his last German reserves committed, questioned his ability to hold at all and insisted on his need for more supplies. By now, everyone was familiar—perhaps too familiar—with Rommel's mercurial temperament: his prognostications of imminent disaster followed by another virtuoso rabbit-out-of–the-helmet performance. The Italians gave their word—perhaps less impressed than they might have been.

Rommel took center stage again, when the 5th Indian Division and the New Zealanders began a major offensive on July 21. The New Zealand Division mauled the 15th Panzer, but in turn suffered heavy casualties the next two days, losing most of a brigade to an Afrika Korps counterattack. The losses among supporting British tanks were heavy, with the New Zealanders becoming so disgusted at the lack of cooperation and coordination that the division refitted as a combined infantry/armor formation. A veteran Indian brigade was overrun as well. But Afrika Korps had shot its bolt, first failing to break through the British front and seeing its tank strength reduced to about forty of all types; then constrained to disperse much of its remaining infantry as "corset stays" for Italians overmatched in material though not in courage.

Mussolini, who arrived in Libya on June 29, fretted impatiently at the delay of his projected entry into Cairo. The German propaganda machine, which initially celebrated its hero's latest triumph, demanded fresh grist. The strength of the British Empire, Rommel noted in retrospect, had begun to tell. For a while, even the bread ration was cut in half—an important deprivation for Germans who saw the heavy, chewy loaves of *Kommissbrot* as a dietary basic. Rommel's German units had been committed time and again without respite or relief, and even the best of them were feeling the strain. Personnel strength was at 30 percent of authorization, tanks at 15 percent. Too many Italian formations lacked the ability to resist the kind of hammer blows the 8th Army could now deliver as a matter of routine. Rommel's scathing indictment of the Italian army's officer corps was accompanied by a directive to his Italian subordinates to make increased use of the death penalty.

Reinforcements were coming on line. Elements of a garrison division from Crete, grandiloquently retitled the 164th Light Africa Division, and a crack four-battalion brigade of paratroopers were transferred to the Panzer Army. But these were both foot formations, useful primarily for stabilizing the Italians and requiring a period of acclimatization to become effective in the North African environment. The paratroopers were picked men, yet within a short time, more than half were sick from heat, jaundice, desert sores, bad food, and worse water. Rommel asked the German High Command for tanks—more of the new Mark III's with the long 50-millimeter gun, and the Mark IV's whose shell guns were so important in the direct support of attacks. Rommel further requested 36 88s and a hundred 50-millimeter antitank guns, more motorized infantry, more antitank gunners, plus at least a thousand trucks.

What he received was a burst of resentment from Italian authorities who stressed the exhaustion of their men by endless marching and countermarching under a German commander who seemed oblivious to the differences between trucks and feet. Rommel, whose rugged constitution and cast-iron nerves were also showing signs of wear, responded that in its present condition, the Panzer Army could meet a major offensive only by being annihilated in place, or by undertaking a strategic retreat as it had done the previous year. The Italian High Command insisted the front must be held under all circumstances. Cavallero added a recommendation he must have enjoyed dictating, that the "state of momentary depression" in Rommel's headquarters must be "combatted." But he also sent across the Mediterranean a full-strength armored division, the Littorio. Untested in battle but equipped with the best Italy could provide, it began arriving on June 28.

The first two weeks of July are frequently presented as the turning point in Rommel's desert war. Two factors stand out. First, only two operational movements were possible in the Western Desert: a frontal attack somewhere from along the coast to about a hundred miles south, and a flanking movement on the desert side. These could be implemented tactically in sophisticated combinations, but the difference in terms of complexity was that between chess and checkers. As in the latter game, the loser was eventually likely to get a reasonable sense of the board. By mid-1942, the British still made the same mistakes, but did so less spectacularly. They were learning how to survive the midgame and force an ending. Second, an Italian army that had been fighting above its weight since 1941 was finally, definitively overmatched. Rommel could no longer rely on his Italian contingent to play successfully the unspectacular static roles that had made his daring maneuvers possible. Instead, he had to expect to support his allies directly.

As the Panzer Army caught its breath, the British introduced a new command team. On August 3, Winston Churchill arrived in Cairo. From his perspective, Auchinleck had succeeded in avoiding another debacle. But the 8th Army remained shaken and confused. Its apparent lack of direction was compounded by Auchinleck's decentralized style of command. When he balked at committing to an offensive to support the projected Anglo-American landings in Tunisia, Churchill replaced him with two generals from Britain. Sir Harold Alexander became commander in Chief Middle East. Lieutenant General Bernard Law Montgomery was transferred from a home defense command to take over the 8th Army.

Auchinleck's reputation has been refurbished by successive generations of postwar British soldiers and historians who highlight "the Auk's" success in learning "desert checkers," and his readiness to try new ideas and new men. Underlying the specifics is a scarcely concealed sense that Auchinleck was an honorable, principled gentleman, just coming into his own, supplanted by a nasty little master of public relations. The other side of the argument is that Auchinleck had had his innings and failed to impress. Montgomery was vain, egoistic, and determined to prove himself to a military system he regarded as a pack of amateurs. But he was also energetic and confident, quickly winning the confidence of subordinates at all levels, succeeding where predecessors had failed in helping the 8th Army to form a collective identity transcending its multicultural origins.

Above all, Montgomery believed in the importance of managed battle. In part, that reflected his solid understanding of the instrument at hand. Flexibility was not a strong point of the World War II British army, particularly at higher levels. As much to the point, its immediate opponent was a master of that kind of war. It made no sense to play by Rommel's rules, with Rommel's deck. Auchinleck had gradually reached the same conclusion. He left Montgomery a plan that influenced the latter's execution, when not his thinking, more than Montgomery was ever willing to admit. Essentially it involved conceding Rommel the initiative in the expectation that he would respond with one of his patented sweeps around the 8th Army's desert flank, followed by a turn north to bring on the encounter battle at which the Afrika Korps excelled. Auchinleck, and later Montgomery, proposed to hold the ridge line at Alam Halfa, then counterattack the Afrika Korps on both flanks, fixing it in position.

Montgomery, however, regarded this operation as only a preliminary to a decisive attack against the Panzer Army elements—mostly Italian—holding the line from the coast south. The 8th Army's new commander projected a set-piece, first taking advantage of the quality of the 8th Army's infantry combined with British air and artillery superiority—the latter not merely in number of guns but in fire control systems—to destroy the Axis infantry. The second phase involved committing what Montgomery called a *corps de chasse* of three full armored divisions to threaten Rommel's supply lines and draw the Panzers north onto a prepared killing ground.

As it took shape, El Alamein was the first of the "colossal cracks" that would come to define Montgomery's way of war. Rommel's best chances of dealing with the blow involved preemption. In mid-August, he calculated he had about three weeks before the 8th Army's reinforcements in men and material could come on line. His own immediate crises of personnel, equipment, and supply were easing. By the end of the month, his staff calculated, the Panzer Army would have up to 250 German tanks and almost as many Italian ones, with enough fuel for a 10-day operation. On the other hand, the tonnage unloaded in North African ports during August fell by almost half compared to July's relative bounty. The tonnage reaching the front continued to diminish relative to the Panzer Army's demands. British aircraft and submarines, directed by ULTRA intercepts, accounted for part of the shrinkage. The shortage of trucks and motor fuel relative to theater requirements remained a major factor. The final element of the logistics crisis reflected Fascist Italy's comprehensive overstretch: its administrative and military systems had useful surge capabilities but could not sustain for any length of time the efforts Rommel's intentions required.

German military writing on World War II makes frequent use of the phrase "force of circumstances" (*Gesetz des Handels*). An opera fan might instead borrow from Verdi and refer to *la Forza del Destino,* for it seemed fate itself was impelling Rommel toward a final dice throw. Rommel recognized that the El Alamein position favored his enemy, both geographically and in terms of institutional characteristics. He recognized that it could not be outflanked or otherwise finessed. Nevertheless, he proposed to take advantage of the full moon at he end of August to break through in the southern sector, destroy the British formations around Ruweisat, then continue operations "in an easterly direction."

This time there was nothing new under the African sun—just Rommel's confidence that the quality of his troops and his own situational awareness would see the Panzer Army through one final time. Rommel's health was by now also becoming a matter for serious concern. He had spent nineteen months in Africa, longer than any officer over the age of forty. He suffered from jaundice, circulation problems, and digestive trouble—that last in part a consequence of a marked indifference to food. Rommel frequently spent a day in the desert with no more nourishment than a package of sandwiches or a can of sardines and a chunk of ration bread, plus a flask of cold tea.

The rest of his physical environment was similarly spartan and has generated corresponding admiration among admirers of muddy-boots generalship. Though Auchinleck paid it the compliment of emulation by deliberately creating a headquarters environment where the staff would be physically deprived, Rommel's unnecessarily minimalist life style arguably did more than the objective hardships of the desert to damage his health and diminish his effectiveness. In Montgomery's words, "Any damn fool can be uncomfortable."

His personal staff babied him as unobtrusively as possible, undertaking fishing and hunting trips to provide fresh protein, scrounging eggs and chickens, having fruits and vegetables flown in. The *Chef* nevertheless endured enough spells of public weakness that Gauss, by now returned to his post as chief of staff, insisted on a complete examination. The doctor, a stomach specialist from Wuerzburg University and Rommel's long-standing medical confidant, reported that Rommel was so debilitated by digestive trouble and low blood pressure that he was unfit to command the coming offensive. Recommended therapy amounted to a long rest.

Rommel himself saw no alternative to at least six weeks of treatment in Germany, which he wrote Lu should bring him around. He informed the High Command that the only officer who could take his place was Heinz Guderian, Germany's leading armored-warfare specialist but under a cloud since Barbarossa's failure. The reply was that Guderian was "unacceptable." Rommel responded by convincing his doctor that he was fit to command after all, with constant medical attention and a replacement ready at hand. Hitler proposed Cruewell's replacement as Afrika Korps commander Walther Nehring for operations and Kesselring in overall charge. The shock was enough to galvanize Rommel into writing by August 29 that his health was "very good again." But to someone like Rommel, having his body turn on him for the first time in his life had a greater psychological effect than on someone who had not enjoyed his lifetime of robust fitness. It was one more bad omen on a growing list.

By the last week in August, indeed, Rommel was sufficiently concerned about his fuel situation to propose mounting a local attack. He changed his mind only when Kesselring offered to release fuel from Luftwaffe holdings and fly it into Africa should that become necessary. For all their personal and professional differences, Kesselring and Rommel by now both saw there was by now no turning back. Hitler and Mussolini each wanted the offensive. Steadily increasing shipments of tanks, ammunition, and aircraft from the United States were rapidly closing any window of opportunity that still existed. It was a time for promises and hopes. "Either," Rommel informed his doctor on the morning the attack began, "the army in Russia succeeds in getting through . . . and we in Africa manage to reach the Suez Canal, or . . ." He accompanied his unfinished sentence with a dismissive gesture suggesting defeat.

Rommel's plan was that the Italian infantry, this time reinforced by German elements, once again fix the British in place along the northern and central sectors of the front. The main effort would be made in the south by the Afrika Korps's old hands, the 15th and 21st Panzer and the 90th Light, and the Italian XX Motorized Corps with the veteran Trieste Motorized and Ariete Armored Divisions and the newcomers of Littorio Armored. Cross the British minefields, their orders stated. Advance as much as thirty miles during the night of August 30. Swing north toward the coast road and through the British supply dumps. Then pivot west and cut off the pocket that by now should contain most of the 8th Army's infantry and much of its armor. Speed and surprise must extend the predictably long British reaction times.

By now Rommel talked and thought less of destroying the enemy than of "giving him a pretty thorough beating." Even the latter prospect began fading when the Afrika Korps's initial attack stalled in minefields exponentially more complex and comprehensive than expected. As pioneers worked desperately to clear paths through them, British air and artillery hammered the tanks and trucks backed up for miles across the desert. The Afrika Korps commander was wounded and the commander of the 21st Panzer killed before their tanks got across the start lines. Not until 8 on the morning of the 21st did the German tanks clear the "death gardens." The Italians, lacking mine detectors, were still probing the sand with bayonets.

Rommel had four choices: play *va banque* and adhere to the original plan, set more modest objectives, go on the defensive behind the now-occupied British minefields—or call off the operation and pull back. Initially, he chose Option Two. Determined resistance by massed British armor combined with diminishing Axis fuel supplies to force a defensive stance Rommel believed would be temporary. Then he received word that the tankers promised him had not reached harbor. Half the expected tonnage had been sunk. More than half of the rest had never left Italy. British fuel dumps were still far away. Around-the-clock air attacks were doing heavy damage to vehicle columns whose camouflage discipline and local antiaircraft defense were alike sketchy.

So much has been said in praise of Panzer Army Africa's use of antiaircraft guns in ground roles that their resulting unavailability for their primary mission is often overlooked. Most of the strikes were at high altitudes by mass formations of medium bombers, American as well as British, with escorts strong enough that an already-weakened Luftwaffe had little impact. Rommel's hehadquarters was bombed no fewer than six times in two hours on September 1. The experience contributed significantly to the field marshal's decision that same day to disengage and withdraw, mostly to his offensive's starting points. By September 6, his offensive was over. In the ranks of the Panzer divisions, cynical Landser joked about the "six-day race," referring to a famous interwar bicycle race back home.

Alam Halfa was the first time Rommel had been engaged head-on and stopped cold. As a morale-booster, it correspondingly overshadowed even El Alamein. Alam Halfa was also the first triumph of the Western allies' version of combined arms. Rommel had taught his enemies lessons at the tactical level through his flexible use of combined arms, his integration of air and ground assets, and his sophisticated reconnaissance methods. The British, by the autumn of 1942, had taken the game to the operational level, developing a plan that took systematic account of their material superiority and their military culture. combining it with the use of air power at theater level and developing sophistication in the use of ULTRA.

Rommel had informed Hitler of his plan of attack by radio on August 13. ULTRA had a translation in Montgomery's hands within forty-eight hours. It confirmed his reading of the situation as opposed to altering it; the synergy was no less critical for a general in his first battle against an opponent of Rommel's quality despite Montgomery's reluctance to acknowledge it.

Ignorant of the ULTRA secret, Rommel in evaluating his defeat emphasized the third dimension. We learned one lesson at Alam Halfa, he wrote: the possiblities of ground action become very limited in the face of air supremacy. He proposed to regain some of the initiative by returning to Germany and restoring his health. In the process, he might gain the Fuehrer's ear and at least secure a greater share of the cutting-edge armored vehicles being sent to the Russian front. He left North Africa on September 23, stopping in Rome before reporting to Berlin. Hitler, who was discussing making Rommel commander in chief of the postwar German army, greeted him with praise for his achievements, concern for his illness, and talk of command of an army group in Russia. He promised more and better weapons: multiple rocket launchers, the feared *Nebel-*

werfer, and the new Tiger tanks, virtually invulnerable to conventional antitank weapons.

Goebbels enthusiastically welcomed Rommel as a house guest and organized a hero's welcome, in part as a distraction from a Russian front where once again the major German offensive was beginning to bog down. Rommel responded with a never-ending supply of war stories, many of them at the expense of the Italians, and most with himself as the hero. From Berlin he traveled to the Austrian Alps and Lucie's company, for the peace and quiet the doctors uniformly considered necessary for his physical and emotional recovery.

Peace of mind, at least, eluded the field marshal. His pleasure in the pubic adulation he received was diminished by having to present a picture of the situation in North Africa that was not merely optimistic, but false. Rommel, acting in his own self-interest and the hope of convincing the British to postpone their inevitable attack, nevertheless resented being thus drawn into the meshes of the Reich's propaganda machine. He resented even more what he considered a dangerously optimistic climate in Hitler's headquarters. When he mentioned that British fighter-bombers were knocking out his tanks from the air with 40-millimeter cannon, Goering scoffed at the impossibility, saying that Americans only knew how to make razor blades. Rommel allegedly replied that "We could do with some of those razor blades" and displayed a round he had brought from North Africa for demonstration purposes.

The story sounds pat in retrospect, but even if it did not happen in quite the way Rommel recorded it, the incident focused and reflected a still unique experience. Rommel was the first German general to face an adversary whose advantages in mass and method could not be rationalized away by emphasizing German operational superiority. The Western allies in 1940 had been embarrassingly outgeneraled. The Red Army of late 1942 was still enough of a heavy, blunt instrument that its opponents might expect to triumph by finesse. The British in North Africa were about where the Austrians had been in 1809, when, in the aftermath of an unexpectedly hard-fought victory, Napoleon reflected "these animals have learned something."

They, and their American allies, could only learn more. Rommel had turned over temporary command of the Panzer Army to General Georg

Stumme. He had led a Panzer corps in Russia with enough success to make him a reasonable choice, and enough common sense to know he had been handed a risk and an opportunity in the same package. He kept Rommel informed: the British offensive could be expected at any time, but the Panzer Army was well entrenched behind 450,000 British and German mines, should be able to stop the attack, and might well be able to resume the offensive in turn. Then, on October 24, Rommel received a phone call from Armed Forces High Command. The British had launched a major attack; Stumme was missing. Was Rommel in condition to return to Africa immediately? Two calls from Hitler confirmed that the situation was serious. On the morning of October 25, Rommel boarded a plane for Africa.

He was going into a fight whose nature was directly opposite to his talents, yet one whose matrix he had created. Rommel understood that to stand on the Alamein Line meant accepting a battle of attrition, rapier against broadsword: 500 tanks against more than 1,300, including 250 Grants and 300 of the new Shermans, whose turret-mounted 75-millimeter gun made it the master of anything across the battle line. The British, moreover, faced the same geographic situation the Panzer Army confronted at Alam Halfa: the lack of an exploitable southern flank to tempt them to seek the 8th Army's enduring *fata morgana* of a mobile battle. Panzer Army Africa lacked the fuel to execute anything but local maneuver operations. A high proportion of his German as well as his Italian troops were straight-leg infantry, at their best in prepared defenses. Given British air supremacy, men on the march in trucks or on foot were likely to be picked off like targets.

Put together, these conditions suggested an operational cloak-and-sword synergy of well-prepared forward defenses and rapid, limited counterattacks—the same scenario Rommel would seek to create as a counter to Operation Overlord. Just before midnight on October 23, the desert silence was broken by a barrage whose intensity was unprecedented in the history of the desert war. More than nine hundred guns flogged the Axis forward positions. Daylight brought the infantry: Australians and South Africans, the New Zealand Division and the Jocks of the 51st Highland Division, reformed after St. Valery and played into action by its pipers. Stumme, driving forward to see the situation for

himself, suffered a fatal heart attack. It was then that Panzer Army headquarters contacted Berlin.

Rommel arrived by Ju-52, Fieseler Storch, and car in the evening of
the 25th. His first act was to order an armored concentration for a counterattack against a fearure the British called Kidney Ridge, where they
seemed to be on the point of breaking through. His second was to send a
signal announcing that he was again in command. The next four days
were a death grapple, as Montgomery's superior forces continued what
he called the "crumbling" of Axis forces and positions. Nowhere did the
British break through. The 8th Army's newly elevated morale began to
sag as its casualties mounted. Tankers and infantrymen resumed the mutual sniping that had characterized their relations since the coming of
Rommel. But the Panzer Army's commander was by now committing armored units to plugging gaps in his forward defensive positions. Fuel reserves shrank hourly. "I hope we'll pull through," Rommel confided to
Lu. He informed Rome that with six thousand reinforcements and fresh
supplies, he could hold. Instead, he received news that two successive
tankers destined for North Africa had been sunk en route. Two more supply ships went down almost in sight of Tobruk, a forlorn hope boring in
through skies the RAF ruled.

That news meant that eventually, and rather sooner than later, the
British were going to break through and out of Rommel's defenses. Given
RAF's control of the air, the result was likely to be a disaster for the
Panzer Army—assuming Montgomery possessed boldness to anything
like the degree he was showing determination. Rommel correspondingly
confronted the necessity for a blitzkrieg in reverse: a rapid withdrawal to
a new position, well behind the current front lines, before the British
grasped what was happening. With his inferiority in the air and increasingly on the ground, he could not risk a fighting, mobile retreat. Instead,
he ordered preparation of a position extending from the coastal town of
El Fuqa, a good sixty miles behind the Alamein Line, south to the Quattara Depression.

A Rommel-organized counterattack by what was left of the 21st
Panzer and 90th Light bought a few hours' breathing space. But at 1 A.M.
on November 2, Montgomery launched Operation Supercharge. The
New Zealand Division, reinforced by a brigade each from the 50th and

51st Divisions, supported by an armored brigade, went forward behind a heavy barrage, to clear the way for the *Corps de Chasse*. Montgomery declared himself ready to accept 100 percent loss of the tanks. The leading brigade launched its attack with 94. Seventy-five were knocked out— a rate close enough for government work. Two brigades that came up to reinforce it were stopped on November 2 by an improvised antitank screen to their front and a tank threat from the flanks.

The latter was increasingly a matter of smoke and mirrors. Afrika Korps reported on the morning of November 3 that it was down to fewer than three dozen tanks. Its infantry and artillery stood at a third of their front-line strength. The same grim figure was reported for the 88s, so vital to the antitank screens. Of the Italian mobile formations, Ariete was still combat-effective. Trieste and Littorio, both hard hammered, were starting to break up.

It was clearly time to go, and by now Rommel was wondering how much he could save even of his armor. An indication of his frustration was an order to take captured British officers as hostages for the bombing of a field hospital that was in hindsight a plain accident. Reluctantly he informed Italian GHQ on the evening of November 2 that nothing could be done for the unmotorized Italian infantry. At 11:30 A.M. on the next day, he notified the German High Command that the front could no longer be held. He requested approval of retreat to Fuqa. Two hours later he received a "Fuehrer Order" from Hitler. A response to his previous signal to the Italians, it demanded the Alamein Line be held at all costs, reminding Rommel that the stronger will often triumphed over the bigger battalions and exhorting him that he could show his troops "no other road than that to victory or death."

Generals on the Russian front had grown accustomed to such exhortations. Rommel was sufficiently shocked to say that for the first time during the campaign he did not know what to do. He had expected an unjustified degree of optimism from his higher headquarters. He had also consistently been given reason to believe Hitler admired him and had faith in his judgment. Now it was plain Hitler regarded not only Rommel but his entire army as expendable on a whim. Rommel had always demanded unconditional obedience. Now he gave it, apathetically issuing ordered for all existing positions to be held at all costs, writing Lu that

"What will become of us is in God's hands" and—perhaps more significantly for a Swabian—sending her 25,000 lire he had saved from his pay. By evening, he was sufficiently upset that when he went to take a walk in the desert, Westphal sent a junior staff officer with him. Instead of exploding, Rommel talked. If the army remained in place, he declared, it would be destroyed in three days. He also called Hitler a lunatic whose self-centered obstinacy would lead to the loss of the last German soldier and the total destruction of Germany.

In despair, Rommel was not without artifice. He ordered his public relations officer Lieutenant Alfred Berndt, who had begun his career in Goebbels's Propaganda Ministry, flown to Berlin, hoping he might somehow back-channel some sense of the truth. His daily report to the High Command stressed the continuing heavy losses: only two dozen tanks left by now in the Afrika Korps. On the morning of November 4th, Kesselring arrived at Army Headquarters. Rommel turned on him, accusing him of contributing to Hitler's "crazy order" by infecting Berlin with his optimism. Kesselring, not for nothing known as "smiling Albert," responded by encouraging Rommel not to take Hitler's order seriously and contacted Berlin with a request to give Rommel a free hand dealing with a situation that became increasingly desperate in the course of the day as the British mounted a final all-out attack.

The Afrika Korps's commander, Lieutenant General Ritter von Thoma, was captured, by some accounts while looking for either a bullet or a chance to desert. He dined that evening with Montgomery, discussing the campaign in a fashion long out of date yet somehow fitting in the desert war's contexts. Ariete went under, its last signals coming in at mid-afternoon and impelling Rommel at 2:50 to issue orders for a general retreat to Fuka. Mussolini approved at a quarter to none that evening, and Hitler five minutes later. Thereafter, if Rommel considered Hitler a lunatic, Hitler reciprocated by referring at regular intervals to Rommel's failure of nerve in the ultimate crisis—proof, if any was needed, to the Fuehrer's increasingly twisted mind, that no army general could be trusted.

The retreat itself went off better than Rommel expected, thanks in part to the relative stateliness of Montgomery's immediate pursuit, in part to the remarkable internal cohesion of the German army, and in part because stragglers had nowhere to go. Those wanting to opt out of the war had only to fall behind and wait for the enemy to pick them up. Otherwise, the alternative was to close up to retreating columns that daily and hourly grew larger and shook themselves into organized formations. Rommel's experience in both world wars had made him something of an authority on panic. It was useless, he argued, to try reimposing order immediately. Let the filght run its first course and try only to channel it into ordered routes until the first fear has run its course.

A head count after the initial disengagement showed 7,500 men, a third of them Italian, 21 tanks, and 65 guns. Not much—but enough to bloody the 8th Army's nose repeatedly, as Rommel again dropped a half-dozen ranks to take personal charge of everything from traffic control to vehicle maintenance. He also grew increasingly convinced that Montgomery would take no serious risks to destroy the Panzer Army's remnants. At the same time, however, Montgomery was emerging as an opponent who would make no serious mistakes. His buttoned-up, buttoned-down style of command left no opportunity for the tactical and operational counterstrokes that were Rommel's trademark, even had the discrepancy between the combatants been less.

The strategic and operational situation changed essentially on November 8, when British and American forces landed in French North Africa. As German and Italian High Commands responded with a massive sea- and airlift of men and supplies, Rommel took time out to think. He might have lacked formal general staff training; it was nevertheless clear to him that fresh perspectives were necessary. He requested Cavallero and Kesselring to join him for a conference. They did not take time from addressing the new crisis. Rommel, after all, was no more than a sector commander in a theater of war that was experiencing a paradigm shift. When Rommel once again dispatched Lieutenant Berndt to Berlin, he received no more from Hitler than a dusty reply to leave Tunisia out of his calculations, combined with more promises of supplies as soon as Rommel submitted his requirements.

By now it was clear that delivery dates would be sometime between the 12th of never and the 31st of June. As Rommel untangled one traffic jam after another, as British air strikes savaged his columns and British armored cars harassed their flanks, Rommel gave up hope not only of mounting a new offensive, but of sustaining a defense anywhere in Italian North Africa. When he finally met with Bastico, Cavallero, and Kesselring on November 24, Rommel presented his views in detail. The Panzer Army was currently holding positions reflecting orders from Hitler to defend them at all costs. Whatever might be the worth of such a policy in Russia, in North Africa it was impossible to implement save at the price of losing most of the survivors of El Alamein. Instead, Rommel recommended a withdrawal all the way to the Tunisian border. The broken terrain around Gabes offered opportunities for a long-term, flexible defense. A "long retreat," moreover, would bring the Panzer Army and the growing Axis forces in Tunisia close enough to enable them to cooperate—perhaps even cripple one or both of the Anglo-American initiatives in the way Frederick the Great had done in the latter stages of the Seven Years War.

Rommel was aware that this scenario was no more than a palliative. It would buy time—but time to what purpose? Any hopes of a grand sweep through the Middle East were long vanished. A debacle loomed in the steppes of Russia, where the o once-triumphant Panzers were fighting for their lives at Stalingrad and points south. In late November, Rommel's headquarters received a treat: movies flown in from Germany. Among them was a newsreel in which Rommel declared that German soldiers would never be forced out of Egypt. The field marshal joined in the explosive, bitter laughter of El Alamein's survivors. By now, junior officers were saying in his presence that the war was lost and it was time for Germany to seek an armistice. One battalion commander described Rommel asserting it was necessary to force Hitler to "abdicate" and to abandon such policies as the persecution of the Jews and the churches.

Credible? Perhaps. Rommel was outspoken but not suicidal; Hans von Luck had forty years and many reasons to put those words in his commander's mouth. Rommel had hitched his wagon to Hitler's star. Perhaps for that reason he was even more punctilious than many of his colleagues in regarding himself as a professional soldier, while at the same time believing Hitler would ultimately respond to professional advice. On November 28, Rommel flew to Rastenburg for one more conference with his commander in chief.

6

INTERIMS

G EORGE Patton's involvement with North Africa began in the aftermath of the fall of Tobruk, when Marshall recommended sending a fully equipped armored division to Egypt. Patton, the obvious choice for its command, was ordered to Washington in June 1942 to plan the deployment. When he proposed that two divisions be sent, Marshall had him put on a plane back to California. When a chastened Patton informed the deputy chief of staff that indeed he could manage with one division, Marshall smiled and said "That's the way to handle Patton." The next month Marshall appointed him, with his I Armored Corps headquarters, commander of the Western Task Force of Operation Torch, the Anglo-American invasion of North Africa.

I

Brian Holden-Reid appropriately likens the Anglo-American relationship in World War II to a long-term marriage on the companionate model, with both partners recognizing the importance of mutual harmony publicly expressed. Mutual incomprehension tempered by occasional fundamental disagreements did not exclude "a measure of tolerance and fruitful union." Dwight Eisenhower, Torch's commanding general, was more blunt: "The British and the Americans came together like a bulldog and a cat."

The Americans were confident—almost exuberantly so at operational and tactical levels. Instead of the improvised formations of 1918, the United States was sending divisions organized since 1940 that had gone through through some of the most elaborate, largest-scale peacetime training in any modern army's history. Under forced draft, the U.S. Army had developed doctrines and weapons systems specifically to wage modern mobile war. Relevant combat experience was nonexistent. The Army had nevertheless come far enough that Americans believed they had little to learn from allies that had spent the previous two years showing their backs to the Germans.

The British ground forces committed to Operation Torch, by contrast, were uncertain both of their general operational effectiveness and their specific readiness to fight the kind of war expected in Tunisia. The British army of 1942 was still learning how to fight on divisional scales, to say nothing of corps and army levels. The divisions sent to North Africa were a distinctly mixed bag, ranging from the regulars of the 4th through the second line Territorials of the 46th to a 78th assembled from three previously independent brigades, with a predictably low level of cohesion. As late as May 1943, Major General Francis Tuker, commanding the 8th Army's elite 4th Indian Division, described the training of the formations out from home as deficient even after six months in the field.

Matters were not improved by a complex command structure that provided a joint Supreme Headquarters, a field army (British), and two corps, one British and one American, for an initial commitment of a half-dozen divisions. Underemployed staff officers of both armies would have much to answer for as relations grew strained. And there was much to strain them. Eisenhower, still feeling his way in command, tended to micromanage. First Army commander Sir Kenneth Anderson had to be reminded to submit his daily situation reports directly to Eisenhower instead of forwarding them directly to London. The initial U.S. field commander, II Corps chief Major General Lloyd Fredendall, made no secret of his Anglophobia despite back-channel admonitions.

Where did Patton fit into this kaleidoscope? Forrest Pogue, Marshall's definitive biographer, suggests that Marshall, knowing he would never have a chance to see combat, regarded Patton as a surrogate whose uninhibited behavior was the other side of the chief of staff's own rigid self-discipline: an id to Marshall's superego. A more mundane explanation involves the lack of senior officers with tested capacity to command divisions and corps in combat: every appointment was a grab bag. The United States, moreover, was waging another war in the Pacific, where Douglas MacArthur was demanding generals as well as men and material. Marshall's first choice to command Western Task Force was Robert Eichelberger, former superintendent of West Point. Instead, he felt constrained to send Eichelberger to the South Pacific, where he rose to Army command and may have saved MacArthur's career by his performance in the Buna campaign.

Considered on his own merits, Patton brought another quality to the table: his potential as a diplomat in uniform. Operation Torch depended heavily on securing at least the acquiescence of the Vichy French governments in North Africa. Western Task Force would be landing in Morocco, a French protectorate where the sultan still exercised significant influence—an unusually complicated situation. Patton spoke French, had spent enough time in France to claim familiarity with the culture, and was accustomed to moving in social circles higher than those open to the average officer of the interwar Army. It was a better package than almost anyone else could offer.

During the two-week voyage to North Africa, Patton fretted constantly. This was the longest-reaching amphibious operation in history, mounted by a comprehensively green force, ending in a landing over open beaches. Possibilities for a fiasco, or a bloodbath should the French choose to fight, seemed infinite. Reality proved less dramatic. French naval and ground forces challenged the landings in Patton's sector in what, on land at least, amounted to a *baroud d' honneur*. By November 10, the French resident in Morocco arranged a surrender.

Patton's picture was again featured on America's front pages, and for the next weeks, he settled admirably into the role of a proconsul. His emphasis on French-American cooperation against a common enemy was accompanied by fingertip sensitivity to the sultan's role and status. Success in Morocco, however, seemed to Patton to be keeping him away from the fighting developing farther east, in Tunisia. Initially, Eisenhower and his subordinates intended to minimize opportunities for friction by keeping British and U.S. contingents under their own respective higher commands. But troop dispositions in Operation Torch were shaped by the distance between the landing zones and the operationally relevant ground farther east. That required the Allies to deploy forward as fast as possible—and encouraged the tendency, already strong in both armies, to fight by improvised task forces rather than by tables of organization. Too often, too many units entered battle under strange commanders and alongside strange counterparts. Hart Force and Blade Force, the consistently reshuffled combat commands of the U.S. 1st Armored Division— all the various combat teams and task forces were sources of uncertainty and confusion to inexperienced officers.

Tensions increased as the Germans opened a Tunisian branch of their school of tactical tuition. In January 1943, Sir Harold Alexander was appointed Ground Forces commander in North Africa. Alexander, a man most histories legitimately praise for his tact, offered a brutal assessment of American soldiers. "They are soft, green, and quite untrained . . . they lack the will to fight," he declared to British army Chief of Staff Sir Alan Brooke. But if the Americans suffered humiliation on larger scales, especially at Kasserine Pass in February 1943, their British counterparts did no better in similar circumstances.

At this point, Eisenhower took his first real steps toward great captain status—not in the field, but by an increasingly ruthless suppression of national backbiting wherever he found it. He informed Fredendall tha when placing American troops under British command he did so ". . . unreservedly and expect any officer receiving an order from his next battlefield superior to regard that order as emanating from me and on up the line from the President himself." No less remarkable in contemporary contexts was Eisenhower's blistering of the war correspondents, warning them that anyone persisting in attempts to initiate British-American controversy would be removed from the theater.

Patton, initially on the controversy's fringes, was drawn in when Eisenhower informed him that if he or anyone else criticized the British, ". . . by God, I will reduce him to his permanent rank and send him home," and a few days later warned him against running his mouth before engaging his brain. Patton was bewildered by admonitions whose roots may have been in the Casablanca conference of January 1942. He was responsible for local arrangements, and for the first time mingled with top British as well as American leadership. Brooke was not impressed: "Definitely a character," he concluded. But "I did not form any high opinion of him . . . wild and unbalanced . . . at a loss in any operation requiring skill and judgment." Brooke made clear that no later events caused him to change his mind.

Eisenhower had decided to give Patton and his corps headquarters the central U.S. role in the Allies' next move: the invasion of Sicily. In mid-February, Mongomery conducted a seminar in Tripoli on "lessons learned" in recent operations. He hoped to attract some American division commanders. He dismissed Patton, the only senior U.S. attendee, as "an old man of about 60." Patton, with the exception of Montgomery and a few others, in turn characterized most of his new British colleagues as "the same non-committal clerical types as our generals." What angered him far more was Eisenhower's apparent deference, not to say submission, to British policies, methods, and personalities that to date had produced no achievements meriting that response.

Rommel's November meeting with Hitler had escalated within minutes into an ugly confrontation, with the Fuehrer asking Rommel how he dared leave his command without permission, insisting the African theater must be sustained for political reasons, and accusing the Panzer Army of collective cowardice. He concluded by ordering Rommel to wait outside for orders.

It was the kind of calculated dressing-down a colonel might administer to a refractory junior officer, and it threw Rommel into a rage. Hitler's assignment of Goering to accompany Rommel to Rome and improve the supply system was small consolation—especially when Goering, Kesselring, and the Italian High Command virtually ignored his presentations, his recommendations, and his recriminations.

Rommel was also increasingly committed to achieving a concentration of German and Italian forces in Tunisia. Only thus was it possible to create a mass of maneuver strong enough to have real prospects of achieving tactical success, as opposed to buying time by days and hours until the British and Americans grew strong enough, or confident enough, to push forward again. Kesselring argued that would increase the air threat to Tunisia. Goering talked of planning a counterattack eastward in the manner of 1941. Rommel returned to Africa on December 2, more convinced than ever both that the Axis higher leadership had lost touch with reality, and that his immediate professional and moral responsibility was to save the Panzer Army from destruction.

Despite repeated orders to hold fast wherever his units found themselves, on January 22, Rommel ordered the evacuation of Tripoli. Four days later, he was instructed to turn over command to a newly formed Italian headquarters—ostensibly, and reasonably, on the grounds of his still-fragile health. The Italian High Command, Kesselring, and Hitler concurred in a judgment reflecting their common conviction that Rommel's time was past, and Rommel was past his best.

Rommel, for his part, "had little desire to go on playing the scapegoat for a pack of incompetents." His spirits were at an all-time low, partly because of his debilitated physical condition and partly because of his deep resentment at being labeled a front-runner, unable to cope when the going got tough. As Panzer Army Africa, under its new sobriquet of First Italian Army, fell back into the Mareth Line, the prewar French defenses along the Tunisia-Libya frontier, it became an open secret that an "Army Group Africa" would be created to command it and the forces facing the Allies in Tunisia, organized by now as the 5th Panzer Army. The commander, it was generally understood, would be the 5th Panzer Army's Hans Juergen von Arnim. He had done well in Russia, and done better pitting his improvised command against the numerically superior Anglo-Americans. He was fresh blood, and at the same time part of the Prussian/German military establishment, with a pedigree that would be the envy of most racehorses. Considered objectively, he was also a better bet than Rommel for a last-ditch holding operation, more inclined to obey than to challenge superior orders. But Erwin Rommel had one more shot in his African locker.

Rommel had been paying increasing attention to the conduct of operations on the Tunisian front. The Axis, he agreed, should concentrate its mobile forces and strike: first to remove the threat of an Allied drive from Gafsa to the sea that would divide the 5th Panzer and the rebaptized 1st Italian Army, then against Montgomery along the Mareth Line. Kesselring agreed, and Rommel and Arnim planned a double blow in

Tunisia. On February 14, the 5th Panzer Army, with the 10th Panzer and Rommel's veteran 21st plus a dozen of the new Tiger tanks with their 88-millimeter guns, struck through Faid Pass toward Sidi bou Zid. The defenders, mostly elements of the 1st U.S. Armored Division, broke and scattered, putting up no more than local resistance. Rommel appeared on the scene on February 15, leading elements of the 15th Panzer Division and the Italian Centauro Armored toward a Gafsa abandoned without a fight. As he drove toward Kasserine Pass through the detritus of the Americans' disorganized retreat, Rommel saw a chance for another Gazala. Give him all three Panzer divisions, he told Kesselring on the 17th. Let him strike for the huge supply dumps at Tebessa and from there on to Bone, and the Allies would be forced to retreat into Algeria.

Kesselring wondered whether Rommel was simply seeking to restore his lost prestige by a gambler's gambit. Arnim, whose vision extended no further than throwing the Allies off-balance, played his tactical cards cautiously. The 10th Panzer's officers thought of time and space in European rather than desert contexts. The Italian High Command temporized, refusing to give either German general full command of the operation. In the face of divided Axis counsels and increasing Allied resistance, the Panzers broke through at Kasserine but were unable to break out. British, Americans, and French North Africans rallied, stood, and held. His forward units low on ammunition and running out of fuel, taking an increasing hammering from Allied air strikes, Rommel halted his attack on the 22nd. In one crucial sector, the American gunners had a fifteen-minute supply of ammunition remaining.

Rommel by now was obviously worn down mentally as well as physically; Kesselring observed that the Desert Fox had turned into a tired old man. He had achieved what he considered the major tactical objective of disrupting the Allied offensive in Tunisia. He had given the Americans a humiliating lesson in armored war. But he retained his situational awareness. What Rommel noted was not that the Americans had initially been easy meat but how rapidly they recovered, and the enormous material superiority they enjoyed, which contributed to the messy battlefield commented on by superficial observers. Sooner or later the African game would be up. All that remained was to minimize the coming catastrophe.

When Kesselring asked if he were interested in taking over Army Group Africa, Rommel initially refused the offer. He had had enough of Italian generals, enough of the Luftwaffe, and enough of superiors who saw everything through rose-colored glasses. The next day, however, he— not Arnim—was formally appointed to the post by the Italian High Command. Von Arnim promptly gave Rommel a dose of his own medicine by independently mounting an offensive about as operationally sophisticated as the beast that provided its code name of *Ochsenkopf* (Oxenhead). It quickly sputtered to a halt against a determined Anglo-American defense.

At the end of February, Rommel summarized the situation. The Tunisian "bridgehead," he argued, was still too large, and correspondingly vulnerable to mobile operations by exponentially superior Allied forces. He urged withdrawal into a perimeter of about a hundred miles. Even preparing that position, he stated, would require 140,000 tons of supplies per month—a figure experience indicated was clearly unattainable. His recommendation that "an early long-term decision be reached" on the future conduct of operations was a fig leaf for the conclusion he favored: commence evacuation as soon as possible.

His recommendations predictably denied, Rommel planned a spoiling attack against an 8th Army continuing to push slowly but inexorably against the Mareth Line. Its intention was to disrupt its assembly areas around Medenine, forestalling the massive offensive Montgomery was sure to launch in the near future. This time, Rommel had all three Panzer divisions, or what remained of them, plus the 90th Light under his hand: the largest armored attack the Germans made in the entire campaign. But ULTRA intercepts gave Montgomery an outline of his enemy's intention, and the 8th Army commander shifted forces to meet it. The attack went in on the morning of March 6, from a different direction than expected, but ran into a multilayered, prepared defense that tore the heart out of the Panzers. I have six hundred antitank guns, four hundred tanks, and good infantry holding strong pivots, Montgomery commented. "The man must be man." At 11 P.M., Rommel ordered a withdrawal from the battle that by all odds ranks as his greatest embarrassment. Perhaps indeed his heart was no longer in it. On March 9, he left once more for Rome and Rastenburg. This time he would not return.

II

Rommel's last African offensive opened the door of opportunity for Patton. The defeat at Kasserine Pass highlighted the tactical shortcomings of the U.S. Army and the professional shortcomings of Lloyd Fredendall. In addition to his increasing inability to get along either with the British or with his American subordinates, he had chosen to construct an elaborate underground headquarters, a bunker that would not have been out of place on the Maginot Line. In the aftermath of defeat, it was bad enough that the senior combat officer of the U.S. Army had emerged as an incompetent. That he seemed a poltroon as well was too much. But again the question emerged: where best to find a replacement?

Ernest Harmon had come up from Morocco to restore initial order in II Corps's demoralized ranks but refused to succeed an officer he had officially described as a "son of a bitch" unfit to command. Perhaps as well Harmon did not want what was so obviously a high-risk job. That left Patton as the next choice, though Eisenhower made plain that the assignment was temporary. At 10 A.M. on March 6, 1943, Patton arrived at corps headquarters. He had ten days to bring it back on line for an offensive ordered by Alexander to distract attention from Mongomery's projected knockout blow against the Mareth Line.

Patton did not consider his new command fundamentally flawed. He had no serious doubts about American doctrine, American equipment, or American training. In any case, there was no time to return to first principles. The immediate problem involved getting II Corps to perform up to the U.S. Army's standards. Eisenhower had given his old friend and new subordinate a free hand, with authority to fire anyone not up to his job. He began at a more basic level, by restoring a discipline badly eroded during the previous six months. Uniform regulations, generally dismissed as "chickenshit" even by field officers, were rigorously enforced, with fines of up to a half month's pay for offenders. Officers were ordered to wear their insignia even if it made them better targets for snipers. Captains and lieutenants, Patton roared, were expendable. He lectured; he harangued; he exhorted. "Let me meet Rommel in a tank and I'll shoot it out with the son-of-a-bitch," he allegedly declared. He took his chances on the line as well as a target for German fighter-bombers, on one occasion almost being killed by artillery fire.

Did it work? Well enough to earn Patton more of the kind of publicity he had attracted in the States. Well enough to mark him as commander and leader even to soldiers calling him "Gorgeous Georgie" and "Flash Gordon." Well enough to bring within a month his promotion to lieutenant general—one rank higher than an American corps commander normally held, but just right for the future commander of a field army. Major General Omar Bradley, a newcomer to Tunisia assigned to the II Corps as Eisenhower's observer, saw Patton as living a role he had created for himself years ago: a cultivated gentleman in private who behaved like a profane thug before the troops. Bradley called it "talking down." What Patton actually did was to appeal to the wish for respect latent in any potentially useful soldier—or person—and get the men of the II Corps believing he could help them earn it. That was his own fundamental desire, and it shone through the posturing and the fustian in a way few could mistake even if they disliked the manifestations.

The first results were manifested on March 23 at a place called el Guettar, when the 10th Panzer Division mounted a limited counterattack against the advancing 1st Infantry Division and was driven back with heavy losses. That was the only time Patton and Rommel would ever command against each other, though the confrontation was indirect. El Guettar was not an epiphany for the II Corps. The 1st Armored Division in particular remained sluggish by Patton's standards. Patton rode Major General Orlando Ward, to the point of insult, on one occasion ordering Ward to ". . . get off your ass, get a pistol in your hand, and lead that attack yourself." Ward responded, was slightly wounded, and Patton himself decorated him with a well-earned Silver Star. But the attack failed, and that was the bottom line. Ward was, by every standard, a more decent man than Patton. He was a capable enough commander. But he lacked the final spark of ruthlessness that takes a division forward in the face of casualties and obstacles. Patton fired him. And under its new commander, Ernest Harmon, the 1st Armored began learning how to win.

One of Patton's first official acts was to issue a report deploring a "total lack of air cover" for his troops. The officer responsible for tactical air support in the theater was Australian-born Air Marshal Sir Arthur Coningham. He had spent years attempting to correct what he considered the dilution of air power by the demands of ground officers who essentially regarded planes as flying artillery. He resented the slur against his USAAF subordinates, who had been following his orders and policies. He responded by suggesting II Corps was not battleworthy in its present condition. Eisenhower ordered Coningham to apologize. After a bitter personal exchange, Patton accepted and was further mollified when the theater's senior air officers, Air Marshal Tedder and USAAF General Spaatz, visited his headquarters to cement relations between air and ground forces.

Another source of friction grew from Alexander's plan to remedy the 1st Army's shortcomings by establishing a system of schools and programs to improve general levels of training. Intended for both armies, they were run by British officers. Alexander also established a network of liaison officers to advise their American counterparts. These men were as a group both experienced and competent. Their presence was nevertheless salt in an open wound. Patton greeted his factotum with "I think you ought to know that I don't like Brits"; though in fact the two officers got along extremely well. In early April, British IX Corps commander Sir John Crocker criticized in the presence of reporters the performance of a U.S. division under his command. Alexander described the same division as being "no good." Patton reacted by demanding in his diary that "God damn all British . . . I will bet that Ike does nothing about it. I would rather be commanded by an Arab." His official response, however, was to tell Alexander that the division in question was a National Guard formation from the Midwest, where isolationism was prevalent. Its removal in disgrace from the front on the authority of a British general would have correspondingly serious political repercussions!

Apart from suggesting that Patton well understood the strategy of the indirect approach, his point was not lost among both British and U.S. commanders beginning to recognize there was blame enough to go around, and displacing one's own command anxieties onto counterparts with different accents led nowhere. To extend Holden-Reid's marital metaphor, it is not unusual for a companionate relationship to develop a significant affective element as well. That is not to be confused with passion. Senior officers in any military system are alpha personalities who

reach the top by force of will and character at least as much as by demonstrated skill in warmaking. That produces levels of stress and antagonism
that can shock the hardiest veteran of corporate or academic feuds, but are
normative in high military commands. The best palliatives—there is no
real cure—are experience and victory. As the Tunisian campaign developed, British and U.S. senior officers might not like each other. They might
not even respect each other. They did develop a culture of cooperation.

Patton's direct contribution to the Allied victory was limited. On
April 15, after only forty days in command, he turned II Corps over to
Bradley and returned to Casablanca. He had hoped to finish the campaign in the field, but Bradley handled the corps well in the final weeks
that took the Americans into Bizerte as Axis resistance collapsed. Patton
rejoiced in a message from Marshall telling him what a fine job he had
done. "I have been gone 43 days," Patton confided to his diary, ". . . lost
about ten pounds, gained a third star and a lot of poise and confidence,
and am otherwise the same."

III

Patton would need that poise and confidence in the coming months. The
invasion of Sicily was an even greater test of Anglo-American cooperation than the Tunisian campaign. At Casablanca, Brooke had argued,
smoothly and convincingly, the advantages of maintaining the momentum gained in the Mediterranean and using the forces concentrated there:
pushing forward with the aims of driving Italy out of the war and using
Allied air and sea superiority to savage the vulnerable Axis southern
flank—what Churchill called the "soft underbelly." By this time, even
Marshall had to concede the impossibility of accumulating sufficient resources in Britain to mount an invasion of northern Europe before spring
of 1944. In turn, even had not Stalin been demanding a second front in
western Europe, it was strategically inadvisable to close down the
Mediterranean and maintain a holding position for a full year. The logic
was as inescapable as it was unpleasant to Americans, who disliked losing the argument. The only remaining question was where best to strike,

and on January 23, 1943, Eisenhower was instructed to plan Operation Husky, an invasion of the island of Sicily, to be mounted in July.

Brooke also argued successfully for a command structure that retained Eisenhower at its apex but put British officers at the head of ground, sea, and air forces. In part, that was no more than an application of a system with which the British were familiar: one considered particularly applicable to joint operations. All three of the appointees, Alexander, Tedder, and Admiral Sir Andrew Browne Cunningham, were experienced officers with established records of success no potential U.S. candidates could match. But Husky's command reflected the British military establishment's continuing lack of confidence in Eisenhower. His performance in Tunisia suggested that at bet he was still learning his job, and an operation as complex as the Sicilian invasion was no place for an apprentice.

For weeks, staff officers argued tactics and priorities. The result, a classic committee product, involved two armies, Montgomery's 8th and the newly created U.S. 7th, landing in ten separate areas with the objective of seizing as many ports and air bases as possible. Such a diffusion of forces was anathema to Montgomery, who informed Alexander that he proposed to develop his own plan for a concentrated landing in Sicily's southeastern tip. His next step was an end run as well executed as any on the battlefield: buttonholing Eisenhower's chief of staff in the headquarters toilet. Eisenhower approved Montgomery's revision, partly because he saw its merits and partly as a way of asserting his shaken authority.

While this was going on, Patton maintained a consistently low profile. As designated commander of the 7th Army, he was the only American among Eisenhower's senior subordinates. He was correspondingly unhappy with Montgomery's plan, which assigned the 7th Army and its three divisions a role that amounted to the 8th's flank guard. There is no basis for the often-repeated assertion that Montgomery sought to maximize his own opportunity for glory at the expense of the Americans in general and Patton in particular. At this stage, what he knew about Patton was that his tenure in field command was measured in days, and that he was a cavalryman, presumably correspondingly indifferent to the details of planning and execution Montgomery considered even more vital in an amphibious operation than in land war. The role he projected for

the 7th Army seemed well within Patton's capabilities, while offering opportunities for expansion should the Americans' performance justify it.

In public, Patton held himself in check. Privately, he told his staff that
Eisenhower had ceased to be an American and become an Ally. He confided to his diary that the United States was being "gypped" and reminded himself to retain his "SELF-CONFIDENCE." With Patton's
assignment to Army field command, he took with him the staff of I Armored Corps, whose core he had assembled before leaving the states. Patton is described—by Bradley in particular—as disinterested in staff work
and surrounding himself with mediocrities. He is also credited with giving staff officers freedom to do their jobs in their own way as long as they
performed well, paying primary attention to results unless an officer became a disproportionate source of friction and correspondingly able to
get more than most commanders from a mediocre staff.

Probably the best approach is to say that Patton followed a pro-
nounced French model in forming a staff. He did not seek yes-men but at
the same time felt no need for whetstones on the German staff model. He
wanted men he knew sufficiently well who he could trust to do things his
way, implementing policy rather than making it. His deputy in North
Africa, Geoffrey Keyes, and his successive chiefs of staff, Hobart Gay and
Hugh Gaffey, all fit that pattern. Patton was indeed almost Napoleonic in
his belief that the duty of a commanding general was to command and,
therefore, a chief must keep his mind clear of details.

Patton continued to emphasize formal inspirational speeches to large
units. His overpowering, not to say overbearing, personality diminished
his effectiveness in dealing with small groups of soldiers in the way made
increasingly familiar by Eisenhower and Montgomery. When he addressed the 505th Parachute Regiment before the invasion, Colonel
James Gavin noted that Patton's stress on the indirect approach in combat depended on sexual metaphors that, though cleverly used, let Gavin
"somewhat embarrassed." It is not the easiest thing in the world to make
a paratrooper blush, and this approach would return to haunt Patton in
a matter of weeks.

When Patton spoke to men scheduled for combat, he consistently reassured them that fear was normal. All soldiers were afraid in battle, he
asserted; a coward was someone who allowed that fear to overcome his

sense of duty. Patton's emphasis on morale reflected his conviction that "battles are won by frightening the enemy . . . Never take counsel of your fears. The enemy is more worried than you are." If he was not, then he must be taught to worry, and to be afraid—"by inflicting death and wounds on him."

"Make the other son-of-a-bitch die for his country" was another constant message. In case of doubt, attack—never an enemy's strengths, but his weaknesses. It was impossible to be too strong oneself. Get every man and gun available, as long as it did not delay the attack. Mortars and artillery were superb when they were firing. When silent, they were junk. See that your weapons fire, Patton insisted. Steel and lead save blood.

These were the kinds of points experience in Tunisia showed were consistently neglected or forgotten under the constant stress of combat. Patton believed in fundamentals. "It is not genus," he wrote, "but memory . . . and character . . ." What may seem like a mishmash of inspirational one-liners was, in fact, an outline of an approach to combat that combined surprise, shock, and mobility, focused and applied by leadership. Patton's experience of combat command added up to little over a month and then his primary task had involved restoring shaken morale. The operational situation he faced had offered little opportunity for his presumed specialties of breakthrough and exploitation. The jury on Patton as a general was still out—and Patton knew it.

He attended church services and noted in his diary that he prayed daily to do his duty and accomplish his destiny. When he thanked the women of a Red Cross club for entertaining some of his officers, he received a reply saying that they had never seen a "he man" general, and could he stop by and let them "Oh" and "Ah" over him. His soldiers agreed that Patton looked like a general. But someone with Patton's background in military history might well have remembered that a general named George McClellan had also looked good in a uniform. He had been brilliant at inspiring the Army of the Potomac. What McClellan could not do was fight.

In the first hours of the Sicilian campaign, the 7th Army benefited from its commander on two levels. Before the landing, Patton convinced Eisenhower to let him replace an inexperienced division with the veteran 1st Infantry in what turned out to be a critical sector. When the Axis defenders mounted a series of armor-tipped counterattacks in Afrika Korps style, Patton on one occasion took charge of calling in the naval gunfire that played a major role in saving the beachhead. He reaped publicity accordingly, with the American press making it sound as though he had been in the front lines. The headlines may have had something to do with Eisenhower's sharp criticism of what he called Patton's inadequate progress reports. The commanding general's outburst of temper was, however, primarily caused by the heavy losses a U.S. parachute regiment scheduled to drop in Patton's sector suffered from the "friendly fire" of naval antiaircraft guns. The incident epitomized a comprehensive breakdown of land-sea-air cooperation despite the months of elaborate preparation, and a formal investigation later concluded no one was to blame. Patton nevertheless saw himself as a scapegoat. His opinions of Eisenhower as a commander and a colleague reached a correspondingly low point—at least in the diary entries and letters home he consciously used as safety valves throughout his overseas service.

Within a week of the landings, Patton's judgment of his immediate superior and his 8th Army stable mate plummeted to similar nadirs. Alexander, who far more than Eisenhower merited the appellation "chairman of the board," had failed to develop a plan for Sicily's conquest that went much beyond Montgomery's original conception as presented in the headquarters men's room. When the 8th Army encountered greater difficulties than expected, Montgomery proposed a short flanking movement, whose implementation required giving the 8th Army the road Patton proposed to use as the 7th Army's principal axis of advance.

Alexander, still highly dubious about American fighting power, assented despite the fact that the switch meant keeping the 7th Army in the supporting role Montgomery originally envisaged. Patton accepted the decision without overt protest. He may have feared Eisenhower was seeking an excuse to relieve him—an unlikely contingency in the context of an efficiency report in which Eisenhower rated him "superior" and described him as an outstanding leader: "aggressive, loyal, energetic." In a wider context, Patton's behavior was consistent with his previous performance as a team player. Superior after superior had offered the same observation: never confuse Georgie's rhetoric with his actions.

Alexander, and by extension Eisenhower, have been generally criticized for neglecting the potential for a 7th Army breakout, taking advantage of superior U.S. mobility to disorganize an Axis resistance already hanging on by its fingertips. Montgomery's "left hook" proved abortive, becoming in the face of resistance with a German core no more than the preliminary to a series of frontal assaults that transformed the Sicilian campaign from the lightning operation originally projected into an attritional struggle prefiguring the long, painful climb up the Italian boot. Alexander, however, had authorized the 7th Army to advance into western Sicily as long as that did not put the 8th Army's flank in jeopardy. And because by no stretch of the imagination did Montgomery's flank ever face serious danger, the 7th Army's commander was free to take a fresh look at his maps.

Alexander, Patton declared, had "no idea of the power or speed of American armies." Patton proposed to show him, multiplying striking power by dividing the 7th Army. Two divisions would drive straight north to the Tyrhennian coast; three more would overrun western Sicily and capture the port city of Palermo. The 7th Army would then advance from the west on Messina, presumably cutting off the Axis forces facing Montgomery. It was a mechanized version of the fencer's *coup de Jarnac:* coming in behind an opponent with a hamstringing slash. The wider the sweep, the better the chances of fundamentally disorganizing the enemy's base and rear areas, throwing him into self-reinforcing confusion.

Patton's critics tend to dismiss the plan as an ego trip designed to increase the visibility of both the U.S. forces in Italy and their commander. On the other hand, Patton's reading of the Germans was that they were particularly accomplished in defensive operations, especially on ground like that along Montgomery's line of advance. The Italians were at their best in set-pieces where their German allies were close at hand. And it was no unfounded disrespect to Montgomery to recognize that his metier was the prepared attack. Put together, this was a recipe for delay. By contrast, the two-stage envelopment Patton proposed responded to the developing tactical situation; to the qualities of the U.S. Army as Patton perceived them; and to Patton's concept of mobile war, which dismissed the German Tiger tank, with its formidable armor protection and its

88-millimeter gun, as a little more than a mobile pillbox, dangerous only when a Sherman was directly in its sights.

With that kind of confidence, Patton had little trouble obtaining Alexander's consent to his plan—and receiving as well an indirect warning from Eisenhower that he must "stand up to Alexander" at the risk of being relieved! Though the operation showcased American logistical capacity and physical endurance more directly than fighting power, Patton exuberantly informed his diary that Fort Leavenworth would study the drive across western Sicily as a classic example of the use of tanks. Scattered Italian forces put up limited resistance, while the 3rd Infantry Division marched more than a hundred miles through mountainous terrain in three days—as good as the Wehrmacht's best. That was paradigmatic for Patton's way of war. "Old Sweat and Guts" would have been a more appropriate nickname than the more familiar version for this believer in maneuver operations. But with resistance in most of the island broken, and the Stars and Stripes flying alongside the Union Jack over Palermo by July 21, Patton was entitled to enjoy the perquisites of establishing his headquarters in the city's royal palace.

Two days later, the 45th Division, showing its high quality in its first campaign, reached the Tyrrhenian Sea and cut Sicily literally in half. At that point, with his own advance still making heavy weather of it in the hills of eastern Sicily, Montgomery requested what the Mafia would call a sit-down, congratulating Patton on his successes and asking him to visit Montgomery's headquarters to discuss the fate of Messina. To his incredulous counterpart, Montgomery recommended that the 7th Army advance east along the coast and occupy the city. Alexander arrived just in time to be informed of the new dispensation.

Montgomery's many critics, most of them Americans, consistently underrate both his professionalism and his egocentricity. To the 8th Army's commander, the operational situation had changed sufficiently in the past week to make his proposed revision of Allied strategy the optimal procedure. It was correspondingly natural that Patton and Alexander agree. Sealing the bargain by giving Patton what the latter described as a five-cent lighter was an equally natural action. After a reciprocal visit to Patton's headquarters a few days later, he noted that, "The Americans are delightful people and are very easy to work with . . ." At least he did not expect Patton to tug his forelock deferentially.

A still-suspicious Patton, for his part, described the capture of Messina as "a horse race in which the prestige of the U S Army is at stake." By now, few American senior officers did not have their own personal mental files of what they processed as insufferable and inappropriate condescending behavior by their allies. American military culture was to a significant degree more overtly competitive than Britain's. Perhaps the British army's heritage of standing in second place to the Royal Navy combined with a history of defeat and embarrassment to leave the soldiers fewer illusions and thicker skins than their American allies. Certainly Patton took the Messina sweepstakes seriously enough to assume what amounted to personal charge of the operation, securing landing craft and fire support for a series of three amphibious end runs around enemy defensive positions, berating his best division commander for alleged lack of initiative and just as quickly standing down when Lucian Truscott pushed back. Patton's behavior did nothing to accelerate the date of Messina's capitulation, which occurred on August 17. But his profane insistence on picking up the pace and his constant unannounced appearances in the front lines had other, far-reaching consequences.

IV

Throughout the war, it was Patton's custom to visit field hospitals unannounced, distributing Purple Hearts and engaging the less seriously wounded in conversations that were no less well motivated for being inevitably one-sided. On the afternoon of August 3, he paused at the 15th Evacuation Hospital. "All were brave and cheerful," he recorded—until he encountered a soldier who informed the general "I guess I can't take it." Patton swore at him and called him a coward. When the man remained motionless, Patton struck him across the face with a glove, dragged him to his feet by his shirt collar, and kicked him out of the tent with a flurry of insults. That night he noted in his diary that such cowards, if they continued to shirk their duty, should be court-martialed and shot. Two days later, he issued a general memorandum to the same effect. The soldier in question was diagnosed as suffering from chronic dysentery and malaria, as well as combat fatigue.

On August 10, the event was repeated at the 93rd Evacuation Hospital. Again Patton began by talking to patients about their wounds. The fourth soldier he encountered told the general, "It's my nerves." The general called him "a goddamned coward," "a yellow son of a bitch," and "a disgrace to the Army"; told him he ought to be shot; and threatened to do it himself, flourishing one of the pistols he habitually wore. When he turned to leave and saw the soldier still crying, Patton hit him hard enough to knock off his helmet liner. "It makes my blood boil," he declared, "to think of a yellow bastard being babied." Later testimony described the patient as having begged to stay with his unit until ordered into hospital by the medical officer.

The slapping incidents have generated more discussion than any single element of George Patton's tumultuous career. To borrow a phrase from novelist Herman Wouk, hounding officers is standard emotional ping-pong for generals, but the regulations bristle with the rights of enlisted men. Patton had committed two court-martial offenses merely by striking the soldiers; zealous perusal of the Uniform Code of Military Justice could probably have unearthed a dozen more.

The commander of the hospital, shocked and enraged by the general's behavior, sent a detailed report through medical channels to II Corps's chief of staff. Bradley ordered it held confidential. Patton was his superior, he explained; loyalty prohibited taking the matter over his head. It was also unnecessary. Patton's behavior was not only as public as it was possible to be; he boasted of it to Bradley, claiming he had put fight into a coward. The corps surgeon received a copy of the report and submitted it to Eisenhower's chief surgeon. The story spread quickly in journalistic, medical, and command networks, losing nothing in the telling, reaching even Alexander's ears. The correspondents attached to the 7th Army verified the incident in general terms, then met to discuss its handling. Although no one was willing to file the story, they agreed that it was their responsibility to inform Eisenhower directly.

The commander in chief's initial reaction was that the incidents, although unfortunate, called for nothing more than a "jacking up." His mind began to change as he thought about the ramifications—and once the correspondents' delegation requested an appointment. Accounts have varied over time as to whether the newsmen wanted Patton relieved in exchange for keeping the story quiet, or whether instead they simply made plain their conviction that Eisenhower take significant action. In any case, the situation was explosive. On August 17, Eisenhower wrote to Patton that if the allegations in the reports he had received were true, then "I must so seriously question your good judgment and your self-discipline as to raise serious doubt in my mind as to your future useful-ness." Eisenhower then instructed Patton to offer "such personal amends to the individuals concerned as may be within your power."

Dwight Eisenhower was no headquarters naïf. The AEF had spawned an underground of anecdotes of soldiers taken into combat on the toe of a shoe or at the point of a gun. As for Patton's language, most regiments of the interwar Army had at least one or two old-school officers who prided themselves in peeling paint off the walls when addressing an en-listed recalcitrant. Nor was Patton by any means the first and only officer to strike an enlisted man in front of witnesses. The resolution of choice was a "man-to-man apology" offered and accepted under the eye of a senior officer of the unit. Egregious or systematic abuse usually resulted in a discreet transfer or a resignation "for the good of the service." But nothing remotely like these incidents had ever happened before in all Pat-ton's history of over-the-top behavior. Indeed, as a young lieutenant he had voluntarily and publicly apologized to a soldier for swearing at him.

Great generals, Eisenhower mused to his naval aide, had often gone temporarily crazy under stress. In any army, he continued, two-thirds of the soldiers are natural cowards and skulkers. Making them fear public ridicule was one way of forcing them to fight: Patton's methods might be deplorable, but his results were excellent. Moreover, even though Patton had exercised operational command for a total of less than three months, Eisenhower considered him the Army's best senior armor officer, a man who would be needed in future campaigns.

Given Patton's still very limited experience, Eisenhower might be de-scribed as "betting on the come." He understood clearly, however, that at the best of it, most of the corps and armies that invaded Europe would be led by men inexperienced in the positions they held. The only other general officer in the Mediterranean who had as yet shown himself even arguably ready for high-level command was Omar Bradley, and Bradley was an infantryman.

Eisenhower's conundrum was a product of the convergence of four separate threads, each in its way highlighting a corresponding aspect of World War II. The first was personal: the character of George S. Patton. The commander of the 93rd Evacuation Hospital characterized him as "a nasty bully." At least one staff officer in Tunisia was so frightened of Patton that he allegedly suffered a breakdown. General John Lucas, whom Eisenhower had assigned to the 7th Army's headquarters as his representative before the invasion, processed the first incident as "Patton being Patton": an unfortunate side effect of the hard-driving personality that made him an effective commander. One of the privates Patton struck later observed that the general seemed to be suffering from combat fatigue himself, and Patton was certainly functioning in a high-stress environment throughout the Sicilian campaign, even if he did generate much of the stress by his own command decisions. He was pushing sixty and had used his body hard most of his life—there were good reasons why Marshall was reluctant to assign older generals to combat commands.

The account Patton offered his patron and former commander Kenyon Joyce is probably as close to a self-critical explanation as he came. He described being overcome to the point of tears by the courage of the desperately wounded men he initially encountered. When he encountered someone who looked and whined like a cowardly rat and rejected admonition to act like a man, "something burst in me . . . I was a damned fool." The second incident had the same background, "and in that I was equally a damned fool."

It is clear enough that Patton regretted his behavior rather than rejecting his belief that battle fatigue was a euphemism for cowardice. For the rest of his life, he believed he had done both men a favor by challenging a manhood that had been temporarily eclipsed. But Patton's behavior had more complex roots. Sucessful generals rarely suffer from inferiority complexes. Clausewitz describes war as the province of danger and considers courage the first quality of a warrior. It is unusual for a physical coward to rise to high rank in any army. At the same time, "to everything there is a season," and the appropriate time to manifest physical courage is in the junior ranks. A senior officer, like an experienced eighteenth-century duelist, is considered to have "given his proofs": a general who routinely behaves like a lieutenant is doing two jobs badly.

Seniors' courage is usually understood in moral terms: the ability to make decisions and abide by them. Erwin Rommel, blunt and matter-of-fact, took charge of front-line situations in what he considered emergencies. Though Rommel was not averse to showing off occasionally to journalists and other rear-echelon types, the courage he demonstrated was essentially a requirement of a particular situation. The high-strung, imaginative Patton by contrast in Tunisia wrote to his wife of his "fear of fear" and then walked through an uncleared minefield. When he went ashore on Sicily, he timed his pulse rate and was "disgusted" at finding it elevated. He systematically recorded his near misses from air attacks and shellfire. Nigel Hamilton, Montgomery's biographer, interprets this behavior as an effort to reject his "shyness" and "timidity," suggesting even that Patton's front-line appearances were "extremely rare" in the context of his heroic reputation. A more nuanced interpretation is that Patton considered moral courage the primary requisite of a commander, believed that form of courage to be directly congruent with physical courage, and believed he best monitored his fitness for command by testing his nerve.

Front-line soldiers cope with terrors more immediate than death—helplessness and mutilation stand out in particular. Patton's fear of being seriously wounded again is a recurring subject in both his diary and his letters home during the preliminaries to the Sicilian invasion. There is a certain irony in Patton, so often presented as a throwback, taking what amounts to a late-twentieth-century approach to his "core issue" by confronting it directly. It seems correspondingly reasonable to suggest that in Patton's case, visiting hospitals was part of an ongoing comprehensive process of self-mastery that he regarded as necessary to maintain his effectiveness as a commander and his identity as a man.

It seems no less reasonable to assert that Patton in Sicily tested himself across the board, to near-destruction. Might there have been a connection between Patton's learning on the morning of July 3 that Eisenhower planned to award him the Distinguished Service Cross for his conduct on the beach, and his apparently impulsive decision to stop off at the 15th Evacuation Hospital to put his courage to another test? Perhaps what Patton's headquarters lacked above all was an aide sufficiently attuned to the Old Man to sense the underlying dynamics of his hospital visitations, and possessing sufficient force of character to steer him away from them the same way his subordinates sought to limit his high-risk trips up front.

In a short story by science-fiction author Roland J. Green published in an anthology titled *Alternate Generals,* Patton visits the hospital and encounters the soldier, but instead of flying into a rage, remembers the men he lost in the Argonne. He declares that it is not cowardly to be scared, that there are no cowards in the American Army. He prescribes a good meal, some sleep, and a stiff drink of medicinal whisky, then leaves before he bursts into tears. In Green's alternate reality, the incident becomes public and Patton becomes a national hero for his insight and his empathy. He commands the invasion of Italy, captures Rome in a matter of weeks, and returns to the United States in triumph on the inside track for command of the Normandy invasion. The irony is that Patton, mercurial and sentimental, was in fact just as capable of the fictional response as the actual one. After the war, he visited the amputee ward of Walter Reed Hospital, resplendent in full uniform. Suddenly he burst into tears, saying, "Goddammit, if I had been a better general, most of you would not be here." That, too, was George Patton.

The slapping incidents also came at a time when military psychiatry was on the cusp of a major change. During the Great War, AEF psychiatrists, like their counterparts in the French and British armies, concluded that battle stress was best treated close to the battle zone, as soon as possible, with everyday responses like food, rest, and showers, and with the stated assumption that the soldier would return to his unit. During the interwar years, a more Freudian approach became dominant. That perspective interpreted battle exhaustion as a subset of all adult dysfunction: a manifestation of childhood trauma. The national mobilization of 1940–1941 institutionalized this approach in the armed forces. Its principal thrust was to avert collapse at the front by screening out those considered susceptible to psychiatric breakdown before they entered the service, or when necessary discharging them during training—the well-known "Section 8." More than a million and a half registrants were turned away on mental or educational grounds. Discharge rates for psychiatric reasons were two and a half times as high as during World War I.

Despite the multiple screening processes, during the North African campaign, the rate of "neuropsychiatric" casualties soared. They were treated essentially like all other casualties: moved away from the combat zones as rapidly as possible, then evacuated to the United States if recovery was prolonged. Because collective medical wisdom considered their circumstances as blameless, in practice, psychiatric casualties received the same levels of what might be called sympathy from doctors, nurses, and orderlies as did men with combat wounds.

There were two problems with this approach. One was medical, and became apparent as the evacuation pipeline developed: psychiatric casualties did not improve in anything like the numbers expected. Instead, their symptoms frequently grew worse the farther they were removed from the front. The second problem was military. The ordinary soldier preferred to consider himself sick rather than afraid. Battle stress offered a correspondingly honorable, potentially permanent way out of combat. A young captain, Fred Hanson, who had previously worked with the Canadian army, was assigned to II Corps in the aftermath of Kasserine Pass—about the same time as Patton. He introduced an alternate form of treatment based on the AEF experience. Built around rest and sedation, it was predicated on keeping patients as far forward as possible, in a context of overt expectation that they would quickly return to duty. Hanson's early figures showed as many as 30 percent of acute cases were back on the line within thirty hours.

It required time and effort to implement the new approach. Not until D-day was army policy on psychiatric casualties fully established. It defined "combat exhaustion" as a medical emergency. Most army psychiatrists accepted what had become collective wisdom in front-line units: everyone is scared; everybody breaks. Exhaustion was a near-universal consequence of somewhere between ninety and a hundred twenty days in combat. Treatment, incorporating sedation for up to seventy-two hours and a matter-of-fact regime of hot food and clean clothes as well as psychiatric consultation, was applied as far forward as possible, even at battalion aid stations. Its objective was to return as many exhaustion cases as possible to the front for as long as possible. Three quarters and more went back to the line, at least for a while.

This harsher, more realistic reorientation of the approach to battle exhaustion certainly had no room for generals cursing and striking privates. It is nevertheless reasonable to suggest that had Patton's loss of self-control occurred a few months later, it would have been in a medical environment, where the approach to combat fatigue incorporated more of George Patton than Sigmund Freud—and just possibly, a climate more sympathetic to Patton's argument that exhaustion cases, however legitimate, left their share of the burden to their comrades. In war, timing is everything.

Patton's behavior was also processed in the context of a paradigm shift in war reporting. For practical purposes, war correspondents did not exist in the United States of 1939. The nation's mobilization was covered by reporters who transferred from other specialties and learned the nuances of their new beat while on the job. One result was a flourishing of a variant form of celebrity journalism. Focusing on personalities was a familiar way of reaching a mass audience: from Babe Ruth or Clark Gable to George Patton was not a major adjustment. Celebrity reporting continued well after the first overseas deployments. In July 1943, *Time* magazine captioned a photo of Patton with a quotation: "It makes no difference what part of Europe you kill Germans in." But the North African campaign inaugurated a change in emphasis.

In part, that was a consequence of an initial policy limiting journalistic access to the fighting. With little real reporting to do, they began filing human interest stories about home-town boys at war in an exotic land. Ernie Pyle proved himself a particular master of the genre. For several yeas before the war, he had written a nationally syndicated column focusing on the lives and hopes of ordinary Americans coping with the depression. He applied the same approach to depicting the lives of ordinary soldiers coping with the war and became a national figure widely imitated by his colleagues.

The Pyle approach did not abandon celebrity journalism. It transformed GI Joe into a celebrity, giving every American in uniform at least the prospect of the proverbial fifteen minutes of fame. In this structure, generals were remote figures, having little to do with the grim, everyday realities of combat. If exceptions were made, they were for those senior officers who came on as homespun, rumpled, and unassuming—men like Omar Bradley. Pyle in particular "discovered" Bradley, consistently depicting him as "so modest and sincere that he probably will mot get his proper credit . . ." "Having him in command," Pyle declared, "has been a blessed good fortune for America."

A few years after the war, T. Harry Williams, then at the beginning of a distinguished career as a military historian, described American military leaders as either "Ikes," open, friendly and down-home, or "Macs." Exemplified by George B. McClellan and Douglas MacArthur, "Macs" were haughty, cold, theatrical, and elitist. Applying the same template to combat commanders and we get the "Georgies" and the "Brads." Both are stereotypes—arguably caricatures, and best not taken too seriously. But Pyle's brand of publicity helped Bradley emerge as the media's archetype of an American general. It also helped nurture Bradley's increasingly open dislike for Patton. Bradley was a poor man's son whose wife was a mortal foe of alcohol in any form. Having spent his military life in obscurity, uncomfortable with the trappings of rank, Bradley was disgusted by the flamboyance that was by now as natural to Patton as breathing. Patton's close supervision of Bradley's corps, amounting to interference on occasion, during the early stages of the Sicilian campaign only exacerbated the friction. Bradley came to consider his superior incapable of thinking through either his personal behavior or his operational plans— "a shallow general" and a glory hunter.

Higher headquarters in any army are nurseries of gossip and innuendo that take their cue from the commanding general. By the end of the Sicilian campaign, Bradley's II Corps was a focal point of anti-Patton anecdotes, with even the nurses invited as dinner guests contributing to a discussion of the 7th Army's commanding general as a posturing vulgarian.

Potentially more serious were a series of atrocities committed against Italian prisoners of war and Sicilian civilians by members of the green 45th Division. The perpetrators' defense was that they had been following Patton's orders to take no prisoners. Their evidence was a speech made to members of the division before the landing, in which among other admonitions Patton said killers were immortal, "We will show no mercy," and urged killing anyone who fought to the last ditch and then attempted surrender. Because the shootings were impossible to deny and the principal ones did not occur in the heat of combat, the only possible defense was to involve the chain of command high enough up the ladder that the system would have to bury the matter.

It did not work. That defense seldom does before a military court. After a detailed investigation, eventually Patton was exonerated by the Inspector-General's office of suborning murder.

The incidents themselves best suggest interpretation as part of the filth of war, reflections of fear, ignorance, and misjudgment rather than command policy. Some of that misjudgment was Patton's. Like most senior officers with experience in Tunisia, he had become increasingly concerned with motivating American soldiers to aggressive behavior: "Keep moving and keep firing." His preinvasion rhetoric was a means to that end. Whether he failed to consider its implications or, in fact, entertained a hidden agenda that accepted a casual approach to accepting surrenders remains unclear. He even had the law of war on his side: those who acknowledge informal, unofficial surrenders assume any risks accompanying the process, and suspicion is a correspondingly good rule.

Patton probably did accept on-the-spot denial of quarter to combatants visibly resisting, then seeking to give up at close range—a technical violation of the laws of war, but one widely practiced and usually overlooked in twentieth-century armies. What is certain is that Bradley, who ordered the initial courts-martial, was outraged—one more point on a mental list of Patton's defects that was growing as long and heavy as Jacob Marley's chain.

It was against this background that Patton embarked on a series of apologies. The two enlisted men were perfectly willing to shake hands—as one of them accurately observed, "I could not imagine anything similar happening in any other army." The hospital staffs remained collectively unimpressed. In addressing the rest of the 7th Army, Patton usually expressed a generalized regret for incidents he described as best forgotten, in the aggressively profane, scatological style that was by now his trademark.

Reactions varied. One regiment is described by a participant as cheering Patton to the echo; other troops of the same division are said to have inflated condoms and released them during his speech. Responses to the apology seem in general to have been influenced strongly by the degree to which units were inconvenienced to hear it; tired men were on the whole more indifferent or antagonistic. The increasingly dominant reaction, for those who gave a damn, seemed close to Eisenhower's original reflections, which shaped the text of his detailed report to the Secretary of War. There was a lot of war still to fight, and if everyone who temporarily lost control of himself were to receive a ticket stateside, those left to fight it would be few indeed.

The story nevertheless continued to snowball. Bob Hope and his troupe, after a command-performance dinner with Patton in Palermo, encountered Ernie Pyle, who described the slapping in detail and called Patton a son of a bitch. The Associated Press bureau chief heard about it in the airport at Marrakesh. Its domestic breakthrough came on November 21, when Washington journalist and radio personality Drew Pearson delivered a broadside on his weekly radio program. Pearson was to journalism what Patton was to soldiering: a flamboyant, controversial polemicist. His admirers called him a crusader; his foes—and targets—denounced him as a scandalmonger. He had been leaked the story by a contact in the Office of Strategic Services but paid it little attention. Pearson's current primary target was Secretary of State Cordell Hull, whom he denounced as delaying a second front because he wanted to see Russia bleed white. Roosevelt replied by calling Pearson a chronic liar. Following his familiar pattern, Pearson sought to change the subject and brought up the Patton story from his files.

Immediately America's journalistic community began bombarding its representatives on the spot for corroboration or denial. This was an era when "scoops" and "inside stories" dominated reporting. There was ample material for both on the wind in Sicily and more to be unearthed by asking the right questions in the right quarters. In the context of the developing cult of the GI, Patton made a vulnerable target even apart from his specific behavior. Novelist John P. Marquand, visiting his headquarters in the immediate aftermath of the scandal, wrote him down—and off—as "a tactless, high-strung, profane officer with a one-cell, juvenile mind."

More was involved, however, than a Fourth Estate feeding frenzy. The eighteen months after Pearl Harbor had been a time of anxiety, a time of rallying around the flag, a time of searching for larger-than-life heroes. Now the emergency was over. The German and Japanese empires were recoiling. The Soviet Union was safe from destruction—an issue important to an American Left strongly conditioned to view Stalin's "grand experiment" sympathetically. As the war moved into its midgame and America extended its mobilization, other questions were beginning to surface. It was increasingly clear that Roosevelt would stand for a fourth term in the coming presidential elections. What might a victory portend for America's democracy and constitution? Yet a Republican Party dominated by Robert Taft and Thomas E. Dewey was an unpalatable alternative to the New Deal intelligentsia. No less to the point, the American people had taken to the war with an unexpected gusto. Was there not a danger of a Man on Horseback emerging as a consequence of victory?

In such contexts, Patton's behavior took on aspects impossible for his military superiors to ignore. Public opinion, perhaps lagging behind the elites, on the whole supported Patton as a colorful winner. Some congressmen and editorial writers demanded his recall. One representative, an Iowa Republican, wondered whether the Army had too much "blood and guts" and expressed concern that parents might worry about "hard boiled officers" abusing their sons in uniform. Marshall and Secretary of War Edward Stimson responded by stressing the need for Patton's "aggressive, winning leadership in the bitter battles which are to come." Marshall, whose iconic status was by this time extending to Capitol Hill as well as the White House, paid similar respects to Patton as a warrior.

They were doing little more than paraphrasing Eisenhower's communication to Marshall of August 27. "Patton," Ike declared, "is preeminently a combat commander . . . the first thing that usually slows up operations is an element of caution, fatigue, or doubt on the part of a higher commander." Patton was never affected by these, and consequently his troops and his subordinate commanders were not affected. Patton was also "a one sided individual . . . apt at times to display exceedingly poor judgment and unjustified temper" when dealing with subordinates. But as Eisenhower put it in a letter of September 6, Patton was "a truly aggressive commander and, moreover, one with sufficient brains to do his work in a splendid fashion." In other words, the Patton package was worth buying, despite its risks.

A consistent element of Eisenhower's discussions of the slapping incident was his assertion, stated or implied, that he could handle Patton.

His chosen approach in the final months of 1943 was to keep him off-balance, reminding him at frequent and unpredictable intervals that his career hung by a thread and Eisenhower had hold of the scissors. Patton grumbled and sulked, resorted occasionally to sleeping pills, criticized Eisenhower bitterly in private, and noted carefully in his diary and letters any signs of Eisenhower's returning goodwill.

On September 2, Eisenhower informed Patton that Bradley would be transferred to Britain as an army commander to participate in planning the cross-channel attack. The news generated no reaction. Perhaps Patton believed it prefigured his own transfer to an even higher command. He certainly believed he and his 7th Army staff, combat experienced and with landings in Morocco and Sicily on their résumé, were professionally qualified to spearhead the invasion. And when it came to inspiring men to the desperate effort required to crack open Hitler's Fortress Europe, Patton considered himself second to none.

Four days later he was undeceived by two cables from Washington. The first stood down the 7th Army, transferring all its combat units, leaving only the headquarters. The second confirmed Bradley's appointment and suggested "the prestige of Seventh Army" would prove of great advantage in the follow-up to the Normandy invasion. Patton had hoped to command that invasion. "The second [cable] ruined me," he wrote in his diary.

Did the slapping incident cost George Patton the command and the role in Overlord that eventually went to Bradley? Its military consequences are best addressed in the context of Eisenhower's professional growth, his focusing and harnessing of his talents in a task no American general had ever faced. In Tunisia, he had been in truth little more than a chairman of the board, brokering among squabbling allies. Sicily took him a long way further on the path to greatness in High Command by testing him at choosing and developing subordinates.

Eisenhower's problem was exacerbated by the Allies' decision, finalized at Casablanca, to pursue a Mediterranean option by invading Italy as in the aftermath of Sicily's fall while simultaneously preparing for the invasion of Northwest Europe. As a consequence, Eisenhower had created two army headquarters. In January 1943, the 5th U.S. Army was activated and given primary responsibility for planning ahead to the Italian beaches.

Its designated commander was Lieutenant General Mark Clark, Eisenhower's deputy for the North African landings. Patton's 7th Army and its commander would be responsible for Sicily and then become available for service as required, presumably in the invasion of Europe. Bradley was designated as Clark's understudy, giving him an opportunity to indicate whether he possessed, or might develop, ability above corps level.

The assignments precisely reflected seniority. Clark outranked Patton; Patton outranked Bradley. Eisenhower understood the axiom that any hand can be a loser or a winner, depending on how it is played. And Mark Clark was a card often overlooked by historians. Eisenhower admired Clark's intellect and regarded him as the U.S. Army's outstanding planner and amphibious specialist. Eisenhower was by now well aware that the choice for supreme command of Overlord lay between him and Marshall. If he could produce a command-experienced, operationally tested senior team of Clark with his reputation for cool intelligence commanding the army group, with the steady Bradley and a chastened Patton each seeking to outdo the other as his subordinates at army level, this would serve the war effort in a way the Washington-bound chief of staff could not match, even should the eventual assignments be different.

Events transformed the prospect to ephemera. Clark's plan for the Italian landings proved seriously flawed. The Germans were waiting at Salerno and came within an ace of driving the invaders into the sea. Clark performed heroically at a captain's level, but his conduct of later operations showed no sign of either superior command abilities or an inspiring personality. In the face of a defense brilliantly organized and commanded by none other than Kesselring, the Allies made haste slowly up the peninsula, stalling in front of a Gustav Line Clark proved unable to breach despite increasingly high casualties. His relations with Alexander, his superior, his British colleagues, and even the French, who made a significant contribution to the campaign, correspondingly deteriorated. At the same time, Clark acquired a reputation among his own subordinates as a cold, contentious, selfish egomaniac.

The metastasizing crisis caused by Patton's self-indulgent behavior was arguably less significant for Eisenhower's future than Clark's failure to step up in the field. Eisenhower abandoned any serious consideration of supporting him for a high command in Overlord. For a time, he even considered relieving his disappointing subordinate. On September 25, Marshall became directly involved when he radioed Eisenhower to the effect that since July he had been under pressure to appoint a U.S. Army commander to work with the British in planning Overlord. His choice was Omar Bradley. Could Eisenhower spare him?

The request was arguably the best news of its kind Eisenhower had heard in months. He respected Bradley's character and ability. Before the landings in Sicily, Eisenhower even mentioned to Patton that should Sicily become a slugging match, he might put Bradley in charge and recall Patton to prepare for the next operation. In Sicily, Bradley had shown more awareness of logistical issues than Patton appeared to. He had demonstrated competence in handling infantry on a restricted battlefield. And by the end of the campaign, he had accumulated more time in combat command than any senior officer in the Mediterranean—Patton included. None of this had escaped Marshall's notice, and Eisenhower's response was the proverbial no-brainer. While making sure the Chief of Staff knew how much he had come to depend on Bradley, Eisenhower characterized him as "the best rounded combat leader I have yet met in our service" despite "possibly" lacking some of Patton's driving power. The rest was a process of cutting Bradley's transfer orders.

For practical purposes, there is no evidence anywhere that George Patton was ever at the top of the short list to command on D-day. There is, indeed, no evidence that a short list for the job existed. The U.S. Army's fundamental institutional problem was more basic: to find anyone at all who could bring an army to shore, keep it there, and break out of the beachheads. As a practical matter, that someone had to be from the European theater. It would be too embarrassing to appoint a D-day commander who had served his apprenticeship in the Pacific under the Navy, the Marines, and Douglas MacArthur. D-day, moreover, was an operation that, for a broad spectrum of reasons, could be mounted only once. That made it a correspondingly unacceptable risk to assign someone like General Devers, who by this time was commanding the administrative headquarters in England. If nothing else, the British, who were putting the last of their resources into the operation, were sure to object.

That left three possibilities: Clark, Patton, and Bradley. Clark took himself out of the running at Salerno and afterward. Taken on the record, Bradley cannot be said to have clearly matched or surpassed Patton in generalship or command ability in Tunisia and Sicily. What he had done, partly by design, was establish himself as Patton's opposite. Whatever Patton did, Bradley came to mind as a counterpoint. It was flamboyance and convention, daring and steadiness, and not least cavalry and infantry—which, in 1943, still mattered.

Neither Eisenhower nor Marshall seem to have regarded Patton as in practice particularly hard to handle. His buttons were obvious and easily pushed. As Eisenhower observed to Marshall, Patton's "intense loyalty to you and to me makes it possible for me to treat him much more roughly than I could any other commander." The problem was that Patton required handling. Bradley did not, and anything diminishing the complexity and the unpredictability of D-day was likely to be welcomed with open arms. A U.S. Army that in 1942 had been almost cavalierly optimistic in evaluating a landing in northwest Europe was increasingly influenced by the British perspective on the difficulties facing that operation. The more specific the planning became, the clearer it appeared that getting ashore would be no bagatelle and might demand special qualities from the responsible generals. Was the high-strung, labile Patton the best choice for an operation that might turn into a meatgrinder? Would not the constricted landing zone offer better scope for Bradley's particular tactical abilities? Bradley might be a good plain cook to Patton's gourmet chef, but he seemed less likely to produce military indigestion. Or—just perhaps—old-time infantrymen like Marshall and Eisenhower preferred to go to war riding a gelding rather than a stallion.

Patton's public behavior remained correct. He turned out a band and an honor guard for Bradley's courtesy call and lent his personal C-47 for the first leg of Bradley's flight to England. Bradley, less than gracious in triumph, responded by describing his former superior as brought to his knees and in a near-suicidal mental state. Patton was certainly miserable enough in the final months of 1943—a condition probably not improved by the stream of advice from friends and well-wishers to keep his chin up while mending his ways. "Send me some more pink medecin," he wrote Bea. "This worry and inactivity has raised hell with my insides." He nevertheless expected his turn to come again. "On occasion it is best to do nothing," he wrote, "and however repellent it is to my character, I am doing exactly that."

By December 1943, President Roosevelt's fear that he could not rest nights without George Marshall in Washington finally outweighed the chief of staff's desire for field command. The prize, as increasingly expected, went to Eisenhower. Patton learned of the appointment on December 7. In discussing his likely future with Assistant Secretary of War John J. Mc Cloy, he was told Marshall approved his having an army. Presidential advisor Harry Hopkins informed him the slapping incident was closed. In preparing Patton's efficiency report, Eisenhower rated him "Superior" for the second half of 1943, ranked him fifth among two dozen lieutenant generals, and recommended him for command of an army. He concluded by saying Patton should always serve under "a strong but understanding commander." Readers were free to fill in the name of that general.

During December, in discussing senior appointments for Overlord with Marshall, Eisenhower reiterated his choice of Patton as one of his army commanders. Bradley would lead the assault; Patton would command the follow-up army. But when that second army took the field and warranted forming an army group, Bradley would move up to command it. "In no event," Eisenhower stated, "will I ever advance Patton beyond army command," and Patton would always serve under the steadier Bradley.

In one sense the question was moot. If Bradley brought victory on D-day, his promotion would be deserved. If the invasion failed, Eisenhower would be in no position to recommend anybody for anything. "I should have a group of armies," Patton commented, "but that will come. I think my luck is in again." He spent most of December in a series of highly publicized tours of the Mediterranean—part of a general plan to keep German attention focused on that theater. He explored ruins, Norman, Greek, Roman, Carthaginian, and ruminated on the follies of history. He visited Malta at the invitation of the governor. He visited the 5th Army in Italy and recorded a set of predictably scathing comments on Clark's ability and his conduct of the campaign. On January 1, he was formally relieved of the 7th Army's command, which was simultaneously tasked with planning Operation Anvil, the invasion of southern France developed by the Allied High Command as a counterpoint to Overlord. Disappointed at leaving a staff that had served him loyally in both victory and adversity, Patton characterized Bradley as "a man of great mediocrity" and wondered if his ultimate fate would be a training assignment in England.

Marshall came up with another possibility when he asked Eisenhower about returning Patton to the 7th Army and placing him in charge of the invasion of southern France instead of Clark, who had been penciled in for the appointment. Eisenhower agreed that if Clark remained in Italy, Patton's prestige, his experience in the theater, and his remarkably good relations with the French favored the move. On the other hand, Devers, who would replace Eisenhower as senior U.S. Army officer in the Mediterranean, and Patton were "not congenial"—a clear reference to Eisenhower's earlier comment about the "strong but understanding commander" Patton needed.

Marshall promptly dropped the subject. Yet it is tempting to speculate on the course of events had Patton led the 7th Army onto the beaches of Marseilles. Devers's previous contacts with Patton offered no indication of inability to work with him. In terms of temperament, Patton and the French 1st Army commander Jean de Latttre de Tassigny were natural stablemates: aggressive risk-takers. Patton was far more likely to have empathized with the complex baggage of emotions and attitudes that accompanied the returning French than either Devers or Alexander Patch, transferred from the Pacific, who in the event commanded the 7th Army in a drive up the Loire Valley against German resistance that failed to cope with even the measured pace set by the two American generals. What might Patton have done as the central figure and the driving force of the "champagne campaign"? The question became forever moot on January 22, when he received a cable ordering him to Britain. He left three days later—no less a collection of paradoxes than when he landed in North Africa in the autumn of 1942.

V

Erwin Rommel spent his first weeks in Germany recovering his health and his equilibrium. He informed his now-teenage son that he had fallen into disgrace and could expect no major assignment for the present. Instead, he underwent a series of "cures" and observed the Reich's declining positions in Russia, North Africa, and on the air over Germany itself. He worried about his generals as the Tunisian situation deteriorated and sought vainly to convince the High Command to organize an evacuation of technicians and senior officers while time remained. As his energy returned, Rommel also began organizing his memories and experiences in North Africa for what he intended as a work similar to *Infantry Attacks* but on an operational instead of a tactical level. He made little progress, though the material he collected formed the base for a memoir published in 1950 by his wife and Bayerlein, suggestively titled *War Without Hate* (*Krieg ohne Hass*).

This interim ended as the Tunisian campaign approached endgame. On May 8, Rommel was summoned to Berlin. The next afternoon he was once more *tête-à-tête* with Hitler. "I should have listened to you," declared the Fuehrer. For the next weeks, he remedied his purported error by soliciting Rommel's views on the emerging Italian crisis. Hitler had long since lost any confidence he might have had in Italy's government, its armed forces, and its Fascist Party. There remained, he declared, only the Duce.

Rommel was scarcely reassuring. Goebbels noted that he dismissed Mussolini as a tired old man and made no secret of his opinion that the Italians would not make even a token resistance to an Allied invasion. Italy's image as a liability instead of an ally was reinforced by the virtual annihilation of its Expeditionary Corps at Stalingrad, by long-simmering disputes over Balkan occupation policy, and by demands for material support that escalated into the ridiculous—in February alone, Italy submitted a wish list including 1,250 tanks, 1,350 antitank guns, and 7,400 trucks, with guns, fuel, and spare parts in proportion.

Hitler was sufficiently concerned to consider canceling the projected offensive in Russia that he intended would reverse the consequences of

Stalingrad. On May 15, he spoke of stripping the Eastern front of a dozen divisions to rush into Italy with or without its government's approval should the Allies invade. The obvious candidate for the job was ordered on May 18 to form a skeleton planning staff for what was christened Operation Alaric—a nice historical touch referring to the sack of Rome by Gothic invaders in 410 C.E.

Rommel, with Gause back in harness as his chief of staff, reported to Berchtesgaden and spent the next weeks planning to move as many as twenty divisions into Italy at Hitler's word—a word that never came. In his spare time, he attended Hitler's war conferences as what he described as "a kind of adviser," but is better understood as living window-dressing. The meetings themselves never came to anything, as much because of their large size and heterogeneous composition as from Hitler's behavior. They enhanced the concern Rommel had earlier expressed on realizing: "Our star was in decline and . . . how little our command measured up to the trials which lay ahead."

He later described to his wife and son a long private conversation building on Hitler's concern for Germany's Italian position. Rommel focused on Allied war production and asked if Germany could keep pace with the entire world. Hitler supposedly replied that he, too, believed there was little chance of winning the war, but that the West would never conclude peace with him. According to Rommel's son, his father had another one-on-one encounter with Hitler at the end of July 1943. This time, the Fuehrer raged that if the German people were unable to win the war, they could rot. The best of them were dead, and in any case a great people must die heroically. "Sometimes you feel that he's no longer quite normal," was Rommel's alleged response when telling the story to Lu.

These kinds of anecdotes, by their nature unverifiable, are correspondingly suspect. The memoir literature of the Third Reich in particular is replete with accounts in which the author either speaks unvarnished truth to Hitler or sees him at an unguarded moment of self-revelation. It is, however, not necessary to take Rommel at his literal word to accept the argument that his time at the Burghof encouraged him to focus his doubts about the course of the war and the future of Germany. Rommel's professional ethos conditioned him to obey the legal political authority embodied in Hitler. He saw Germany's cause as both legitimate and righteous: the preservation of a Europe ordered under German hegemony. Certainly nothing from either the Russian front or the Combined Bomber Offensive suggested the Allies would be merciful or generous in victory. The "unconditional surrender" proclamation that concluded the Roosevelt-Churchill meeting in Casablanca earlier in the year suggested just the opposite. Was Adolf Hitler the man to bring Germany through the greatest challenge of its history? Once, perhaps, yes. Now—?

Another encounter, suggesting a different perspective, also took place in July. On the first of the month, Hitler returned to his East Prussian headquarters for the start of Operation Citadel. Rommel accompanied him, to the benefit of a headquarters rumor mill that quickly had the Fuehrer naming Rommel commander in chief of the army. Erich von Manstein, another of the army's masters of armored war, was recalled to Rastenburg for consultation during the Battle of Kursk and met Rommel for the first time under casual circumstances—as casual as possible, because Manstein was enjoying a swim *au naturel* in a nearby lake. Rommel informed his colleague that he was taking a sunlamp cure: soaking up sun and faith. Lest he meaning be mistaken, when Manstein asked if they would meet later Rommel replied, "Yes, under the sunlamp." The reference to Hitler was impossible to miss.

Was Rommel in fact seeking a renewal of his optimism in Hitler's dynamic presence? Or was there a hint of irony, even sarcasm, in his choice of words? Rommel was seldom given to verbal subtleties. At the same time, he did not know Manstein save by reputation—which at that time still included high standing with the Fuehrer. The possibility that he would even hint of doubts to a complete stranger, even a fellow tanker, is vanishingly small, especially given the passionate desire to return to active command reflected in another July meeting, this one with Fritz Bayerlein.

Bayerlein had been evacuated sick from Tunisia just before the collapse, with a brilliant record as both a staff officer and a troop commander that he considered owed much to Rommel's mentoring. He, too, was summoned to Rastenburg for a consultation, and Rommel took the opportunity to discuss the need for a completely new approach to the war. For the next few years, he declared, there was no possibility of resuming the offensive anywhere. That meant a comprehensive shift to the defense: producing fighters instead of bombers; increasing exponentially the number of heavy antitank guns in a division from the current thirty or forty to a hundred or two hundred. (Eventually, he would request no fewer than four hundred.) Generals like Guderian, who called for increasing tank production, were missing the point. It was impossible for Germany to keep pace with the Allies' outputs. But guns, cheap and simple to manufacture, were another story. Rommel talked of antitank screens six miles deep on the style of the Russian *pakfronts* currently chewing up the Panzers at Kursk. When the troops saw they could hold their ground, morale would soar again.

Nothing there indicates loss of hope. Erwin Rommel in the summer of 1943 maintained an opacity worthy of his Swabian ancestors, hinting at the contents of his hand but never tipping it in a performance any poker player must admire. Destiny did not allow a full-scale clash of armor between Rommel and Patton. Rommel and Eisenhower in an all-night game of five-card draw might have been no less memorable.

Rommel played his cards close enough to the chest to bring him the command he wanted. On July 10, the Allied invasion of Sicily began. Initially, Rommel's staff was ordered to Greece to prepare for the contingency of a second landing in the peninsula. Then on July 24–25, a palace coup deposed Mussolini. The new head of state, Marshal Pietro Badoglio, promptly opened armistice negotiations with Eisenhower. A confused Hitler ordered Rommel back to Germany and put him in charge of implementing the German response: occupying Italy before either Badoglio or the Allies could react.

Rommel, though forbidden by Hitler to cross the frontier himself, by most accounts enjoyed the assignment as a chance to settle scores with Italy's establishment. His original plan was to infiltrate as much of the country as possible by what were masked as routine troop movements, then pounce. Success depended particularly on controlling the rail lines through the Alps. At the same time, Rommel insisted that everything possible be done to sustain good relations with Italian officials, troops, and citizens. The Germans were entering Italy as allies—though resistance was to be broken by force. Rommel understood his own reputation for hostility to Italians and denied it at every opportunity. He nevertheless expected Italy's new government to change sides as quickly as possible—

"Even the Pope is now wanting to lean on us." Why, he mused, did Italy go to war in the first place with its inadequate armed forces? In any case, better to fight there than at home.

Not until August 15 was Rommel authorized to enter Italy. Accompanied by Alfred Jodl, Chief of the Armed Forces High Command, he promptly flew to Bologna for a meeting with the Italian High Command. Its ostensible purposes, arranging the logistics of the new German arrivals and deciding which army would be responsible for what, rapidly segued into a discussion of Italy's policies and Germany's intentions. An indication of the mutual ill will informing the proceedings is that the German officers carried pistols. Plans for the occupation continued—with the particpation after August 30 of an SS contingent tasked to study internal security problems. It was Rommel's first systematic contact with an organization he had done his best to avoid since 1940.

On September 3, elements of the British 8th Army began landing in Calabria, at the toe of the Italian boot. For two weeks previously, the Italians had been making difficulty about German rail and road movements. They had even redeployed some of their units from the south. Rommel, summoned to Rastenburg once more, found Hitler essentially in agreement with his own views that Italy could no longer be trusted and enjoyed Hitler's criticism of Kesselring for his excessive credulity where Italians were concerned. Considering himself fully restored to favor, Rommel suggested that he be given command of all German forces in Italy, with his army group headquarters near enough to Rome to lay a thumb on the Italians' windpipes if—or when—it should be necessary. Kesselring would presumably resign or be transferred: the smart money was on his being reassigned to Norway. Rommel found that particular fringe benefit pleasant to contemplate.

On September 8, the 5th Army went ashore at Salerno. Eisenhower also announced that Italy's leaders had agreed to an armistice. A project to land the 82nd Airborne Division in Rome was abandoned on the grounds of excessive risk. Instead, Badoglio and the king slipped through a still-nominal German security screen to the Allied zone of occupation, perhaps with Kesselring's knowledge. They left no orders for a disorganized army and a demoralized administration, beyond forbidding taking any initiative against the Germans. Some Italian units, especially in

Greece and the Balkans, fought back and paid the price of annihilation. Others disbanded themselves and went home. And still others grounded arms and awaited the course of events.

That course was largely determined by the Germans. The Allied High Command, from the beginning dubious about the value of its new partner, had no interest in a power drive up the peninsula, nor anyone on the ground capable of leading it. By September 19, Army Group B reported that more than 400,000 Italians had been disarmed. The process was initially facilitated by Rommel's orders to treat the Italians as former comrades, appealing to their soldierly honor to prevent needless killing. But a policy of deporting disarmed Italians to the Reich as forced labor—accepted and implemented by Rommel without any hesitation—quickly disillusioned soldiers and civilians alike. Resistance movements began springing up everywhere north of Rome. Mussolini's rescue by German special operations troops, and his installation as head of a shadow Salo Republic did nothing to mitigate a Fascist/Nazi occupation that grew increasingly brutal. As defeat came to stare the Third Reich and its representatives in the face, all the masks of civilization were dropped in favor of a merciless oppression whose consequences finally engulfed Mussolini himself.

Rommel was not involved in Italy's partisan war, though the orders he issued prescribing death for Italian soldiers taken in arms and Italian civilians sheltering escaped British prisoners do not suggest he would have behaved significantly different from his Wehrmacht counterparts. Rommel's focus was on Italy as a theater of war where he expected to be named commander in chief. His final projected approach to operations was an economy-of-force plan that reflected both his respect for Allied air and naval superiority, and the conviction expressed to Bayerlein that Germany must now switch to a defensive mode. He advocated abandoning the south, with its vulnerable coastlines and long lines of communication—even Rome itself. The forward line of defense, he argued, should be in the Apennines north of Rome, from the Rapido River on the Mediterranean side to Ortona on the Adriatic, roughly along what later became the Gustav Line, with the main positions established south of the Po. Even then it was necessary to guard against amphibious landings behind the front—and here Rommel first introduced his emphasis on stopping landings at the coastline as the best practical counter to Anglo-American air strikes and naval gunfire.

Rommel's plan reflected an exaggerated calculation of Allied amphibious capabilities. The demands of the Pacific theater created a comprehensive shortage of landing craft from mid-1943 to just before D-day. Churchill himself grumbled that it seemed impossible that strategic planning for a global war could be determined by the presence or absence of things called LSTs: the ungainly cargo carriers that were the backbone of over-the-beach invasions. Rommel also overrated his potential opposition. The Allied campaign in Italy remained characterized by a stupefying lack of imagination and initiative that underwrote Kesselring's preference for an extended fighting withdrawal.

The wisdom of the German decision to make any kind of fight for the peninsula remains debatable. Central Italy's mountainous terrain, its narrow valleys and swift-running rivers, combined with the winter weather mocked the familiar images of World War II as a war of movement and technology. The Germans proved masters of defense, creating networks of observation posts and killing grounds that turned what open ground existed into tactical deathtraps. Yet when the final figures were in, the Allies suffered 312,000 casualties while inflicting 435,000—attrition on the wrong side of the balance sheet.

What might Rommel have done with the Italian theater had he been given command there? Would he have made the shift from master of mobile warfare to coordinator of a protracted defense? Hitler's decision on the appointment was still hanging fire when in mid-September Rommel suffered an appendicitis attack and underwent emergency surgery that kept him hospitalized till the 27th. Three days later, he was summoned to Rastenburg. Kesselring was also present, and in what was becoming a typical situation, each general made his case before a Fuehrer who, observers agreed, demonstrated none of the vitality he usually brought to these sessions. Hitler's summary showed his line of thought. Every day the Allies could be contained in southern Italy was vital. They were running out of men and material; sooner or later they would become war-weary enough to give Germany victory by default.

Shortly after the meeting, Kesselring made a concrete proposal for a defense south of Rome, which he said he could maintain at least over the winter. Previously he had not asked for reinforcements; now Hitler was sufficiently impressed to order Rommel to send troops south. Rommel warned of the near-certainty of amphibious landings behind the proposed defensive line and repeated his doubts Rome could be held for any length of time. Kesselring protested Rommel's interference. On October 17, Hitler told Rommel he would be named commander in Italy but was expected to take over Kesselring's deployments. Rommel answered by setting three conditions: he wanted to inspect the front himself; he demanded clear instructions allowing him operational flexibility; he would submit his plan only when his appointment was confirmed.

At this stage of the war, no one spoke to Hitler in that fashion. Rommel, never a model of tact, was frustrated by the failure to resolve the kind of divided command situation that had caused so much trouble in North Africa. He must also have been in a fair amount of pain despite his legendary toughness: "minor surgery" is what another person has. Air force general Wolfram von Richthofen, himself no shrinking violet, described Rommel at this period as "pigheaded" and "worn out." One of Hitler's adjutants mentioned how difficult the field marshal was to get deal with. Rommel did not help his situation by referring to Jodl and High Command operations chief Wilhelm Keitel as "assholes"—an epithet much stronger in German than in English and no less an insult.

Hitler vacillated for a couple weeks. Then, on November 5, he informed Rommel he had a new job for him: inspecting the Atlantic Wall, the major barrier to Allied invasion of Northwest Europe. He would leave on November 21. That same day, Kesselring would become Commander in Chief, Southwest—which meant Italy. "Smiling Albert" had taken the pot, and Rommel was disgruntled. When he bade farewell to those of his headquarters who remained in Italy, he described the war as lost and said Germany's soldiers were led by people whose fantasies amounted to delusion. "Do we make peace then?" asked one officer. Rommel replied that there could be no question of peace with the Russians. Four months earlier, in his conversation with Bayerlein, he had declared that if the British and Americans were once thrown back into the sea, it would be a long time before they returned. Now he was responsible for evaluating that prospect—and for considering its implications.

The Atlantic Wall began when, at the end of 1941, Hitler ordered the construction of a line of fortifications along the Atlantic coast. He intended this as the main position securing the conquered continent and Germany's western provinces. Initially no comprehensive plans for the system were developed, though by 1942, it was clear to the newly created High Command West that the Allies would eventually strike northwestern Europe in force. The Command's initial response was to deploy whatever divisions were available to cover directly what seemed the most vulnerable ports and landing sites. It was a wing-and-a-prayer proposition, but point defense seemed the most promising immediate response to the German experiences in Norway and Crete. These indicated that not merely the first hours, but the first minutes of an invasion could be crucial.

That perspective seemed validated on August 19, 1942, when a division-size assault with heavy air and naval support was decisively broken on the beaches of Dieppe. Terrain favored the defenders. Fortune smiled as well that day on the men who fought under the swastika. The Germans nevertheless won their victory with military pocket change, and Dieppe generated a new optimism among the senior officers who contemplated the burned-out tanks. In September 1942, Hitler ordered the coastal defenses increased by no fewer than 15,000 strong points. Given enough concrete and barbed wire, the Wehrmacht's leftovers might be able to make "Fortress Europe" a reality.

As Hitler's initial vision of kicking in the Soviet Union's front door drowned in blood, France increasingly became a rest-and-recuperation zone for burned-out front-line units. A few weeks in France to absorb equipment and replacements, to forget the war as far as possible, was a dream that ran a close third to a long furlough or a million-mark wound. Even the West's supreme commander as of March 1942, Field Marshal Gerd von Rundstedt, received his appointment after being removed from his army group in Russia. At the same time, the "hero-thieves" of the replacement service staged comb-out after comb-out in the formations that watched the coasts.

The Germans who remained, the lame and the halt, the elderly and the invalid, saw themselves as garrison troops. Some historians of World War II have argued that the United States–initiated projects for a full-scale landing in the spring of 1943 would have caught the Wehrmacht at its lowest ebb. German fixed defenses in the west were still embryonic. At sea, the argument runs, the Allies were supreme. In the air, they could count on a significant margin of superiority. The disaster at Stalingrad and the preparations for Kursk reduced the German army in the west to a shell primarily concerned with rebuilding shattered divisions, providing cadres for new ones, and conducting training courses at all levels. For a good part of 1943, High Command West had fewer combat-ready divisions than it possessed in 1942. *Ostlegionen,* battalions recruited from Russia's Asian communities or from prisoners of war, filled out its orders of battle. The invasions of Sicily and Italy and the German occupation of Vichy France increased the stresses on already-overstretched field forces. The growth of demands for forced labor from a conquered Europe converted what had been large-scale compliance to a seemingly permanent occupation first to sullenness and hostility, then to opposition and resistance.

The case for a 1943 invasion of northeastern Europe nevertheless becomes plausible chiefly because of distractions caused by Anglo-American initiatives in the Mediterranean. Without Operation Torch and its consequences, High Command West would have been correspondingly free to concentrate on preparing for a major landing from Britain. Despite the challenges generated by the Russian and Mediterranean theaters, the Atlantic Wall began taking on a life of its own. By mid-1943, particularly around the major ports, the Wall looked authentic, with trenches, ditches, minefields, machine-gun nests, concrete strong points, and heavy artillery emplaced in what even to men who knew better seemed impregnable bunkers. By June 1943, more than 8,000 permanent installations were operable. By November, more than 2,300 antitank guns and 2,700 guns larger than 75 millimeters were in place.

The building program, however, tailed off in the final months of the year. Allied air raids drew away skilled workers. German firms that had obtained sweetheart contracts or low-balled their bids produced unsatisfactory work or failed to meet commitments. Nor were the commanders on the spot exactly sure what to do with the system in place. The defense of western Europe, originally regarded as a joint-service undertaking, had by late 1943 become an army responsibility. The *Kriegsmarine,* defeated in the U-boat campaign, its remaining surface vessels penned in harbor, could expect to do little more than conduct coast-defense operations with a mixed bag of small craft. The Luftwaffe's attention had shifted to the Eastern Front and, increasingly, to the Reich itself. Staff and operational assignments to Air Fleet 3, responsible for Western Europe, were viewed as either dead ends or rest cures.

On October 25, 1943, Rundstedt submitted a comprehensive memorandum describing the challenges and requirements of a sector that in the next year could expect to become a major theater of operations. The field marshal pulled no punches. The Allies already had as many divisions available as Rundstedt could muster in his entire expanded theater. Most of them were first class: young men, sound of wind and limb, and equipped with the best American and British industry could provide. Rundstedt expected an invasion no earlier than the spring of 1944, and probably not much later. He believed the Allies would land first in the Pas de Calais, then in Normandy and Brittany. Admittedly, that would pit them against the best-defended sector of the Atlantic Coast. On the other hand, those invasion sites offered the easiest passages across the Channel, the shortest supply lines to Allied bases in England, and the closest distances to Germany's frontiers. Anglo-American air and naval supremacy meant they could shut down German reconnaissance at will, thus securing tactical surprise.

Rundstedt went on to argue that trenches, pillboxes, and strong points were only half of a successful defensive system. Depth was also necessary: fall-back positions in the rear areas, mobile artillery, and enough troops for counterattacks to seal off the inevitable breakthroughs. High Command West, however, not only lacked anything resembling an effective mobile reserve, it also lacked enough static troops to do more than observe and patrol much of the endangered area.

These weaknesses paradoxically made the Atlantic Wall more important than ever. Abandoning the coast without a fight would sacrifice the advantage of the channel as a moat. It would mean the loss of a heavy investment in fortifications. Above all, it would require the conduct of a mobile battle in northeastern France against an enemy whose strong point was a capacity for mobile warfare. Therefore, Rundstedt argued, the coastline must be defended to the last. Experience in both world wars showed that landings in force would nevertheless succeed. But local counterattacks, combined with the concentrated blows of a massed reserve, provided the window of an opportunity for defeating the invasion, or at least so bloodying the Anglo-Americans' noses that they might reconsider their military and political options.

Hitler read this complex document with a level of attention by this time unusual. Instead of responding by insisting on the importance of willpower, a Fuehrer Directive of November 3, 1943, accepted most of Rundstedt's basic propositions. For two and a half years, the Reich's energies had been directed against Asiatic Bolshevism. Now an even greater danger had emerged: the Anglo-American invasion. An Allied breakout from a successful landing would have prompt and incalculable consequences for the Reich. No longer could the West be stripped for the sake of other theaters. Instead, its defenses must be strengthened by every means possible. Panzer divisions must be created or reequipped with the latest models of heavy tanks and assault guns. The supply of antitank, infantry, and artillery weapons must be increased. High Command West was ordered to reduce the garrisons of less-threatened areas and improve the counterattack capacity of static formations by improvising their mobility through internal resources.

Hitler believed even more than Rundstedt that victory in the West ultimately would depend on throwing the Allies into the sea at all costs. Was Rundstedt, a man of advanced years and fixed opinions, the general to perform that mission? Kesselring seemed to be bringing Italy under control. Time then to plug another hole by the well-tried method of personal competition in true National Socialist terms: survival of the fittest. Rundstedt, not one of Rommel's chief admirers, was nevertheless familiar enough with that process, and pleased enough with the Fuhrer's newfound interest in the West, that he offered the newcomer full cooperation. Rommel, for his part, recognized the awkwardness of his position and took pains to avoid stepping on his senior's toes. But these men, the army's senior and junior field marshals, were like oil and water. Rundstedt had been to the circus and seen the clowns. He tended to let situations develop before he acted, all the while commenting on those developments with an irony that could alternately inspire admiration or fury in his associates. Rommel was a driver, accustomed to seeing every situation as an emergency, making snap decisions, and making those decisions work.

The problem was exacerbated because both men were respected and admired by their subordinates. Each possessed charisma: Rundstedt the "last Prussian," patrician, dignified; Rommel the frontline commander who talked like a first sergeant and paid little attention to formalities. The old pro and the new broom—small wonder that within weeks even senior officers in the theater were uncertain who was really in command.

It was Rundstedt who broke the ice. On December 30, he made a formal proposal to bring the headquarters of Army Group B under High Command West, with direct responsibility for the region most exposed to invasion. Rundstedt's command style, like that of most of his old-army contemporaries, was based on the delegation of authority. His responsibilities as theater commander had been so extended by recent Allied initiatives that he could not hope to supervise directly every area under threat. And if, as was frequently murmured behind closed General Staff doors, Rommel was no more than a good corps commander, his tactical record was nevertheless sufficiently distinguished to make him a solid choice to command western Europe's most likely hot spot.

Rommel applied the energy that had made him famous to strengthening and vitalizing the Atlantic Wall. He estimated that no fewer than fifty million mines would be needed to establish a viable belt around the coast! Such an astronomical number was of course unattainable. Nevertheless, between October 1943 and May 1944, the number of antitank and antipersonnel mines in place rose from two million to six and a half million. Rommel also oversaw the introduction of underwater obstacles at the most likely landing sites. These ranged from angled wooden stakes to steel Belgian antitank barriers transplanted from their original sites on the German border. By mid-May, more than 500,000 of these passive defenses had been installed, many of them with mines attached. Behind the coast the field marshal planted "Rommel asparagus"—pointed stakes driven into the ground on terrain deemed suitable for paratroops or glider landings.

Rommel brought new vigor as well to the construction and renovation of manned defenses. He was shocked to find that many of the gun positions and machine-gun emplacements were open, offering no significant protection from air strikes or naval gunfire. Engineers and workers from the Organization Todt began bringing as many heavy weapons as

possible under bombproof protection. Camouflage and camouflage discipline improved sharply. Local commanders assigned troops to the construction efforts, which included establishing dummy positions in hopes
of deceiving the by-now ubiquitous Allied reconnaissance aircraft.

On paper and in reality, the results were impressive. In 1944, the
Germans laid more than four million land mines—well over double the
number that had been put in place since 1940. Between January and May,
more than five thousand new permanent fortifications were erected: no
small number even though the figures included the French Mediterranean
coast. In the Pas de Calais sector, 93 of 132 heavy guns had been put under concrete, as were 27 of the 47 heavy guns in Normandy.

In his initial report, submitted on December 31, Rommel said the major Allied effort would most probably be made in the Pas de Calais,
largely because that would be the sector from which the projected V-
weapon offensive against London would be launched. Rommel's ideal
was to defeat the invasion on the coast, fighting the main battle in the fortified zones. The most difficult phase of a landing was its beginning: the
movement from ship to shore. The Germans, Rommel insisted, must take
every possible advantage of this fact. Passive defenses, mines, and off-
shore obstacles must complement the fire of artillery, antitank guns, and
automatic weapons covering the landing sites. Infantry should be deployed as close to the beaches as possible. But the heart of Rommel's tactics was his proposal to deploy the Panzer formations so close to the coast
that combined-arms battle groups would be able to engage the enemy in
the invasion's first hours.

Without the immediate help of mechanized reserves, the field marshal
insisted, the German divisions holding the coastline could not expect to
maintain their positions. Once the Allies disembarked, their fighting
power multiplied exponentially. Left undisturbed, they would flank the
defenders out of their fixed defenses and roll up the Atlantic Wall like a
rug. Rommel's approach offered the advantage of employing the mechanized divisions in ways grown familiar to their officers in recent years:
counterpunching a tactically vulnerable enemy, with dash and tactical
skill compensating for inferior numbers. It offered as well a closer link
between the two tiers of the defense, the infantry divisions at the water-
line and the mobile formations. His plan made it less likely that the for-

mer would regard themselves as pawns for sacrifice, and correspondingly less likely that they would break or capitulate quickly.

Rommel had experienced a similar situation in Africa with the Italians. One of the reasons for the German infantry's Homeric combat record on the Eastern Front was the widespread knowledge that surrendering to Ivan involved high levels of immediate risk and complete certainty of subsequent discomfort. By contrast, conditions of British or American captivity were so favorably mythologized that not a few prisoners taken during the D-day campaign seemed surprised when their first meal did not include steak.

Rommel's principal critic was not Rundstedt, but Leo Geyr von Schweppenburg. An experienced staff officer and longtime commander of armored forces, with extensive experience on the Russian Front, Geyr had been appointed commander of Panzer Troops West in July 1943 and immediately began developing his own plans for using armor against an Allied invasion. Geyr recognized the potential impact of Allied sea and air power but was no admirer of the battle group tactics he believed had emerged in Russia and Africa as a response to a chronic shortage of tanks. These small formations, Geyr argued, would be particularly vulnerable to Allied firepower. What was needed were large-scale counterattacks against the invasion beaches, counterattacks in divisional strength or more. Hold the mechanized forces back from the beaches, he argued, and commit them in mass. Air power could not stop movement—only delay it. Properly trained troops under competent officers could expect to arrive in time where they were needed.

Rommel, unlike Geyr, had spent a fair amount of his time in North Africa personally dodging Allied aircraft. He expected the invasion to have higher levels of air support than anything previously seen in history. The terrain, moreover, was ideally suited for tactical air power. In contrast to the wide-open desert, northern France was so heavily built up that only a relatively few roads could be used for major troop movements. These led across rivers and through cities. Bridges and buildings alike offered inviting targets for Allied medium and heavy bombers. Rommel did not expect any feelings for the French people to restrict such uses of air power. The French resistance was also likely to be a factor, both directly in partisan operations and by providing up-to-date intelligence to the Allied airmen. It was unreasonable, Rommel argued, to expect divisions positioned according to Geyr's proposals to reach the battle zone, reorganize, and refit in less than ten days or two weeks. That was all the time and more the invaders would need to establish a bridge-head impregnable to anything High Command West was likely to bring against it.

The decision was Rundstedt's, and the field marshal remained torn between his own belief that the invasion was best defeated at the water line and the lure of Geyr's arguments for attempting something more decisive. As more and more armored and Panzer grenadier divisions joined High Command West, Rommel sought Hitler's intervention. The Fuehrer was reluctant to decide, particularly because a decision in Rommel's favor meant the corresponding necessity of relieving Rundstedt. Geyr did not have Rommel's access to the supreme commander, but his patron, Heinz Guderian, was in renewed good odor at the *Fuehrerhauptquartier.*

With more and more armored divisions arriving in France, in February 1944, Rommel's Army Group B was given the right to command any formations of Panzer Group West in its operational area as part of its preparation for the invasion. Rommel also received the right to recommend sector assignments and command appointments for the mobile formations directly to Rundstedt, thus bypassing Geyr. The result was an increase in friction among the senior officers that finally led Hitler to intervene directly. He began in April by stating he reserved the decision to determine when mobile formations should be assigned to Army Group B. Until that point, High Command West retained full control of those divisions. A month later, the Fuehrer became even more specific. He created a new Army Group headquarters under Rundstedt to control southern France and assigned it three Panzer divisions: the 9th, 11th, and 2nd SS. Rommel's Army Group B also received three Panzer divisions: the 2nd, 21st, and 116th. The mobile units that remained were the cream of the crop: the 1st and 12th SS Panzer, 17th SS Panzer Grenadier, and the army's Panzer Lehr. They remained under control of Panzer Group West—but not exactly under Rundstedt's command. Instead, the Panzer Group was designated part of the Wehrmacht High Command reserve, which in practice placed it under Hitler's direct control.

The reorganization invites dismissal as no more than another example of Hitler's high-test meddling in matters outside his competence. Assigning three mechanized divisions to southern France left seven available for the decisive sector. Either massed as a central reserve or posted close to the prospective beaches, they represented a force strong enough to shape, if not decide, the coming battle—not a queen, but properly used, perhaps a pair of knights. Their division not only created the obvious possibility of being too weak everywhere. It generated a subtler risk of making everyone just strong enough to generate a false sense of security. Rundstedt's sarcastic comment that Hitler's decision left him only the authority to move the sentries in his headquarters was, however, at best a half-truth. The field marshal had forgotten a fundamental military axiom. The first duty of a commander is to command: in this case, to decide the organization of his theater. War abhors vacuums. Adolf Hitler filled that created by Gerd von Rundstedt.

Rommel's direct contact with the Fuhrer was more recent and more extensive than anyone else in High Command West. His faith in "final victory" had been correspondingly weakened. In that at least he had much in common with almost every senior officer west of the Rhine River. But while Rommel's counterparts were content to play the cards in their hands with a cynical shrug, Rommel thought in wider terms. Repulsing the landings at the shoreline would buy military time that might be exploited politically. A decisive victory presented to the Fuehrer by his favorite marshal might well prove an entering wedge for a negotiated peace. If not, there was always a developing military resistance, whose plans and hopes for direct action against "history's greatest warlord" were increasingly open secrets among those in the know at High Command West.

7

RESOLUTIONS

PATTON arrived in England on January 26 and learned from Eisenhower the next day that he was to command the 3rd Army. Ike simultaneously administered a sharp lecture whose burden was "Think before you act; look before you leap." "As far as I can remember," Patton noted, "this is my twenty-seventh start from zero since entering the U.S. Army. Each time I have made a success of it, and this time must be the biggest."

I

The developing chain of command for the Northwest Europe campaign slotted Patton as one of seven army commanders under three army groups. Dressed in his regulation best, cavalry boots gleaming, a riding crop in his hand, he began by informing his new headquarters that "I mean business when I fight. I don't fight for fun, and I won't tolerate anyone on my staff who does . . . Ahead of you lies battle. That means just one thing. You can't afford to be a goddamned fool, because in battle fools mean dead men."

By the time he finished, he had made believers out of the first thousand of his new command—at least most of them. As new divisions arrived, they received a similar speech to the effect that "No bastard ever won a war dying for his country." It was a bravura performance, prefiguring the rock concerts of a later era. "Americans love to fight," was the typical beginning. From there, Patton usually went on to insist on the importance of obedience and alertness; the superiority of American food, equipment, and men; and the vital contribution made by every member of the 3rd Army, no matter how mundane and inglorious his duty might appear. "We all want to go home," he concluded. "But the quickest way home is through Berlin and over the Boche. And thirty years from now, when your grandson asks what you did in World War II, you won't have to say, 'I shoveled shit in Louisiana.'"

With his audiences growing larger, Patton acquired a loudspeaker truck. A proportion of his listeners were put off by the language. Another proportion, many of them college graduates, prided themselves on being impervious to inspirational rhetoric of any kind. One young officer described the speech made to his division as "worthy of a Latin American general or a southern demagogue": mostly bombast larded with profanity. But to soldiers fresh from home, facing the unknowns of combat without even war movies as a guide, who knew Patton only by reputation, "The Speech" conveyed a sense of someone in charge, someone with a grip on a situation as frightening as it was unfamiliar.

"Soldiers, all men in fact, are natural hero worshippers," Patton wrote his son. Because he believed what he was saying, Patton gave them a hero. Sixty years later, on a cruise commemorating the invasion's anniversary, a cross-section of veterans briefly described their service at a reception in the ship's main lounge. Airmen, sailors, and rangers, medics, truck drivers, and MPs stood in their turn. They mentioned ships and divisions, or anonymous small units long since disbanded. But only one name emerged, as again and again old men repeated "I was with the 3rd Army!" "I rolled with Patton!" And each time the room shook with applause.

Patton understood that he would be operating on a scale far larger than in Tunisia and Sicily. He had four corps headquarters, all green, assigned for training and planning. He could not be everywhere at once, as he had tried to be in those theaters. Although he never expressed such an idea overtly, Patton also seems to have at least considered the possibility that stress and fatigue had contributed to the behavior that had brought him low. In emergencies, he noted, everyone must work all the time. But "[p]ersons who did not rest did not last."

As the 3rd Army took shape during early spring, Patton spent increasing amounts of time working with his senior officers. The old cavalryman knew when to dismount and use cover. Displeased with the "finish, class, and polish" of the newly arrived 5th Armored Division, Patton suggested its corps commander take the CO with him when inspecting another division that was getting it right, then "to avoid invidious comparisons," take that division's commander with him when he inspected the 5th. The idea was to bring the 5th up to standard "as painlessly as possible." By V-E day, the 5th Armored's record stood comparison with any in the ETO.

Patton also prepared and issued a series of papers setting forth his principles of combat. The first of them, dated March 6, emphasized leading in person. In World War I, and now in the Mediterranean, too many officers commanded from headquarters until the situation collapsed, then appeared at the front when it was too late to do any good. The 3rd Army's commanders and staff officers were to visit the front daily, to view the situation with their own eyes and at the same time to be seen by their men. Maps were necessary, but there could never be too much reconnaissance: information was like eggs, the fresher the better. Orders must be short, telling "what to do, not how"—the concept of "mission tactics" surfacing again. At the same time, commanders must remember that issuing an order was the first 10 percent; insuring its "proper and vigorous execution" was the other 90. In that context, "[I]f you do not enforce and maintain discipline, you are potential murderers." Remember, however, that praise was more valuable than blame. Decorations must be awarded promptly. Visit the wounded personally and frequently. And in the final grim analysis, a commander who did not gain his objectives and was not dead or severely wounded had not done his full duty.

Military mantras, to be sure: copybook maxims. But they set a tone in the inexperienced formations of the 3rd Army, a tone its commander was constantly reinforcing. "You will not simply mimeograph this and call it a day," stated the instruction of April 3. "You are responsible that these usages become habitual in your command." "I wish we had more of the killer instinct in our men," Patton wrote to Bea. "They are too damned complacent—willing to die but not anxious to kill . . . The B[rit-ish] have suffered and are mad, but our men are not." To his officers and men, Patton insisted, "You can never be too strong," but battles were ul-timately won by frightening the enemy. The successful soldier won cheaply in terms of his own casualties; violent attacks might be costly at the time, but saved lives in the end.

Not until his third letter of instruction on April 13 did Patton address in detail the employment of armor, and then he stressed armor-infantry cooperation. Because of a "slavish" notion that tanks should be used in mass, the independent tank battalions attached to the infantry divisions were too often neglected or misused. Infantry should lead against anti-tank guns, minefields, and fixed defenses. Tanks should keep out of vil-lages, where their shock and fire power were neutralized. It was a long way from Louisiana and California, but it was solid advice for the hedgerows of Normandy and the built-up country of northwest Europe. It was also easier said than done: one of Patton's major criticisms of the 3rd Army's training exercises was the consistent failure of tanks and in-fantry to keep together. "I gave them hell," he grumbled to his diary, "and hope they improve."

As Patton oversaw and overhauled the preparation of his troops, he added a major element to his operational repertoire. From the beginning of Operation Torch, controversy had existed between the air and ground forces about the best approach to cooperation. To simplify a complex structure of argument, the airmen tended to prefer centralized control and deep deployment, with air assets held under air command to influ-ence operations at sector and theater levels. The soldiers favored direct support and immediate presence. They liked to see planes overhead or at least have them on call for emergencies, like taxis.

Experience gained in the Mediterranean generated compromises and modifications. The revised Army Air Forces field manual issued in July 1943 stated in capital letters that "LAND POWER AND AIR POWER ARE COEQUAL AND INTERDEPENDENT FORCES." Pursuant to that concept, the 9th Air Force, responsible for supporting the field armies in Northwest Europe, organized Tactical Air Commands, one to work with each field army. Brigadier General Otto P. Weyland arrived in

England in January 1944 to take command of XIX TAC, the 3rd Army's designated stablemate.

Patton was a predictably outspoken advocate of the ground-pounders' position. He also enjoyed baiting his AAF colleagues as chocolate-cream soldiers who enjoyed such luxuries as hot food and hot showers in the frequent intervals between their brief encounters with the foe. "Nobody was *really envious* of me, let's put it that way," Weyland later described his assignment. He was in for a surprise. Patton understood clearly that the firepower he considered vital to mobility must come in good part from the air, particularly in view of the Army's decision to provide only a limited amount of heavy artillery. His official report on the Sicily Campaign, virtually forgotten in the uproar over the slapping incident, showed a solid grasp of tactical air power's strengths, limitations, and potential. He did not advocate direct control of air operations by ground commanders—a general had enough to do conducting the land battle.

Above all, Patton emphasized the importance of joint training and joint planning. He was willing to work closely with Weyland, to learn from him, and to give him full control of air operations. "The decisions were mine," Weyland noted later, "as to how I would allocate the air effort." Otto Weyland was himself extremely capable and deeply committed to working with ground forces. Two ranks junior to Patton, he saw no percentage in arm-wrestling over details and surface matters. While Weyland was not directly under his command, Patton's typical approach to staff officers and senior subordinates was to give competence free rein. Patton saw in Weyland something of a kindred spirit: committed to providing ground support however necessary, even at the expense of orders and doctrine. He believed as well in positive reinforcement and found no difficulty in regularly praising the command staff and the fighter-bomber groups assigned to it. Patton described the XIX TAC–3rd Army relationship as the most successful example of air-ground cooperation in his experience. Later research bears out his contention.

"I am a pretty good judge of a fighting man when I see one," Mrs. Marshall wrote to Patton, "and I am expecting great things of you." Then in April, Patton blundered again. It began when he was invited to say few words at a local club for American soldiers operated by British civilians. For one of the few times in his life, Patton sought a low profile, arriving late and declining an invitation to stay for dinner. When the chair introduced Patton, she took pains to mention he was not present officially; and Patton took pains to acknowledge the loveliness of English ladies. He even quoted George Bernard Shaw when he praised the club and others like it for promoting understanding between the British and Americans—whose evident destiny it was, along with the Russians, to rule the world!

It was an innocuous exercise in hands across the sea. But there was a local reporter present. He filed a story that appeared in British papers and was picked up by U.S. wire services. Some editors saw a chance to improve circulation by reviving the slapping scandal. Others, both Democrat and Republican, in an election year were disturbed by what seemed not only inappropriate meddling in politics by a senior officer, but the casual depiction of a postwar world order that seemed to deny every statement of cooperative internationalism from the Atlantic Charter to the United Nations. The *Washington Post* in particular described Patton as progressing from individual assaults on soldiers to collective attacks on nationalities. Perhaps even more serious in the eyes of Patton's colleagues, the *Post* recommended disapproving a list of permanent promotions that included Patton's name.

This time Marshall got the news literally with his morning papers. The chief of staff, though not a man who reacted well to surprises, made it plain to Eisenhower that Patton's experience against Rommel and his skill at mobile war justified keeping him in command if at all possible. "You should not weaken your hand for Overlord," he cabled on April 2. "Everything else is of minor importance." Marshall's question whether Courtney Hodges could assume command of the 3rd Army and perform as Patton might be expected to was self-answering. Hodges was an infantryman, in the Bradley mold only more so, intended to take over Bradley's 1st Army when the latter moved up to Army Group. Expecting him to conduct a campaign of exploitation meant ignoring everything Hodges had shown to date that he could and could not do.

Nevertheless, "Patton's fate is hanging in the balance," observed the secretary of war. Eisenhower was "just about fed up." "Sick and tired of having to protect [Patton]," he was on the verge of relieving him—at least according to Bradley. The Supreme Commander ordered Patton to report to his headquarters, and on May 1, the two generals met privately. Their accounts could not be more different. Patton describes Eisenhower admitting his need for Patton's talents and upbraiding him for putting Eisenhower in such a difficult position. Eisenhower told of showing Patton the documents authorizing his relief and seeing the "tough old soldier" literally begin to cry on Eisenhower's shoulder, then standing to rigid attention as Eisenhower told him "keep your goddamned mouth shut."

The generals' interaction may remain a mystery. The most accurate depiction of their respective reactions is probably in the 2004 made-for-TV movie *Ike: Countdown to D-Day,* in which each is shown contrapuntally congratulating himself on having outmaneuvered the other. What is certain that on May 3, Eisenhower notified Patton that he would keep his command, and on May 4, he informed Marshall that relieving Patton would be counterproductive. D-day was a month away, and it was no time for a tempest in a teapot.

There was another reason why the Knutsford incident so angered Eisenhower. Patton's presence in England had been kept secret as part of the general deception plan underwriting Overlord. Since 1940, the entire network of German spies in the United Kingdom had been operating under British control. The Double Cross system involved providing accurate information to the German *Abwehr*—but information of no importance or just out of date. To the Double Cross was added in late 1943 an even more elaborate complement. Operation Fortitude created entire armies out of whole cloth and radio call signs. It suggested possible invasion sites from Norway to Marseilles and was spectacularly successful in encouraging Hitler to retain thirteen divisions in Norway to secure the bases of a U-boat arm that had been ineffective for almost a year. By the end of May, Fortitude persuaded High Command West's intelligence that the Allies had no less than eighty-nine divisions, with enough landing craft to bring twenty of them ashore in the first wave. The actual figures were forty-seven and six, respectively.

Fortitude's core, however, was its effort to convince the Germans that the major invasion would take place in the Pas de Calais. To that end, a nonexistent 1st U.S. Army Group (FUSAG) was created, with a mixture of real and imaginary divisions under its command that made it seem not merely a pistol, but a cannon aimed at the area that, years before Rundstedt had described as posing the greatest long-term risk to Germany's "Fortress Europe." As a final touch, the notional Army Group was placed under command of the very real George S. Patton.

Patton's stature among his opponents at this period is usually exaggerated, generally on the basis of quotations from his Allied colleagues describing how much the Germans feared him: "a Sherman and a Sheridan combined in one," according to an American admiral. With a résumé based on a month in Tunisia and a few weeks of mopping up against halfhearted Italians in Sicily, Patton's was not yet exactly a name to conjure with in Wehrmacht circles. Patton was regarded as the Western Allies' most daring commander. He did not, however, have much competition for that title. Patton's surfacing in England as an army group commander, and his simultaneous absence from the headlines that had been his métier, did seem to confirm the Allies as preparing for a massive thrust directly across the channel, led by one of their few generals experienced in command at the highest levels. German intelligence picked up and reported the slapping incident. But a Wehrmacht that formally executed almost 50,000 of its own men during the war was unlikely to believe such a bagatelle could adversely affect a senior officer's career.

The course of Operation Fortitude is a classic illustration of the risks of tunnel vision in intelligence operations. Had part of the energy devoted to monitoring and analyzing Fortitude's communications been directed instead to commonsense evaluation of possibilities, it seems likely that some bright colonel or major might have questioned whether an exhausted Britain and a United States fighting a two-ocean war could in fact provide such huge forces even for a decisive operation. German intelligence, like the Wehrmacht of which it was a part, tended to focus on tactical and operational problems rather than production statistics and manpower pools. That, in turn, ironically, added to Eisenhower's difficulties should he relieve Patton. The more he was in the news for any reason, the correspondingly greater became the chances of the Germans picking up a thread that would enable them to unravel Fortitude's entire web.

Patton attended the final briefings as D-day approached, but as a marginal participant, he was not kept in the information loop for the events of June 5th and 6th. Patton toasted Montgomery's health and wished Bradley well when his onetime subordinate went over his final plans. He rejoiced at the invasion's success but found it "Hell to be on the sidelines" and had "horrible feelings that the fighting will be over before I get in." For Patton, June 7, not June 6, was "the longest day I have ever spent." He took to wearing his shoulder holster daily "so as to get myself into the spirit of the part." And as the invasion stalled in the hedgerows of Normandy, above all Patton fretted at the loss of time and lives.

II

The D-day landings were close-run, especially in the American sector. June 6 was a German defeat as well as an Allied victory, and the roots of that defeat ran deeper than Hitler's control of operational details. What was important was not the Fuehrer's alleged late sleeping on that morning, but his uncertainty as to whether the Normandy landings were only a diversion. That uncertainty was shared at all levels in High Command West, however much it was denied later. Committing the armored reserves meant the die was indisputably cast, and for all their alleged battlefield virtuosity, the German generals were reluctant to throw that final switch.

One man who might have made a difference was absolutely elsewhere. Rommel, despite Hitler's repeated compliments on his achievements, remained concerned at the weaknesses of his army group. He wanted at least two more Panzer divisions removed from Geyer's command and moved forward to the coast. As a field marshal, he was entitled to direct access to Hitler and believed his best chance was in a personal discussion with the Fuehrer. He planned his trip for early June. Weather and tide conditions were expected to be unfavorable for an invasion. Lu's fiftieth birthday was approaching, with all the traumas accompanying that particular number. Rommel proposed to spend a couple days with her at Herrlingen in Bavaria, where the family had relocated from Wiener Neustadt, and where he would be readily available to reply if Hitler gave him an appointment at Berchtesgaden. Rundstedt approved; Rommel phoned Hitler's headquarters and left on the morning of June 5.

Might Rommel's presence at his headquarters have generated a different German response on the morning of June 6? Certainly his propensity for taking immediate action would have been felt everywhere along the German chain of command. Based on his previous record, Rommel was more likely to be willing to make a mistake in calling the invasion than to wait another hour, another half hour, to be sure. He might have insisted on speaking to Hitler personally earlier in the day and persuaded him to release the Panzer reserves. He might have convinced Rundstedt and Geyer to move the reserves without orders, or taken charge himself and expected victory to justify him.

Such speculations by staff officers and junior commanders arguably incorporate a serious element of wishful thinking. Rommel's personality was as forceful as any in the Third Reich—but his track record of actually changing the decisions of his superiors was definitely spotty. The chain of command in France was much more rigid than it had been in Africa. As much time might have been lost in arguing as was sacrificed by indecision. Rommel would almost certainly have gone forward to organize and galvanize counterattacks, as he had done so often in Africa. On the other hand, Rommel could not repeal the laws of space and time. The reserves were a long way from the landing beaches—particularly when the delaying effect of Allied air power is considered. The 21st Panzer Division, the armored formation closest to the invasion zone, was according to its commander so dispersed by Rommel's previous orders that it was unable to mount a counterattack until afternoon. Even if Rommel had relieved him, the prospects of a new man doing better were slim. Had the two additional divisions Rommel requested been available, the story might have been different—but that was why he was absent in the first place.

Rommel, notified early on the morning of the 6th by his chief of staff that something big was happening, returned to France and reached his headquarters around 10 P.M. By then the initial Allied lodgment was reasonably secure, with more than 150,000 men ashore on five beaches. But the 12th SS Panzer and Panzer Lehr had been released and were on their way. The SS and what remained of the 21st Panzer counterattacked the

3rd Canadian Division west of Caen the next day, beginning a series of operations that stalled Montgomery's projected British-tipped breakout in its tracks and nurtured hopes from Hitler's headquarters downward that the Allies might after all be driven into the sea. Otherwise, Germany faced once again what had been its military nightmare since the days of Frederick the Great: a land war on multiple fronts.

Rommel, as sector commander, had three concerns. The first was the continued possibility of a second invasion in the Pas de Calais. The second was containing, then rolling back, the British in the Caen sector. The third was keeping the Americans from breaking into the Brittany peninsula and capturing the port of Cherbourg. As the Allied buildup continued, the formations of Army Group B responded by mounting the sharp local counterattacks Rommel had intended as the first level of response. Anything larger was frustrated by Allied air supremacy. "The enemy has total command of the air up to 60 miles behind the front," Rommel recorded on June 10. "[B]y day the movement of our troops on the battlefield is almost completely paralysed."

To the air strikes were added the effect of naval guns with what seemed unlimited supplies of ammunition. On land, Allied artillery had a devastating effect on German concentrations. Their Sherman and Cromwell tanks might be individually inferior to the Panthers and Tigers, but there were so very many more of them. The material superiority of which Rommel had warned since his North African days was battering his troops into submission, in a theater whose geography prohibited trading space for position, as could be done in the desert.

The alternate solution, grabbing the Allies by the throat and hanging on, was working for the present. Its success depended heavily, however, on the enemy's tactical shortcomings. These were in good part a function of inexperience, which from the German perspective was a wasting asset. Even before the invasion Rommel observed that "we are facing an enemy who applies all his native intelligence to the use of his many technical resources . . . Dash and doggedness no longer make a soldier . . . he must have sufficient intelligence to enable him to get the most out of his fighting machine. And that's something these people can do . . ."

Aside from the operational problems accompanying any attempts at redeployment and concentration, Rommel dragged the ball and chain of another of Hitler's "no retreat" orders. Almost every troop movement needed the approval of the Wehrmacht High Command—a bureaucratic process that significantly inhibit the quick responses Rommel considered vital to maintaining a successful defense against superior forces. Though the British continued to drive hard around Caen, Rommel advocated hammering the Americans, still tangled in the bocage and showing increasingly the weaknesses accompanying first-time combat. Casualties especially in the infantry divisions were so heavy that the informal means of transmitting battlefield lessons were breaking down. Command was inadequate, or at best inexperienced. Morale was beginning to sag among veterans and replacements alike. Instead, the Fuehrer insisted that the theater reserves be concentrated against the British in the Caen sector, and Rundstedt followed him in taking the bait.

In December 1943, Manfred had decided to volunteer for the Waffen SS, who "were far better equipped than the army, and they had a more handsome uniform." Rommel dismissed the idea as "out of the question." When pressed, according to Manfred, Rommel said he did not want his son serving under a man like Himmler, who was authorizing mass killings. Now the men in black who wore the lightning runes formed an indispensable component of his armored force. Rommel had to work with party hard cases, like Sepp Dietrich, commander of the I SS Panzer Corps. He had to come to terms as well with the fact that Dietrich and his subordinates gave him the same kind of loyalty as his old Africa hands had done when the going was desperate, while their men fought with no less courage and skill than the men in army *Feldgrau*.

In the weeks after the landing, Rommel continued to spend time up front. By now, however, "front" usually meant a divisional headquarters. As an army group commander, Rommel had moved a long way up the chain since the days when his responsibility extended to three or four divisions. The "hussar tricks" that frustrated the Allies at the sharp end were the province of the young studs: Hans von Luck, now commanding a regiment in the 21st Panzer Division, or Kurt Meyer, who took over the 12th SS Panzer when its CO was killed by naval gunfire.

The close and broken terrain of Normandy also did not lend itself to the kind of in-and-out, "now you see him, now you don't" interventions characteristic of Rommel's command style in France and North Africa. Allied tactical air forces were close to their peak strength on D-day, and the force-ratios they could apply to the still-constricted beachhead were exponentially higher than during the rest of the campaign. In the British sector especially, fighter-bombers were circling the battlefield looking for targets of opportunity—"cab ranks," British tankers and infantrymen called them, invoking the taxis that circled Piccadilly seeking a fare. Air power's dominant role in Normandy has been questioned as a self-serving excuse offered by German generals to explain their defeat. The direct effectiveness of air attacks against German tanks. especially the heavies, was in fact limited. The effect of constant bombing and strafing on morale and effectiveness was, however, beyond doubt even in the best divisions. Too many veterans insist they experienced nothing like that anywhere during the war, even in the worst days of the Russian front, to dismiss their testimony as hyperbole. Staff cars, traveling alone or with small escorts, made even more tempting targets. Casualties mounted among senior officers trying in the German tradition to keep touch with their forward units. Others like Geyr von Schweppenburg had the kinds of narrow escape that left brave men shaken for days, judgments clouded and perspectives skewed. Fritz Bayerlein, hardly the exemplar of a timid man, assigned "broomstick commandos" to sweep away tire tracks left in roads and fields by the vehicles of Panzer Lehr.

Was it time to begin thinking of cutting the Reich's losses in Normandy and falling back into France? And even then, was it possible to establish any defensive positions short of the Rhine itself that the Allies could not eventually break through or outflank? Had it become necessary to consider stabilizing the situation in the west as a step toward a political solution: seeking at least to open negotiations at some level with the British and Americans? Again Rommel kept his own counsel. But on June 17, when Hitler summoned Rundstedt and Rommel to a conference at Soissons, Rommel described conditions at the front as impossible and challenged Hitler to come and see for himself. Instead of debilitating the Panzer divisions' strength by using them to shore up local weaknesses, he proposed a limited retreat, drawing the Allies out of range of their naval guns and then attacking into the flank of the major offensive he expected to develop around Caen. Rommel said later that the project offered no more than a one in four chance of success, but even that was better than the certain defeat looming in Normandy.

Hitler's reply was a declaration that the Allies were committed to developing their beachheads and, therefore, the front as it stood must be held at all costs. The *Kriegsmarine* and the Luftwaffe would interrupt Allied supplies. Additional reserves, including two SS Panzer divisions from Russia and the 2nd SS Panzer from southern France, would be brought into the theater for a massive attack on the beaches as their logistic support diminished. This last was no off-the-wall Fuehrer insight, but conventional general staff wisdom: seizing the initiative and seeking a decision by a single major operation. The very next day, however, the Allied High Command decided the first phase of Overlord had succeeded and began implementing its own plans for a breakout. Ironically, the operation was delayed by a four-day storm that did what the Germans were in the event unable to do: disrupt the movement of supplies and reinforcements to France.

For the next ten days, the German situation nevertheless worsened along what to Rommel were predictable lines. The initial decisive point of the Allied offensive, insofar as one existed, was in the British/Canadian sector, where Montgomery mounted a series of offensives named after famous British races. Their purpose, whether to open the way into France or to engage and fix draw the German armor reserves, has been intensively debated, usually along national lines. Their result was to draw more and more German armor into what became killing grounds that absorbed formations High Command West and Army Group B intended for the major counterattack, that in terms of tanks pitted numbers against quality in a series of tactical standoffs, and whose casualty rates on the British side compared with the worst weeks of the Somme and Passchendaele.

Meanwhile, the Americans under Bradley chewed through the bocage with more determination than finesse, moving into the Cotentin peninsula, capturing a devastated Cherbourg on June 26. First Army's broadfront attack on St. Lô, beginning on July 3, was another grind-it-out process that filled aid stations and hospitals rapidly but made slow progress forward. "By July 10," Bradley admitted, "we faced a real danger of a World War I–type stalemate in Normandy."

On June 29, Hitler once again summoned Rommel and Rundstedt, this time all the way to Berchtesgaden. In a rambling and convoluted presentation, he ordered the beachhead contained while the navy counterattacked with all available resources and the Luftwaffe regained air superiority with jets, rocket planes, and a thousand newly produced fighters. "Special bombs" were to be used against allied battleships, whose destruction Hitler considered outstandingly important.

The presentation could hardly have been less relevant to the situation. In his previous meeting with Hitler, Rommel had taken advantage of an air-raid warning that temporarily disrupted the recording procedures to tell the Fuehrer that politics must come into play before the situation deteriorated beyond saving. On the way to Berchtesgaden, he and Rundstedt had spoken together—a conversation ending when Rommel said loudly, "I agree with you. The war must be ended and I shall tell the Fuehrer so, clearly and unequivocally." Now he spoke openly and in public. On behalf of the German people, to whom he was also answerable, Rommel declared it high time that Hitler learned of the real situation in the west—beginning with the political situation. Hitler slammed down his hand and told Rommel to confine himself to military matters. Rommel replied, "History demands of me that I should deal first with our *overall* situation." Ordered again to stick to military matters, Rommel fell silent. Solicited for his views, he said again he must speak on the subject of Germany. Hitler ordered him from the room.

Rommel returned to his headquarters expecting to be summarily relieved. In fact, it was Rundstedt who was dismissed, replaced by Field Marshal Gunther von Kluge, Rommel's old commander from 1940. He had established a formidable reputation in Russia but had been out of action for months as the result of a car accident. Hitler spent several days convincing him the pessimism of Rundstedt and Rommel was the main problem in the western theater, and one of Kluge's first actions on assuming command was to insist Rommel obey Hitler's orders unconditionally. The resulting exchange grew so heated the staff officers were sent from the room. Rommel also prepared a report and forwarded a copy to

Hitler. It set forth in measured language "the reasons why it has been impossible to maintain a lasting hold on the Normandy coast, the Cherbourg peninsula, and the fortress of Cherbourg . . ." Most of them involved the rejection of his ideas by the High Command, especially failure to complete the coastal fortifications and poor deployment of the armored reserves.

Kluge, a competent field soldier and a quick study, rapidly came around to Rommel's view of the military situation's desperate nature, in particular the effect of Allied air strikes on troop movements above the battle group scale. For the first two weeks of July, the front held, but as Allied strength and allied pressure increased in his sector, Rommel prepared another report. Allied material superiority was inflicting such high casualties that the fighting power of the German divisions was rapidly disappearing. Fewer than six thousand replacements had arrived to balance almost a hundred thousand casualties. For tanks, the ratio was 17 to 225. Conditions in the rear were so bad that "only the barest essentials" were reaching the front. A breakthrough somewhere on the overstressed Normandy front, followed by a deep thrust into France, must be expected in the foreseeable future. "[T]he unequal struggle," Rommel concluded, "is approaching its end. It is urgently necessary for the proper conclusion to be drawn from this situation . . . I feel duty bound to speak plainly on this point."

Rommel had submitted the report to Kluge on July 16, who forwarded it to Hitler with an unexpectedly positive endorsement. The next day, Rommel undertook another of his visits to the front. He had grown increasingly concerned about the prospect of a breakthrough attempt in the Caen sector, and his destinations, ironically, were the SS units that had taken heavy casualties in the recent fighting. Ironic, too, was an elliptical discussion with Sepp Dietrich. According to Rommel's aide, he asked whether Dietrich would execute his orders even if they contradicted Hitler's. Dietrich offered his hand and said, "You're the boss, Herr Feldmarschall."

Was this last visit to the front an effort to kill two birds with one stone? Since his return from Berchtesgaden, Rommel had been talking with officers he felt he could trust—initially his old comrades from Africa, then a wider and more senior circle. As later reported, the thrust of the conversations was generally the same. Rommel spoke of taking advantage of his positive image to negotiate a truce with the Western Allies even against Hitler's will.[1] Should the Fuehrer remain obdurate, Rommel proposed to open the front—that is, to order resistance to cease in Army Group B's sector. The optimal time would be when the inevitable breakout began: whatever Kluge did, the entire western front could be expected to unravel in chaos. At best, the Allies would allow Germany to hold the line on the eastern front. At worst, they would reach Berlin before the Russians.

Did these encounters represent a developing intention, a sequence of ruminations, or exaggerations by men who after the war had every interest in connecting Rommel, and by extension themselves, with the German resistance? Sometimes in those conversations Rommel discussed and rejected suicide. Sometimes he drifted, on one occasion speculating that Germany might eventually become a British dominion like Canada, and on another talking of securing Hitler's permission to request a personal meeting with Montgomery—"one old soldier to another." On the other hand, Rommel had already opened radio links with the Americans for the purpose of directly exchanging severely wounded and their medical attendants—on July 2 and July 9, such exchanges actually took place.

As for Hitler's fate, Rommel both before and after the assassination attempt went on record as calling it a political mistake in that it risked making Hitler a martyr, and a moral error in that if Hitler had acted unjustly he should be brought to trial—all very logical and very high-minded. But there is a familiar German proverb that to eat sausage it is necessary to butcher the swine. It is unlikely that Rommel did not reckon with a certain swine having a fatal accident in the course of the projected regime change. A hundred years earlier, a general had led part of the Prussian army in a revolt against Napoleon that eventually won over the rest of the generals and the king as well. Rommel in his own mind was still the Desert Fox—still the master at turning breaking situations to advantage by moving decisively at what more timid men called the last

---

1 An indication of Rommel's continued high reputation across the line was the dispatch of a British Special Air Service team to kill or kidnap him. The order was issued on July 20.

minute. But given what he might have to do, deniability was essential. His hands must remain as clean as possible.

The question became moot on the late afternoon of July 1, when Rommel's car was attacked by two fighter-bombers. He was so badly wounded the initial diagnosis was that he was out of the war for the rest of the year. In any case, he would have had only three days to decide. On July 20, the U.S. 1st Army unleashed Operation Cobra: the long-awaited breakthrough that eviscerated the German front in Normandy.

III

The Germans might be reeling under the Allied sledgehammer, but what dominated thoughts and emotions on the other side of the line was the maddeningly limited progress through Normandy. Patton had spent June chafing to get into action. On July 6, he arrived in France by C-47, landing on an airstrip near Omaha Beach and promising the soldiers who gathered around him to "personally shoot that paper-hanging goddamned son of a bitch . . . when we get to Berlin." For the next three weeks, his destiny was more pedestrian as he adjusted to the circumstances of a new theater of war. He had not been Bradley's first choice as an army commander, and after six weeks of frustration, Bradley was anything but amenable to the barrage of suggestions and recommendations his new subordinate offered for ending the stalemate. Patton, for his part, described Bradley and Hodges as "nothings" who pushed all along the front, developed no power anywhere, and believed "all human virtue depends on knowing infantry tactics." "I could break through in three days," he declared. "All that is necessary now is to take chances by leading with armored divisions and covering their advance with air bursts."

Patton's criticism of his colleagues ironically paralleled Montgomery's denigration of Eisenhower for favoring a broad-front approach instead of developing a grip on the campaign. At this stage of the operation, the British field marshal was if anything pleased to see Patton in the field. He considered him the hardest driver in the Allied camp and correspondingly valuable despite a continuing willful disinterest in administration and preparation. As for Patton's disciplinary issues, Montgomery had taken pains to stay out of what he insisted to his British subordinates was an American affair. Patton's opinion of Montgomery both as a field commander and a general who knew how to inspire and lead troops was no less positive: he was the best of the British generals despite a definite lack of boldness. The negative references in his diary and correspondence to date had overwhelmingly involved what he considered Eisenhower's readiness to be "bound hand and foot by the British."

Montgomery, in any case, was enough of a general to appreciate the difficulty in which he found himself as July began to wane. He had planned and hoped for deep penetrations on D-day. Instead, the Allied front had virtually stabilized. Only with the capture of Caen on July 9 was he able to implement plans for a breakout. The heavy concentration of German armor against the 21st Army Group might not have been part of the grand strategic design Montgomery later described—some say invented—but he took advantage of it once it developed. The first phase of the offensive, Operation Goodwood, was a full-scale attack by the British 2nd Army, intended both to pin down the German tanks and to break through them into the open country around Caen. The second phase involved the 1st U.S. Army's attacking south, clearing Brittany and swinging east into France.

Bradley was also enough of a general to perceive the necessity for breaking out of the confines of the beachhead, as opposed to grinding through them. The result was Operation Cobra. Bradley's plan, reduced to its essentials, was to concentrate against a sector of his front where the road network facilitated movement, blow it open, then break through the German defenders into the open country beyond. Frequently described as uncharacteristic of Bradley in particular and the U.S. Army of World War II in general, Cobra, in fact, combined fire power and exploitation in a way familiar to American interwar thinking. It worked magnificently despite a series of costly short drops by heavy bombers integrated for the first time in the war into ground operations.

As Goodwood and its successors held the Panzers in check and were checked by them, what began on July 20 in the American sector as a breakthrough became a breakout.

German reserves were exhausted. German commanders who had spent six weeks responding to local, specific threats were unable to readjust their thinking to the changed scale and pace of events. The general they most trusted, who might have understood what was beginning to happen, was in a hospital. Resistance eroded, then crumbled, then collapsed. On July 31, the 4th U.S. Armored Division captured the key road junction of Avranches, and Kluge described the situation to High Command West as a *Riesensauerei* (ratfuck), with the Americans on the verge of being able to do what they wanted.

On August 1, the 3rd Army officially took the field, with Bradley moving up to command the 12th Army Group. Patton's initial mission was the overrunning of Brittany. In one sense, the operation was a sideshow, as far away from the decisive sector as Bradley could arrange. Brittany's ports were nevertheless considered vital for the invasion's logistics—even more so given the damage in Cherbourg and the June storm's effect on over-the-beach supply facilities. Bradley wanted the peninsula cleared expeditiously. Patton proposed to put some tempo into the war wherever he began: "rush them off their feet before they get set."

The 3rd Army initially committed two corps to Brittany. The battle-tested VIII under Troy Middleton, transferred from the 1st Army, led through the Avranches corridor; Wade Haislip's XV followed, deploying as space became available. Avranches was choked with rubble. There were two roads south, both mined, and both blocked with wrecked vehicles and dead men. In one of the campaign's best examples of staff work, the 4th and 6th Armored Divisions pushed through in twenty-four hours, Patton himself profanely directing traffic for ninety minutes in the center of Avranches. Within three days, a hundred thousand men were clear of the bocage and the Brittany Sweepstakes was well under way.

The 4th Armored was to take Rennes, then Lorient; the 6th would advance on St. Malo and drive for Brest. The tankers, bouncing off episodically determined resistance, outran their initial objectives, then outran wire and radio communications, then ran off their maps. Middleton kept touch by using light planes, as the Germans did in 1940. Patton has been criticized for the energy with which he pursued what rapidly became a diversion, and for eventually leaving the crack 6th Armored Division to play a static role for a month in front of Brest and Lorient. When the 4th Armored captured Rennes, its commander, John Wood, argued strongly for turning east toward Germany instead of west into the peninsula. But given the importance of Brittany and its ports to long-term Allied planning, Patton can scarcely be faulted for pursuing his assigned objective energetically in his first action as the 3rd Army's commander—particularly given his distinct probationary status in Bradley's eyes.

With VIII Corps driving deeper into Brittany and XV Corps following in its wake, Bradley feared a German counterattack into Patton's increasingly exposed flank. "Some people," Patton observed, "are more concerned with headlines and the news they'll make rather than the soundness of their tactics." Patton in any case considered tactics the province of battalion commanders. "If generals knew less tactics, they would interfere less." As XV Corps cleared its sector against limited resistance, as the toll of German prisoners mounted into the thousands, above all as American casualties remained unbelievably low by previous standards, Bradley's anxiety gave way to a concept of using Avranches as the base for a turn north and east. The 3rd Army had two other corps, XX and XII, in its order of battle. Feed them through Avranches, join them to XV Corps, strike into the German rear—suddenly Paris itself did not seem out of reach.

Patton had spent part of his time in England studying the routes used nine centuries earlier by William the Conqueror in his campaigns in Normandy and Brittany, reasoning accurately that those roads had to be on good terrain. He spent time as well studying maps of western Europe, noting—again accurately—the places he expected to fight. He was already anticipating an order to turn XV Corps toward the Seine when Bradley explained his expanded vision to Eisenhower. Eisenhower was no less enthusiastic, informing Marshall that in two or three days the 12th Army Group would be in a position to destroy the German forces in its sector and exploit forward "as far as possible."

The crushing defeat of the German counterattack on August 6–7 at Mortain left most of what remained of High Command West's mobile troops in a salient whose flanks were completely exposed. On August 3, Bradley had ordered Patton to complete operations in Brittany with a minimum of forces and prepare for "further action with strong armored forces to the east and southeast." Now he was attracted by a "short hook" option that would send XV Corps into the immediate German rear, through Argentan, and toward Falaise, where it would meet the

newly activated 1st Canadian Army advancing on that road junction from
the north and cut off the German forces in a developing "Falaise pocket."
In the aftermath of that victory, the drive on Paris would be a milk run.

Montgomery, still officially the overall ground force commander until Eisenhower's Supreme Headquarters Allied Expeditionary Force
(SHAEF) became operational, accepted Bradley's concept but saw Falaise
as an element of a deeper envelopment, with the 21st Army Group turning left and driving east for the Seine while the Americans cut across the
now-open German southern flank and eventually turned north toward
Paris. Patton, his eyes as well on the French capital as the objective of a
strategic maneuver, wanted to complete the Falaise operation quickly
while turning the rest of the 3rd Army loose in the German rear. Instead,
the Canadian 1st Army advancing from the north made headway slowly
against resistance as skilled as it was determined. Patton responded by
ordering XV Corps on August 12 to take Argentan and push toward
Falaise. He was convinced Haislip could close the gap and hold the line
until he was reinforced or the Germans collapsed—whichever came first.

When Patton sought confirmation from Bradley's headquarters, he
spoke of "another Dunkirk," in the sense of driving forward until his
spearheads found the Canadians—the probable original source of the
often-quoted one-liner about driving the British into the sea. Bradley
replied, "Nothing doing. You're not to go beyond Argentan." He explained his decision in terms of intelligence reports of German troops
massing for a counterattack, saying then and later that he preferred "a
solid shoulder at Argentan to the possibility of a broken neck at Falaise."
An alternate explanation describes Bradley as an orthodox infantrymen
who ". . . just didn't understand these crazy Armor people."

Accounts focusing on the Canadian/Polish advance from the north
use the fierce resistance encountered in that sector as evidence that Patton
proposed to bite off more than he could chew. Had XV Corps pushed
past Argentan, the argument runs, it would almost certainly have found
itself in a pitched battle with the rough equivalent of eight or ten German
infantry and Panzer divisions, desperate to break out of the pocket. The
accompanying implication is that the Americans were not *that* much better than their allies, especially when it came to close-quarters fighting.

In the event the Canadians did not capture Falaise until August 16; the pocket was not officially declared closed until three days later. Under unprecedented levels of air attack, the German army dissolved, abandoning vehicles and equipment helter-skelter in a desperate effort to push through the Allied gauntlet. Only ten of the fifty divisions committed to Normandy remained combat-effective. The fifty thousand men who escaped, including a high percentage of headquarters and staff officers, would in a matter of weeks become the nucleus of a revived German effort in the west. That they survived to do so was not the responsibility of George Patton.

Patton and his supporters ever since have depicted Bradley at Falaise as taking counsel of his anxieties. Alternatively, it might be said that Bradley was micromanaging. If Patton believed XV Corps could hold the gap, the responsibility was his—and so would be the voyage back to the States if he was wrong. Martin Blumenson and Carlo d'Este combine to develop a strong alternate-history case. Had Patton commanded the 12th Army Group instead of Bradley, he would have acted more decisively than Bradley; cooperated more closely with Montgomery, whose strategic vision in this case he shared; and been able to convince Eisenhower, his friend of many years, to endorse the risks of a long thrust into France.

Perhaps—but the Germans would have had something to say about it. The Reich possessed substantial reserves of men and material positioned for deployment in the western theater. The German army in the west may not have been the first team, but it was nevertheless a formidable opponent, able to charge high tuition for the tactical and operational lessons it taught its opponents. What is certain is that Falaise became for Patton a springboard. At the head of the 3rd Army, he was about to embark on a run of victories that changed the face of the war in Northwest Europe. Instead of head-on engagements, flanking became the norm. Instead of the grind-it-out attrition of Normandy, advances of twenty, thirty, or fifty miles at a bound became the standard for judging success.

It began when Patton responded to Bradley's halt order by suggesting instead that he turn east with the bulk of the 3rd Army and drive toward the Seine and Paris. Walton Walker's XX Corps and Manton Eddy's XII had begun fanning out across France even as XV Corps turned toward

Falaise and VII Corps mopped up in Brittany. When Bradley ordered the halt, Patton convinced his superior to turn Haislip and two divisions eastward as well, leaving three divisions to hold the Falaise sector until the 21st Army Group should finally arrive.

"It is really a great plan," Patton exulted, "wholly my own and I made Bradley think he thought of it." Bradley, no less impatient for great results than his subordinate and arguably even more anxious to show up Montgomery for his slowness, had entertained a similar vision since the end of July. He needed correspondingly little convincing. The result for Patton was the culmination of a lifetime's worth of dreams. As the 3rd Army exploded into France, he had been constantly at the front, exhorting corps and division commanders to keep moving, testing his nerve under fire, and recording his reactions. He transformed an entire mechanized cavalry group, two squadrons, into an information service on the lines of Montgomery's Phantom, operating in small units across the 3rd Army's front, reporting directly the state of affairs on the line. When infantryman Manton Eddy, new to corps command, asked how far he was expected to advance in a day, Patton replied it depended on the state of his nerves. Told to go fifty, Eddy turned pale—at least according to Patton. "[T]he lambent flame of my own self-confidence burns ever brighter," he wrote as early as August 6.

Some of his subordinates thought that flame burned too brightly. Fourth Armored Division's John Wood excoriated after the war Patton's commitment of the 4th and 6th Armored to a Brittany offensive that went in the wrong direction. In fact, the 4th Armored was warned for movement east as early as August 11 and changed direction in time to establish a lambent reputation in the drive across France. Bradley as well entertained second thoughts, ordering Patton on August 16 not to go beyond a line Dreux-Chartres-Orleans, on the very edge of the Orleans-Paris gap. His concern for a developing fuel shortage and his fear of exposing the 3rd Army's flanks too greatly lasted only a day. Patton's lead divisions were meeting no more than scattered resistance from broken formations and improvised battle groups. The successful Franco-American landing in the south of France on August 15 and the subsequent drive up the Rhone Valley diminished concern for the 3rd Army's southern flank. Courtney Hodges, seeking to establish himself in command of the 1st Army, was unlikely to admit for the record that he could not cover Patton's left. On August 17, Bradley lifted his stop order. On the 20th, the 3rd Army's 79th Infantry Division reached the Seine. Patton made a personal pilgrimage to the river to urinate in it. He then convinced Bradley to let him send the XX and XII Corps across the Seine in hot pursuit of the dissolving Germans along the highways running east to the old Franco-German frontier.

The 3rd Army's triumphant advance owed much to its evolution as an air-ground combt team. One anecdote, which deserves to be true, has Patton sending for Weyland on August 1 and greeting him with a quart of bourbon. By the time the bottle was empty, the two generals had sworn brotherhood. Of more practical use were the series of joint planning projects the XIX TAC and the 3rd Army headquarters conducted in the weeks before Operation Cobra; the careful attention they paid to the relationships of the 1st Army to its companion IX TAC; and such technical innovations as the installing in Sherman tanks of radios able to communicate with aircraft and experienced pilots to control the strikes thus called in. It did no harm that XIX TAC was junior partner to IX TAC and its colorful and competent commander, Major General Elwood Quesada. Patton's attitude, and his patronage, were correspondingly welcome in Weyland's headquarters.

From the beginning of the breakout, XIX TAC's P-47 Thunderbolts covered the ground troops like a blanket. In a simplified description, Weyland's pilots specialized in close support, armored column cover with an entire group of seventy-five aircraft assigned to work with each of an armored division's two combat commands, and "armed reconnaissance" missions, usually flown in squadron strength of around two dozen planes. Weyland threw away the air power book, decentralizing operations, delegating command, and dispersing assets as the situation dictated. Patton recommended that bomb lines be abolished and aircraft allowed to strike any target of opportunity. "Friendly-fire" casualties were an acceptable risk.

Although the P-47 could carry up to 2,500 pounds of bombs, and later an equivalent payload of air-to-ground rockets, pilots considered strafing a more effective form of attack, especially against unarmored targets. The Germans agreed. Thunderbolts carried eight .50-caliber machine guns in their wings. By this time obsolescent relative to cannon in fighter combat, the "fifty" was formidably intimidating as its rounds chewed their way across a road or kicked up lines of dust in a nearby field, leaving survivors to calculate just how close a call theirs had been as the *Jabos* pulled away.

On August 17, Patton wrote to General H. H. Arnold, commanding general of the U.S. Army Air Forces, "For about 250 miles I have seen the calling cards of the fighter bombers, which are bullet marks in the pavement and burned tanks and trucks in the ditches." When asked if he worried about his flanks, he answered, "The Air Force takes care of my flanks." The pilots did more than that. Weyland's fighter-bombers hammered the garrisons still holding out in the fortresses of Brittany. They kept watch along the Loire River, screening the 3rd Army's southern flank and shooting up German forces retreating from the south. They roamed up to 35 miles ahead of the main line of the 3rd Army's advance into the heart of France, attacking Luftwaffe and army targets where they found them, reporting road and terrain conditions, and informing headquarters just where their subordinate formations were located. As the advance progressed, two other missions developed. One involved reporting, then keeping an eye on, possible counterattacks. Another turned the Army Air Forces traditional interdiction mission inside out. Instead of keeping enemy forces from entering the battle zone, Weyland's fighter-bombers were tasked with preventing troop movements away from the fighting, keeping them within killing range.

Patton was back in the headlines with a vengeance. Slapping incidents and political incorrectness were forgotten as America's front pages trumpeted the 3rd Army's drive across France, into the frontier province of Lorraine, and toward the German border. He was insecure around the correspondents compared to his earlier years, reminding them regularly that the best way to get him sent home was to quote him. But like any born actor, he found it difficult to resist the lure of the footlights. On one occasion, when asked about his next plans, he pounded a map and declared that if Eisenhower gave him the supplies he needed, the 3rd Army would go through the German frontier defenses "like shit through a goose."

Patton's leitmotif from the beginning had been to attack without letup, giving the Germans to his front no time to regroup. "We can be in Germany in ten days," he wrote on August 21. By August 26, the 3rd

Army had advanced more than four hundred miles and liberated fifty thousand square miles of France. Critics have argued that Patton's success was based on avoiding battle as opposed to seeking it, to a point where movement became a goal in itself, neglecting the disruption of communications, the overrunning of road junctions, and similar measures described by interwar armor theorists such as Fuller and Liddell-Hart. Patton would probably have agreed. Since the 1920s, he had argued for the prospects of destroying an army by bypassing resistance, using speed and shock to get inside the enemy's decision loop, throw him off-balance, and keep him there until he could be killed or captured—or, preferably, until organized resistance simply collapsed.

Some analyses describe this concept as reflecting Patton's understanding of the strengths and shortcomings of the American soldier and the U.S. Army. GIs understood machinery and what it could do. They had been formed by a culture of speed and power: home runs and the Indianapolis 500. On the other hand, so the argument runs, the American infantry in particular lacked the tactical ability and the moral tenacity of their German opponents. Manpower procurement policies allowed the skilled and the motivated to volunteer for the Navy and the Marines. The best of the draftees were assigned to the technical arms and services; the best of the rest volunteered for the paratroops. The infantry got what remained.

Institutionally, U.S. armored divisions were reorganized prior to the invasion, the number of nearly useless light tanks reduced from two-thirds to one-fourth of their strength. The reconfigured divisions, with three battalions each of tanks, infantry in half-tracks, and self-propelled light howitzers, were significantly more mobile than their German and Soviet counterparts. But with a strength of slightly more than ten thousand men, their shock and staying powers were significantly limited—so limited that after the war, a General Board recommended doubling the number of infantry battalions and virtually doubling the size of the division. The new field manual released in January 1944 addressed more than its predecessor the destruction of enemy forces in combat, but continued to stress the armored division's primary role as exploitation: offensive operations in enemy rear areas. This was a sharp contrast to the Panzer divisions, which as the war progressed were increasingly configured as big, powerful formations designed for spearheading breakthroughs and counterattacks.

Patton who understood the consequences of both sets of decisions, played to their strengths. He did not delude himself about the depth of American combat motivation. His own need to reaffirm his courage gave him a visceral understanding of the emotions of the ordinary tanker or rifleman going into battle. Patton comprehended as well the effects of a replacement policy that for practical purposes kept men on the line until they became casualties. He understood that the "ninety division gamble," which kept the ground forces at a minimum for the sake of maintaining war production and increasing air and naval power, made it impossible to withdraw formations from the rapidly expanding front for any length of time, either to rest and assimilate replacements or to form operational and strategic reserves. In those contexts, maneuver warfare, based on movement and momentum, was an optimal approach in the same way that someone running down a hill best sustains balance by increasing tempo. "We are going so fast," he wrote Bea on August 21, "that I am quite safe."

Nor was Patton performing in isolation. On August 19, Eisenhower, Montgomery, and Bradley agreed to bounce the Seine rather than pause to regroup. On August 30, a SHAEF intelligence summary declared the end of the war in sight. It was in those contexts that Montgomery began pushing for a "single thrust" northeastward by the 12th and 21st Army groups into the heart of Germany. He considered this the 1914 Schlieffen Plan in reverse, the most colossal of his long series of "colossal cracks," and not least the final affirmation of his standing as a Great Captain. The Americans were given a significant role in the operation—that is, the 1st Army and the newly arriving 9th Army, which would deploy on Hodges' left. To guarantee the logistical support necessary for this massive thrust, however, the 3rd Army must be grounded, forbidden any but local initiatives and receiving only a minimum amount of fuel.

Bradley countered with his own idea: a drive across the Frankfurt Gap and into central Germany by the 1st and 3rd Armies working in tandem, the British covering its left flank. If a thrust to the heart of the Reich was what was wanted, that was the most direct route. "Give us gas," Patton raged, "we can eat our belts. We have, at this time, the greatest chance to win the war ever presented. . . . It is such a sure thing that I fear these blind moles don't see it."

Eisenhower's decision to deny both Montgomery and Bradley in favor of a "broad-front" approach combined political and military elements. Montgomery's proposal might in fact be an Allied operation—but it was unlikely to look like one to an America that had spent four years building a massive Army designed to operate as an independent force. Bradley and Patton already were submerging their differences all too readily, finding common ground in accusing Eisenhower of sacrificing decisive victory to Allied cooperation.

At the same time, Eisenhower was better aware than his fractious subordinates that the breakout and advance from the beaches had created a logistical problem that defied command solutions. In the aftermath of D-day, enough material was landed to fill 90 percent and more of the front-line units' needs—including fuel. The problem was transportation—and by extension, administration. By September 14, the Allies had reached a line the quartermasters had not expected until May 1945. Martin van Creveld describes Overlord's logistics planners as conservative to the point of pusillanimity and dismisses them as "prudent accountants." Certainly the chief of the supply services, Lieutenant General J. C. H. Lee, was a man of balanced books and sharp pencils, unwilling by principle and unable by temperament to address the unexpected. Even had Lee been an inspired logistician and a good deal less of an obnoxious empire-builder, the damage done to an originally obsolescent French transportation system by weeks of preinvasion bombardment and years of neglect under German occupation defied rapid repair. The emergency use of trucks on a round-the-clock basis, the American Red Ball and its British counterpart Red Lion used up men, vehicles, and fuel at unsustainable rates.

The result was a SHAEF constrained to allocate fuel with what seemed medicine-dropper stinginess to the forward commanders, especially Patton, whose 3rd Army in its rush across France was using a daily average of 350,000 gallons of the 800,000 gallons consumed by the Allies' vehicles. On August 29, Patton noted his army was 140,000 gallons short of "our share" of gas. His complaints proved futile—in part at least because Walter Bedell Smith, Eisenhower's chief of staff and the designated master of gasoline allowances, was not averse to curbing what he considered Pattton's risk-taking propensities by cutting back his fuel. By the turn of the month, daily deliveries shrank to 32,000 gallons, and the

3rd Army's fuel tanks were literally running dry. Captured German supply dumps, creative administrative finagling, and occasional plain hijackings could not bridge the shortages created by Eisenhower's decision to provide extra logistical support to Montgomery in the first two weeks of September.

Eisenhower's original intention was that Montgomery concentrate on capturing the port of Antwerp and opening the Scheldt River. Antwerp had thirty miles of docks and more than six hundred cranes. It could handle sixty thousand tons of cargo daily, and the Belgian resistance had taken the facilities virtually intact. Instead, Montgomery pursued what turned out to be the *fata morgana* of a combined airborne and ground assault designed to bring the 21st Army Group onto the north German plain. As the multiple fiascos of Operation Market-Garden absorbed SHAEF's attention and resources, the 3rd Army's allocation of supplies shrank to around 2,500 tons a day, despite Bradley's regular promises of more.

The accompanying authorization to cross the Moselle, attack the Siegfried Line, and go as far as the Rhine meant nothing without fuel, ammunition, and spare parts. On August 30, Patton again denounced the 3rd Army's being denied gas in favor of a 1st Army that did not know how to use it. "We should cross the Rhine . . . and the faster we do it, the less lives and munitions it will take. No one realizes the value of the 'unforgiving minute' except me." On September 1, elements of the 3rd Army captured Verdun. Patton was thirty-five miles west of the key fortress of Metz, seventy miles from the Siegfried Line. The next day at a conference of the 12th Army Group's senior officers, Eisenhower discussed the coming great battle of Germany. "We assured him," grumbled Patton, "that the Germans have nothing left to fight with if we push on now. If we wait, there *will* be a great battle of Germany."

By September 14, gas was arriving to the 3rd Army by rail, but Patton did not enjoy the luxury of two days' reserve supply until late October. Give me 400,000 gallons of gas, Patton told Bradley, and "I'll put you inside Germany in two days." The fuel was ultimately not Bradley's to allocate. Nor did he seriously challenge Eisenhower's decision to support Montgomery by directing the 1st Army north, away from the eastward-driving 3rd and toward the head-on confrontation with good German troops that eventually took its riflemen into the slaughterhouse of the Huertgen forest.

Sustained Allied progress all along the front in the last half of August reinforced the impression that the German army in the west was finished. Eisenhower's chief of intelligence proclaimed "the end of the war in Europe within sight, almost within reach." From the other side of the front, Siegrried Westphal, one of the most perceptive of senior German staff officers, agreed that the Allies until mid-October could have thrust deep into Germany, unopposed for all practical purposes. Patton's effervescent optimism was fuelled specifically by ULTRA reporting German fears of a breakthrough in the Metz-Trier sector: the 3rd Army's zone of advance. Perhaps as well, like the German Panzer generals in 1940, Patton was influenced by the relative speed and ease which the killing grounds of World War I had been overrun. "The Boche has no power to resist," he noted on September 1. "You can't have men retreating for three hundred or four hundred miles," he noted at a press conference on the 7th, "and then hold anything."

Four interrelated problems nevertheless hovered over the 3rd Army's planning. One lay outside Allied control: the remarkable recovery of the Third Reich and the Wehrmacht in the west during the autumn of 1944. In the aftermath of the failed attempt on Hitler's life on July 20, in the aftermath of the Red Army's colossal breakthroughs in the East, the Nazi regime and the German people mobilized their last reserves of ferocity and fanaticism. Rationality was giving way to passion—and to fear, as retribution loomed for a continent's worth of crimes committed "in the name of the German people."

Operationally, that meant organizing defenses to take advantage not only of broken, wooded terrain ideal for German defensive tactics, but of the pillboxes and bunkers of a never-finished Siegfried Line and of a half-century's worth of permanent fortifications constructed on the old Franco-German frontier between 1870 and 1914. Institutionally, that meant the reconstruction of shattered divisions, the filling of their ranks by new draftees or men combed out of the increasingly moribund navy and air force. It meant their rearmament by an industrial system that continued to defy the best efforts of the Combined Bomber Offensive. It meant morale enforced by field courts-martial that seemed to impose only one sentence: death; and by laws making a soldier's family liable for any derelictions of duty.

Hitler concentrated the bulk of the newly available reserves in Patton's sector. The 3rd Army had advanced the farthest eastward of the Allied forces; its momentum suggested it would be the first to enter Germany if unchallenged. A successful counterattack in Lorraine would also at least delay the joining of the 12th Army Group with the forces advancing up the Loire from southern France. In the coming weeks, the 3rd Army would go up against elements of eighteen German divisions, including a half-dozen Panzer and Panzer Grenadier. The 11th Panzer, tempered on the Russian front, proved such a master of riposte and counterattack that it earned the nickname "Fire Department." Some of the others were still recovering from Normandy. The infantry's quality also varied, but none of the German divisions would prove walkovers.

The second problem confronting the 3rd Army was fatigue. The drive across France had worn out divisions, generals, and privates alike. The experience of World War I had made the Army strongly committed to minimizing losses by all possible means. Casualties had nevertheless been unexpectedly heavy in the infantry—so heavy in fact that some rifle companies had turned more than 100 percent. From Omaha Beach to V-E day, GIs proved able to improvise and fight their way out of the tightest of situations, even those of their own making. The Army system did not always help them. The U.S. replacement system, based on feeding individuals forward, meant too often that men who had been shuttled anonymously from replacement depot to replacement depot found themselves still anonymous in front-line foxholes. Leadership correspondingly tended to be personal and from the front, with predictably heavy casualties among company officers and sergeants: the men most difficult to replace.

Senior officers also found their judgment affected by stress. Command relationships at all levels soured as what might have been manageable tensions escalated into full-blown feuds. Patton, for all his fire-eating reputation, had a light hand when considering relieving a subordinate for cause. "Wholesale beheadings," of the kind familiar in the airborne divisions and increasingly in Hodges's 1st Army, in Patton's mind created "fear and lack of self-confidence." He preferred to stick with an inexperienced man, giving him time to find his feet, and to consider lapses on the part of his veterans as part of the "fog and friction" inherent in war. But by the end of November, the physical and emotional states of John Wood and his corps commander Manton Eddy had generated a confrontation sufficiently bitter that Patton was constrained to relieve Wood, the junior, on the ostensible grounds of fatigue and send him home despite his brilliant record. Eddy's blood pressure continued to rise until his own relief in April 1945.

Critics, and Wood himself, argue that Patton made a bad choice. Eddy, nervous, pedestrian, was less qualified for corps command than the general Liddell Hart called "the American Rommel." Though he considered Wood "one of my best friends" and deeply admired him as a battle captain, Patton also questioned Wood's potential above the division level. Wood was intellectually arrogant and unwilling to compromise. Whether he could handle a complex combined-arms formation like a corps in a technical sense was less important than whether he could work harmoniously with subordinates and superiors who did not match his capacities or share his approaches. In the end, Patton swung the axe with no sense of irony about a decision whose rationales were no less applicable to him.

The effects of fatigue were exacerbated by a crisis in technologies. The U.S. Army's institutional self-image in World War II was as the best equipped in the world. Comprehensively that may have been so. But when Eisenhower evaluated the machines most important to the ground war, his list included the C-47 transport, the DUKW amphibious truck, the two-and-a-half-ton truck, and the jeep—not a weapons system among them. American infantrymen were armed with individual weapons, the Garand and the Browning Automatic Rifle, designed to fit a tactical doctrine emphasizing individual marksmanship as opposed to fire power. American tankers in Europe would repeatedly seen a half-dozen and more of their Shermans disabled at long range by a single German heavy tank. The Germans' grim nickname for the gasoline-engined version of the Sherman was "Tommy cooker": a recognition of its propensity for bursting into flame before the crew could get out.

Even before the end of the North African campaign, U.S. designers began work on a new gun for the Sherman, a 76- millimeter design primarily designed to engage tanks with armor-piercing rounds rather than destroy obstacles with high explosives. Design of a heavy tank with a heavy gun received correspondingly limited priority. The question was not whether U.S. factories could retool to produce a heavy-tank successor to the Sherman. The issue instead was whether such a changeover represented the best use of material and technical resources, and whether anyone with a say in the matter wanted such a tank in the first place. In North Africa, then in Sicily and Italy, American tankers had regularly encountered not merely up-gunned Mark IV's but Panthers and Tigers, the former with a 75-millimeter high-velocity gun even more deadly to tanks than the vaunted 88. On the whole, the Shermans had coped––not perfectly, but they had coped, and that was enough. The 76-millimeter gun seemed an adequate response to the German innovations.

Patton was not involved in tank development or production even before he left the United States for Operation Torch. His technological awareness correspondingly atrophied. In preinvasion conversations with Liddle-Hart, Patton echoed conventional American wisdom in expressing his preference for light tanks in quantity as opposed to fewer and larger ones. The Sherman, he said, was invincible given suitable terrain and skilled crews. He was correspondingly unenthusiastic about the design that would become the M-26. Weighing 48 tons, with a 90-millimeter gun and much thicker armor than the Sherman, it was a medium/heavy tank along the lines of the Panther. It could be expected to have all the bugs and teething troubles inherent in a new design. It was also slower and required more fuel than the Sherman. For Patton, with his understanding of armor as an instrument of exploitation and his belief that tanks should engage tanks only in exceptional situations, versus tank, the M-26 at best fell into the category of "nice to have"—certainly nothing he was willing to encourage or promote. Similarly, no 76-millimeter Shermans were assigned to the 3rd Army before it went to France.

In the first weeks after D-day, in the close terrain of Normandy's bocage, German tanks proved so formidable even in small numbers that the 1st U.S. Army ran a series of tests to determine exactly what would reliably knock out a Panther. The 76-millimeter gun was not merely ineffective but dangerous, as overconfident crews learned to their cost that the gun's round was more likely to glance off than pierce the frontal armor of German tanks. As for the tank destroyers, the M-10 soldiered on with the 3-inch gun. The new M-18 Hellcat, introduced in late 1943, could make the incredible top speed of 55 miles per hour, but carried the same 76-millimeter gun as the rearmed Sherman.

U.S. crew losses mounted; U.S. crew morale declined. Omar Bradley and then Dwight Eisenhower were sufficiently disconcerted that Eisenhower contacted Chief of Staff George Marshall demanding that tanks and tank destroyers with 90-millimeter guns be made available as soon as possible. As early as December 1942, a 90-millimeter gun had been experimentally mounted on a modified M-10 tank destroyer chassis. The new vehicle, the M-36, went into production—in April 1944! By the fall of 1943, the Army possessed, in inventory and on order, 11,500 tank destroyers. It had a unit requirement for fewer than 3,000. But tank destroyer doctrine considered a heavy gun an example of overkill until the weeks after D-day made believers. As for the M-26, not until May 1944 was the original order of 50 prototypes completed. The War Department wanted to begin a small production run in the summer of 1944. In the face of the general indifference among senior ranks typified by Patton, the first M-26 was not standardized until March 1945. Fewer than 1,400 had rolled off the line by the end of the war in Europe. Two hundred were issued to armored units, thirty of them to one of Patton's divisions in April.

In contrast, beginning in 1943, the German army introduced another wave of "platoon technologies" that reshaped the tactical battlefield. The MG 42 light machine gun, with its high cyclic rate of fire, the various models of assault rifles, the man-portable antitank rockets, the *Panzerfaust* and the *Panzerschreck,* lifted the German infantryman to what might be called a "post-modern" level the rest of the world's footsoldiers would not reach for thirty years. In their developed versions, the Panther and Tiger tanks, with their high-velocity guns and well-sloped armor, their state-of-the-art optical and radio equipment, differed essentially from their predecessors of 1940 in favoring individual—or crew—*virtu,* arguably even at the expense of higher tactical effectiveness.

These innovative weapons systems were originally intended to redress strategic and grand-strategic imbalances. Instead, their qualities and limitations proved ideal for the long fighting retreat toward Germany. They proved ideal as well to enhance significantly exponentially the fighting power of the Reich's new-model warriors, not least by appealing to that fighting power's vitalist aspects. The MG 42 might devour ammunition and use up barrels—but nothing beat "Hitler's buzz saw" for stopping enemy infantry in its tracks. Rocket launchers were an equalizer in the face of what seemed—and often were—overwhelming numbers of Allied tanks. German tank crews knew and cursed the short-comings of their new mounts: the unreliable engines and the refractory suspensions, the optics that were as fragile as they were precise. But the firepower and the protection of the Tigers and Panthers time and again gave them "battlespace dominance" against long odds. The effectiveness of Wehrmacht "platoon technology" meant, moreover, that not everyone had to be a hero. At the last ditch, a Tiger's five-man crew, three in-fantrymen with an MG 42, a single Landser with a Panzerfaust, could do a good deal of killing before going down themselves—often in what seemed a kind of exaltation that less-inspired witnesses, Allied and Ger-man, described as fanaticism or *Blutrausch*.

The final challenge confronting the 3rd Army was geography. During the sweep across France, Patton had hundreds of miles to play with. He was able to seek and exploit German weaknesses on all four points of the compass. As the 3rd Army closed up into Lorraine and the German fron-tier, it was increasingly sandwiched between the 1st Army on its left and the 7th Army advancing from the south. Opportunities for operational-level thrusts were restricted by Army and Army group boundaries even Patton could not violate at random. Eisenhower and Bradley highlighted the changing conditions by transferring the XV Corps to the 7th Army. Bradley was pleased to be rid of the logistical burden and give the 7th Army a boost. Patton mourned the loss of this experienced corps and its commander, Haislip, who had shown himself so proficient in mobile operations.

The Lorraine plateau, surrounded by natural barriers, with its rivers running north-south and the successive lines of high ground that had shaped tactics in earlier wars, did not lend itself to overrunning or by-passing by armored forces even without the overlapping networks of man-made fortifications that crisscrossed the region. The 3rd Army re-quired more than 3 months and paid 50,000 casualties for the region. The operation was the sternest test of Patton's generalship during the war. Constant rain, heralding one of the worst winters in years, turned fields into glutinous mud and highlighted the cross-country limitations of the

Shermans, with their narrow tracks. "I hope," wrote Patton, "that in the final settlement of the war, the Germans retain Lorraine. I can imagine no greater burden than to be the owner of this nasty country where it rains every day and where the whole wealth of the people consists in assorted manure piles."

In the first days of September, the XII and XX Corps both failed initially to get across the Moselle north of Nancy. Wood's 4th Armored carried the weight of the limited exploitation when the river line was eventually breached, and Nancy fell in mid-September after what Patton called "as bitter and protracted fighting as I have ever encountered." He did not expect to do "any broken field running till I cross the next river"—a pleasure the Germans proposed to deny him. On September 18, the 5th Panzer Army under Hasso von Manteuffel launched Hitler's long-projected counterattack, structured along the lines of the ripostes at which the Germans had become so expert in Russia. This was the first time Patton's army had faced one of these strokes on a large scale. In some of the heaviest armored fighting since Normandy, "Tiger Jack" Wood took advantage of the prevailing fog to bring the 4th Armored Division to close quarters with the Panthers. His subordinates, including such future Army luminaries as Bruce Clarke and Creighton Abrams, further reduced by sophisticated tactical maneuvering the advantage of superior German guns and armor—Patton's tank units were still almost entirely equipped with 75-millimeter Shermans. Losses on both sides were heavy, particularly in some of the newly organized German units. Manteuffel was ordered to push on regardless. The Americans held around, claiming a kill ratio of ten to one; and on September 29, Manteuffel's superiors finally ordered him to stand down the troops and tanks he had left.

Throughout the fighting, Patton had been primarily concerned with the consequences of the German attack for the breakthrough to the Rhine he expected to achieve. On September 22, his fears were confirmed—but from a different quarter, as Eisenhower informed Bradley that the British advance toward the Ruhr would continue to have priority for supplies. "Bradley and I would like to go to China and serve under Admiral Nimitz," Patton recorded—that last, for an Army officer, the supreme expression of disgust! As for the 12th Army Group, the 1st Army would continue supporting Montgomery's right. The rest—meaning the 3rd Army—"would take no more aggressive action than that permitted by the maintenance situation after the full requirements of the *main* effort have been met."

Even Patton could not mistake that language. As the 21st Army Group hammered vainly into fierce resistance on the lower Rhine, the 3rd Army underwent its "October pause" while Patton chafed. In his frustration, he overlooked the 3rd Army's remarkable success in once more diminishing High Command West's revitalized capacity to conduct mobile operations at anything but sector levels. Not until December would the German capacity for strategic maneuver in the west be restored.

Patton had also, albeit involuntarily, repaid Montgomery for attracting German reserves and facilitating the U.S. breakout at St. Lo. Now it was the 3rd Army whose hard-driving advance, across the Moselle, drew Hitler's attention and the bulk of the Panzers into Lorraine—and away from the 21st Army Group's drive through Holland toward the Ruhr. Had they been available along Hell's Highway, Operation Market-Garden might well have gone into the books as a disaster instead of an embarrassment.

"Hold present position until supply situation permits resumption of the offensive," ran Patton's new direct orders. He was not inclined to take then literally. As part of a sequence of local attacks designed to improve the 3rd Army's position, the 5th Infantry Division clawed into Fort Driant on the outskirts of Metz in early October. That it did not hold should not have been surprising. Metz had been regarded since the sixteenth century as a key to the frontier zone developing between France and Germany. The fortress system begun by the Germans after 1871 and developed by the French after 1918 was designed to absorb an entire field army. The individual works were designed to resist bombardment above even Great War scales. For the sake of mobility and to save shipping tonnage, the U.S. Army had gone to war with limited numbers of heavy guns. Air strikes eventually proved vital to the reduction of Metz, but XIX TAC was spread thin, and the weather restricted the number of sorties that could be mounted. Commanders were forced to rely on the tactical skill of their infantry—which did not extend to conquering such formidable defenses in what amounted to hand-to-hand combat.

Motivation had less to do with that than training—something Patton, generally considered a master trainer, should have recognized. To a degree, he was distracted by vanity, unwilling to see the 3rd Army accept even a minor defeat. He was engaged as well by the prospect of capturing a world-renowned fortress by assault. But Patton's ultimate reason for insisting Metz must fall was his belief that he now lacked the maneuvering room to leave a strongly defended fortress in the rear of his next offensive. On October 4, Patton ordered the Fort Driant attack pushed home "if it took every man in the XX Corps." In practice, he proved too much the cavalryman to throw away lives against concrete. A week later, he noted the Driant operation was ". . . going sour. We will have to pull out." He informed Bradley that the glory of taking the fort was not worth the losses its capture would entail. Bradley agreed. By October 13, the last of the 5th Division's troops had withdrawn, and the XX Corps began planning the capture of Metz, Patton style—by indirection.

Compared to his counterparts in Allied command at such places as Monte Cassino and the Huertgen Forest, Patton was a quick study. His learning curve was rendered steeper by his still-regular practice of seeing for himself—a particularly sharp contrast to Huertgen, where the absence of senior officers was sufficiently noteworthy to remain something of a scandal among historians of the operation. Noteworthy, too, for those who argue Patton discouraged staff work in favor of action, is the precision of the XX Corps's plan: so detailed that maps showed every house in Metz known to be occupied by the Germans. Weather and logistics, however, continued to impose delays. Patton's temper grew worse. So, arguably, did his judgment. When XX Corps commander Major General Walton Walker had continued nibbling at the Metz defenses, Patton called him off. Now he began ordering other limited attacks, justifying them on the grounds of "blooding" newly arrived divisions by giving them combat experience on a small scale. Too often the attrition was on the wrong side of the ledger. "For God's sake, George, lay off" was Bradley's reaction. Patton, in turn, informed Bradley that he could mount an army-scale offensive on two days' notice and reach the West Wall in two days more.

The final version of his plan involved the XII Corps swinging up from the south and connecting with a northern pincer provided by the III

Corps, freshly transferred from the 1st Army, to isolate and contain
Metz. The XX Corps would take Metz itself—according to Walker, by infiltration tactics instead of assaulting the forts directly. As Patton supervised the training of Walker's infantry in antifortress training conducted
against old pillboxes, the 3rd Army's heavy artillery was significantly reinforced. Weyland, whose XIX TAC had been concentrating on interdiction missions, cooperated with Patton's staff in developing a plan for a
coordinated series of bomber and fighter-bomber strikes in the battle
zone.

As preparation proceeded, Patton focused his fretting. Though his ultimate intention was to establish bridgeheads across the Rhine, he seems
to have recognized that weather, terrain, and the quality of the German
resistance combined to impel a short-yardage approach, at least in the
initial stages. He spent increasing amounts of time with his staff officers,
working out details. "Touring France was a catch-as-catch-can performance, where we had to keep going to maintain our initial advantage," he
noted. "In [the Metz offensive] we had to start moving from an initial disadvantage." It was a disadvantage not to be overcome by inspired improvisation, and the 3rd Army headquarters rose well to the occasion.

The 3rd Army's attack jumped off on November 8. The rain was
heavy; the rivers and streams were high and running fast. The night before, Eddy and the 6th Armored division's Robert Grow recommended
postponement. Patton insisted the attack would go in and gave Eddy the
chance to name his successor if he disagreed. Unable to sleep, he took up
a book that included a description of a battle fought in similar weather. It
was Rommel's *Infantry Attacks* and reassured Patton that "if the Germans could do it, I could."

The heaviest artillery bombardment in the 3rd Army's history opened
the proceedings, and XIX TAC made the most of breaks in the foggy,
rainy weather, itself taking heavy losses from flak. Manton Eddy's XII
Corps included two of the best armored divisions in the ETO: Wood's 4th
and Grow's 6th. Patton's intention, reflected in Eddy's orders, was that
they take the lead as soon as possible and strike for the Rhine, bypassing
pockets of resistance in the way made familiar by the race across France.
Wood was less sanguine, denying that he entertained "illusions about any
rapid advance."

Some critics charge Eddy with misunderstanding the capabilities of armor, fighting his armored divisions by combat commands instead of employing them as a concentrated striking force. Others focus on professional and personal disconnections between infantryman Eddy and the tankers Wood and Grow. The official historian accurately notes that mud negated a plan based on surprise and speed. Rain continued to swell watercourses and wash away bridges. Mines, many of them new designs based on wood or plastic and immune to detectors, took a heavy toll in casualties and tactical initiative. The cold and wet exacted a parallel cost in respiratory diseases, and even more in trench foot. Dry socks became no less important than gasoline in maintaining the pace of an advance that from the beginning was channeled along a relatively limited number of reliably hard-surfaced roads.

The best explanations for the 3rd Army's floundering come from the other side of the battle line, beginning with the new commander of Army Group G, which completed its retreat from southern France by assuming responsibility for the western front's southern sector. Hermann Balck, son of one of Germany's best-known tactical theorists, was a master of applied tactics and a charismatic leader, six times wounded. The advancing Americans encountered not the fragmentary last stands of the sweep across France, but a sophisticated resistance initially based on mines, roadblocks, and determined small units, then shaped by the 11th Panzer Division, whose mobile defense based on company-strength tank-infantry teams was a model of an economy of force operation. The apparently limited strength of the opposition encouraged the American armored divisions to fight exactly the kind of battle least suited to their capacities: a head-on fight against a flexible defense. It was retiarus against secutor, and the 11th Panzer, with its Russian experience of cape-and-sword tactics, inflicted heavy casualties on Patton's elite tankers in the first days of the offensive.

Metz was another bone in the 3rd Army's throat. Not until November 14 was Walker sufficiently satisfied at the progress of the encirclement that he began the final attack Hitler had ordered Metz defended as a fortress: no retreat and no surrender. The commander, who had done the trick twice on the eastern front, hoped to escape with his garrison at the last minute. He got most of his men out before falling wounded into American hands on the 21st; but not until November 25 was the city sufficiently under control for Patton to make a ceremonial entrance. "Your deeds . . . will fill pages of history for a thousand years," he informed the troops he reviewed in the city. A few days earlier, visiting a hospital, Patton told a wounded man the headlines might read "Patton Took Metz," but that was "a goddamn lie. You and your buddies are the ones who actually took Metz."

Rhetoric could not dry out the fields of Lorraine or clear the sky over them. Patton sought to engage a Higher Power, asking the senior army chaplain if he had a good prayer for weather. The padre's request to grant fair weather for battle remained unmet. By the end of November, it was clear that the fighting in Lorraine had devolved to a level not merely of corps and divisions, but regiments and battalions. For a few days after the fall of Metz, Walker's XX Corps drove forward into the rolling country west of the Sarre River. Then it encountered another elastic defensive system anchored by Panzer Lehr Division, refreshed since its hammering in Normandy and still commanded by the hard-charging Bayerlein. In Eddy's sector, the 11th Panzer orchestrated a similar holding action.

Progress, in Patton's words, was "not very brilliant." "I believe that the enemy has nearly reached his breaking point," he wrote in a letter of December 5. "As a matter of fact, we are stretched pretty thin ourselves." Despite all the negatives, on December 3, the first elements of the 3rd Army finally moved into the Reich's West Wall. For Patton, the next step was to the Saar and forward to a Rhine River still seventy miles away. Within days, however, the German Ardennes offensive would begin a new chapter in the history of the 3rd Army and its commander.

By comparison with the drive across France, and by comparison with his own concepts of generalship, Patton is open to charges of losing his grip on the latter stages of the Lorraine campaign. His German opponents suggested Metz could have been taken in half the time the 3rd Army required. While Patton continued, and indeed increased, his presence at front-line headquarters, he did not seek to impose his will to increase the pace of the advance. Nor did his overall plan emphasize generating and maintaining momentum to the degree of its predecessors and successors. Even his complaints about Bradley, Eisenhower, and Montgomery seem flat and lifeless. When informed that "Patton for President" clubs would soon be forming in the States, he replied that like

General Sherman, he would neither run if nominated nor serve if elected. When the war was over, Patton continued, he intended to remove his insignia but would continue to wear his short coat—"so that everyone can kiss my ass."

George Patton, in short, was copping an attitude. But his moroseness was a consequence of his situational awareness. Patton considered himself still on trial as the 3rd Army's commander. Being relieved was by autumn of less concern than being marginalized: finding himself in a position where his ideas and his presence carried no weight in the councils of war that to a significant degree determined operational policy in both the 12th Army Group and SHAEF. Patton also understood that the old Army mantra, "Shut up and soldier," applied to generals as well as privates, especially when the going became as rough as it did on the French frontier in the autumn of 1944.

As winter set in, trench foot and respiratory sickness increased their toll. Infantry strength fell at alarming rates. Ninety percent of the XII Corps's casualties in November wore the crossed rifles. "We are closely approaching a 40 percent shortage in each rifle company," Patton noted in early December. In some veteran divisions like the 95th, the figure was closer to half. Armored divisions, already weak in organic infantry, were growing seriously unbalanced as replacement depots emptied. One of the 4th Armored's battalions was down to 160 men, another to 126, of their authorized thousand. Patton fumed at Eisenhower for letting himself be caught short of men. He wrote of combing out headquarters and rear echelons, but knew better than to believe cursorily retrained clerks and truck drivers were able to do much more than swell casualty lists.

Patton was a horseman and knew better than to drive the most willing mount against an impassable obstacle. In the autumn of 1944, logistics, terrain, fatigue, command policies, and not least the Germans combined in a barrier that constrained him to recast, albeit temporarily, his approach to war. That he was uncomfortable in his new operational skin, that he made decisions hindsight highlights as questionable and worse, should come as no surprise. Considered from an alternative perspective, Patton showed a situational awareness, a flexibility, sufficiently remarkable among senior army officers in the European theater that it merits consideration as unique.

Patton in Lorraine clearly was not at his best in conditions unfavorable to his style of command. War, however, resembles baseball in that the ultimate test of a pitcher's ability is whether he "knows how to pitch"—that is, whether he can win on those inevitable days when he lacks his "good stuff." In Lorraine, Patton showed that he could perform competently under unfavorable circumstances. In a zero-defects model, Patton's scores may be low. In the real world where war is fought, he enhanced significantly his claim to greatness.

IV

Patton was not so preoccupied with his own sector that he lost interest in the rest of the front. As his requests for more divisions were turned down time and again, he grasped more fully than his colleagues the fundamental problem the ninety-division army posed to Eisenhower's strategy. Given the supreme commander's commitment to a continuous front, weak spots must inevitably emerge. The obvious one in the American sector was in the Ardennes Forest, where the VIII Corps, now assigned to the 1st Army, controlled a static sector manned by a mix of green divisions and veteran outfits burned out in the Huertgen Forest. "It is highly probable that the Germans are building up east of them," Patton noted on November 24. Higher headquarters were more sanguine, despite increasing evidence from ULTRA as well as more conventional intelligence sources that the German High Command was coordinating a concentration that by mid-December gave the Ardennes sector a three-to-one advantage in men and a two-to-one advantage in tanks.

Hitler's intention, shared and underwritten by High Command West, was to replicate the success of 1940 by striking through the Ardennes for Antwerp. The port's capture would both create a logistic crisis for the Allies and divide the British from the Americans, opening the way to their defeat in detail and—just possibly—to a decisive falling-out between partners whose squabbling, egalitarian relationship was never really understood by German strategic planners who believed in client systems rather than alliances.

That the Allies still had absolute control of the air over the front, or that German fuel supplies were about enough to get their tanks halfway to Antwerp, did not concern the Fuehrer. Nor were his generals excessively disturbed. The planners of High Command West preferred in principle a more limited operation but were never able to convince even themselves why Germany's last reserves should be used that way. What was to be gained, except a drawn-out endgame? At least the West was geographically small enough to offer something like a strategic objective. The eastern front presented only the prospect of a second Kursk, with the last of the Panzers feeding themselves into a Russian meat grinder fifty or seventy miles east of the existing front line. And if Operation Watch on the Rhine proved instead a Twilight of the Gods, then it would at least be a virtuoso performance as far as the army's professionals and the zealots of the SS could make it.

The German attack began before dawn on December 16. From the beginning, its pace was slowed by stubborn American resistance—the kind of tactical triumphs critics of U.S. "fighting power" tend to assert lay outside the American soldier's capacities. Ironically, the initial successes of the troops on the ground delayed the 1st Army, 12th Army Group, and SHAEF in developing an understanding of what was happening. Initially, Bradley and Hodges believed it a local counterattack to disrupt the 1st Army's drive through the Huertgen Forest. Eisenhower realized it was more than a spoiling attack, but (the ninety-division gamble again) had no reserves to send in except two U.S. airborne divisions, both badly mauled in the fighting for Arnhem.

Patton's G-2 had been anticipating trouble in the Ardennes for weeks, and Patton was regularly briefed on the growing German buildup. The plans that emerged from the 3rd Army headquarters for dealing with the contingency of a major offensive were themselves offensive. As early as the morning of December 17, Patton called "the thing in the north . . . the real McCoy" and also an opportunity to finish the war. The attack reminded him of the German offensive of March 1918, and like it nothing would be left—if the battle were managed properly. If we roll with the punch, Patton's operations officer (G-3) declared, in a week it should be possible to cut off the main German force west of the Rhine. "That isn't the way those gentlemen up north fight," Patton relied.

The night before Bradley had called Patton—reluctantly—and asked him to send an armored division north, Patton believed this kind of piecemeal commitment played into the German hands, but concluded Bradley was in bigger trouble than he could discuss over the phone. On December 18, Bradley requested Patton and his senior staff officers to report to Army group headquarters. When they arrived the next day, Bradley showed Patton on a large-scale map that the German penetration was much larger than Patton had thought, and was expanding steadily as pockets of American resistance were broken. The broad outlines of a response were nevertheless in place: first contain the offensive, then control and defeat it. What, Bradley asked, could the 3rd Army contribute?

In one sense, the question was rhetorical. The discussion had made clear that the 3rd Army was expected to send more divisions north, at the price of abandoning its offensive into Germany. Yet in the worst crisis of the campaign, Bradley did not approach Patton with orders. One account has him reluctant to increase his burdens by sparking an argument. In the past six months, however, Bradley had come to understand Patton better than he had in Tunisia and Sicily, as someone most effective driven with a loose rein. "I feel you won't like what we are going to do, but I fear it is necessary," were Bradley's words.

Patton's response was to guarantee to send a division, the 4th Armored, north starting at midnight, a second the next morning, and a third within twenty-four hours if necessary—cross-country in the dead of winter. Bradley not only believed him, but the next morning phoned that the situation had worsened, asked for the redeployment to be stepped up, and ordered Patton to report to Verdun the next day for a conference with Eisenhower and his principal subordinates.

Patton spent the early morning of the 19th with his staff officers and corps commanders, explaining and outlining his plan for turning north into the Ardennes on any of three possible road axes, and enjoining rapid movement once the orders were issued. By then, he had concluded that the best way to deal with the German offensive in the long term involved allowing it to keep on going, to a depth of forty or fifty miles, then drive into the base of the now-developed salient and cut it off. It was a high-risk solution, demanding cast-iron nerve at command levels. It was also a potential war-ender. And it was a galvanic shock to the officers who assembled at Verdun. None of them brought specific plans. Most of them feared the worst. Even Eisenhower's characteristic bonhomie seemed forced. When he described the situation as "one of opportunity for us, and not of disaster," Patton burst out, "Let's have the guts to let the sons of bitches go all the way to Paris. Then we'll really cut 'em up and chew 'em up!" The room burst into laughter, and Eisenhower replied "George, that's fine."

The Supreme Commander's intentions were nevertheless more modest: to contain the German offensive behind the Meuse River, then counterattack. When Eisenhower told Patton he wanted him to command the operation, "under Bradley's supervision, of course," he was recognizing the 12th Army Group's loss of touch with its subordinate headquarters and conceding as well that the 1st Army headquarters would be doing well to avoid disaster on its immediate front. Eisenhower wanted a strong counterattack: at least six divisions."When can you attack?" Patton replied, "On the morning of the 21st, with three divisions." Eisenhower, thinking this was more of Georgie's hyperbole at a most inopportune time, told him, "Don't be fatuous." There was laughter from other quarters as well, especially among the British officers present. But Patton's aide noticed "a stir, a shuffling of feet . . . through the room excitement leaped like a flame."

Patton stepped to the map and used a cigar to illustrate his intentions: "The Kraut's stuck his head in a meatgrinder. And this time I've got hold of the handle." Thanks in good part to the previous work of his staff, Patton came to the conference with more than a strategic generalization. He had specific plans for switching the 3rd Army's axis ninety degrees, specific replies to questions and criticisms. When Eisenhower questioned whether three divisions were enough, Patton answered that waiting for more would cost the advantage of surprise but agreed to mount a larger attack in six days. Within an hour, all was settled: the divisions to be used, their objectives, the new army boundaries that had the 7th Army taking over much of the 3rd's old front. As the conference broke up, Eisenhower, recently promoted to General of the Army, remarked, "Every time I get a new star I get attacked." "And every time you get attacked, I pull you out," was Patton's rejoinder.

The Verdun conference is frequently described as Patton's finest military hour, the culmination of a thirty-year career as a thinking soldier, the justification of all of Eisenhower's forbearance. It was all those things. But as Russell Weigley reminds us, other generals had accomplished similar shifts in direction and commitment against competent opposition. The difference at Verdun was that Patton was, to borrow his own phrasing from another context, "The only son of a bitch around here who knows what he's trying to do." Kipling's words remain appropriate: "If you can keep your head when all around you are losing theirs—."

The next few days were also a triumph of teamwork. Before leaving Verdun, Patton phoned his headquarters: the 4th Armored and 26th Infantry Divisions to Arlon; the 80th Infantry and 3rd Army headquarters to Luxembourg. Patton's colleagues had consistently low-rated the 3rd Army's staff as "a mediocre bunch." In fact, the staff had developed since the breakout into exactly the kind of organization Patton wanted: one able to rise to occasions and handle emergencies. Minor problems of traffic control and command authority did not hinder the ninety-degree turn: another indication of Patton's willingness to give his subordinates rope that they could turn into either a lifeline or a hangman's noose.

Patton himself took the field as a one-man headquarters—two if his driver is counted. On a single day, he cheerfully wrote to Bea, "I visited seven divisions and regrouped an army alone . . . Destiny sent for me in a hurry when things got tight. Perhaps God saved me for this effort." His first order read, "Everyone in this army must understand that we are not fighting this battle in any half-cocked manner. It's either root hog—or die." The corps headquarters controlling the advance, and its general, were new to the 3rd Army, having joined only in October. As a consequence, Patton kept much tighter control over the details of the attack than was usual. He prescribed in detail the tactics to be employed by the 4th Armored Division. His high-pitched voice was heard everywhere, exhorting and inspiring. "This will get the bastards out of their holes so we can kill all of 'em," he encouraged his corps staffs. "When one attacks, it is the enemy who has to worry," he reminded himself. And within forty-eight hours, after a hundred-mile march over largely secondary roads in snow, fog, and bitter cold, three divisions were in place to mount the first counterattack of the Ardennes campaign.

Patton initially still entertained some hope of allowing the Germans to continue overextending themselves, even considering abandoning Bastogne to lure them deeper into Belgium. But Troy Middleton, whose VIII Corps was making the principal fight in the Ardennes, was an old friend whose competence Patton respected. On the afternoon of December 20, Middleton advised Patton to take a close look at the map. With six roads converging on it, Bastogne was too important for the Americans to abandon or the Germans to bypass. Patton agreed, and his attack's first objective became the relief of the Belgian market town and its garrison, the 101st Airborne Division's "band of brothers."

"Drive like hell!" Patton exhorted at his final meeting before the offensive. But the twenty-mile breadth of the American front acted as a check on a single massive thrust toward Bastogne. Elements of the 4th Armored, a company each of tanks and infantry, actually entered the town on December 20, only to be ordered out again by the division's new commander, Major General Hugh Gaffey, whose main body was strung out along country roads in a snowstorm, its path barred by elite German paratroopers. German counterattacks combined with the weather to frustrate hopes of relieving Bastogne by Christmas. By now, Patton was for practical purposes running the III Corps directly, and he forced the pace to the limit. When the 4th Armored was pushed back, Patton blamed himself for insisting around-the-clock attacks—". . . all right on the first or second day of the battle . . . but after that the men get tired." "With a little luck I will put on a more daring operation just after Xmas," he wrote to Bea on the 22nd.

By Christmas the worst was over—at least in hindsight. The determination and the tactical skill of the Americans in the offensive's path; Patton's military broken-field running; and not least a break in the weather that enabled the C-47s and the fighter-bombers to reassert control of the sector's air space, had shifted the initiative to the Allied side of the line. "Lovely weather for killing Germans," Patton noted on Christmas Day. He spent most of it visiting front-line units, a pattern he continued throughout the fighting. Despite the German insertion of special operations forces with a mission of killing senior officers, Patton rode in an open armored jeep, a parka or overcoat his only concession to the biting cold. His face was regularly frostbitten. When strafed by an American plane, he took refuge in a ditch like any high private. Patton's purpose was to be seen and to see; word of his presence spread wherever he went. Even the two pistols he habitually carried did not seem as much of an affectation in the looming forests of the Ardennes as they might appear on maneuvers. Contrary to legend, these were ivory-handled: Patton insisted in and out of season that no one but a bawdyhouse pimp would carry a pearl-handled sidearm. Besides, he considered pearl "unlucky."

Patton, for good and ill, was still Patton. On one occasion, he allegedly was talking with a number of stragglers from units initially overrun by the Germans when he singled out one man, sulfurously denounced him as a coward, and ordered him arrested. The terrified soldier was later released—again on Patton's orders. The incident remained buried in the files; doctors and reporters had other matters occupying their attention in the winter of 1944. Army cartoonist Bill Mauldin, the ETO's successor to Ernie Pyle as celebrant of the common soldier, whose admiration for Bradley extended to contributing a foreword to his memoirs, responded to a personally administered tongue-lashing with what remains among the more perceptive summaries of Patton. "If you're a leader, you don't push wet spaghetti, you pull it . . . Patton understood. . . . The stupid bastard was crazy . . . but I certainly respected his theories and the techniques he used to get his men out of their foxholes."

Years later another soldier told Beatrice of a miserable late afternoon: "We [were] stuck in the snow. He yelled at us to get out and push, and first I knew, there was General Patton pushing right alongside of me. Sure I knew him; he never asked a man to do what he wouldn't do himself." A sergeant in a forward outpost at St. Vith, where the German pressure was greatest, heard that the 3rd Army was attacking. "That's good news," he replied. "If Georgie's coming, we've got it made." On December 30, in an editorial titled "Patton of Course" the *Washington Post* said, "It has become a sort of unwritten rule in this war that when there is a fire to be put out, it is Patton who jumps into his boots . . . This is the same Patton who has a number of indiscretions on his record, but who has again and again demonstrated that when a jam develops he is the one who is called upon to break it." The Army and the country had come a long way from Tunisia and Sicily.

On December 26, the 4th Armored broke into Bastogne to stay. Its tanks that night escorted in a forty-truck supply train and a convoy of seventy ambulances: grim evidence of the Airborne's sacrifices. "[T]he outstanding achievement of the war," Patton bragged to Bea. To the correspondents who flocked to the town after the shooting stopped, he urged remembrance of "the men who drove up that bowling alley out there from Arlon." In his conversations and correspondence, he urged an immediate counterattack with every available division and dismissed Montgomery, who had been given temporary command of Allied forces north of the breakthrough, as "a tired little fart."

Patton argued to Bradley and Eisenhower for deep-penetration envelopments by the 3rd Army south of the Bulge and the 1st to its north. Bradley was reluctant; Hodges complained the roads in his sector would not support such an operation. Eisenhower no less than Patton believed the German salient offered a major opportunity: the annihilation of the German army west of the Rhine. *"We must be prepared to use everything consistent with minimum security requirements to accomplish their destruction,"* he wrote to Montgomery on December 29.

When it came to a decision, however, he shared the cautious perspective of Bradley, Hodges, and not least Montgomery, opting to cut the salient at the waist. The Supreme Commander intended that the 1st and 3rd Armies link up inside the Bulge, then drive side by side through the Eifel toward Bonn and the Rhine. The next and final stage of the operation would be a long joint thrust across Germany through the open ground from Frankfurt to Kassel, and a meeting with the Russians. Montgomery, retaining the 9th U.S. Army to bulk up his army group, would simultaneously stage his own drive into and across Germany north of the Ruhr.

Eisenhower's decision to strike the salient's middle reflected his belief that Patton's proposal was too risky for a small force and required too much time to concentrate a large one. At the same time, he wanted Patton to do the heavy work of reducing the Bulge. Neither Hodges nor Bradley stood especially high in the Supreme Commander's standing after their performances in December, while Montgomery's Yank-baiting, deliberate and otherwise, was reaching a point where his relief seemed a distinct possibility. The Germans fought with desperate courage and consummate skill to hold the shoulder of the salient by keeping pressure on Bastogne. They were helped in Patton's sector by the nature of his attack. Like its immediate predecessor, it was on a broad front, twenty to twenty-five miles, and correspondingly tended to devolve into a series of small-scale encounter battles: the sort of fighting in which the Germans excelled.

"All my troops are just where they should be," Patton noted on New Year's Day. "So if we lose it will be due to better fighting on the part of the enemy . . . not to any mistakes which I have made." Patton, like every other senior U.S. general in the ETO, nevertheless had to address an unexpected consequence of the "ninety-division gamble": the regular necessity for using armored and airborne divisions in the same way as infantry divisions, despite their shortcomings in staying power. The paratroopers suffered disproportionate casualties in the Ardennes due to their lack of armor and artillery. Armored divisions, with only three battalions of infantry, eroded no less rapidly. Only the 6th Armored Division, "better than the 4th only without the PR," according to its veterans, achieved anything like a breakthrough before icy weather and German counterattacks slowed its progress.

Patton muttered that the "super planners" seemed more scared than the soldiers and expressed "fear we have not got the mental equipment of one big push." He sought, more than usual, to use time to compensate for restricted space and lack of mass. His handling of the 3rd Army in the later stages of the Bulge, notably his initial attempts to establish contact with the 1st Army, was frequently characterized by a level of haste that the Germans were experts at punishing. Not until January 16 did elements of Patton's 11th Armored Division connect with the 1st Army's vanguards at Houffalize. "Now we will drive them back," Patton noted, and the 1st and 3rd Armies pushed eastward as thousands of Germans turned from soldiers to fugitives under massive air and artillery strikes. It had not been elegant, but it was effective, and on January 31, Bradley began discussing with Patton and Hodges how best to implement Eisenhower's general plan for the 12th Army Group's push for the Rhine.

Patton's sun was nevertheless at noon. He had emerged from the Bulge a national hero. The army newspaper *Stars and Stripes,* which he openly loathed as "subversive of discipline," regularly featured articles praising the general and his army. Charles B. MacDonald, who commanded a rifle company in the Bulge and became one of World War II's most distinguished historians, asked rhetorically—and legitimately—what it mattered to a GI in a foxhole who commanded him at the top? But one day in the battle's later stages, someone recognized Patton as his jeep met a convoy of trucks carrying infantrymen toward the front. Within minutes, men were standing up and leaning out, cheering their commander to the echo. Even Bradley went on record that Patton's generalship during the relief of Bastogne was "one of the most brilliant performances by any commander on either side in World War II . . . rapid, open warfare combined with noble purpose and difficult goals."

Patton now held his liquor better than most. Praise was another matter, and Eisenhower steadily refused to join the public chorus of acclaim. Yet he told one of SHAEF's most notorious gossips that "George is really a very great soldier, and I must get Marshall to do something for him before the war is over." Patton, as expected, received that news within days. "Leadership . . . ," Patton noted about the same time. "I have it—but I'll be damned if I can define it." Dwight Eisenhower had it as well. The old Army's best poker player knew how to encourage someone to stay in a game by extending the promise of a big win.

Bradley would soon be wearing four stars—a promotion Eisenhower justified to Marshall on the grounds that not promoting him would be the same as affirming an American failure in the Ardennes. That did not prevent his losing the 9th Army to Montgomery, but when SHAEF phoned a proposal to transfer several more divisions to the 6th Army Group, Bradley exploded: "The reputation and the good will of the American soldiers and the American army, and the good will of its commanders are at stake . . . you can take any god-damn division and/or corps in the 12th Army Group, do with them as you see fit, and those of us that you leave back will sit on our asses until hell freezes." Patton himself could have done no better, and shouted over general applause, "Tell them to go to hell, and all three of us will resign. I will lead the procession."

From then until the end of the war, Patton was Bradley's biggest ally—especially once he became aware of Eisenhower's developed plan for the war's final stages. Montgomery would mount his offensive north of the Ruhr. Once across the Rhine, the 9th Army would swing south and the 1st Army north in a pincers that would envelop the Ruhr and crush the forces holding it. The 3rd Army, along with the 6th Army Group, would drive across Germany and into Austria and Czechoslovakia, overrunning any remaining German resistance and eventually meeting the Russians.

Not only did the Supreme Commander again appear from Patton's perspective to be assigning the Americans a set of supporting roles. The 12th Army Group's attack into the Eifel, which achieved greater initial success than at least the Germans expected, was shut down in favor of reinforcing the 9th Army and supplying a 21st Army Group whose commander nevertheless said he would be unable to launch his offensive until February 10. The 1st and 3rd Armies could continue attacking until that date as long as the casualties and the ammunition expenditure were not excessive.

Patton called it "a foolish and ignoble way to end the war." The 3rd Army's supply and replacement situations were better in the first weeks of 1945 than they had ever been. Patton argued for a simultaneous attack all along the front—an attack, he argued, the Germans lacked the resources to stop. He received authorization to continue "probing attacks now in progress" to draw German resources from Montgomery's front. His response was to repeat his behavior in Lorraine. "Making rock soup," he called it in an elaborate shaggy-dog story about a hobo who began with a rock and a pot of hot water and showed an incredulous housewife how to make rock soup by borrowing the real ingredients for a mulligan stew from her one at a time.

This meant scrounging extra supplies, avoiding contact with higher headquarters, and keeping his divisions committed in the line so they could not be transferred elsewhere. He fooled neither of his superiors, who were pleased enough to see some progress in an American sector. Eventually, Patton proposed to force a situation that would compel Eisenhower and Bradley to support a full-scale offensive: achieve a local breakthrough, then push two or three armored divisions through to develop and exploit the success. That would leave practically nothing to hold the rest of the 3rd Army's front—but with three American armored divisions on the loose, there would be no line left to hold.

The Battle of the Bulge had shown Patton the limitations of the 75-millimeter Shermans against the German heavy ranks. His ordnance units were working on a way to up-gun them in the field. Patton also authorized additional frontal and turret armor for all the 3rd Army's 76-millimeter tanks, including the new ones arriving from the states in increasing numbers, contracting the work to Belgian factories when it proved beyond the limits of his own ordnance people. Then, on February 10, Bradley dropped the hammer. Patton must transfer an infantry division and a corps headquarters to the 1st Army. And how soon could the 3rd Army shift to the defensive?

Patton replied that he was goddamned if he would comply. As the Army's oldest serving general, he would resign first. When Bradley said he owed it to his troops to stay, Patton responded that "there was a lot owed to me, too." "The only army group I would like to have," he wrote to Bea, was "one in China without Allies."

What Patton got was permission to continue an "active defense" in the Eifel. As the VIII and XII Corps pushed across the Our and Sauer Rivers, their commander spent a few days in Paris. In what Patton could only regard as a major policy shift, Chief of Staff Bedell Smith informed him that he had "quite a few" divisions available and asked how many Patton would require to resume his offensive, advancing into the Palatinate toward Kaiserslauten and Sarreguemines. Told "five," Smith replied, "I think you should have twelve." Smith took the pleasantly shocked Patton hunting. He attended the Folies Bergere, came away with an offer to consider the theater his home, and returned to the front, where he promptly rediscovered the worth of a staff officer's word.

Asking Bradley for up to three more divisions, Patton received one, with restrictions on its use and a sharp reminder that SHAEF had decided to make the main effort elsewhere. When Bradley visited the 3rd Army headquarters to drive home the point personally, Patton and his corps commanders begged to continue to advance, at least until the capture of Trier. "I wonder if ever before in the history of war, a winning general had to plead to be allowed to keep on winning," Patton confided to his diary.

Bradley had his own recipe for rock soup. When Trier proved more of an obstacle than expected, he told Patton to keep on until "higher authority" intervened and said he would not listen for the telephone. After the city fell on March 1, Patton received directions to bypass it, because its capture would require four divisions. Patton answered, "Have taken Trier with two divisions. Do you want me to give it back?" Vintage Georgie—and a counterpoint to Bradley's order of March 3 that the 12th Army Group close up to the Rhine north of the Moselle.

Ironically, Simpson's 9th Army and Hodges's 1st both reached the Rhine before Patton, with Hodges's 9th Armored Division bouncing the first crossing at the Remagen Bridge on March 7. Patton congratulated his colleagues suitably, indeed fulsomely, while pursuing the opportunity offered by Trier's capture to break south into the Bavarian Palatinate. What to a conventionally minded general might seem an excursion would from Patton's perspective enable the 3rd Army to envelop the West Wall's remaining defenses from the north and in cooperation with the 6th Army Group overrun southern Germany in a replication of the dash across France. Bradley underwrote the maneuver, and in the first half of March, the 3rd Army seemed omnipresent. The 4th Armored Division was again the star of the show as it broke loose for the Rhine, reaching the last ridge line west of the river on March 7 after covering fifty-five miles in two days, bypassing and scattering retreating German columns, taking five thousand prisoners and losing only a hundred of its own men.

Had Patton or Gaffey been a bit more opportunistic, the 4th might well have picked off a Rhine bridge of its own. Instead, it turned south toward the Moselle. Walker's XX Corps drove its armored spearheads through terrain even the Germans considered virtually impassable to link up with the 4th, and German resistance on Patton's front collapsed. When Eisenhower asked the 7th Army's commander if he had any problems with Patton staging a "hot pursuit" into his sector, Alexander Patch answered, "We are all in the same army." He had lost his son in the long run up from Marseilles—something that can change a man's priorities and perspectives.

With the end in sight, Eisenhower felt he could risk generosity. After the capture of Trier, he told Patton's staff that the 3rd Army did not appreciate its own greatness and was not cocky enough! Now he said to Patton, "George, you are not only a good general, you are a lucky general, and as you will remember, in a general, Napoleon prized luck above skill." Patton appreciated the flattery, but commented that Eisenhower would be running for president after the war, and the 3rd Army represented a lot of votes! He was more grateful for the allocation of an additional armored division to support his drive for the Rhine as the remnants of two German armies sought to escape across the river, blowing bridges behind them.

On March 24, Patton's 12th Armored Division met the 7th Army's 14th Armored, closing off the main lines of retreat. Two days earlier, elements of the 5th Infantry Divison had crossed the Rhine without serious opposition. The crossing was not entirely improvised. On March 21, Eisenhower had ordered the establishment of a "firm bridgehead" across the Rhine. Patton had ordered bridging equipment forward even earlier. As his engineers drove pontoons across the fast-flowing river, he telephoned Bradley. "Don't tell anyone, but I'm across." "Well I'll be damned," was Bradley's unvarnished reply. With a day to stabilize the bridgehead, Patton phoned Bradley again. This time he wanted his superior to tell the whole world the 3rd Army had crossed the Rhine—without the elaborate preparations characterizing Montgomery's long-delayed setpiece, which also took place on the 23rd.

"We are the eighth wonder of the world," Patton boasted of the 3rd Army. "And I had to beg, lie, and steal to get started—now everybody says 'that is always what we wanted to do.' I hope things keep smooth. It seems too good to be true." On March 24, he crossed the Rhine, stopping midway to urinate in the river, then, on reaching the German side, deliberately stumbled and picked up two handfuls of dirt as William the Conqueror had done on landing in England in 1066.

Patton had not been on the recent list of senior officer promotions, but he had been in the Army too long not to understand the elements of hierarchy that for the present kept him a three-star general. "At the moment," he declared, "I am having so much fun fighting I don't care what the rank is." On March 13, he wrote to Marshall, asking to be considered once the war in Europe was over for any kind of command from a division up in the Pacific. He was old enough that this would be his last war, and he wanted to see it through till the end.

George Patton's war might well have ended even earlier, and under a cloud of disgrace. It began with a minor adjustment of the 3rd and 7th

Army boundaries, one that put a POW camp near the small city of Hammelburg in Patton's zone of responsibility. A reasonable body of evidence indicated his son-in-law John Waters, captured in Tunisia, was confined there, and Patton's letters to Bea strongly suggest he believed it. Over the reservations of the corps and division commanders involved, Patton insisted that a raid be mounted to liberate the camp. His motivations were not entirely familial. American forces under Douglas MacArthur had recently and to much fanfare liberated two prison camps in the Philippines—a red flag to the competitive Patton. The operation itself was risky, but not more so than many others undertaken under the 3rd Army's auspices. The division Patton selected was the 4th Armored—most likely of any in all of SHAEF to pull off such a stroke.

The problem was, in mocrocosm, that confronting the U.S. Army throughout the campaign in Northwest Europe: force ratios. The 4th Armored's commander, new to the job, believed the mission required a full combat command: a third to a half the division. Eddy was unwilling to divert that large of a force. Patton also believed something smaller would suffice for what he regarded as an in-and-out operation depending heavily on speed and surprise. The raid was eventually mounted by a company each of Shermans and infantry in half-tracks: about three hundred men. The task force moved out on March 26, reached the camp easily, but on its return was surrounded and destroyed. The camp was overrun a second time a few days later by a division of the 7th Army. Patton's son-in-law, badly wounded in the earlier fighting, was among the liberated.

Patton made every effort to turn the Hammelburg raid into a "black operation" or, better yet, send it down a black hole. In this he benefited from President Roosevelt's death on April 12, which dominated the news to the extent that "you could execute buggery in the streets and get no farther than the fourth page." Patton nevertheless insisted at a press conference that he had not known of Waters's presence in the camp and described the raid as reflecting concern that the prisoners might be murdered. His behavior prior to the raid speaks eloquently to the first point. As for the second, it had validity in the Pacific, where American prisoners were not only regularly killed but at times eaten. The Wehrmacht, however, had been consistently correct, if not always scrupulous, in its treatment of U.S. prisoners; there was no need to panic over this particular camp.

Patton expected a public reaction something like that to the slapping incident. Hammelburg was in fact far worse; neither a lapse of personal judgment nor a "rank has its privileges" personal indulgence. Hammelburg was an egregious abuse of command power for personal reasons. Even had it succeeded it was grounds enough to break Patton out of the service.[2] Bradley responded by publicly accepting most of Patton's story, regretting what he called "just a spectacular stunt . . . doomed from the start" and "deploring" the "impetuousness" prompting it. "Had he asked permission I would have vetoed it"—yet Bradley neither rebuked Patton personally nor reprimanded him officially. "Failure itself was George's own worst reprimand." Eisenhower explained it to Marshall as "a wild goose chase . . . I hope the newspapers do not make too much of it. . . . Patton is a problem child, but he is a great fighting leader in pursuit and exploitation." In war, they send for the hard men and bury the consequences wholesale. George Patton was far from the only hard case in SHAEF's upper echelons.

By now the bulk of the 3rd Army was across the Rhine, with the 6th Armored Division reaching Frankfurt on March 26, then crossing the Main on the 28th to catch up with the 4th Armored. These two divisions had been for the 3rd Army what the 2nd and 3rd Armored were for Hodges's 1st: the pace-setters. Now they led Patton's drive toward Giessen and into the Fulda Gap, meeting only scattered albeit occasionally fierce opposition. In the first week of April, Patton's spearheads were as much as forty miles ahead of those of the 1st and 9th Army. Bradley, however, had come to share Eisenhower's belief that the 12th Army Group's next best step was the encirclement of the Ruhr—both because it promised an American Cannae and guaranteed the return of the 9th Army to Bradley's command as the northern arm of the pincers. The al-

---

2 According to one account, the commander of the raid, Captain Abraham Baum, inspired Moshe Dayan in 1948 by describing the effect of using maximum firepower on an unsuspecting enemy, recommending "shoot and drive" as an optimal method that was adopted in essence by Israel's fledgling armored forces. Robert Slater, *Warrior Statesman: The Life of Moshe Dayan* (New York: St. Martin's 1991), pp. 89ff.

ternate prospect, a drive into Germany toward the Elbe River by the 1st and 3rd Armies, had terrain in its favor, but not politics.

By now there was little doubt at SHAEF that American field armies could plan and execute large-scale, armor-tipped advances. Patton with the bit in his teeth could drag Hodges and Bradley in his wake across what remained of the Reich. But to what end? The Yalta Conference earlier in the year had established postwar zones of occupation. The pace and mass of the Red Army's offensive in the east had brought it so close to Berlin that Eisenhower no longer believed the Western allies had a chance to take the city without high risk and heavy casualties. Instead of turning the 3rd Army loose, Eisenhower and Bradley stood it down until April 10, giving Hodges and Simpson chance to close up. Their leashes slipped once more, the 6th Armored made fifty miles in a day to the Napoleonic battlefield of Jena, only to see the 4th Armored catch up the next day. But the armor, and the 3rd Army as a whole, was being slowed by improvised defenses based on the large concentrations of heavy anti-aircraft guns that had defended Saxony's industrial zones and were now turned Rommel-style against tanks and half-tracks that proved as vulnerable in central Germany as in North Africa.

When on April 12, Eisenhower informed Patton of his decision not to strike for Berlin, Patton nevertheless protested. When Eisenhower asked who would want the devastated city, Patton answered that history would answer that question. The Supreme Commander, however, had another, more pressing concern. Since the autumn of 1944, Allied intelligence had been warning of a "National Redoubt" being developed in Germany's southern mountains—a fortress to which the Reich's remnants could withdraw and prolong the war for months and years. Combined with growing concern for the prospects of underground resistance in occupied Germany, the so-called "Werewolves," the notion of a broken-backed resistance in near-impassable terrain, alarmed SHAEF sufficiently to make destroying organized German forces in the south a high priority.

The initial responsibility fell to the 6th Army Group. But on April 15, with the 9th and 1st Armies holding in place on the Elbe to await the Russians, Bradley was ordered to send the 3rd Army south into Austria and help eliminate the last possibilities of continued organized resistance. The decision was motivated in part by Eisenhower's wish to have Bradley and Patton share in the war's final headlines—an emotion in part fuelled by an ongoing, long-term dislike of Devers. Patton, denied a shot at Berlin, basked in what he considered the Supreme Commander's favor, and its concrete manifestation of a 3rd Army increased to four corps and eventually no fewer than eighteen divisions.

"We got the ball for what looks like the final play," he wrote to Bea on April 17. He was a full general now, with date of rank from April 14— one day ahead of Courtney Hodges! As the 3rd Army drove down the Danube Valley, resistance to its fast-moving spearheads eroded, with more and more Germans discarding their uniforms and making for home as best they might. Everywhere swastikas were replaced by the white flags of surrender. The 3rd Army's longtime foe, the 11th Panzer Division, threw in the towel on May 4, the last of the Panzers. Patton, with his eye on Prague, had his staff working on plans to cross the prewar border, and on May 4, he received Eisenhower's approval. Two days later, he was informed that Eisenhower had negotiated a stop line with the Soviet forces in Czechoslovakia to avoid possible friendly fire incidents. The line ran through Pilsen, just a few miles north of Prague, and the 3rd Army was drawing up to it when George Patton's war ended on May 7, 1945.

CODA

ERWIN Rommel's war had come to an end six months earlier. He was in the hospital when the final and most nearly successful assassination attempt against Hitler took place on July 20, 1944. But the conspiracy had two loci. One was in Berlin, where Claus von Stauffenberg and his immediate followers sought to seize control of the centers of power in the aftermath of the bomb explosion. The other was in Paris, where another more group of officers centered on the Military Command of France, but with links to High Command West as well.

The German army historically prided itself on identification with the state but detachment from the government. In a modern state, however, the conscience of the armed forces is a public matter in the public keeping. Public dissent from public policy by serving soldiers is seldom tolerated even—or especially—in democracies. Even when military doubters began comparing moral notes, they did not easily find common ground. Merely agreeing that the Hitler regime's crimes were sufficient to merit its overthrow absorbed a disproportionate amount of energy. The Western conspirators, while more loosely connected to each other than were their counterparts in Berlin, nevertheless understood that any successful putsch undertaken in wartime depended on transferring the loyalty of the armed forces. More specifically, Germany's future was likely to depend on what happened in the West. Continuing the war with Russia was for these men a military and political given. The Western theater offered possibilities, however limited, for negotation. If some kind of surrender proved the only option, in the last analysis it would be surrender to civilized peoples. But for even these shabby alternatives to be meaningful, the troops must be willing to accept the new order. In practice, that meant following their generals—or at least obeying orders in the first crucial days and hours of the putsch.

The problem was complicated by the large number of SS and Gestapo men present in France because of the occupation, and even more by the central role of the Waffen SS in High Command West's order of battle. It was possible to arrest the former, but a half-dozen elite mechanized divisions could not be disarmed against their will by the stroke of a pen. That was where the field marshals came in. Rundstedt had served Kaiser, Republic, and Reich with detached loyalty; his age alone suggested that he would serve a fourth government for the brief time needed. His relief by Kluge was an unexpected bonus. During his tenure in Russia, Kluge had been sufficiently committed to Hitler's removal that he allowed the junior officers of his headquarters at Army Group Center not merely to discuss but to plan Hitler's assassination during a projected visit to the front. That project had come to nothing, but Kluge now agreed to cooperate once Hitler was dead.

Keitel and Rundstedt were sidebars. It was Rommel whose reputation and presence made him the most likely—arguably the only—senior army officer able to override SS field commanders' residual loyalty to a dead Fuehrer. It was Rommel whose public persona still shone brightly enough to give a new government the public legitimacy it needed. It was Rommel whose prospects were the best of any German officer's when it came to negotiating with the Western Allies. And it was Rommel who, to the end, kept his own counsel.

Rommel's involvement with the events of July 20 is in the final analysis best understood as a structure of inferences informed by wishful thinking. Although many key records are missing, it is clear that as the day for the assassination approached and the military situation worsened, the conspirators in France spoke more openly with Rommel. His responses, including facial expressions and body language, allowed his interlocutors to believe the field marshal had been won over, at least to the degree that he would support a new government after Hitler was deposed or killed. That information was, in turn, passed on to like-minded colleagues in France and communicated to Stauffenberg's group in Berlin—almost certainly in an embellished form

It has been suggested that colleagues more comfortable than Rommel with the art of intrigue sought to "set up" the field marshal, enveloping him in a web of innuendo that gave him no choice but to support the anti-Hitler conspiracy. It seems more reasonable to take into account the high levels of unaccustomed stress under which the men of July 20 were working. Aesopian language, allusions, and pregnant pauses were *de rigeur* in any case. Rommel's support was considered so vital that it was scarcely remarkable that men whose own lives and honor were committed saw in him what they needed to see, and sought to use their belief as leverage on less-committed associates—who, in turn, understood as a given what at best had been a wink and a nudge.

The same pattern holds for the investigations that succeeded the assassination's failure. Apart from the effects of "rigorous interrogation" at the hands of the Gestapo, the temptation for accused majors and colonels to suggest or assert that ultimate responsibility rested with higher ranks was strong. Command responsibility in armed forces everywhere is usually understood as including taking care of one's own when "the system" seeks scapegoats. Devolving responsibility upward in the hope of involving such high levels that the investigation will be abandoned is a feature of all bureaucracies. The Reich's post–July 20 practice of *Sippenhaft*, punishing families for the behavior of one member, created serious and legitimate questions of where one's ultimate loyalty belonged. In the weeks after July 20, Erwin Rommel's name appeared in an increasing number of dossiers and reports.

While in hospital, Rommel continued to tell his uniformed visitors openly that the war was lost. By the time he returned home in early August, he was more guarded. Kluge was dead, a suicide. Hans Speidel, Army Group B's chief of staff, had been dismissed and would be arrested in September. Rommel still had numerous contacts and well-wishers in the army and the regime at large. He was sufficiently concerned at the prospect of assassination that he carried a pistol on his daily walks. He did not as yet seem to consider himself a subject of "legitimate" suspicion. His long conversations with his son, however, suggest an alternate possibility. In them, Rommel made no secret either of his belief that the war was lost, or of his criticism of the attempt on Hitler's life. Manfred Rommel took both seriously. At sixteen, he was of an age when a father's first adult confidences are especially important. It was impossible for Rommel to deny his "defeatism"—itself by now a capital offense. But might he have been playing one last hand close to the chest, hoping that if he should be arrested, his family might escape the worst consequences by swearing, legitimately, that to the end Rommel had denounced the Fuehrer's would-be assassins?

On October 7, Rommel was summoned to Berlin—a special train would be sent, Keitel assured him. Rommel pleaded ill health, telling trusted friends he believed he would never get there alive. A week later, two generals called on him. Hitler, the field marshal was informed, had judged him guilty of involvement in the conspiracy against him. Despite his deep sense of betrayal, the Fuehrer offered a choice: public trial for high treason or "the officer's way": suicide and a state funeral, with no harm to his family. For the last time, Rommel made his decision in seconds.

George Patton's dying took a bit longer. He realized that his hopes for a Pacific assignment were futile. Marshall would never send him to serve under MacArthur; MacArthur would never ask for him. When a head-quarters was designated for assignment to the Pacific, it was the pedestrian 1st Army and its pedestrian commander Courtney Hodges. A man of war, Patton saw his reason for existing vanish like smoke. The call was for demobilization, and Patton's age meant he would be among the first on the retirement list. Even as the guns fell silent, he perceived himself as a back number.

Designated as Military Governor of Bavaria, Patton spent a month in the States before assuming his new duties. It was a time of triumph, despite Bea's suspicion that her husband had resumed his brief affair with Jean Gordon. Jean had arrived in Europe in the summer of 1944 as a Red Cross volunteer and worked an assignment to the 3rd Army. Bea's concern and Patton's pooh-poohing are matters of record. So are the diary comments of Colonel Everett Hughes, a close friend of Patton's at SHAEF, indicating that the two enjoyed a relationship something more than platonic.

Here at least Patton had something in common with Eisenhower, who seems to have spent almost as much time assuring his wife of the innocence of his relationship with his driver Kay Summersby as he did dealing with the German army. In each case, the most reasonable verdict must be "not proven." Patton's history of demonstrable infidelity resembles his record of physically abusing enlisted men: both are limited. He frequently equated prowess in the bedroom with performance on the battlefield. But while he welcomed Jean's peripheral presence, Patton was rising sixty when she reappeared in his life. Although he was hardly a burned-out wreck, those who knew him often commented that the war had aged him significantly. He was under constant, intense stress—seldom an aphrodisiac for anyone past his twenties. Patton would have been neither the first nor the last aging rooster to encourage among his male associates the notion that he could still crow at will. There are worse follies.

Patton's month at home, for the first time since 1942, was on the surface a triumph on a Roman scale. From downtown Boston to the Los Angeles Coliseum, he was greeted by cheers, broke into tears, and made generally appropriate speeches. The public relations personnel assigned as his bear-leaders usually had cutoff switches on the microphones. They were not needed. Patton was a public hero, second only to Eisenhower, far overshadowing the other senior generals of the ETO. In private, however, Patton frequently referred to his luck having run out, saying, "It was too damned bad I wasn't killed before the fighting stopped."

Such sentiments were far more common among returning GIs of all ranks and grades than would, or indeed could, be acknowledged until far later in the century. They nevertheless indicated a growing darkness of spirit that boded ill for Patton's return to Europe. His superiors, specifically Marshall and Eisenhower, considered his usefulness at an end with the end of large-scale mobile warfare. Eisenhower openly questioned his mental balance. Yet nothing was done to clear a senior vacancy in the United States as a preliminary to his retirement with the honor his service merited. Perhaps Eisenhower believed Patton was best kept under his direct authority until something better could be arranged. In the event, Patton's assignment as Military Governor of Bavaria ranks among the most ill-considered senior appointments since Emperor Caligula made his horse a consul of Rome.

In the years of the Cold War, a myth a rose that Patton had advocated continued national mobilization and a hard line, to the point of using force, against the Soviet Union. Reality was a good deal more pedestrian. As early as V-E day, Patton declared the impossibility of doing business with the Russians and argued for keeping America's armies intact to counter what he considered an inevitable Soviet challenge. Like many of his counterparts, he supported some form of compulsory, universal peacetime service but believed Russia's intentions were best tested and Russia's ambitions best deterred while the United States still had large, experienced military forces in hand on the spot—and before he retired, just in case it came to shooting!

The creation of NATO in the 1950s and its endurance into the twenty-first century suggests that Patton's concept of keeping the Americans in, the Russians out, and the Germans at least under control was not entirely the product of a belligerent imagination. But even by the time he returned to Bavaria, it was apparent that demobilization was the order of the day, with veteran divisions shrinking to cadres as their experienced men departed for home. As for denazification, Patton regarded it as a shibboleth, unrealizable in the context of simultaneous policies of restoring German self-sufficiency and bringing American boys home. The antifraternization aspects of occupation seemed to him even more ridiculous, as long as the occupation forces' supplies of penicillin held out.

Again, in the long term, Patton was scarcely isolated in his approach. The American occupation was arguably a "retreat to victory," most successful in changing German hearts and minds when it was at its most pragmatic. Patton's observation that it was no more possible for a civil servant in Germany to have avoided paying lip service to the Nazis than it was for an American postmaster to avoid cooperating with the Democrats or Republicans acquired fresh force when the collapse of the Soviet Union and the Warsaw Pact demonstrated anew the problems of reweaving history. Individuals may achieve catharsis; cultures never do. But in the waning months of 1945, retribution was still the officially reigning paradigm, with Eisenhower warning that "Nazis should not be allowed to retain wealth, power, or influence" and reminding Patton in particular that the "obliteration" of Nazism was a major U.S. war aim.

The endgame began at a press conference on September 22. Asked why Nazis were still occupying governmental positions in Bavaria, Patton began by asserting his loathing of Hitlerism, but reminded his questioner that "more than half" of the German people had been Nazis, and to get anything done it was necessary to "compromise with the devil a little." When he called "this Nazi question . . . very much like a Democratic and Republican election fight," he was referring to the necessity for post-election cooperation no matter who won. Three days later, he made the same point, referring to a relative who had kept his postmastership by "judicious flip-flops" between the parties. But a four-star general of the U.S. Army who said that "Nazism might well be compared to any of the parties at home, Republican or Democrat," was throwing a bucket of manure into the proverbial fan.

Patton supporters then and afterward depict a journalistic conspiracy to discredit Patton for his anti-Soviet views and his undisguised loathing of the Eastern European displaced persons, particularly the Jews, whom he considered responsible for most of the still-prevalent disorder in Bavaria. A simpler explanation involves a journalistic version of post-traumatic stress disorder. Reporters and editors, accustomed to the unceasing drama of war, were finding it difficult to accept the more nuanced events of peace. Here was a ready-made red-meat story virtually demanding feature status.

Eisenhower had met with Patton only a few days earlier and discussed the possibilities of a stateside appointment. Patton suggested President of the Army War College and commander of the Army Ground Forces. When Eisenhower temporized on both, Patton said the only thing left was retirement. Eisenhower asked him to stay another three months. Patton, ever the team player, agreed. The problem of his disposal seemed settled. Now Georgie appeared to have done it again.

Eisenhower exploded, then tried to give Patton the opportunity to say he had been misquoted. When Eisenhower summoned him by telegram to discuss the issue, Patton noted that this was not the first time he had been in trouble and had it turn to his advantage. Yet in a wider context, it hardly seemed to matter. Patton's wars were over. Eisenhower's foot was on the threshold to a wider stage. Eisenhower gave him a choice: immediate resignation, or command of the 15th Army, a headquarters whose primary responsibility was preparing a history of the ETO.

Patton not only accepted reassignment, he galvanized his new subordinates into doing some serious work and himself composed another of his *Notes on Combat*, stressing the difference between infantry and armored divisions and the generals best suited to command each type. But like an old gunfighter in a Sam Peckinpah film, Patton was playing out his string. He talked not of merely retiring, but resigning at the turn of the year, then "doing all the talking I feel like." What he might have said remains a subject of speculation. On December 9, he was seriously injured in a traffic accident. He died on December 21, and Bea had him buried in the American military cemetery at Luxembourg, among so many of the men he led.

I

Neither Rommmel nor Patton seemed a promising candidate for legendary status in the late 1940s. Patton had always been, to put it gently, a man of strong opinions about his fellow men. They shock current sensibilities by embracing so many categories that have become sacrosanct: blacks, Jews, organized labor, to name a few—even Arabs. Patton's political, social, and ethnic antagonisms were, however, unusual neither for his milieu nor his self-definition as a warrior aristocrat. Nor, in those contexts, were they unusually consequent. Nothing in Patton's record indicates that he regularly or occasionally did a deliberate bad turn to a subject of his prejudice. His frequently graphic language was largely confined to outlets understood at the time as private: his diary and his personal correspondence. Even there his tone as a rule invites comparison to expressions of opinion common among other kinds of elites at the turn of the twentieth century on Kenneth Starr, George W. Bush, Texans, neoconservatives, and similar upstarts who do not accept their places. The underlying motivation in each case is the same: a comprehensive, unreflective, uncritical sense of superiority.

In the final months of Patton's career, however, he began steeping himself in radical anti-Soviet literature. His reaction to the controversy over his treatment of displaced persons expanded into a vitriolic anti-Semitism that went beyond the more generalized prejudices against Jews common in the contemporary officer corps even after World War II. Had Patton resigned and spoken out, as he talked of doing, his probable themes bade fair to carry him deep into the fever swamps of postwar

American politics, to a place beyond McCarthyism. Patton's death in a traffic accident, mundane though it was, may have been Bellona's final gift to one of her last and most fervent devotees. The Goddess of War can be an ironist.

As for Rommel, he was another dead general in a Germany whose emerging definition of "Zero Hour" (*Stunde Null*) involved for millions of Germans a rejection of war and the men who made it. There were no heroes' receptions for the men of a defeated Wehrmacht, no GI Bills, no veterans' preference, for a while not even pensions. Nor was the talk of Rommel's involvement in the Resistance necessarily to the advantage of his memory—except in Allied circles, where wartime mythologies of the chivalrous foe who waged a clean war readily segued into the notion of Rommel as a principled foe of Hitler.

A major contribution to the process was the biography *Rommel, the Desert Fox*, published in 1950 by Desmond Young, a British officer captured by Rommel in the desert, and in 1951 made into a movie, "The Desert Fox," with James Mason in the title role. The film focuses on Rommel's growing disillusion with Hitler, and Mason reinforces the trope by playing Rommel as a proper English gentleman, fundamentally out of place among the thugs and poseurs of the Third Reich.

The Rommel legend was fostered as well by his former comrades. Rommel was a major figure in B. H. Liddell Hart's *The Other Side of the Hill*, also first published in 1950. The German generals interviewed by Liddell-Hart were disproportionately old Africa hands, who not only stressed Rommel's opposition to Hitler, but unsubtly described him as a disciple of Liddell-Hart's concepts of armored war. The next steps in the process were taken as the new Federal Republic considered rearmament. Men who had served with Rommel in Normandy, particularly Hans Speidel and Friedrich Ruge, saw the value of constructing an image of the field marshal as simultaneously a heroic leader of Germany's armies and a principled conspirator against Hitler's Reich. West Germany needed, if not exactly heroes, then military exemplars whose shields were as clean as possible. The best place to seek them was among those who had fought and fallen against the Americans and British. West Germany's developing armed forces also needed senior officers and sought them among those who learned the lessons of the Reich. With their links to Rommel as a springboard, Ruge and Speidel would rise to the tops of their respective services and make honorable names for themselves in NATO. The first large ships of the West German navy not safely named after cities were the *Luetgens,* the *Moelders,* and the *Rommel.* Perhaps it was all just as well. A living Rommel, with his limited tolerance for fustian and hypocrisy, might have challenged the cardboard characterizations built around his name in an emerging new Germany.

Patton, by contrast, tended in the years after 1945 to be relegated to the supporting cast of America's World War II heroes as a character actor—sometimes almost as comedy relief. His single-minded devotion to war seemed a dangerous anomaly in a thermonuclear age. His conscious flamboyance appeared unseemly posturing in an era of gray flannel suits and anonymous generals. His achievements as a commander diminished to parochial in the best-selling memoirs of Bradley and Eisenhower.

The turning point in Patton's status was, appropriately, provided by Hollywood. Studios had long been interested in the Patton story but were deterred by family opposition and Department of Defense reluctance. A difficult subordinate who had assaulted enlisted men, made anti-Semitic remarks in public, wanted to fight the Soviet Union, and dragged his heels on denazification hardly seemed a poster boy for the armed forces. Not until 1965 did 20th Century Fox finally embark on the project; not until 1970 did the film finally appear. The nuanced script, the direction and production, earned an award as Best Picture while appealing to Americans from then–President Richard Nixon down to the ticket-buyers who made it the most profitable military film ever. But it was George C. Scott's sophisticated performance in the title role, which won him an Academy Award he refused to accept, that continues to define the movie.

Scott brilliantly illuminated the conflicting aspects of a complex personality in the complex contexts created by war. The slapping scene, for example, presents simultaneously an insensitive and unsympathetic man and a man with a strong sense of morality, purpose, and conviction. Patton the general emerges as a necessary evil who America was lucky to have in an emergency and a living indictment of war's specious promises of glory and its very real indifference to human life. If a Patton is needed to win wars, can victory have any moral meaning?

The Patton brought to the screen by George C. Scott emerged in fully developed form from Martin Blumenson's two-volume edition of *The Patton Papers*. Published in 1972, the culmination of more than a decade of scholarship, this ranks among the best works of its kind: a model of selection and presentation that admirably fulfills Blumenson's intention of presenting a synergy of Patton's personal and professional development. Turning the pages is nevertheless like turning the tube of a kaleidoscope. Pieces seen in clear relationships suddenly reform into something entirely, perhaps even essentially, different. Arguably, it is these interactions that make Patton World War II's postmodern hero: his unresolved contradictions, in turn, create unresolved issues in place of those that seemed so simple in 1945.

II

Perhaps paradoxically, the development of Patton and Rommel as mythic figures inspired a still-cresting wave of critical analyses of their respective military performances. They have surprisingly common features. Each general is more admired by the descendants of his erstwhile adversaries. Rommel is an iconic figure at West Point, where cadets are more likely to do term papers and research projects on him than on anyone except Robert E. Lee. The most favorable analyses of Rommel as a commander have been done by American and British soldiers and scholars, who have praised his grasp of the initiative, his mastery of improvisation, and his ability to maximize the effect of inferior numbers and limited resources.

German interpretations tend, in contrast, to emphasize Rommel's focus on tactics at the expense of logistics, strategy, and ultimately policy. He is criticized for getting too easily discouraged and for blaming his allies and his superiors for defeats better put to his own account. His resistance connections are dismissed as tenuous at best, and more probably muthic. He gets high marks for quick reactions and for leadership, but the usual evaluation describes him as a superb division commander, adequate or a little better at corps level, and miscast in higher roles.

Patton similarly gets his best press among Germans, who during the war and afterward have consistently described him as the closest thing to a Panzer general the Western Allies produced, unique among British and Americans in his mastery of mobile warfare at the operational level. "Patton is your best," Rundstedt informed his postwar questioners. Fritz Bayerlein compared Patton to Heinz Guderian and commented on the aftermath of El Alamein, "I do not think he would have let us escape so easily." In the United States, civilian historians tend to be similarly generous. Aficionados and popular writers in particular credit Patton as the only U.S. senior officer who understood and practiced the concept of mobile warfare based on shock and finesse, as opposed to attrition based on mass. They tend as well to see in Patton an appealing combination of military intellectual and rebellious outsider, a model of professionalized effectiveness as opposed to the GI-general, everyman-at-war images projected by such earlier icons as Eisenhower and Bradley. In an age when leaders' feet of clay are regularly sought out and exposed, Patton's various indiscretions appear less unusual than they did in 1943. And Patton at least was no hypocrite. His behavior reflected his beliefs, a welcome congruence in an increasing age of spin.

British and U.S. military scholars tend to criticize their counterparts for overlooking the practical complexities of warmaking—paticularly against the Wehrmacht. They agree that Patton was a first-class battle captain, at the top of his form in exploiting victory. But when it came to the hard fighting necessary to set up the mobile operations, Patton is described as falling short—a quintessential cavalryman in an army whose heritage is dominated by the infantry and artillery and a corresponding commitment to a firepower/attrition model of warmaking. In that same context, although Patton may have been denied command above army level because of his personal behavior, a certain subtext lingers regarding his staying power in a higher post.

It is possible, in short, to muster arguments at all points of the spectrum for both officers. Fate denied soldiers and historians the guilty pleasure of a direct engagement between the two. Direct comparisons are rendered even more difficult by the lack of congruence in their professional backgrounds and their operational experience. Patton was a son of privilege, a cavalryman when that still met something, not merely a student and scholar of war but an insider on issues of doctrine and planning.

Rommel was a muddy-boots infantryman who owed his place and position in the Reichswehr to his achievements as a field soldier. Patton had access to the resources of the world's greatest military-industrial power. Rommel fought his war on a shoestring; even the 7th Panzer went to battle in looted tanks. Rommel excelled as a division and corps commander; Patton led an operational corps for slightly more than a month. Rommel finished in command of an army group; Patton never rose above army level. Rommel's position as an army commander was in many ways nominal, an administrative extension of his position with the Afrika Korps. Patton molded the 3rd Army in his own likeness, into a fighting force Martin Blumenson legitimately compares with those of Hannibal, Cromwell, and Napoleon. The general and the command remain identified in the same way Robert E. Lee is synonymous with the Army of Northern Virginia.

When all those points are made, what remains to be said about George Patton and Erwin Rommel that has not been said and is worth saying? Patton was far more than the sum of his public achievements and public performances. He cultivated a complexity of character that defies explanation and developed a personality whose force was terrifying. Stronger than the individual or the collective personalities of his soldiers, it tapped into the spectrum of motivations for making war. It appealed to blood lust and vengeance as well as courage and comradeship. And it generated rapport with the citizen soldiers of a democracy—to a degree that still makes Patton's critics uncomfortable.

Patton was a trainer. In the States, he first made his mark at senior levels by his successes in developing the Armored Force out of a collection of regiments and battalions. In North Africa, his primary achievement involved compelling the II Corps, from its staff and division commanders down, to begin taking the war seriously. In Europe, perhaps the most outstanding characteristic of the 3rd Army's order of battle was the constant accretion of green divisions with everything to learn at all levels: even the cadres were raw, and few commanders had any combat experience in the current war. While all U.S. field armies had the same problem, the 3rd Army's new formations seemed to adjust more quickly and suffer fewer casualties relative to their early missions. On another level, Patton's racism did not deter him from being the first army commander to employ, and personally welcome, black tank battalions, or to integrate black volunteers into the 3rd Army's replacement-starved rifle platoons during the Battle of the Bulge.

Patton was both an educated soldier and a military intellectual. A lifetime of reading and reflection focused on war developed a mental sophistication that enabled him to think ahead, anticipating moves and developing counters, forcing the pace of battle to points where neither his enemies, his superiors, nor his subordinates could readily keep pace. Patton's concepts of war led him away from conventional approaches, toward a nonlinear paradigm whose pace and impact compelled the enemy to fight at a disadvantage, to surrender, or to flee. Often presented as designed to avoid enemy contact, Patton's way of war accepted combat, but sought to make it brief and decisive: the final element in throwing the enemy fatally off-balance through sophisticated use of time, space, and mass.

Patton compensated for his personal and intellectual apartness by being professionally cooperative. A survey of his military career suggests strongly that the familiar image of Patton the outlaw, Patton the rebel, is significantly overdrawn. When the fustian is subtracted—and when the distinction is made between public behavior and private comments intended to discharge steam—Patton emerges as a team player whose superiors had in common a confidence that they could handle him. Even his feud with Montgomery has been exaggerated on both sides. The admittedly high degree of tensions at SHAEF during the D-day campaign owed much to wider political factors. The pressures caused by Roosevelt's bid for a fourth term in the United States and the increasing fragility of Churchill's wartime coalition in Britain generated corresponding pressure on the respective generals. It was Eisenhower, moreover, not Patton, who was Montgomery's principal bete noire throughout the campaign. Monty, in fact, though well aware of Patton's habit of insulting him in public, seemed to find the American mildly amusing much of the time—like a poorly housebroken dog whose messes others clean up.

Compared to Patton, Erwin Rommel spent his early days in World War II in what the Germans call a "made bed." The German army had a doctrine for mobile war, an organization to implement it, and training methods that produced officers and men able to execute it. Rommel brought strict discipline, high standards, and incandescent energy to his command of the 7th Panzer. The result was the most spectacular record of the ten mobile divisions that essentially decided the campaign of 1940. Sent to North Africa, Rommel again enjoyed the advantages of commanding in the Afrika Korps, a force that knew what it was supposed to do and responded positively to its commander's hard-driving style. Rommel offered few second chances to units or commanders—largely because the Afrika Korps and Panzer Army Africa had so little margin for error. His German formations might be defeated, but they seldom failed him. In time, the Italian mobile divisions as well adapted to Rommel's methods as far as their deficiencies in equipment and command allowed.

Rommel brought to the desert a set of qualities well adapted to that theater's balance of space, time, and mass. Ultimately, the Axis forces were not consistently outnumbered and outgunned because the British held Malta, or because the Italian navy was ineffective, or any other immediate reasons. North Africa was a tertiary theater for Hitler and a secondary theater for Mussolini, while it was the primary theater of engagement for Britain. Those respective priorities shaped the governments' respective commitments and put Rommel in the position of a short-money player in a table-stakes poker game. His only hope of keeping the field against superior British force, and British generalship that was not always as inadequate as Rommel made it look, was to use his assets as though they were not wasting assets, needing to be husbanded like a miser's coins.

Rommel's boldness in maneuver, his feel for the pace of a battle, his personal intervention at crucial points, and above all his risk-taking were necessary force multipliers at the cutting edge. Because Rommel was constrained consistently to push the envelope, he made mistakes in conceptualization and execution. Yet in the contexts of policy and strategy, the ambition and the recklessness often attributed to Rommel by his critics acquire a different dimension. So does his approach to logistics, which was in no way as cavalier as it is frequently described. So does his relationship with his Italian allies and superiors—again, on the whole, more politic than admitted in most general accounts. If Rommel in North Africa was essentially a virtuoso corps commander of mobile forces, it was in good part because such a general was absolutely essential to sustaining the Axis position, no matter whether it was defined as a springboard or an outpost. Absent that virtuosity for any reason and the result, as indicated by the course of events from El Alamein to the surrender in Tunisia, was an endgame, likely to be completed sooner than later.

Rommel demonstrated a level of intellectual growth unusual for someone under the kinds of pressure he faced in the desert. He continued to emphasize tactics and operations because he believed, like the German officer corps as a whole, that wars are won by winning battles, and that strategic opportunity develops as a consequence of tactical and operational success. But even before leaving North Africa, Rommel grasped the consequences of a developing Allied air supremacy on future operations. He understood the potential of Allied amphibious operations long before he engaged any landings. In Italy and later in Northwest Europe, Rommel showed that his approach in North Africa had been a matter of tactics rather than principles, that maneuver war as he had practiced it was no longer feasible—at least on the German side of the line. He wrote down his ideas. He discussed them frequently. He became a mentor to the commanders and staff officers of High Command West: someone to turn to in the hope that somehow the worst might be averted, if not through combat, then by means initially barely thinkable: Hitler's removal.

Patton defined and constructed himself as a hero. He spent his life preparing for the opportunity to fulfill his destiny on the battlefield, and when opportunity came, however late and truncated, he seized it with both hands. Rommel, while he sought and enjoyed the public acclaim that came to him as the Desert Fox and Hitler's general, saw himself as essentially a warrior for the working day, making the best of tools that lay to hand and circumstances as they developed. And there, perhaps, lies a final paradox.

Heroes in the epic mold like their way of life and are deeply committed to it. They are ultimately limited not by external values or official codes, but by internal standards individually derived and personally held. In the modern world, the real world, with its complex institutional and social organizations, a hero's virtues are correspondingly likely to seem ambiguous. He tends to assume the status of a clown or an outlaw. In the context of America's World War II, George Patton was a hero out of his time. But in the context of Hitler's Reich, what might someone with both heroic stature and heroic aspirations have achieved in the contexts of 1944? Correspondingly, where might Rommel's commonsense approach and his skill at maneuver war have carried him on the other side of the line, as part of Eisenhower's command team and with America's military resources behind him? Erwin Rommel with an endless supply of tanks and all the fuel he needed! It's worth discussing, over another drink down at Fiddler's Green.

INDEX